Tonino Valerii

ALSO BY ROBERTO CURTI
AND FROM MCFARLAND

Italian Gothic Horror Films, 1957–1969 (2015)
Italian Crime Filmography, 1968–1980 (2013)

Tonino Valerii
The Films

Roberto Curti

Foreword by Christopher Frayling
Afterword by Ernesto Gastaldi

McFarland & Company, Inc., Publishers
Jefferson, North Carolina

LIBRARY OF CONGRESS CATALOGUING-IN-PUBLICATION DATA

Names: Curti, Roberto, 1971– author. | Frayling, Christopher author of foreword. | Gastaldi, Ernesto, 1934– author of afterword.
Title: Tonino Valerii : the films / Roberto Curti ; foreword by Christopher Frayling ; afterword by Ernesto Gastaldi.
Description: Jefferson, North Carolina : McFarland & Company, Inc., Publishers, 2016. | Includes bibliographical references and index. | Includes filmography.
Identifiers: LCCN 2016031483 | ISBN 9781476664682 (softcover : acid free paper) ∞
Subjects: LCSH: Valerii, Tonino, 1934—-Criticism and interpretation.
Classification: LCC PN1998.3.V346 C87 2016 | DDC 791.4302/33092—dc23
LC record available at https://lccn.loc.gov/2016031483

BRITISH LIBRARY CATALOGUING DATA ARE AVAILABLE

**ISBN (print) 978-1-4766-6468-2
ISBN (ebook) 978-1-4766-2618-5**

© 2016 Roberto Curti. All rights reserved

No part of this book may be reproduced or transmitted in any form or by any means, electronic or mechanical, including photocopying or recording, or by any information storage and retrieval system, without permission in writing from the publisher.

Front cover: United States movie poster for *Day of Anger* (1967)

Printed in the United States of America

*McFarland & Company, Inc., Publishers
Box 611, Jefferson, North Carolina 28640
www.mcfarlandpub.com*

Table of Contents

Foreword by Christopher Frayling	1
Preface	5
Introduction	7
One. Childhood, Vocation and Early Experiences	13
Two. In the Lion's Den	24
Three. A Taste of Directing	31
Four. Oedipus in the West	39
Five. Death of a President	50
Six. The Anomalous Venetian	57
Seven. "There once was a little girl…"	66
Eight. Once We're Dead…	71
Nine. Nobody's Fool	79
Ten. Beware the Gorilla!	99
Eleven. A Sting in the Desert	107
Twelve. The Long Silence	115
Thirteen. The Naked Charm of the Bourgeoisie	121
Fourteen. Too Late the Hero?	125
Fifteen. Yojimbo vs. Cosa Nostra	130
Sixteen. His Master's Voice	133
Seventeen. Twilight's Last Gleamings	141
Epilogue	146
Afterword by Ernesto Gastaldi	149

Appendix: Interviews   **151**

    Andy J. Forest 151   Saverio Marconi 175
    Gianni Garko 153   Franco Nero 177
    Giuliano Gemma 154   Pasquale Rachini 178
    George Hilton 159   Beatrice Ring 180
    Peter Hooten 161   Bud Spencer 184
    Marco Leonardi 163   Bo Svenson 185
    Roberto Leoni 165   Pamela Villoresi 186

Filmography   189

Chapter Notes   207

Bibliography   217

Index   219

Foreword

Christopher Frayling

I first met Tonino Valerii during a Festival of "Euro-Westerns" at Udine in April 1997; one of the reasons the organizers had called them "Euro-Westerns" was to get away from the phrase "Spaghetti Westerns" which they thought was a put-down. In my presentation I tried to persuade the audience that "Spaghetti Westerns" was intended as a term of endearment—but opinions were still divided, especially among Italian film students. Some of the Westerns Tonino Valerii had directed in the 1960s—notably *Day of Anger* (1967), with its classic rifle-loading duel on horseback—were prominently featured in the Festival, and I took the opportunity to interview him at length as part of the research for my biography of Sergio Leone. After all, Tonino Valerii had worked for Jolly Film/Unidis as head of the editorial department—as the *whole* of the editorial department, actually—while Leone was preparing *Ray the Magnificent* or *The Mysterious Stranger* (later renamed *Fistful of Dollars*); he was involved in post-production on that film; he was Leone's assistant director on *For a Few Dollars More* and took part in early preparations for *The Good, the Bad and the Ugly*—plus he directed *My Name Is Nobody*, Sergio Leone's first film as a producer. So he had been intimately involved in Leone's working life during those crucial years, and had experienced it first-hand. He was a key witness.

I had researched and prepared an interview with Valerii, which had been filmed for the BBC television documentary *Viva Leone!* first broadcast in the year Sergio Leone died, in 1989. But I had never met him face to face before Udine. When we did meet, in a hotel foyer, I found him to be a well-informed, cultured, articulate filmmaker—not an extrovert or an ego-tripper—with clear memories of the period of 1963 to 1973 and a quietly forceful way of expressing them. It was a surprise to discover that he was a graduate of film school, CSC in Rome, and that he had studied under the distinguished veteran director Alessandro Blasetti. Until then, I had assumed that the directors of Italian-Spanish Westerns in the 1960s tended to be hardened professionals who had worked their way up in the industry since the glory days of "Hollywood on the Tiber"; Valerii was clearly an exception. He reminisced to me about Sergio Leone's fateful visit, with his wife Carla, to the Arlecchino Cinema in Rome in autumn 1963, to see Akira Kurosawa's *Yojimbo*, which had been made in Japan a couple of years before; about the casting of Clint Eastwood, his arrival in Rome, and the choice of locations in Spain for *The Mysterious Stranger*. He recalled the post-synchronization of the film—the shooting script had somehow been mislaid in all the excitement—and the shaping of the release print. And he described the initial distribution of *Fistful of Dollars*, around which several myths about miraculous happenings were in circulation. On the subject of Kurosawa's understandable reaction to *Fistful*, Tonino Valerii admitted that it was his idea to introduce Carlo Goldoni's play *Harlequin, or The Servant of Two Masters* into the case for the defense—giving lawyers the opportunity to claim that both *Fistful* and *Yojimbo* were distantly derived from the same source—a mid-eighteenth-century Italian one! After sharing his memories of the casting and locations of *For a Few Dollars More*—I immediately travelled to Almeria to check them out—and the evolution of the character of the bad guy Indio (originally called Tombstone), he described in detail the background to the making of his own Westerns *Taste of Killing* (1966); *Day of Anger*; *The Price of Power* (1969); and *A Reason to Live, a Reason to Die!* (1972, which I had seen as *Massacre at Fort Holman*). All of them had reached England in truncated forms, in the pre-video age, as "B" movies on the bottom half of double bills. The print of *Day of Anger* screened at Udine was the longest I had seen: part of his aim in making these Westerns, he said, was to avoid the pyrotechnics of some directors, to adopt a more "classic" style, and to try and put some heart—and some credible relationships—into an increasingly cynical genre.

Then we turned to *My Name Is Nobody* (1973). Tears welled up in his eyes, and he became noticeably more emphatic, as he explained to me the exact circumstances of Sergio Leone's personal involvement in the film—and the ways in which Leone had, over the years in published interviews, claimed more and more responsibility for directing as well as producing it. Leone's well-known tendency to exaggerate, in a Falstaffian way, here had real human consequences. This had evidently cast a shadow over the rest of Valerii's professional life, and as he passionately expressed his reaction—more in sorrow than in anger—I could see for myself how deeply he still felt about it many years later. He was evidently conflicted between gratitude for the opportunity Leone gave him, and bewilderment about why Leone was claiming credit for someone else's work when he didn't need to.

I met Tonino Valerii several times after this, at festivals including Madonna di Campiglio in July 2001 and for a BBC World Service radio interview as part of my series "How the West Was Shot." On that occasion, he showed me one of his treasured possessions—a very competent, small landscape painting by Lee Van Cleef. He sent me articles he had published on film history, including a fascinating one on the origins of the "wandering stranger" figure in Italian film culture—the stranger of *Fistful of Dollars* and countless derivatives—in the Gino character (played by Massimo Girotti) from Visconti's *Ossessione* (1943), itself based on the drifter Frank Chambers in James M. Cain's crime novel *The Postman Always Rings Twice* (1934)—an American figure radically reworked in an Italian cultural context, just like Clint Eastwood. This man certainly knew a lot about film history. His own Western, *A Reason to Live, a Reason to Die!*, had its long-term origins in Augusto Genina's *L'assedio dell'Alcazar* (1940), which Valerii remembered seeing as a child in his local cinema, growing up in Fascist Italy; instead of Republicans besieging Nationalists, it became Confederate and Union troops. When my book *Sergio Leone: Something to Do with Death* (2000) was first published in English, Tonino Valerii was generous enough to say—publicly—how highly he regarded it, and he campaigned for the book to be published in Italy (which it eventually was, in 2002, as *Sergio Leone—Danzando con la morte*).

In my earlier book *Spaghetti Westerns* (1981; a controversial title in Italy!) I had made an error about *My Name Is Nobody*—and I felt bad about it. I had claimed that Leone directed the opening sequence in that film—the sequence in the barber-shop—as well as the drinking/shooting contest in the saloon involving Terence Hill, part of the village carnival and the jokey interlude with the train-driver in the public urinal. And I had claimed the barber-shop sequence, I subsequently realized, through the misinterpretation of a publicity still which showed Leone directing Henry Fonda in a barber-shop chair for *Once Upon a Time in the West*—a comedy sequence, and a reference to John Ford's *My Darling Clementine* (1946), which was deleted by Leone from all versions of *West* which went into release. The only trace of it in release prints was that Fonda as Frank suddenly walked clean-shaven and well-groomed into the Flagstone saloon, for no apparent reason. I had also over-interpreted the publicity stills of Sergio Leone posing on location in the Spanish desert for the climactic showdown with the Wild Bunch in *Nobody*—a sequence which, incidentally, inspired one of Ennio Morricone's best-ever musical gags, *The Bride of the Valkyries*, rearranged for car-horns, as if it was a traffic jam at rush hour in the Via Veneto!

Roberto Curti's book conscientiously puts the record straight on *My Name Is Nobody*, and on much else besides. It covers Antonio ("Tonino") Valerii's early life in Abruzzi, his time at film school—"Blasetti had shown me the way, Leone gave me the opportunity to follow it"—and contributions, with fellow graduate Ernesto Gastaldi, to scripts for horror movies; his apprenticeship in the industry, and work for Papi and Colombo at Jolly Film. Valerii, it transpires, gravitated towards Italian Westerns almost by chance, at a time when they were flavor of the month: Blasetti had advised him not to miss opportunities as they arose—even when they were far from ideal. And the Western gold-rush was in full swing. There follows a detailed analysis of each of Valerii's films in turn (he made nine of his fourteen films in just eleven years), including the ones which came after the five Westerns—much less well known outside Italy—notably *Go Gorilla Go* (1975) and *Sahara Cross* (1977). It is extraordinary that this is the first full-length study of Tonino Valerii's life and work to appear in English, half a century or so after the events it describes.

If you search the internet for "Valerii," you currently encounter (a) a pilot from *Battlestar Galactica,* (b) assorted ancient Roman generals, members of the Valerii tribe, and (c) a dietary supplement derived from Valerian root…

Maybe after the publication of this book, you will at last find Tonino Valerii there as well—heading up the references. It is where he deserves to be. His finest film—the one Steven Spielberg rates more highly than the other Leone films, perhaps because *Nobody* treats Henry Fonda and the world he represents with childlike wonder—has been misattributed and underrated for far too long. His name is, or should be, Somebody.

Christopher Frayling is a former rector of the Royal College of Art, chairman of Arts Council England and of the Design Council, trustee of the Victoria and Albert Museum and a governor of the British Film Institute. A radio and television broadcaster he has published more than 20 books about art, design and popular culture. He was knighted in 2000 for "services to art education," and is currently a professor emeritus of cultural history at the Royal College of Art, a research fellow at the V&A and a fellow of Churchill College, Cambridge.

Preface

I first met Tonino Valerii in 2001, in Roseto degli Abruzzi, during the festival "Roseto opera prima" which he had created in 1996, and thanks to my friend Tommaso La Selva, who had interviewed him for the magazine *Nocturno Cinema*. I vividly remember the four of us—Tonino, Tommaso, my wife and I—having a pleasant conversation while sitting outside a bar, on a sunny day, and Tonino's well-hidden Abruzzi accent turning up every now and then, whenever he became too passionate during the recollection of an episode of his career as a director. What I remember the most, though, are Tonino's pale blue eyes, mobile and attentive, like those of one of the many gunslingers of the Italian Western, but with an unmistakable goodness, almost childlike, in them.

Having admired Valerii's work since an early age—my first encounter with one of his films being an early viewing of *Day of Anger*, which deeply impressed me as a kid—it seemed natural to choose him as the subject of one of the two essays I was commissioned to write (the other being on political Westerns) for a special issue of the Spanish magazine *Nosferatu*, which came out in October 2002, dedicated to the Euro Western. On that occasion, I submitted quite a few questions to him; much to my surprise, he faxed me a dozen typewritten pages in just a couple of days. His answers were witty, thorough and frank, with a surprising number of anecdotes and production details to his recollections. Around the same time I wrote a piece on his underrated crime film *Go Gorilla Go* for *Nocturno*, and on that occasion as well Tonino was quick, gracious and prodigal of information.

Over the years we kept in touch via email, and the idea of a book on him started taking shape. We met several times during 2007 and 2008 at Tonino's house in Rome, and he paid me visit in Tuscany, in Cortona, and I recorded hours of video interviews with him. The result formed the basis for my book *Il mio nome è Nessuno: Lo spaghetti western secondo Tonino Valerii*, published in late 2008 by Un Mondo a Parte. To me, in addition to exploring Valerii's career as a scriptwriter and director, as well as the rise and fall of the Italian genre film industry as seen through the eyes of one of its protagonists, it was the occasion to try and set the record straight (at least, as far as possible, that is) on the vexing question regarding *My Name Is Nobody*, Valerii's most popular and successful film, but also the one that undermined his reputation as a filmmaker due to the alleged interference of the producer, Sergio Leone, who later claimed to have directed much of the film himself.

The present edition is greatly expanded, with important additions that shift the book's focus from the original's heavy focus upon the Spaghetti Western more squarely upon the work of Valerii. The result is, in the author's opinion, a much more fitting tribute to and assessment of the films and television productions of Tonino Valerii. Since the publication of the original work in my home country, the Italian Western has been experiencing a renewed, ever-growing popularity, thanks also to the works and words of such personalities as Quentin Tarantino, who repeatedly paid homage to it and acknowledged the *oeuvre* of Italian filmmakers, including Valerii, as a major source of inspiration. Consequently a new and expanded treatment in English seemed timely, even overdue. In addition to revising the original manuscript, I decided to drop a few additions which I felt were superfluous and add as many interviews I could with people who worked with Valerii—actors, technicians, scriptwriters—in order to give a full-fledged portrait of the filmmaker and the individual as well.

So, all's well that ends well? I wish it were so.

Unfortunately Tonino's health got worse and worse in the last couple of years. I sincerely hope that when this book is out he is still with us and appreciates the result. I hope his pale blue eyes shine when he sees it, like Hank Fellows' when he finally gets his reward.

First and foremost, then, I want to thank from the deep of my heart Tonino Valerii, who opened his house, his personal archives, his memory to me and, most important, gave me his friendship and trust. All his quoted excerpts that appear in the book, unless otherwise noted, come from our conversations and email exchanges spanning over the course of seven years, from 2001 to 2008.

My deepest gratitude goes also to Sir Christopher Frayling, the author of the most exhaustive book on Sergio Leone and one of the most prestigious scholars of the Euro Western, who graciously agreed to write a new foreword for the occasion; to Ernesto Gastaldi, one of Tonino's best friends and his long-time collaborator on many movies, who already contributed to the 2008 edition with his personal recollections, and who penned a moving afterword; to scriptwriter and friend Roberto Leoni, one of the wittiest and wisest individuals I have ever met in the movie business, to Rita Valerii, a most gracious landlady; and to the following actors, directors or technicians who shared their memories about Tonino Valerii for this book: Sergio Donati, Andy J. Forest, Gianni Garko, George Hilton, John Peter Hooten, Marco Leonardi, Gianni Macchia, Saverio Marconi, Franco Nero, Pasquale Rachini, Beatrice Ring, Bo Svenson, Pamela Villoresi—and, last but not least, the late, great Giuliano Gemma, Carlo Lizzani and Carlo Pedersoli, a.k.a. Bud Spencer.

My gratitude goes also to Carlos Aguilar, who gave me precious advice during the writing of the Italian edition; Tom Betts, whose contribution was vital in compiling the filmography; Daniel Bird, who did an invaluable job on the Arrow Blu-ray of *Day of Anger*; Philip Dittman, who identified character actors and extras and provided other useful information; Steve Fenton, who helped me polish most of the pictures that illustrate the book; Mario and Roderick Gauci, my trusted proofreaders; Troy Howarth, who put me in touch with the lovely Beatrice Ring and helped with the proofreading; Stefano Lecchini, whose invaluable friendship made possible for me to include Franco Nero's recollections at the eleventh hour. Thanks also to Mark Thompson Ashworth, Lucas Balbo, Howard S. Berger, Marco Bertolino, Stefano Isidoro Bianchi (*Blow Up* magazine), Simona Carlini, Davide Cavaciocchi, Pierpaolo De Sanctis, Matteo Di Giulio, Roberto Donati, Giovanni Ferrari, Marcello Gagliani Caputo, Gabriele Giuli, Langdon Hammer, Peter Jilmstad, Tom Lisanti, Fabio Melelli, Domenico Monetti, Luca Pallanch, Alberto Pezzotta, Roberto Poppi, James T. Prickette, Davide Pulici, Federico Vitella; and, last but not least, my dear friend Tommaso La Selva, who introduced me to Tonino Valerii, and to my beloved wife Cristina, without whom my very existence would be pointless and unbearable.

For Tonino. He deserves it.

Introduction

With only fourteen feature films and a handful of television movies to his name in a career spanning over forty years, Tonino Valerii is one of the less prolific filmmakers in Italian genre cinema. He is also one of the most underrated—a lack of critical recognition that is curiously at odds with the popularity of many of his pictures. Virtually every Italian Western movie fan has seen and probably loves efforts such as *Day of Anger* (*I giorni dell'ira*, 1967), starring Giuliano Gemma and Lee Van Cleef; *A Reason to Live, a Reason to Die!* (*Una ragione per vivere e una per morire*, 1972) starring James Coburn, Telly Savalas and Bud Spencer; and especially *My Name Is Nobody* (*Il mio nome è Nessuno*, 1973), which pairs Henry Fonda and Terence Hill. Still, film scholars have somehow overlooked Valerii's body of work compared with other cult Italian directors. Valerii was perhaps the victim of his most successful film, *My Name Is Nobody*, which succumbed to the overwhelming personality of its producer Sergio Leone, to the point of being attached from then on to the latter's filmography, with Valerii reduced to the humiliating role of an executor, to say nothing of a mere front (which, as this book will prove, he definitely was not). To many, Valerii was and will always be "Sergio Leone's assistant"—a role he played on *For a Few Dollars More* (*Per qualche dollaro in più*, 1965)—despite the fact that his Westerns (with the exception of *My Name Is Nobody*) are poles apart from the filmic language, the style and the themes of the man who helmed *A Fistful of Dollars* (*Per un pugno di dollari*, 1964).

Unlike most of his contemporaries, former cameramen promoted as directors on the field but without any formal training, Tonino Valerii graduated in Filmmaking and Scriptwriting at Rome's prestigious CSC (Centro Sperimentale di Cinematografia), under the guide of the renowned Alessandro Blasetti—something which should make one aware of his technical skills. At the same time, Valerii's first steps in the filmmaking business indicate that he started out with higher ambitions, and adapted to shooting Westerns—the genre that he visited more frequently, with five films out of fourteen, starting with his 1966 debut *Taste of Killing* (*Per il gusto di uccidere*)—out of necessity, during the gold rush that followed *A Fistful of Dollars'* exceptional worldwide success. Nevertheless, Tonino Valerii was never a soulless *metteur en scène* but an eclectic narrator, who explored the genres not to ride their commercial wave, but to keep telling the stories that were close to his heart.

Still, what is missing in Valerii's filmography is precisely the *auteur* movie, the one which calls for the critics to raise their eyebrows and elect a director above the range of his fellow genre filmmakers. Partly, this was the result of the vicissitudes typical of Italian cinema: an emblematic episode had Valerii meet a producer to illustrate his intention to adapt for the screen Livia De Stefani's prestigious novel *Black Grapes* (*La vigna di uve nere*) … only to find himself saddled with a film adaptation of the scandalous paperback *La ragazza di nome Giulio*. But Valerii's peculiar trajectory within genre cinema was also due to the director's own temper, introverted and stubborn: he was a painstaking professional who did not suffer from solipsistic temptations but was equally far removed from the sloppiness of many of his peers. Even the most obviously work-for-hire efforts in the latter part of his career, such as the erotic thriller *Unscrupulous* (*Senza scrupoli*, 1986), the war movie *Brothers in Blood* a.k.a. *Savage Attack* (*La sporca insegna del coraggio*, 1987, with Martin Balsam) and the Mafia flick *Shatterer* (1987, featuring Toshirô Mifune) possess an undeniable formal dignity.

As a result, Valerii's body of work is episodic, consistent in quality but numerically small: nine films in eleven years, between 1966 and 1977, almost all commercially successful. Then, eight years of silence, before a comeback that was not up to his previous output, and the inevitable drift to the small screen, common to so many filmmakers of his generation: Valerii's *buen retiro* on television was characterized by a stoic professionalism and an ill-concealed irritation towards the continuing decline in quality, with sloppiness as the norm and a wealth of know-how blissfully ignored in the race for reaching wider audiences.

Valerii's name is mostly associated with the so-called Spaghetti Western, a postmodernist phenomenon if ever there was one, which deconstructed the formulas and stereotypes of its Hollywood models, so as to detach the genre from the tyranny of tradition and recover it under a different, new light. The Italian Western galloped on the fertile plains vacated by American filmmakers, using with feverish impetuosity its "materials" (guns, horses, farms and saloons) to shape a hybrid which nonetheless had its own unmistakable identity. Among the directors who ventured in such territories, Valerii can be labeled as the most classic of the postmodernists. His classicality can be found first and foremost in the themes, even though his cinema cannot escape the basic contradiction of the Spaghetti Western, a genre populated by "places, stories, men that are a thousand miles from our own Italian culture and our horizons"[1] as he himself pointed out.

Therefore, if Sergio Leone's cinema is postmodern, more and more with the theoretical awareness of all its epigones—that's especially the case with *Once Upon a Time in the West* (*C'era una volta il West*, 1968), starting with the title itself—even a superficial viewing of Valerii's five Westerns reveals how their peculiarities stand out: they lack the gruesome excesses of Sergio Corbucci's films, even though *Day of Anger* and *A Reason to Live, a Reason to Die!* exude a pessimism that has nothing to envy to *The Great Silence* (*Il grande silenzio*, 1968); the political subtext, when it comes to the fore, as in *The Price of Power* (*Il prezzo del potere*, 1969), is treated in a very different way than the dialectic between civilization and barbarism that characterizes most of Franco Solinas' scripts—such as *The Big Gundown* (*La resa dei conti*, 1966, Sergio Sollima), *A Bullet for the General* (*Quien sabe?*, 1966, Damiano Damiani) and *Tepepa* (*Id.*, 1968, Giulio Petroni); the characters played by Giuliano Gemma leave aside the ironic vein displayed by the actor in Duccio Tessari's *Ringo* diptych and Michele Lupo's *Arizona Colt* (*Id.*, 1966). On top of that, Valerii's encounters with the kings of Western comedy, Bud Spencer and Terence Hill, resulted for both actors in unusual, anomalous moments in their career: in *A Reason to Live, a Reason to Die!* Valerii had Spencer reinvent the physicality of his Bambino character from *They Call Me Trinity* (*Lo chiamavano Trinità ...*, 1970, Enzo Barboni) and discover within himself a surprising tragic vein; on the other hand, Hill's eponymous gunslinger in *My Name Is Nobody* is a one-of-a-kind figure in Euro Western, a reflection (and a criticism) in real time on the

Tonino Valerii

Trinity films, a metafilmic and even metaphysical creation, a spectator, demiurge and apocalyptic destroyer of myths—all crammed into one.

Valerii's favorite themes are not, however, the epic of frontier expansion, the myth of progress or the necessity to "print the legend": the center of attention is the individual—not Leone's cynical icon of "the man with no name," mind you. The director's anti-heroes—with the important, significant exception of Nobody—are tormented and restless outsiders, closer to the characters embodied by James Stewart in Anthony Mann's films than to Italian Western's unerring and picturesquely-named gunmen, and are marked by inner conflicts far more harrowing (and interesting, it must be added) than the gunfights that punctuate their paths. Valerii likes to dwell on the difficult choices, on men at symbolical crossroads, on the weight and responsibility arising from the necessity to take a decision. Therefore, he borrows themes and types from tragedy, history and literature, so as to give a specific weight to the genre's empty, shiny shells. Here are Oedipus and Tiresias (*Day of Anger*), JFK (*The Price of Power*), Ambrose Bierce's Civil War stories (*The Price of Power, A Reason to Live, a Reason to Die!*).

The style is classical too. The camera is far less intrusive than in many Westerns of the period: how distant are the Pop experiments of Tinto Brass' *Yankee* (Id., 1966) and the bewildering, wonderful madness of Cesare Canevari's *Matalo!* (Id., 1970)! What is more, the editing is less aggressive and showy, and the odd cinephile reference never becomes an academic wink or a tongue-in-cheek joke, nor does it boil down to mannerism. What is missing in Valerii's films is precisely "the duty not to ever fully identify with the game that is being played, by taking some distance—now ironic, now ideological—and underlining in every shot, or at least in every sequence, that, indeed, it is just a game."[2] There is, in

Valerii during the shooting of *The Price of Power* (1969), directing actress Norma Jordan.

short, the ability to define the world while describing it: that is, the very essence of classicality.

During the Seventies Valerii deviated several times from the paths of the Wild West to confront himself with the present. *A Girl Called Jules* (1970), the adaptation of *La ragazza di nome Giulio*, despite being essentially a work-for-hire job, is perhaps the closest thing to an *auteur* movie Valerii ever made, starting with some very unusual calligraphic self-complacency: the earnestness of approach here becomes chisel craft, in the attempt to ennoble a matter that the director still does not feel his own. *My Dear Killer* (*Mio caro assassino*, 1972) stands out for technical mastery and thematic density among the other *gialli* made during the period, and is in stark contrast to the paths traced by Dario Argento (who, together with Leone, has been Italy's postmodernist filmmaker *par excellence*): with its stylistic dryness, it is also one of the better aged products of the *giallo* season, far removed from pulp excesses even when it sporadically bows to truculence. Similarly, the robust crime film *Go Gorilla Go*, a.k.a. *The Hired Gun* (*Vai gorilla*, 1975) follows a *sui generis* route compared with the contemporaneous *poliziottesco*, and only marginally touches the genre's revanchist tendencies, whereas the exotic adventure flick *Sahara Cross* (1977) implies on the one hand the desire to escape a present (the so-called "Years of Lead") which generated anguish, and on the other hand the attempt to detach himself from an industry that was becoming increasingly asphyxiated.

What is more, these films display an inexhaustible curiosity and a will to explore film language and develop technology, never for its own sake but always aimed at the story's necessities. That is the case with the craftsman-like inventions of *My Dear Killer*, the pioneering use of blue-back projection in *Go Gorilla Go*, the innovative employment of the Steadicam—only a few months after its debut in U.S. productions—in the sadly underrated *Sahara Cross*. This implies a desire to get involved, to learn, to test one's own limits and knowledge, which reaches up to the most recent works, such as the experiments with high-definition in *Un bel dì vedremo* (1997). All this, without ever assuming *auteur* airs, but with the humility and determination of someone who has a job to do, and wants to do it as best he can. And that is the greatest praise for a natural-born filmmaker like Tonino Valerii.

Chapter One

Childhood, Vocation and Early Experiences

My memories of childhood? The first dog I had, Less—my own childish mispronunciation for Lassie. A puppy that grew up with me, accompanied me to kindergarten every morning and came back to take me home in the evening. Nobody had taught him to; he decided to be my friend. He left me as soon as I set foot in kindergarten, waited for me at the exit, when the bell rang, and followed me all the way home. From his behavior I developed a feeling for loyalty and friendship that I have maintained throughout my life; and when it happened that someone betrayed such loyalty, I suffered a lot. And to this day I still suffer.

—Tonino Valerii

Antonio Valerii was born on May 20, 1934, in Montorio al Vomàno, a municipality of about 8,000 inhabitants, in the province of Teramo, in the region of Abruzzi e Molise (which in 1963 split into two separate regions, Abruzzo and Molise), in Southern Italy. The fourth of seven brothers, as a child he was a skinny little kid, and right from the start everybody called him Tonino (Italy's common diminutive for Antonio)—and that's how he was to be known by all, from then on.

The surname Valerii, with those final twin "i"s, one of which would usually be forgotten by the press in the first stages of his career, is a quite peculiar one, since the common version is, indeed, "Valeri." The director claimed it was an Italization of the French *Valery*. "Some years ago I made a heraldry search: the surname belonged to an ancestor of mine, a Captain of the French army who came to make war at the Civitella del Tronto fortress [...]. He never came back to France, and started a family, which obviously is my own family. One of my great-grandfathers, who did not like the foreign surname, had it changed, curiously enough, to Valerii."[1]

The Valerii family was a wealthy one. The father, Riccardo, was a landowner from Campli; the mother, Francesca Candelori, was the daughter of a well-to-do notary who practiced for free; in Montorio, a basically agrarian town, the only richness was the land itself. "They got married very young—she was 16, he was 18—but they had known each other since childhood. They met when they were only kids, on the beach of Roseto degli Abruzzi, a place which is still very dear to my heart." About 27 miles from the hill town of Montorio, Roseto is a little town facing the Adriatic sea. For the citizens of Montorio, it was the obvious holiday destination, and a place where summer loves would blossom, just like roses. "It was given this name of Dannunzian ardor ('Roseto' means 'rose garden') after changing three [earlier names]: Le Quote (that is, the lands divided into unit shares among the landowners from the hills who would move near the sea); Rosburgo, ugly-sounding but at least pertinent; Borgo delle Rose, that is Rosburgo explained to the folk; and eventually Roseto."

Valerii's father had been a member of the Fascist Party from the very beginning; the Fascist press labeled him a *"camerata della vigilia"* (early comrade), enrolled in the PNF since March 2, 1921 (over one year before the March on Rome), and attributed him the title of *"squadrista marcia su Roma"* and *"sciarpa littorio."*[2] Due to the regime's notorious aversion to foreign names and terms, Riccardo Valerii's surname was spelled on the official papers as "Valeri" during the Fascist era, when he eventually became Montorio's *podestà* from 1930 to 1934.[3] According to local historians, he was a respected one. "Valeri, whose image of 'respectable Fascist' of moderate nature and alien from the pursuit of self-interest has settled into the collective memory, remained in office until the supervening incompatibility with the prestigious position of deputy secretary of the provincial PNF federation. [...] Until the fall of the regime (25 July 1943) the city was entrusted to prefectural officials, frequently accompanied by Valerii as 'sub-commissioner' or 'additional Commissioner.'"[4]

Little Tonino attended school up to primary during wartime. Life went on quietly, between daily lessons and the weekly mass at the local San Rocco church. Then, the boy discovered a new, burning passion: the manager of the village's only movie theater was a family friend, and his son was Tonino's classmate: that meant free entrance to all shows for both kids. "Movies were being screened only on Saturdays and Sundays, and in those days I entered the theater at 2 p.m. and came out at midnight. I used to watch the same movie again and again, four or five times in a row..."

Being bitten by the film bug did not just result in the bi-weekly rite of binge-watching: Tonino was curious, and his was a voracious and restless curiosity. He wanted to unravel the secrets of such a magical wonder, that beam of light that reached the silver screen, carrying images and stories within itself. Since celluloid was flammable—and sometimes the screenings were brisquely cut short by a sudden fire, with the smell of fumigant film spreading among the audience's buzz—the projection booth was separated by the auditorium, and could be reached only by climbing a line of iron hooks in the building's rear wall. Climbing that rudimentary ladder was to Tonino the equivalent of Jim climbing atop the *Hispaniola*'s mainmast in *Treasure Island*, or Huck Finn reaching his tree fort. There, the boy discovered how the magic did work. "There was an old Prevost projector, one of those with the starter motor detached from the body. Every time you changed the reel, you had to start the mechanism by way of a pulley that you had to bring into the roll of the electric motor, and operate a crank handle. There was a young dude doing this job, and one day he asked me to help him roll the crank. It was then that I really fell in love, watching in awe how the tiny, upside-down figures passed through the magnifying lens, and magically became huge and overturned again. I couldn't wait for Saturday afternoon to come, to run to the projection booth, climb the back ladder, turn over the film, help putting it into the projector and so on. Remember *Cinema Paradiso*? It was all exactly like that..."

Even in the town of Teramo, where he attended secondary school, the weekly ritual did not change: Saturdays and Sundays were reserved to spend the pocket money at the local Apollo theater.

> I watched mostly American films, sophisticated comedies, pirate flicks, Westerns.... I distinctly recall the first time I saw *Stagecoach*.... I remember that above the screen there was an inscription in Latin, that read

iucunda oblivio vitae, "pleasant oblivion of life." Each time I sat in the auditorium, I read it again and again. Later on in my existence I was struck by another inscription, at Teramo's asylum, run by a student of Freud's, Marco Levi Bianchini, who turned it into a cozy place where the mentally ill were treated humanely. Over the front door, he put a writing: "*Questi soltanto i pochi / forse neppure i veri.*" (These only a few / Perhaps not even the true). These two sentences have marked my concept of life. That is, maybe the crazy people are not those who are kept inside the nuthouse, but those who are outside, and cinema ultimately can only be a *iucunda oblivio vitae*.

However, the mere cinephile passion was destined to turn into something more. While attending the first class at secondary school, Tonino came across a weekly magazine, *Hollywood*, published by a house named Vitagliano, whose editor-in-chief was the renowned journalist Adriano Baracco.[5] "It was a tabloid mag, just 16 page sheets, but it featured news on American and European movies: even in Italy we were beginning to understand what the star system was all about. There, I read words that I had never even heard of, and for the first time I read about what was called 'film directing.' And then I realized that a motion picture is not something that was born spontaneously, like a flower, but is the fruit of a long and difficult job which needs special skills: knowing how to tell a story, sketching the characters effectively, and not losing the audience's attention."

Always an avid reader, as a teenager Tonino started collecting movie magazines, including the new series of *Cinema*—the mag on which such renowned directors as Michelangelo Antonioni, Giuseppe De Santis and Massimo Puccini had moved their first steps as film critics—and the weekly *Novelle Film*. "The latter was published by the same company as *Hollywood*, and it was one of the most brilliant mags ever conceived. Each issue told the story of a successful movie as if it was a novel—hence the title, which literally meant 'movie tales'—by way of pics from the film, the actors' roles explained to the reader, and so on. Reading *Hollywood* and *Novelle Film*, imagination galloped: and one could understand how a story was constructed, and why these movies were so successful."

At first Valerii dreamed of becoming an actor. He began mailing around his photographs, mostly half-body pics shot at the Roseto beach, to agencies and production companies alike. "I was thin as a rail, so of course no one ever answered back. Then I said to myself: after all, I am not as good-looking as movie actors, so perhaps I'd better stay *behind* the camera. And when one day I read in *Hollywood* about a contest to attend the Centro Sperimentale di Cinematografia[6] in Rome, from that moment on I couldn't think of anything else. A university degree was required, which I did not have, but a paragraph stated that if a candidate showed particular aptitude, he or she might be accepted regardless of it. So I started doing my homework: besides regularly going to the movies, I began collecting and reading all kinds of mags and books on cinema. *Hollywood* was some kind of agenda, and whenever a new volume about the subject was reported out, I purchased it…." At the local bookshop, besides school textbooks, young Tonino ordered a growing number of film books, and had them put on his account. Unbeknownst to his father, we shall add. "My dad was amazed: 'This year's textbooks have reached unbelievable prices!' he complained. He could not imagine that, in addition to my accountancy manuals, he had paid for Eisenstein's *Film Form and the Film Sense*, Pudovkin's *Film Technique and Film Acting*, and so on…!"

Eventually, Valerii managed to enroll at the CSC. He graduated in 1957, in screenplay writing and film directing, after studying with the prestigious Alessandro Blasetti, the director of such milestones of Italian cinema as *1860* (1934), *La corona di ferro* (1941), *The Jester's*

Supper (*La cena delle beffe*, 1942) and *Fabiola* (1949), who was also one of Centro Sperimentale's foremost teachers. "Blasetti was my real mentor, the one who taught me what being a filmmaker means. But there are no masters of art who are not masters of life as well. Blasetti taught me honesty, since when you are making a movie the money you spend is not yours but someone else's, and you must keep it in mind. And he taught me the physical fatigue of being a film director, the need to take care of your body ('Strength comes from the guts,' he used to say.) Then, the language of film, the rule of looks, the 180-degree rule, people coming in and out of shots, and so on, are all things you learn in just a few days."

Il diario di Anna Frank, Valerii's final essay at the CSC, was a 26-minute adaptation of *The Diary of Anne Frank*. Shot in an evocative black-and-white, featuring only four characters (Anna, her father, her older sister Margot, and the young Peter Van Daan) and entirely set in a few interiors, it is a solid and occasionally remarkable effort despite the actors' shortcomings (the sole professional involved was Carlo D'Angelo, who played Anna's father) and a few didactic excesses. The plot consists of a few sketches taken from the diary: Anna prepares to meet Peter and borrows Margot's necklace; Anna and Peter are studying together and the boy courts her; she tells her father about her feelings for the boy; she goes up to the cellar to take some apples, and flirts with Peter; the Franks listen to Radio London; Anna and Peter have their first kiss; the arrival of the Gestapo. Valerii uses the claustrophobic setting coherently: he often has Anna look out of the window, but never shows the sky, underlining the characters' state of *de facto* prisoners in their clandestine Amsterdam refuge; still, he manages to avoid a feeling of theatricality by adopting well-thought camera movements, and develops the extended dialogue scenes with just the right touch of intensity and dynamism. The opening, in which Anna and Margot happily dance and fantasize about their future, is impressive, and so is the final breakout of the Nazis, suggested only through sound effects and off-screen voices. The featurette ends with archive footage of concentration camps, marking a vivid contrast with the final pages of Anna's diary, whose hopeful words are recited in voice-over.

Il diario di Anna Frank was screened at many cinema school retrospectives, and, according to Valerii, when Otto Frank heard about it, he claimed a copy for Anne Frank's memorial. The director vividly recalled the excitement of the first screening to CSC's faculty committee. "Blasetti came out of the projection room visibly moved. 'Where's Valerii?' He patted me on the shoulder and said: 'You *are* a filmmaker.' And then he went back in. One of my classmates stepped forward: '*Bravo*, Tonino! I'm so happy for you!' It was Ernesto Gastaldi."

Born in Graglia, in the province of Biella, Piedmont, on September 10, 1934, Gastaldi did not harbor ambitions to become a film director, but wanted to be a screenwriter instead. He came to Rome with two friends, on a midsummer's night, following the dream of that big exciting adventure.

> Being admitted at the CSC was, and perhaps still is, a lottery. For someone like me, then, who came from the province, as they say in Rome, it was really hard. There were only three seats left for the course on film directing and screenplay writing, plus a couple more reserved for auditors. When I resigned my job as a clerk at the Sella bank in Biella to move to Rome and give it a try, half the city laughed behind my back: three seats! Imagine! They'll end up being assigned to the son of the MP, the nephew of the cardinal and the cousin of the famous film director! Nevertheless, I was sponsored by Blasetti, who had seen an amateurish film I had scripted, and which had been directed by Giuseppe "Peppo" Sacchi, who one day would break the government monopoly on television.[7] Its title bode well: *La strada che porta lontano* (The Road That Leads Far Away). And away it led me.[8]

There were fifteen students in the course: Valerii, in Gastaldi's memories, stood out for his thinness, pale blue eyes and vast cinephile culture. "I found *Battleship Potemkin* a bore, whereas Tonino went into a rapture over the celebrated Odessa steps sequence and Eisenstein's use of editing; I laughed at the big maggots on the sailors' steaks and Tonino was moved by the sight of the baby in a carriage falling down the flight of steps. He could even manage to stay awake when, in the postprandial hours, professor Montesanti served us three hours' worth of silent films, such as Greta Garbo's break-out role, *The Saga of Gosta Berling*." The two provincial young men became close friends: Tonino, who had rented a room by a local family, often invited Ernesto—who had to tighten his belt due to the constant lack of money—to the Sunday lunch. "The landlady, *Sora* Giggia, was an amiable matron in her fifties, who cooked dense and nutrient sauces. On Sundays I used to eat for the whole week, and stuffed myself with an incredible quantity of food," Gastaldi amusingly recalls. "The matron often stood behind my back in admiration, and exclaimed: 'You eat so much, my little boy, you eat so much....' We laughed, without stopping chewing."[9]

After graduation, the two friends took different paths. Ernesto continued to struggle to make ends meet, whereas Tonino was granted a job by his father, who was quite worried about his son's future, at the Cassa del Mezzogiorno bank, thanks to the elderly man's friendship with the head of the staff. But he was not happy. Being a clerk was like a humiliation to him, it meant being pigeonholed in the greyness of everyday life, the farewell to the dreams—that is, *the* dream—of a lifetime. He suffered through it to the point of sinking into a depression. "Every day I went to the ambulatory to be given antidepressant injections. Until one day the doctor told me that I was not ill, but I had to leave that job, and my health would benefit from it." So he did: he stayed home, benefitting from health insurance, and started to look for his own path in life.

It was 1959. Valerii's first attempt at building for himself a future in show business was through the national public broadcasting company, RAI.

> I participated in a contest, together with Liliana Cavani, who back then was a lovely little girl. She passed it, I didn't. However, I ended up working at RAI for quite some time as a freelance contributor: I was the assistant director for Bruno Beneck, one of Italy's most renowned TV directors, specializing in sports-related programs. Beneck helmed a broadcast for ANICA,[10] called *Questo nostro cinema* (This Cinema of Ours), dedicated to newly released movies. Since it was a weekly program, within four or five days we had to put together one hour's worth of material: footage from the featured pics, interviews with filmmakers, actors and critics, plus some very amusing cinema-related couplets by the comedian Gigi Reder. We spent whole nights editing it, Cleofe Conversi and I.

Perhaps a job consisting in editing presentations of other people's movies was somehow diminishing for someone who graduated in film directing; still, to Valerii it was better than nothing: at least it meant being closer to the object of his passion.

However, despite the prospect of a secure job, the love of movies was too strong. Through a friend, film critic and scriptwriter Vinicio Marinucci, Valerii started working at the Jolly/Unidis film company as head of the editorial department, at the princely (so to speak) wage of 25,000 *lire* a week. Jolly had been established in 1950 by Arrigo Colombo and Giorgio Papi: in the immediate post–World War II years, in the absence of Italian-based dubbing facilities, Colombo (1916–1998) had been in the United States, taking care of the dubbing of American pictures to be exported to Italy, together with another producer, Dario Sabatello. At first he even lent his own, rather strident voice to dub James Cagney and Edward G. Robinson for the Italian releases. In 1956 Jolly merged with Unidis; the former produced motion pictures, and the latter distributed the films financed by its associated company, as well as other movies purchased on the market.

Do not be misled by the high-sounding title tied to the willing new recruit. "It's not that there were any other people there; actually I was *the whole* editorial department: head, clerk and errand boy—all in one!" This also included performing such humble jobs as clearing a foreign film through customs or bringing a negative over to the printing and developing lab … which meant having to carry a dozen heavy aluminum cans across town. "Since they were flammable, I was not allowed aboard streetcars, so after just one stop I had to get off and walk all the way to the lab!"

In his comings and goings to Ettore Catalucci's SPES printing and developing lab, in Via Campo Boario, Tonino noticed a neat-looking female employee, in black apron, white collar and lace shirt. Her name was Rita Scannavini. "I knew that she walked her way from the lab to the bus stop, and since we got to know each other as I turned up at SPES quite often, as soon as I bought a car—my first one, a Fiat 500, which meant an end to my endless walks to the lab—I offered her a ride home. 'No, thanks.' I insisted … and after ten times or so she finally said yes." It was 1962; three years later Tonino and Rita got married.

At Unidis, Valerii started following all the phases of post-production—editing, dub-

Valerii and his wife Rita in Japan, during the promotional tour for *Shatterer* (1987) (courtesy Beatrice Ring).

bing, mixing—up to the sample print. This included splicing together a trailer and rewriting the dialogue, either after censorship cuts or editing changes, or due to the syllabic adaptation when translating from a foreign language. Among the films for which he took care of the Italian edition were *Soviet Spy* (*Qui êtes-vous, Monsieur Sorge?*, 1961, Yves Ciampi) and the re-releases of *Comradeship* (*Kameradschaft*, 1931, Georg Wilhelm Pabst) and *Devil in the Flesh* (*Le Diable au corps*, 1947, Claude Autant-Lara). The latter had had quite a few problems with the Italian board of censors, because of its then "scandalous" theme of adultery. Initially forbidden to minors, it then had its visa withdrawn after an intervention on the part of the then-undersecretary to the Presidency of Council Giulio Andreotti, who basically was the absolute monarch of Italian film censorship from 1947 to 1953, following protests by religious groups and the Catholic press. Autant-Lara's film stayed out of circulation for over a decade, until Papi's Unidis resubmitted it to the board of censors, with sensible alterations in the editing and dialogue ... courtesy of Valerii's efforts. It eventually passed with a V.M.18 rating. Valerii was very proud of his work for the re-release. "When I was asked to splice together a trailer, I realized that the film was beautiful but a little dated. Moreover, it was very talky, although the highlight was the famous fireplace scene, that is the first time the two protagonists make love: Gérard Philippe and Micheline Presle kiss on the bed, the camera pans around the room until it frames a fireplace where the flames are burning. Cross-dissolve: the fire has extinguished, the camera resumes the panning shot until it returns to the two lovers, now exhausted after lovemaking. It caused a sensation, back in the day." To try and make the film more palatable to 1960s audiences, Valerii suggested to Papi they hire Mario Serandrei, one of Italy's greatest film editors ever, to prepare a striking presentation. Serandrei stipulated 300,000 *lire* for the job, and demanded that the film be screened for him at double speed. Eventually, his response was: "Look, Valerii, the only thing we can do about it is to try and make it look like an Antonioni movie." To which the reply: "If only!" The trailer came up pretty effective, *Devil in the Flesh* did well at the box-office, and Papi—initially wary about whether to take on Valerii permanently, unlike his partner—took a liking to the young man.

Around the same time, Valerii's name made its way to the literary world, in a rather offbeat manner: in 1961, the Milan-based Lerici Edizioni published *Laura nuda*, "Tonino Valerii's novel based on the film of the same name by Nicola Ferrari," as the cover proudly stated. Directed by Nicolò (not Nicola) Ferrari and starring Giorgia Moll, Nino Castelnuovo and a very young Tomas Milian, *Laura nuda* was a rather daring motion picture for the period, and underlined the troubled relationship between production and distribution companies on one side and the board of censors on the other, which, the following year, led to a new discipline of the matter, with Law 161 of 21 April 1962.[11] Valerii's novelization closely followed the script, the story of a young, bored woman who marries a man she does not love and has a series of sexual encounters which lead to her own tragic demise. Written in a stark, effective style, the book is illustrated with set stills and publicity material from the film (no doubt one of the book's selling points, with the odd glimpse of bare female flesh), among which the arresting cover image of the half-naked Giorgia Moll, lying on a bed, stands out. Even though Valerii never mentioned the book in interviews—and understandably so, it being a mere work-for-hire job—*Laura nuda* predates the director's subsequent approaches to eroticism.

In addition to his work in the editing room, the time came for the aspiring filmmaker to take his first steps on a movie set. Once again, the credit was Blasetti's, who allowed his ex-student to be his assistant on *I Love, You Love* (*Io amo, tu ami...*, 1961), a documentary—subtitled *Antologia universale dell'amore* (Universal Anthology of Love)—along the vein of the director's earlier *European Nights* (*Europa di notte*, 1959), which had started a whole thread of flicks that spliced together a number of saucy night-club acts. Valerii's name was not even mentioned in the credits, though. "It was a precarious job, which I volunteered to do, only for the part of the shooting that took place in Rome (a couple of weeks if I'm not mistaken), with no weekly pay and without even the lunchbox, which nevertheless someone passed on stealthily." Blasetti's film featured a scene set on the beach, where a handsome and athletic young man made a brief appearance—a former stuntman who was trying to find his way in the movies, by the name of Giuliano Gemma. He and Valerii would meet again in a few years, under quite different and more favorable circumstances for both.

Blasetti wanted Valerii again by his side on the set of *The Best of Enemies* (*I due nemici*, 1961, Guy Hamilton), starring David Niven and Alberto Sordi. The Roman director, officially head of the second unit, in fact directed a number of scenes, including the fire in the lake and the sequences featuring Sordi. Then came Tonino's first official screen credit, for Camillo Mastrocinque's *I motorizzati* (The Motorized Ones, 1962), produced by Jolly Film, one of those typical anthology comedies—a genre introduced by Blasetti, incidentally, with his diptych *Altri tempi (Zibaldone n. 1)* (1952) and *Tempi nostri (Zibaldone n. 2)* (1954)—which became immensely popular during the decade. Like its peers *I motorizzati* was built as a series of sketches around a recurring theme; here it was the passion and an obsession for cars, which were becoming more and more widespread among the middle class after the rise in wealth brought by the economic boom. As Dino Risi's masterpiece *The Easy Life* (*Il sorpasso*), made the same year, mordantly pointed out, owning a car had suddenly become a status symbol, in a country which had just left behind the miserable post–World War II years. "*I motorizzati* was a very nice little movie, featuring all the most popular comedians of the time: Nino Manfredi, Ugo Tognazzi, Franco and Ciccio, Walter Chiari, Aroldo Tieri.... I was credited as Mastrocinque's assistant, but he already had one, Nino Zanchin. So he asked me to be Zanchin's assistant. I even played a bit role, at Manfredi's suggestion." Eventually Valerii's childhood dream materialized, even if only for a minimal screen time, but the character he plays has more than a slight resemblance to his real self: he turns up as the loafer employee and cinephile, who, as his colleague complains he has been to the movies and seen a "stinker," replies testily, in a passable Roman dialect: "Serves you right ... you coulda joined me at the arthouse theater, couldn't you?"

The encounter with veteran filmmaker Mastrocinque, born in 1901 and having helmed well over 50 films since his debut behind the camera in 1937, was to be a felicitous one. "He was a fine elderly gentleman, always generous with anecdotes about his life and loves, and we used to gather around him during lunch break, to hear his stories. He always carried a bag with a dozen silk handkerchiefs, cashmere design, custom made, and a one-liter bottle of *eau de cologne* 'Jean Marie Farina—*extra vieille*.' He used to take a handkerchief, soak it in cologne, and pass it over his face. And every now and then he asked me: 'Tonino, will you please do me a favor? Go get me a one-liter bottle of "Jean Marie Farina." But *extra old*, I implore you...,' as if perfume aged like a liquor and there were also a *vieille* version!"

Around the same period Valerii was the assistant of another important Italian filmmaker, Raffaello Matarazzo, on the latter's penultimate film, *I terribili 7* (a.k.a. *I cagasotto*,

1963), an unpretentious comedy aimed at kids. He was also credited as assistant director on *Tutto è musica* (Everything Is Music, 1963), a *musicarello* (a term coined for unassuming comedies featuring musical numbers by singers and bands, which were very popular then), directed by and starring the renowned singer Domenico Modugno, with a special appearance by the ubiquitous Franco Franchi and Ciccio Ingrassia. In fact, according to Valerii, his contribution was much more decisive. "I was put under contract as a.d., but Modugno came and told me: 'You have to direct the film, you know that, don't you?' and he would sign it." Valerii also wrote the screenplay with Modugno and songwriter-cum-music producer Franco Migliacci: "Well, screenplay is a big word…. It was rather a matter of finding a narrative thread that would allow us to switch from one song to another. The script practically did not exist, it was a basic outline like this: 'The film starts with *Nel blu dipinto di blu*, then we move on to *Lu pisce spada*, then to *Piove…*.'[12] and so on." Valerii is not exaggerating: The film's title refers to Modugno's opening monologue, in which the singer (as himself) explains that everything is, indeed, music (from the sound of a car's horn to the wind blowing through trees) before the film cuts to a sort of primordial video clip of Modugno singing *Nel blu dipinto di blu*. The rest is a series of slapdash vignettes that vary wildly in tone: a Felliniesque segment following two rather grotesque vendors on a beach (one is Eddra Gale, of *8½* fame), Franchi and Ingrassia's usual comic routine (Franchi here posing as a dog and then as a siren, to fool a credulous tourist), a Neorealist segment on swordfish fishing, akin in tone to Vittorio De Seta's documentaries, and accompanying Modugno's song *Lu pisce spada* (The Swordfish), a *sceneggiata* bit with Modugno in a dual role as a man who has himself arrested in order to kill his wife's lover (also Modugno) in prison, and so on. It would be a futile exercise to try and glimpse anything personal in the result. The film's best asset is Gábor Pogány's color cinematography, worthy of a better cause.

In that period, Valerii and his friend Ernesto Gastaldi had started writing screenplays together, initially without much luck. They either processed the scripts as a team, scene by scene, or developed them during long discussions, "like two friends that chat about a story that happened to them for real, but with the wonderful ability to play the part of God Almighty, and change those events and characters at will."[13] They worked quite well together: Ernesto focused on the stories, Tonino gave depth to the characters. Their first scripts that made their way to the big screen were two horror stories. Those were the years of Italian Gothic, with such works as Mario Bava's *Black Sunday* (*La maschera del demonio*, 1960) and Riccardo Freda's diptych *The Horrible Dr. Hichcock* (*L'orribile segreto del dr. Hichcock*, 1962) and *The Ghost* (*Lo spettro* (1963). The genre's icon was the British actress Barbara Steele, raven-haired, with voluptuous lips, huge black eyes—"De Chirico–like" as Freda would brilliantly describe them—and sunken vampire-like cheeks: a sensual heroine and her evil double in Bava's masterpiece, and a recurring presence in a number of Italian horror flicks of the period, such as Antonio Margheriti's *Castle of Blood* (*Danza macabra*, 1964).

Often hiding behind the pseudonym Julian Berry,[14] Gastaldi quickly became one of the Gothic's specialists: he penned Renato Polselli's *The Vampire and the Ballerina* (*L'amante del vampiro*, 1960), Italy's first canonic vampire film,[15] on which he was also assistant director, as well as Freda's *Hichcock* and Bava's *The Whip and the Body* (*La frusta e il corpo*, 1963), two of the very best efforts in the genre. On top of that, the two horror flicks Gastaldi wrote with Valerii are among the most interesting examples of the Italian way to the Gothic. *Terror in the Crypt* (*La cripta e l'incubo*, 1964) was concocted in record time: according to

Valerii, only three days—or rather, three nights, since Gastaldi preferred to work after sunset, like vampires do. The overturning of circadian rhythms had its side effects, though: "Night shifts were certainly more tense and productive, but I think I slept only five hours out of 72!" Valerii commented. According to Gastaldi, the script was nailed in a mere 24 hours, in a bout of creative frenzy, *Seven Keys to Baldpate*-style: not by way of a bet, but out of mere economical necessity. "While chatting with a producer, Tonino and I told him the story—we had just a tiny little sheet. We caught his interest, and he told us he would produce the movie, but he needed the script at once, because he wanted to start shooting in a few days, for economical reasons. Lying shamelessly, I told him that the script was ready, and he happily told us that he would wait for us the next morning in his office with the screenplay, so that we would read it together. So, Tonino and I spent the night writing the script on my terrace, with Mara Maryl providing coffee."[16] It is truly a memorable example of how the Italian film industry worked those days. During coffee breaks, the two exhausted friends found relief singing ramshackle sonnets on the melody of a popular Paul Anka tune: "*Ogni giorno un poco / questa Laura mi muore ogni giorno un po' / e il dottore dice che mi muore di sindrome anemica. Sarà forse Cedric / sarà Ljuba sarà Frederic / sarà infine Rowena a succhiarle le vene? / Ma il sospetto più atroce è che / si tratti di froce!*" ("Each day a bit more / This Laura o' mine is dying each day a bit more / And the doctor says she's dying of an anemic syndrome. Could it be Cedric / Could it be Ljuba or Frederic / Could it be Rowena that sucks blood from her vein-a? / But the worst suspicion so far is that they both lesbians are!")

Although at the time it passed almost unnoticed on audiences and critics alike, *Terror in the Crypt* revisited Joseph Sheridan Le Fanu's *Carmilla*, already adapted for the screen a few years earlier by Roger Vadim with *Blood and Roses* (*Et mourir de plaisir*, 1960). Yet Valerii and Gastaldi (that is Robert Bohr and Julian Berry, in accordance with the habit of adopting Anglo-Saxon pseudonyms to cheat the audience) sweep away the arty conceitedness of Vadim's film, and indulge on the homosexual attraction between the two female protagonists, the sensual brunette Laura (Adriana Ambesi) and the blonde, angelic Ljuba (Pier Anna Quaglia)—the latter turning out to be the vampire, in a nice inversion on the genre's clichés. "I insisted that he cut the niceties and get down to sex," Valerii recalled.[17] Laura's central nightmare sequence, which ends with the young woman awakening and inviting her friend Ljuba to come in her bedroom and "keep her company," is one of Italian Gothic's most significant moments, because of the way it summarizes the central motif, the erotic seduction of evil, which in this case is troubling not a man (as in *Black Sunday*) but a woman: since, as we will later discover, Ljuba is the vampire, the implied erotic offer becomes the symptom of ruin, and the bedroom door which closes behind the two women seals the ongoing vampire seduction.

Terror in the Crypt starred Christopher Lee, in one of his Italian forays of the period, as Laura's stern father. It was shot almost entirely at the Balsorano Castle (one of Italian Gothic's recurrent locations, in Abruzzo), with Valerii acting as assistant to director "Thomas Miller," that is, Camillo Mastrocinque—for the first time in his career, the old specialist in comedies tried his hand at horror, a genre which he thought did not suit him at all. As Valerii recalled, "*Terror in the Crypt* was to be directed by Antonio Margheriti: he met Ernesto and I at his home to talk about the script, but eventually he could not make it and the film passed on to Mastrocinque. When this elderly gentleman, who had always directed light comedies, such as Totò's films and so on, was given the opportunity to make a vampire flick, he felt lost. He said, 'You have to be help me out shooting this, I don't know anything about it...' There were things that made him shudder: hanged men, severed hands with burning candles over the fingers and so on ... and he made me shoot that stuff!" Valerii claims to have directed the scene with the so-called "Hand of Glory,"[18] Ljuba's vampiric kiss as well as the macabre sequence of the tramp hung in the bell tower, with a dog trying to release the body and provoking each time a mournful tolling. Still, in spite of Mastrocinque's alleged disinterest towards the genre—which on the other hand did not stop him from inserting a delightful homage to Bava's *Black Sunday* in *I motorizzati*,[19] *Terror in the Crypt* is a rather accomplished work, as is the director's second and final Gothic, *An Angel for Satan* (*Un angelo per Satana*, 1966), starring Barbara Steele.

The second Gothic horror written by the Bohr/Berry firm, *The Long Hair of Death* (*I lunghi capelli della morte*, 1964), produced by Felice Testa Gay, had an equally hasty genesis, and was the result of a number of diverse influences and sparse borrowings, from *Diabolique* (*Les diaboliques*, 1955, Henri-Georges Clouzot), to the shock ending from Roger Corman's *The Pit and the Pendulum* ("*The Pit and the Pendulum* was a big influence on Italian horror films. Everybody borrowed from it," Gastaldi confirmed[20]), plus curious analogies with popular Italian comedies—namely Pietro Germi's *Divorce—Italian Style* (*Divorzio all'italiana*, 1961) and Dino Risi's *The Widower* (*Il vedovo*, 1959)—reworked in an ironically horrific way, which hinted at the disenchanted, mordant vision of marriage that characterized the Italian Gothic horror film style, and which is emphasized by the dialogue ("You are my wife, Elizabeth!" "You have not yet possessed me. What if I refuse?" "You can't refuse, for I am your master!"). On the other hand, the final scene suprisingly predates the mocking epilogue of Robin Hardy's *The Wicker Man* (1973), and demonstrates the lively approach to the genre on the part of the scriptwriters.

The Long Hair of Death was meant to be a trampoline for Valerii's debut as a filmmaker, but things went in a different way. As Gastaldi told Tim Lucas, "Valerii tried to direct that film, but the producer didn't want him because, at that time, he hadn't directed any movies. Antonio [Margheriti] was called when the script was finished, and we met only once, so that I could explain some details to him. He didn't change the script and I never went on the set."[21] One wonders what might have happened had Valerii started his career with this little, atmospheric horror film. But fate had other plans for him.

One day in 1963, a certain individual destined to change the course of events forever had made his first appearance in the 29-year-old aspiring filmmaker's life. "At Jolly Film I was usually the first to arrive at the office. I loved the job, even though the pay was scant. Papi and Colombo would not show up before noon, and in the morning, from 9 o'clock onwards, I did a little bit of everything: revised the dialogue of a movie we were dubbing, checked the mail, answered the phone, and so on. Early one morning I heard the phone ring: it was a deep, baritonal, authoritative voice. 'Is Mr. Colombo in?'" I told him that Mr. Colombo would arrive about one hour later at best, and asked who it was at the other end.

"Leone. Sergio Leone."

CHAPTER TWO

In the Lion's Den

"It is a very fine film, but it is my film."
—Akira Kurosawa, letter to Sergio Leone

In 1963, whereas in America Westerns had been steadily carving out an increasingly large spot on the television screen with such series as *Bonanza* and *Rawhide*, in Europe the genre was taking its first tentative steps with the films produced in West Germany by Horst Wendlandt, and inspired by Karl May's Winnetou novels, such as *The Treasure of the Silver Lake* (*Der Schatz im Silbersee*, 1962, Harald Reinl). The true initiator of the thread in the Old World had been Joaquín Luis Romero Marchent, with his films centered on the masked avenger El Coyote: *El Coyote* (1955) and *Judgement of Coyote* (*La justicia del Coyote*, 1956), followed in the early 1960s by several pics inspired by the character of Zorro.

In the years of Francisco Franco's regime the Spanish film industry was virtually isolated; under the Catholic-military dictatorship of El Caudillo autarchy prevailed, but local products were subject to strict supervision and censorship on the part of the State. Eisenhower's visit to Madrid in 1959 marked the beginning of an international thaw towards Spain, but it was the appointment of the Galician-born Manuel Fraga Iribarne as Minister of Information and Tourism in July 1962 which kicked off a slow process of censorship relaxation. Moreover, Fraga promoted the development of the tourist industry, and in the following years he favored the loosening of morals that had stifled the country's image abroad. The slogan "Spain is different!" was the punchline for attracting visitors and foreign currency in the country. Tourism soon became the main source of income in the national economy and favored an increase in living conditions; but the contact with other cultures was also an important factor in the change of Spanish mores, and of the film industry as well. In this respect, another vital moment had been the advent on the Iberian peninsula of mogul film producer Samuel Bronston, who in the late fifties had turned Spain into fertile ground for U.S. capitalists by establishing his own production company in the country. As Valerii recalled, "The occult purpose was to actually *lose* money, producing very expensive movies to justify the losses. Whereas, once he moved to Spain, Bronston started making important, landmark films, such as *El Cid*, *55 Days at Peking*.... When the Americans left, in Spain there was a wealth of costumes, horses, unused props, which were recycled to make the first Westerns." Besides, of course, a whole army of technicians, workers and extras. In Italy, however, about 20 Westerns had been produced over the years up to the early 1960s, but the genre had not yet taken root: the critics snubbed the local products, and the public seemed to appreciate the spoofs—such as Mario Amendola's *Terror of Oklahoma* (*Il terrore dell'Oklahoma*, 1959)—rather than the serious attempts, which were seen as awkward imitations of the American models.

It is a known fact that by the end of 1963 Sergio Leone wanted to make a film called *Le aquile di Roma* (The Eagles of Rome), which Adriano Bolzoni described as "*The Dirty Dozen*, peplum-style," set between Rome and the Teutonic forests—one more trickle from a source nearing exhaustion, after the exploits of the many musclebound heroes that had dominated the screens since *Hercules* (*Le fatiche di Ercole*, 1958, Pietro Francisci), and one which Leone had attended with little success with his debut *The Colossus of Rhodes* (*Il colosso di Rodi*, 1961), not to mention his disastrous experience on the set of Robert Aldrich's stab at the Biblical movie *Sodom and Gomorrah* (*Sodoma e Gomorra*, 1962), on which he was hired to shoot second-unit photography. But it was the providential viewing of Akira Kurosawa's *Yojimbo*—released theatrically in Italy in the fall of 1963 as *La sfida del samurai* (The Samurai's Challenge)—that changed Leone's own destiny and that of the whole Italian cinema, which in that period was undergoing an alarming economic crisis. It was a feat all the more dramatic since it came from a filmmaker fresh from having been fired on the set of *Sodom and Gomorrah*.

The genesis and production vicissitudes of *A Fistful of Dollars* (*Per un pugno di dollari*, 1964) are the object of a flourishing mass of anecdotes: a lively Vulgate which, according to each of those who had to do, if only tangentially, with the founder of the so-called "Dollars Trilogy," often becomes contradictory, labyrinthine and difficult to decipher. Kurosawa comes to mind again; this time, however, it is *Rashomon* (1950). Where does the truth end, and where does the wish, even unconscious, to claim "I was there, too" begin, to earn one a spot, even in the back rows, on the motion picture which marked so deeply the history of the Italian film industry?

It is not surprising, then, that so many take credit for pointing out *Yojimbo* to Leone. Sergio Corbucci claimed, "It was I who told him to make it [*A Fistful of Dollars*], I had seen *Yojimbo* with friends [...], which had been recommended from [Enzo] Barboni, and liked it very much. Sergio had Rory Calhoun available, who had starred in his *The Colossus of Rhodes* and had played many cowboy roles in America, but was looking for something suitable. I told him: 'Take this Kurosawa film, draw from it!' He copied it at the moviola, slavishly, changing only the setting and the dialogue, and asked Calhoun to star in it. Calhoun read the script and said: 'It sucks, I'll never do it!.'"[1]

According to Valerii, the merit should instead be ascribed to Enzo Barboni and Stelvio Massi, who met Leone outside the Arlecchino theater in Rome, where they had just seen *Yojimbo*, and told him that it might be turned into a good Western. Barboni and Massi, both cameramen, would become top-notch directors of photography and later directors, and would leave their mark on Italian cinema, the former with the two *Trinity* movies—*They Call Me Trinity* (*Lo chiamavano Trinità...*, 1970), and *Trinity Is Still My Name* (*Continuavano a chiamarlo Trinità*, 1971)—and with other pics starring Bud Spencer and Terence Hill; the latter with his crime films (the so-called *poliziotteschi*) starring Maurizio Merli, made in the late 1970s. "Barboni was an outstanding cameraman," Valerii recalled. "They said he could stick a pencil and a piece of paper under the lens of his Mitchell camera—which has two crank handles, one for vertical movements and one for horizontal movements, and it is extremely difficult to harmonize them—and could write his name on the paper by working the cranks!"

One of Leone's best friends, actor Mimmo Palmara, told a substantially similar version, with minor variations: "One evening, we were having dinner together when Enzo Barboni showed up and told us he had just seen a wonderful movie, *Yojimbo*. The next day we went to see the film, myself, he [Leone] and his wife Carla. When it was over we told each other it was ideal as the basis for a Western." Palmara added it was his suggestion to have a villain who was a Winchester fetishist, and claimed the authorship of one of *A Fistful of Dollars*' most memorable intuitions: "The idea of the iron plate which Eastwood wears to protect himself was mine. And so was the poncho, which had to conceal that armor. He gave these ideas to the scriptwriters without telling them that he had spoken with me."[2]

Other versions differ radically. In an article published in 1978 on the weekly magazine *Il borghese*, screenwriter and film director Adriano Bolzoni revealed himself to have had a role of primary importance in the genesis of *A Fistful of Dollars*; moreover, he attributed the idea of taking inspiration, to put it mildly, from Kurosawa's film, to general manager Franco "Checco" Palaggi, "clever as the Fox and the Cat put together, and convinced that within the woods of cinema industry the Field of Miracles does exist, and that golden coins indeed can be grown into trees."[3] Palaggi sent Bolzoni to the head office of the Italian distributor of *Yojimbo*, Rizzoli Film, armed with paper, pen and tape recorder, to watch *La sfida del samurai* and take notes. Bolzoni and Duccio Tessari wrote down a first draft of the script, then the project passed into Leone's hands. "I am not credited, I disappeared.... Same for Tessari, who wrote the majority of the script [...] I took my money, 300,000 *lire*, and left."[4]

Lastly, Fernando di Leo has claimed a key role in the project. "Leone's first two Westerns were written by me and Tessari, not him and [Luciano] Vincenzoni," he recalled in Franca Faldini and Goffredo Fofi's monumental interview book on Italian cinema, *L'avventurosa storia del cinema italiano raccontata dai suoi protagonisti*. In the case of *A Fistful of Dollars* he stated: "Leone got the idea, Tessari wrote the script and I gave him a hand."[5] Years later, on the pages of the monthly magazine *Nocturno Cinema*, Di Leo told what in his words was "the true story of the screenplays for *A Fistful of Dollars* and *For a Few Dollars More*, narrated by someone who has knowledge of the facts. ... Being Tessari's long-time collaborator ... I attended the first meeting between Duccio and Sergio, when they talked about what 'kind' of movie to make out of Kurosawa's work. We agreed to risk an accusation of plagiarism, and therefore detach from the model only as far as the diversity of genre implied. [...] Leone did not like the first draft, and said that Walter Chiari[6] would have been fine as a protagonist. Then I drastically intervened and laid down the script—always with Duccio—and the movie became 'hard,' very similar to the Japanese one. That was what Leone wanted, and he had the script he wished for."[7] In the notification of the start of production, which still bore the title *Il magnifico straniero* (The Magnificent Stranger),[8] the story is credited to Víctor A. Catena and Jaime Comas Gil, and the screenplay to Leone, Duccio Tessari and Hans Billian, but of course the Spanish and German names served only to play the usual co-production tricks in order to get financing from their respective countries. Later, Leone would keep much of the credit for himself, liquidating Tessari as a mere executor: "I conceived the whole treatment in five days with Duccio Tessari. Tessari did not quite understand what I was doing. He spread the rumor in Rome that I had become a bit weird. Then I wrote the adaptation alone, in a fortnight."[9]

Script under arm, Leone and Palaggi knocked at Jolly Film's door, since Palaggi had been working for the company as executive producer, and still had a pending litigation with it. "Palaggi proposed to Jolly that they produce this Western, which he would act as guarantor for, and the matter could be considered closed," Valerii explained. Meanwhile, Jolly had set up production for another Western to be shot in Spain, *Bullets Don't Argue* (*Le pistole non discutono*, 1964), to be directed by Mario Caiano; Colombo and Papi accepted Palaggi's proposal, provided that a couple of sets already built in the studio—a bedroom and a saloon—would be re-used. *A Fistful of Dollars* was thus born as a "recovery production," a fairly common practice in those days to save time and money.

The choice of the leading actor was an ordeal. Palaggi and Leone got in touch with Americans (the aforementioned Calhoun, Guy Madison, Richard Harrison, Steve Reeves, Charles Bronson, Frank Wolff), many of whom had by then settled down on a permanent basis in the country, and with Italian actors as well (Gianni Garko, Luciano Stella, a.k.a. Tony Kendall[10]). Everyone declined. The only one available would be the Brazilian Antonio de Teffé (Anthony Steffen), whom the director did not like. The most stinging "No" came from James Coburn, who demanded 25,000 dollars, too high a sum for Jolly. That Coburn was this close to playing the protagonist in *A Fistful of Dollars* is proven by the papers kept at Rome's Pubblico Registro Cinematografico (Public Film Registry), which indicate him in the leading role, in a sensibly different cast from the definitive one—among others, it features Mario Adorf (in the role later assigned to Gian Maria Volonté) and Karin Dor (then replaced by Marianne Koch). Colombo and Papi suggested the 53-year-old Rod Cameron, the star of *Bullets Don't Argue*, but Leone refused, and started looking for his protagonist elsewhere. "One day, a young female assistant from an acting agency in Rome, Claudia Sartori, brought us a 16mm reel of an episode of the American TV series, *Rawhide*, which featured a young guy who looked suitable for the part, provided that we chop off his very American-like tuft, a certain Clint Eastwood," Valerii recalled. "I screened the reel to Leone, who was not at all convinced; but Eastwood would accept the 15,000 dollars offered by the producers. One day I told him: 'Listen, if you don't want to do the movie, find another excuse.' I think I made him realize that things were looking bad: I heard the producers say that Sergio was difficult to work with, maybe they were thinking of replacing him. He understood and softened up, and eventually accepted Eastwood, in order to make the film."

Whether Valerii's alleged intervention was really decisive in changing Leone's mind is unknown. However, there is no doubt that initially Leone considered Eastwood a fallback: He would have rather cast the Greek Vassili Karamenisis (a.k.a. Vassili Karis), whom he even auditioned for the role. And when the American actor arrived in Rome, Leone did not even go pick him up at the airport; instead he sent Mario Caiano, who at least spoke English.[11]

Here is how Valerii recalls the actor's arrival. "Eastwood was carrying a fiber suitcase: he opened it and pulled out a hat, a poncho, a leather armlet and the two wooden cheeks to be screwed to the revolver's handle. 'Coming to Italy to do a Western seemed like a strange thing' he said, 'and since I didn't know how you'd manage to I brought over the costumes I used on *Rawhide*.'" Still, other versions differ radically on the details of the protagonist's arrival and the creation of his costume. According to Carla Leone, Eastwood did not bring anything, whereas the actor claimed he even brought (quite improbably) the cigars. The most obscure detail concerns the poncho, which Eastwood said he bought in Spain, but which can already be found in a prep sketch by costume designer Carlo Simi.

Slowly, then, the "Man with No Name"[12] began to take shape. Leone asked Eastwood to cut his hair and get rid of that tuft, and grow some beard so as to make the character more realistic, and add the detail of the cigar (a Tuscan cigar, to be precise) that the hero always keeps in his mouth; Eastwood did not smoke, incidentally, and the taste of the unlit cigar bothered him, but he adapted to it. And so his screen persona was born. "Clint realized he was not surrounded by amateurs—or rather, amateurs, yes, but quite good ones" Valerii joked, "and decided to trust them blindly. American actors understand immediately whether a director knows how to do his job or not. I never heard an argument between Eastwood and Leone on the set of *For a Few Dollars More*, except when it came to modifying certain terms used in the English translation of the script, and make them more adherent to the spoken lingo."

Valerii's role in *A Fistful of Dollars*, initially quite marginal, took on a greater importance as a result of a mishap: the original editing script got lost in Spain, and Valerii, as the head of Jolly's editorial department, had to rewrite the dialogue on the basis of the original script, changing it when necessary, in the parts where the story had been changed.[13] According to others, Valerii "simply took care, in collaboration with specialist Vinicio Marinucci [...] of *A Fistful of Dollars*' post-production, adapting here and there, as it often happens in this stage, a few lines of dialogue."[14] Valerii's comment: "Marinucci did not have anything to do with the film. He was my teacher in this job, and helped me in other movies, such as *Soviet Spy* and *Comradeship*, but on *A Fistful of Dollars* there were only Sergio and I at the moviola. Some lines, we invented them on the spot, during post-production. Leone stayed next to me and told me what the characters would say, and sometimes it was my turn to do the syllabic adaptation: I leaned on the original script, and whenever it did not fit, I would change it." One day, editor Roberto Cinquini pointed out to Leone that a scene badly needed a close-up of a burning fuse, before the explosions at Baxter's house. "Leone turned and said to me: 'Call Giovanni Corridori[15] and go shoot it!'"

A Fistful of Dollars came out on a hot Friday in August 1964. After a few days it was taken down—except for one theater in Florence. Then, in a short while, it started grossing a lot of money, the result of incessant word of mouth. The rest, as they say, is history. Or legend. And when one day a letter came from Japan, signed Akira Kurosawa, that accused Leone of plagiarism ("I have just had the chance to see your film. It is a very fine film, but it is *my* film"), Valerii and his bosses at Jolly had to try and come up with something to fix things up. First of all, there was that receipt of a private screening of *Yojimbo*, which Colombo and Papi had viewed at Leone's suggestion, to get rid of. And, most of all, there was the problem of facing the accusations on the part of Kurosawa's lawyers with a convincing line of defense, coming up with some Western literary source to the story of the hero who puts two families one against the other. And Valerii came up with quite an inventive one. "I came across the advertising for a theatrical performance of Carlo Goldoni's *Arlecchino servitore di due padroni*. I called Gastaldi, the lucky owner of a copy of the *Dizionario Bompiani delle opere e dei personaggi* (Bompiani Dictionary of Works and Characters) and asked him to read the plot for me on the phone."

Written in 1745, *Arlecchino servitore di due padroni* (Arlecchino, Servant of Two Masters) is one of the most popular of Goldoni's comedy plays, and in the tradition of the Commedia dell'Arte its original draft had large sections reserved for improvisations. It is the story of a young woman named Beatrice, who traveled to Venice disguised as a man, in search for the man who killed her brother. A series of complications and misunderstandings ensue. Meanwhile, Beatrice's servant, Arlecchino (known abroad as Truffaldino), is always trying to satiate his hunger by eating everything in sight; when the chance comes for him to serve another master, he sees the opportunity for an extra dinner, throwing himself into more trouble trying to fill the orders of two masters at the same time, playing both sides and running the risk of being uncovered. Vaguely, very vaguely, it could pass for some kind of a distant inspiration for Leone's film ... if, among other things, the judge closed one eye on the fact that Truffaldino was a comical character, while Eastwood's was definitely not. "That very afternoon I brought my idea to Papi, with a hint of shame for the irreverence [towards] the paragon. It was passed over to their lawyers who were enthusiastic about it. I was given an extra benefit of 300,000 *lire* for it. So it was that Goldoni became the inspiration for the Italian Western."[16] Not that Valerii's idea was of much use, though. Kurosawa won the trial, and Colombo and Papi probably cried all the way to the bank.

Soured by the strict contract signed with Jolly for *A Fistful of Dollars*, and by Papi and Colombo's refusal to pay him the set percentage, for his second Western Leone made a deal with Alberto Grimaldi, a Neapolitan lawyer who wanted to make the leap into the movie business and had already produced a couple of films. This time, Leone hired Valerii as his assistant. "Blasetti had shown me the way, Leone gave me the opportunity to follow it," the latter commented.

The genesis of *For a Few Dollars More* (the title is a patent jab directed at Papi and Colombo) is, again, fertile ground for conflicting versions. According to the most popular one, the movie would have originated from a treatment written by Fernando di Leo and Enzo Dell'Aquila, *Il cacciatore di taglie* (The Bounty Hunter), which Leone purchased and turned into a script together with Luciano Vincenzoni; Sergio Donati, uncredited on the film, was called in to make several passages more incisive. Valerii, who did not work on the script, nevertheless claimed to be the creator of the villain (who was initially called Tombstone and was a mere bandit), suggesting that Leone turn him into a psychotic *mestizo* who smokes marijuana and is prey to terrible withdrawal symptoms: El Indio.[17] However, Vincenzoni also claimed to have rewritten the character as it is in the film. Fernando di Leo's version of the facts is quite different, and he repeatedly stated that he had written almost the entire movie, after Tessari bowed out of the project: "I wrote the treatment all by myself, shaping the different characters and their psychologies; I called in Enzo Dell'Aquila because Sergio was in a hurry." According to Di Leo, the script, provisionally titled *La collina degli stivali* (Boot Hill), was "almost ninety percent the film that Sergio shot," including the character of El Indio, and with the exception of Sergio Donati's additional scenes, whereas Vincenzoni's contribution was little more than nominal.[18] The director of *Milan Calibre 9* (1972) added: "For the screenplay of *For a Few Dollars More*, the Neapolitan lawyer who produced the film gave me 300,000 *lire*, which [...] I gave to the group of Ben Bella's militia,[19] because back then such gestures had a meaning."[20] Di Leo's presence in the credits as assistant director—given that he never set foot on the set—was to be interpreted, in his own words, as "Sergio's homage: a subliminal 'thanks for existing.'" Dell'Aquila's take is somewhat different: "We were given 300,000 *lire* to write the treatment, then the thing passed on to Vincenzoni, who took away our names and re-wrote the film. It was the classic ghost-writing job."[21]

Valerii recalls the enthusiasm that overtook the entire crew during the making of *For a Few Dollars More*. Perhaps there was an awareness of being at work on an important motion picture, which was destined to make history just as much as the previous one, or perhaps there was just the dedication of a team of professionals who worked exceptionally well together. As the assistant director, Valerii chose the actors for bit parts, oversaw the preparation of the costumes and sets, and did location scouting for the outdoor scenes. Leone was so happy with his work that he gave him the task of preceding the crew in moving from one location to the other, and setting up everything in advance. On the set, the Abruzzi-born assistant also acted as a counselor of sorts. "I am often trenchant in my judgments, when I am convinced of something. And back then Sergio needed someone to back him up and give him certainties." It so happened that the camera operator Leone wanted, the Spanish-born Eduardo Noé ("An incredible talent, a great professional, the correspondant to what Barboni was to Italy") was busy in an American co-production. The Spanish assistant Julio Sempere suggested his own brother as a temporary replacement, but the new crew member quickly showed himself uncomfortable with the elaborate camera movements required by Leone.

> We soon realized he was not up to the job. Sergio called Julio and told him. But the cameraman had already shot several scenes, including a couple of difficult shots. What to do, then? Reshooting them meant losing one day, maybe two. Sergio turned to me: "But what we have already shot, was it good?" And I, instinctively: "Very good!" Actually, I did not know myself whether that scene was good, but that way I saved him a couple of days' extra work ... and at the end, watching the rushes, we found out it was indeed quite good, the cameraman's uncertainties were not visible.[22] Moral of the story? Sergio did not need anyone to tell him what to do, because he knew it all too well. He just needed someone who told him "*Bravo!*," who supported his ideas, who reassured him. And I believe that my small contribution to the film has been of this kind.

Chapter Three

A Taste of Directing

"I never go where I can send a bullet"
—Hank "Lanky" Fellows, *Taste of Killing*

By the mid–Sixties, Valerii knew the practice of moviemaking inside-out. He had mastered scriptwriting, gained experience on the set, and taken charge of post-production at every stage. He even tried his hand at the unsung art of film doctoring for Alberto Grimaldi, in one of those crazy recycling jobs that were typical of the era.

> In a blind purchase, Grimaldi had secured the reels of an incomplete German film: 30 cans, 2000 feet each. "I've already sold it to the distributor with the title *A 001: operazione Giamaica* [A001 Operation Jamaica]. Now it's your turn...." I began to watch the footage with the editor, and it made no sense whatsoever! I had to build a story based on what I saw: the problem though was that there was no sign of Jamaica in it! I asked around and finally retrieved a copy of an exotic documentary shot in Jamaica. With Grimaldi's approval I bought some footage, 15,000 *lire* per feet, and stitched some Jamaican view here and there in the film: landscapes, a funeral, and so on. Grimaldi paid 30 million *lire* for that crap, and in the end found himself with over 100 million grossed at the box office![1]

Finally, at 32, Valerii felt he was ready to take the big leap, and make his directorial debut. "I wanted to adapt a book called *Una volta sola nella vita*, published by Mondadori," he explained, referring to Tom Hanlin's novel *Once in Every Lifetime* (1945), which came out in Italy in 1947. "It was the story, set in a Scottish mining town, of a young miner who sees his friend die in a pithead collapse; the mine manager asks him to carry the news to the widow. The young woman arouses such pity in him, that the young man returns several times to visit her, and decides to marry her. My idea was to transpose it to Italy, in the Tuscan town of Larderello, among the geysers, changing the cultural context but not the degraded and miserable environment in which the story takes place."

Valerii's idea was fascinating, and would provide for a visually striking film. Larderello is truly one of the world's unique and fascinating places. The village is sited in a volcanically active area, with plenty of hot springs and explosive outbursts of steam, which earned the valley in which it is located the eerie name of *Valle del Diavolo* (Devil's Valley). In the 19th century, it became one of the first places in the world to exploit geothermal energy to support local industry. In 1827 the French scientist François de Larderel invented a way to extract boric acid from the volcanic mud. His work was supported by Leopold II, Grand Duke of Tuscany, who awarded Larderel the title of Count and funded a town, named Larderello in honor of his work, to house the workers in the boric acid production factory. In 1904, the zone was the site of a pioneering experiment in the production of energy from geothermal sources, and in 1911 the first geothermal power plant was built in the valley. It was the world's only industrial production site of geothermal energy until 1958, when another one was built in Wairakei, New Zealand. The choice of Tom Hanlin's novel underlined Valerii's penchant towards poignant melodrama, and would have made it one of the very few Italian films to deal with the Industrial expansion of the late 1800s and early 1900s—another being Mario Monicelli's extraordinary *The Organizer* (*I compagni*, 1963), set in a textile factory in Turin and starring Marcello Mastroianni, which had sadly been a box-office flop. But in full Spaghetti Western fever, fate commanded otherwise. And besides, Blasetti had warned the aspiring filmmaker that the important thing was not to miss an opportunity, even if it was not an ideal one, because it might not come again.

Opportunity came in an unexpected way, as Valerii was starting prep work on Leone's third Western, on which again he would act as assistant director. "I was preparing the shooting schedule for *The Good, the Bad and the Ugly* when the Genesi cousins called Leone to ask his advice on who to hire as the assistant for a Spanish filmmaker, Ricardo Blasco, who had to shoot a low-budget Western in Italy and Spain as Blasco's assistant director. Sergio said: 'Well, I am sorry to lose my assistant, but Tonino Valerii would do for you.'" In the meantime, though, Blasco had an argument with the producers, and took away the script with him. What to do? "The Genesi cousins had a meeting scheduled in Spain with their local co-producer, José López Moreno, within one week, and had to provide a screenplay. So they called me, and asked me to knock out a script."

Francesco and Vincenzo Genesi were the owners of Tecnostampa, one of the biggest printing and developing labs in the country, and were active in production as well. Thanks to engineer Mario Calzini, Tecnostampa had developed Cromoscope, a substitute for Techniscope,[2] the 35mm panoramic aspect ratio introduced in Italy in 1963 by Technicolor engineers Giovanni Ventimiglia and Giulio Monteleoni. In Techniscope, also known as 2P, each individual non-anamorphic frame was not spanned between four perforations of the negative as in the standard 35mm format, but between just two perforations, with a device that allowed to save 50 percent of film, drastically cutting the negative's cost. In addition to the economic benefits, there were more advantages: shooting with 2P did not require the expensive anamorphic lenses (and thus were avoided certain distortions of the image caused by the use of said lenses), and allowed for the employment of extreme focal lengths (such as wide-angle or telephoto lenses) and the zoom, with a more pronounced depth of field, and a smaller minimum focusing distance. The new format was not widespread in the U.S., but soon became very popular in Europe, and was employed by, among others, Leone himself on *A Fistful of Dollars* and in his subsequent films, as well as in dozens of Italian Westerns, becoming "the" Spaghetti Western format par excellence.[3]

Valerii had been toying with the idea of a Western centered on a bounty hunter who speculates on the lives of the wanted criminals as if he was playing on the stock market: When the criminal has a cheap reward on him, the bounty hunter leaves the former free to kill or steal; then, when the reward has been raised as a consequence of such deeds, he kills him and collects the money. A variation of sorts of Blondie and Tuco's routine in *The Good, the Bad and the Ugly*, if you will, but one with some punch, and nasty humor to boot. Now he had to write a script around that premise in record time, the same way he and Gastaldi had done with *Terror in the Crypt*.

> I went home, asked my sister to move to Rome, and locked myself in my bedroom for a week; every now and then she brought me a plate of spaghetti or a coffee, and I wrote and wrote.... The producers had to leave for Spain on a Wednesday; on Tuesday morning the script was finished. I gave it one last read, brought it

over to a copy center and got it back that evening. On Wednesday morning—the plane took off at 11 a.m.—I drove to Fiumicino with the script. The producer read it during the flight, and as soon as he landed in Madrid he called me, almost shouting: "It's great!" The Spanish co-producer liked it as well, and the film got made.

For the usual co-production reasons, the script is credited also to the Spanish writer Víctor Auz Castro, a former member of the Spanish censorship *junta*. As Valerii pointed out, "He signed the screenplay without even seeing it!"

The making of *Taste of Killing* (*Per il gusto di uccidere*)—Valerii's original script was titled *Cacciatore di taglie* (*Bounty Killer*)—brought many good memories for the novice director. On October 16, 1965, Tonino and Rita got married. They then headed to Madrid, for an adventurous honeymoon in a Volkswagen Beetle, on a journey that also touched Lourdes and San Sebastián, and was the occasion to do some location scouting for the film. "They told me to take the opportunity and visit some sets, and see the horses, the costumes, the upholstery. I got in touch with the co-producer, José López Moreno, and with him I did a small survey in Hoyo de Manzanares and La Pedriza, near Colmenar Viejo. I saw the *cuadras* with the marvelous Arab horses, and visited the tailoring workshop of the awarded Cornejo firm, specialized in stage and cinema wardrobe."

The budget was small, and filming went on for four and a half weeks. On the set, Valerii reunited with a pair of old acquaintances: executive producer Lucio Bompani, who recommended him as Modugno's assistant director on *Tutto è musica*; and Stelvio Massi, who also had a past at Leone's court as camera operator (credited as "Steve Rock" on *A Fistful of Dollars*) and was making his debut as director of photography. Massi and Valerii would work together again on *The Price of Power* and *A Girl Called Jules*. "I hired him on Bompani's advice. Stelvio was fast and technically prepared, and his contribution to my films has never been poor. He even improved over time, and became a good director. And he was a lovely person."

Shooting took place in Almería, in the Western town designed by Carlo Simi and already used in *For a Few Dollars More*; the bank where the gold that Hank Fellows must guard is kept is the El Paso bank in Leone's film. The cast was made up largely of Spanish actors who specialized in the genre, like Fernando Sancho and George Martin, along with Italian character actors such as Piero Lulli and Franco Ressel. The mustachioed, burly Sancho was a ubiquitous presence in co-productions of the period, because of his hypercharacterized physical appearance, which invariably relegated him to villain parts, on top of his own role within the then very powerful Spanish National Union of Performing Arts. A former athlete who recycled himself in films as a stuntman and master of arms before finally landing acting roles, the handsome George Martin (alias Francisco Martínez Celeiro) moved from Westerns to spy flicks and action thrillers, standing out more for his athleticism than for his acting skills.

For the leading role of Hank Fellows (actually, just "Lanky Fellow" in the script and in the Italian version, in a literal translation of his looks), the Italian distributor Titanus chose a young American actor whom Valerii had noticed on a photo resume. He had "an extraordinary face, looking a bit like Sean Connery, but younger. Handsome, virile. We hired him on the spot, he comes in and all hell breaks loose." The director did not recall the actor's name, but a penned notation on the title page of the script kept at the CSC library in Rome, and dated December 13, 1965, features precious details on the film: not only the director's name ("A. Valer," [sic]) and the estimated budget (125 million *lire*, whether overall or only for the Italian participation is anyone's guess), but also the indication "shooting: Italy and Spain" plus four actors' names: "R. Warren, C. Estrada, Ressel, Meli." This seems to imply that, whereas Franco Ressel was the first choice as Aarons, Spanish actor Carlos Estrada was initially considered for the role of Kennebeck. One wonders whether the mysterious "R. Warren" was the lead Valerii had settled for.

However, plans had to be drastically changed when the unnamed actor arrived in Italy stuffed with amphetamines: He created an uproar on the plane and that night he had to be taken away from the hotel to avoid a formal complaint. The young man was admitted to a clinic where he stayed for a few weeks. When he came out, the film had already been shot without him. "We had to choose a replacement overnight. An agent came, I think Pippo Cortini, and suggested Craig Hill, available the very next day. He showed up, we dressed him up in his costume and started shooting the very next day." The then-39-year-old Hill was a rather well-known face because of a television series entitled *Whirlybirds*, co-starring Kenneth Tobey and broadcast in the U.S. between 1957 and 1960. He had arrived in Italy in the following years and played in Rafael Romero Marchent's *Hands of a Gunfighter* (*Ocaso de un pistolero*, 1965). Hill would become a recurrent face in Euro productions.[4] He was a makeshift protagonist, and not a particularly skilled actor, but his lanky physique and cerulean eyes make him quite a compelling presence.

Italian poster for *A Taste of Killing* (1966).

Taste of Killing

A military convoy which carries money is attacked by the ferocious Sanchez and his gang. After the robbery, the bandits split: Sanchez and a couple of henchmen head across the border with the loot, the others wear the the dead soldiers' uniforms to rob the Omaha City bank. Bounty hunter

Hank "Lanky" Fellows, who witnessed the assault, follows Sanchez, kills him and retrieves the money; then he returns to Omaha City in time to foil the robbery and collect the 10,000 dollar reward. The wealthy mine owner Collins, who has just sold 100,000 dollars in gold to the state of Texas, offers to Fellows the job of guarding the gold—which will be deposited in the bank for three days until the army arrives to take possession—using the reward mone as insurance. If the gold is stolen, Fellows will lose his money; otherwise, it will be doubled. Meanwhile, a bandit named Gus Kennebeck, who three years earlier had killed Lanky's brother, finds out about the load of gold from his brother John, who leads a honest life, and kidnaps the latter's daughter, Peggy. Fellows foils a first attack on the gold, then takes away the chest from the bank and hides it in a secret place. After arresting the bandit's right-hand man, Machete, who confesses the gang's plans, Lanky has Kennebeck's son kidnapped. The bandits arrive in Omaha City, but are welcomed by snipers and decimated. The survivors manage to get into the vault, but have a nasty surprise: instead of the gold, there is a barrel of explosives, which Lanky sets off from a distance. Only Kennebeck is left alive: Lanky faces off the bandit in a duel and kills him. The gold—which had always been in plain sight, disguised as bricks on the front steps of the bank—is safe. Lanky leaves Omaha City and lies in wait on the top of a hill, waiting for the military convoy that has left the city with the gold to be attacked by yet another gang of desperados.[5]

Tonino Valerii's feature film debut opens on the profile of a man on horseback who rides in silhouette on a sand dune, before advancing toward the camera, accompanied by a typical Western ballad written by Nico Fidenco. It is an iconic image, which seems to corroborate a mythical vision of the Wild West, and suggest a heroic and romantic model—a premise denied by the rest of the movie. The opening titles, based on concentric multicolored circles and the cast and crew credits blown away to the sound of gunfire, immediately pay homage to the master, but Valerii is seeking his own way into the genre, and a different one than Leone's. Craig Hill's "Lanky" Fellows is, indeed, a close relative of Clint Eastwood's Man with No Name: he speaks in one-liners ("I never go where I can send a bullet") and is driven not by nobility but by money—to the point of postponing his revenge upon the bandit who killed his brother in order to speculate on the reward.

Even though his deeds are often juxtaposed with the humorous musings of an old man (Eugenio Galadini) who acts as a semi-serious chorus to the story, Lanky is indeed an exterminating angel of sorts. He never gets his hands dirty, though, except when absolutely necessary: He remains on the sidelines during Machete's beating (but it's he who suggests kidnapping Kennebeck's son), and sends the best sharpshooters in Omaha City into the fray against Kennebeck's gang without even personally firing a single bullet, simply making sure that his plan reaches fruition. Lanky is a distant and ubiquitous observer, who turns up on top of mountains, behind dark corners or curtains, and never reveals himself but watches the action at a distance, often through the lens of the telescope which he has attached to his rifle. In a way, it can be said that Valerii's bounty hunter orchestrates the events like a film director *ante litteram*—hence the detail of the telescope, acting like a substitute for the movie camera. But whereas Clint Eastwood's cigar-chomping stranger is, after all, a character who captures the viewer's imagination and earns sympathy—especially in *For a Few Dollars More*, where the script serves Eastwood some of the best lines of his career—*Taste of Killing*'s unflappable, cold-eyed bounty killer is a "hero" completely devoid of ethics, who in the opening scene allows a gang of marauders to rob and massacre a convoy of soldiers so as to recover the stolen goods and earn the reward, and who is about to do exactly the same in the cynical ending. At least those that Leone's stranger pit against each other were members of two criminal families.... And if Fernando Sancho's sweaty Mexican bandit Sanchez—who laughs out loud and waves his arms like any *bandido* worthy of such a name, and proclaims "The only time a soldier's your friend is when he's lying dead at your feet.... I want lots of friends like that!," a line which recalls El Indio's notorious motto in *For a Few Dollars More*—is a traditional villain, the boundaries become more blurred in the confrontation between Fellows and Kennebeck. For one thing, the "good guy" repays the bad ones with the very same methods, starting with the kidnapping of innocents. At the end, Valerii reserves the dead bandit a short requiem, as Kennebeck's lover (Rada Rassimov) mourns over his body after the final duel. Significantly, these characteristics come off more evidently in the film than in the script, which included an unfilmed prologue where Lanky falls into an ambush set up by Kennebeck and Machete, is gravely injured and left for dead and then thrown into the Rio Grande. He survives and goes on what is primarily a revenge mission, a trait almost totally erased in the film, where there's barely a mention of Lanky's will to avenge his brother—definitely a less urgent need than the one for money.

Even though he is at his career debut, Leone's ex-assistant already shows a keen eye for framing and pacing. "Everything I had to do, I had it written down in the script. The only way to save myself was to do it as best I could: every little thing, from the gags to the action scenes, were minutely described in the script," he explained, and it is indeed true, as the *Cacciatore di taglie* screenplay features extremely detailed indications of camera movements, shots and cuts. Valerii even dared some elaborate shots, such as the one that shows the fleeing bandits jumping on the bandwagon as the camera pans leftwards as it rises on a dolly towards the balcony where Fellows is taking aim, or the one in which the camera follows a fuse which comes out of the bank, unfolds on the ground, passes on the telegraph wire and finally ends right by Lanky, on the roof, ready to light it. Overall, however, the style is classic, respectful of the rules. "In my first film I scrupulously stuck with the ABC of film-making: master shot, inserts, camera movements, the dialogue spoken before cutting, the classical way. There were no such inventions as in Monte Hellman's films, which are apparently very messy but are actually very free, experimental in the use of film language. *Taste of Killing* was an honest little movie, made according to the rules, and applying them to the letter. Whereas *Day of Anger* was already shot in a much looser manner."

With the partial exception of Peggy's kidnapping, and the bloated, if barely touched upon, love story between the girl and her jailer—the story's real weak point—the canonical ninety minutes flow seamlessly. The outbursts of violence—partially softened at the demand of the board of censors to get an "all audiences" rating,[6] and stigmatized by some reviewers at the time[7]—comply with the escalating brutality of Leone's epigones without reaching the paroxysm of Monco's prolonged beating by El Indio's gang in *For a Few Dollars More*, not to mention the Grand Guignol excesses of *Django* (1966, Sergio Corbucci). Machete impales a guy with the weapon that gives him his nickname, and Kennebeck tortures his brother by pouring hot coffee in his face, in a moment that recalls Fritz Lang's *The Big Heat* (1953). The final duel between Lanky and Kennebeck stands out: The two men swap their weapons, the bandit takes aim through the telescope, and Lanky shoots him in the eye through the

Spanish poster for *A Taste of Killing*.

viewfinder. It is a show-stopping moment, likely to have had audiences of the time cheering and applauding in awe, that Valerii would recycle verbatim in the final confrontation between Marco (Fabio Testi) and the biker-cum-hitman (Antonio Marsina) in the climax of *Go Gorilla Go*, and which possibly influenced other filmmakers—think of the notorious sequence in *Opera* (1987, Dario Argento) in which the murderer kills Mira (Daria Nicolodi) by shooting through the door's peephole and through her eye.

Irony is the point where Valerii's debut comes off with greater clarity than Leone's model, moving beyond the "crude, earthy sense of humor" (as defined by Sir Christopher Frayling[8]) of the Roman filmmaker to a sharper black humor, and punctuating the film with visual gags that soften its tone, such as the twin bartenders who rub the saloon bench in unison, and at the slightest danger of a shooting drop down an iron gate to protect the bar, or the "pigeon house" atop a building on the main street from which the old man observes events through a mirror device. Even more exquisite, though, is Valerii's handling of the way Fellows hides the gold in plain sight, most likely a reference to Edgar Allan Poe's *The Purloined Letter*, and a hint at the director's literary taste, which would manifest itself in his following Westerns.

However, a biting aftertaste remains: Violence is everywhere, to the point that in a scene we see Kennebeck's young son intent on assembling bullets, and in the end it is not the "good guys" who win, but the wealthy ones—such as the big-time shark Collins (Piero Lulli), who, we sense, has built his fortune by extracting mining licenses from the weakest, like Gerald Mohr and his gang of claim jumpers did in Don Siegel's *The Duel at Silver Creek* (1952). The West depicted in *Taste of Killing* is already a paleocapitalistic one, which has moved on from the accumulation of the "fistful of dollars" to its investment. Hank Fellows is a stock market speculator ahead of his time, who ups the ante and lets rewards reach the limit, until he is sure to be able to collect the highest possible sum. "How much you worth now?" he asks a bandit, in a line virtually identical to one in *The Good, the Bad and the Ugly*: "1000 lousy dollars!" "That's your limit, you're not worth more than that..." he comments before shooting him. He is an illiterate ("I'm only able to read the figures on banknotes and bounty posters") who nevertheless has figured out how to do business in a capitalist system, so much so that his motto is "You can never have too much money." A way of saying, between a shot and a smile, that history is made by the rich, those who already are and those who will become so, and when the man with the gun meets the man with the money, the one who will come out on top is always the man with the fat wallet.

CHAPTER FOUR

Oedipus in the West

"When you start killing you can't stop it."
—Frank Talby, *Day of Anger*

Taste of Killing was greeted with rather positive reviews, sometimes surprisingly so for a genre product. It was too bad that the debuting director's name (not hidden behind a pseudonym, unlike many of his peers) was invarialby misspelled as "Valeri" in newpapers.[1] Box-office grossings were fairly good: almost 500 million *lire*, far from the year's most successful Westerns—*The Good, the Bad and the Ugly* grossed well over 3 billion *lire*; the second, Giorgio Ferroni's *For a Few Extra Dollars* (*Per pochi dollari ancora*, 1966) was outdistanced at 1,300 billion; *Django* slightly topped the 1 billion figure)—but more than enough to swell Genesi's coffers. Valerii recalled with pleasure the first screening of *Taste of Killing* at Fonoroma. "There was a large auditorium where film music was recorded, and which sometimes was used as a projection room. It was packed full. I find myself an empty seat and sit down. The film ends. A man next to me gets up, calls Genesi. 'What was the guaranteed minimum we'd arranged?' '30 million...' 'I'll double it up, the movie's good! Where's the director?' It was Goffredo Lombardo. The next day he summoned me at his office and I signed a contract for two films."

Meanwhile, on Stelvio Massi's advice, Valerii—who had just become the father of a little girl, Francesca, born on January 4, 1967—signed a deal to make his second feature film with Alfonso Sansone and Henryk Chrosicki's Sancrosiap (formerly Sancro Film), the production company behind such works as Marco Ferreri's *The Conjugal Bed* (*L'ape regina*, 1963) and *The Wedding March* (*Marcia nuziale*, 1965), Antonio Pietrangeli's *The Magnificent Cuckold* (*Il magnifico cornuto*, 1965), and Gian Luigi Polidoro's *Run for Your Wife* (*Una moglie americana*, 1965). As Valerii recalled, *Day of Anger* was the brainchild of a young man from Biella, Renzo Genta: "He paid a visit to Ernesto Gastaldi, said that he wanted to make movies, and told him this story about an old gunslinger who, starting to feel arthritic hands and fearing of not having a fast draw anymore, teaches a boy how to shoot in his place. In a way, it is the tale of a corruption."

Genta and Gastaldi knocked out a story, *Il ragazzo e il pistolero* (The Boy and the Gunman) which Sansone and Chrosicki liked. For the role of Scott "Mary," the young man born in a brothel and the victim of a hostile environment, Valerii wanted Lou Castel: "He seemed to me the most suitable actor for the role of this tormented kid, a character in his ropes after Bellocchio's *Fists in the Pocket*.[2] But I was told that Castel was not a name appreciated by the distributor since he was not commercial enough, whereas if we had cast Giuliano Gemma the film would be made immediately."

Launched by the semi-parodic *peplum* flick *My Son, the Hero* (*Arrivano i titani*, 1962), Duccio Tessari's directorial debut, the handsome and athletic Giuliano Gemma (1938–2013) had moved on to Westerns with *A Pistol for Ringo*, a.k.a. *Ballad of Death Valley* (*Una pistola per Ringo*, 1965) also directed by Tessari, who applied to the newborn genre the same method with which he'd experimented on the sword-and-sandal, softening its rough edges. With such titles as *Blood for a Silver Dollar* (*Un dollaro bucato*, 1965, Giorgio Ferroni), *The Return of Ringo*, a.k.a. *Blood at Sundown* (*Il ritorno di Ringo*, 1965) and *For a Few Extra Dollars*, Gemma (initially credited as "Montgomery Wood") had consolidated his image of nice-guy-in-the-West, loved by the young and old alike, "a sympathetic and socialite replica of the impassive U.S.-born Eastwood."³ Moreover—Valerii would learn about this only later—Gemma was an associate of the Bologna-based distribution company Cidif, a fact that would guarantee the film's commercial fortunes. A chance meeting near Porta Portese between director and actor led to the deal.⁴ Gastaldi and Valerii rearranged the script in order to suit it to their star, but the producers informed them of having entered into a co-production agreement with a German company: therefore, it was necessary that the resulting movie be the adaptation of a Western novel by Ron Barker, *Der Tod ritt dienstags* (Death Rides on Tuesday), published in Germany in 1963. "It was crap, absolutely impossible to film," Valerii commented. "'Oh well,' they said, 'you just put something from the book into the script, so that we can claim that it's based on the book.' We took very few things from it, I think perhaps just the scene in the saloon, while the rest is all flour from my sack and Ernesto's." Gastaldi confirmed: "They forced us to slip in a few pages of the book in the second half of the film, which in fact in those moments has a rather awkward break."⁵

Then, it was time to cast the actor who would play the gunslinger, Frank Talby. "At this point we thought: given that we are spending so much money on Gemma—whose salary was already several million *lire* at the time—why not cast a big name for the U.S. market? And we chose Lee Van Cleef." The aquiline-nosed and lynx-eyed character actor, invariably doomed to die before the end credits in his brief appearances in Hollywood films, from *High Noon* (1952, Fred Zinnemann) to *Ride Lonesome* (1959, Budd Boetticher), to *China Gate* (1957, Samuel Fuller) to *The Bravados* (1958, Henry King), had experienced an unexpected professional rebirth thanks to Sergio Leone, who had gone all the way to America to find him, armed only with an old photograph. By that time Van Cleef had abandoned all hope of making it in the movie business and earned his living as a painter. With *For a Few Dollars More*, where he played Colonel Mortimer, and *The Good, the Bad and the Ugly*, as the ruthless gunslinger "Sentenza," Van Cleef's name had become a box-office lure, and the actor had turned into one of the Italian Western's most recognizable icons. For *Day of Anger*, Van Cleef abandoned the flat-brimmed hat and belt worn in the previous works, but kept his inseparable meerschaum pipe. Rounding out the cast were the German-born Walter Rilla, the father of film director Wolf (*Village of the Damned*) and Christa Linder, and Yvonne Sanson, the veteran of so many films by Riccardo Freda, Alberto Lattuada and Raffaello Matarazzo, in the brief role of the brothel's madam ("She was an old cinephile love of mine. I said to myself that, as soon a the opportunity arose, I would find a role for her in one of my films"), plus a number of Italian and Spanish character actors, such as Andrea Bosic, Ennio Balbo, José Calvo and future Jess Franco regular, Ricardo Palacios.

Shooting lasted nine weeks, of which only two were spent in Spain; there, Valerii filmed the exteriors. The scenes in which Scott follows Talby on the back of a mule were shot at Llano Mellado, Rambla Del Cautivo and Rambla Lanújar; the village of Los Albaricoques (Agua Caliente in *For a Few Dollars More*) became Wild Jack's (Al Mulock) hideout; Cortijo El Sotillo near San José (seen in *A Fistful of Dollars*' opening scene) posed as the Stafford Ranch; Talby's torture and the duel on horseback between Talby and Owen White were also filmed near El Sotillo. The rest, including the scenes set in Clifton, was filmed in Rome. "The town was rebuilt on the ruins of the small village set where Sergio had shot the scene of the telegrapher forced to transmit a message in *For a Few Dollars More*," the director pointed out: "In fact, it was rebuilt from scratch." Among the additions, there was Judge Cutchell's imposing house, and one of the most significant expenses in the budget concerned the saloon which is destroyed in a fire started by Talby in a scene (a rare occurrence in Euro Western, where sets were usually recycled from film to film) and replaced by the surreal "Forty-Five Saloon." The "Old Mill" on the outskirts of Clifton, where Scott is ambushed, was filmed at the ranch set at Mazzano Romano, in Lazio.

Filming went on smoothly enough, despite the American actor's drinking problem. "Lee Van Cleef was an adorable man, but only up to a certain time of the day," Gemma explained. "Then, unfortunately, he started to drink."[6] The director recalled only one unpleasant episode occurred on the set:

> His wife had left the set a few hours earlier, and recommended us not to let him drink, but Van Cleef had gone to the catering desk, drank two or three glasses of Chinchón, that strong anise liquor which contains 73% alcohol, and got drunk. He could not tell fiction from reality. Giuliano was shooting a scene with Al Mulock, in which Mulock breaks a bottle and puts its neck close to Giuliano's throat. At that point, Lee turned up on the set, shirtless, approached Al shouting: "You don't treat my friend Giuliano like that!" and kicked him in the balls! Then, behind me, Benito whispered, "If you're a smart guy, now you call it a day and send everyone home..."

Day of Anger marked the beginning of the working partnership between Valerii and Benito Stefanelli, one of Italian cinema's most respected masters of arms. In Westerns, as it would be with the crime films, the relationship between a director and the master of arms is essential for the success of the action sequences, which are studied in detail before shooting. It is up to the master of arms to recruit the stuntmen and train them. "When the Americans made *Ben-Hur* in Rome, one full year before shooting started, the head stunt Yakima Canutt came to Rome with his two sons, to train the stuntmen for the chariot race, and the first thing they did was to recruit athletes in circuses. It is from there that many of the most famous stuntmen and masters of arms came, such as Nazzareno Zamperla, who was Giuliano Gemma's trusted stuntman." Yet Stefanelli was not from the circus: during Fascism his family had settled in Libya, from where the young Benito, born in 1928, had been repatriated to Italy during World War II. He entered the film business due to his skills as horseman, and after years of apprenticeship he debuted as master of arms in 1960, with Guido Malatesta's *Road of the Giants* (*La strada dei giganti*). He and Valerii had first met on the set of Leone's film, where Stefanelli also had a small role under the alias Benny Reeves. In *Taste of Killing*, the debuting director had been entrusted by Bompani with stunt coordinator Remo De Angelis, who "did beautiful things, but relied on rather 'heavy' effects. Benito's was a more modern way to be a master of arms, compared with De Angelis, whose fight scenes looked somewhat forced at times. Those coordinated by Stefanelli were more spontaneous, they looked real." At the first opportunity, then, Valerii called Stefanelli, and

Giuliano Gemma in *Day of Anger* (1967).

also had him play the role of the gunslinger Owen White, nicknamed "The Saint." The two would work together again on *The Price of Power*, *A Reason to Live, a Reason to Die!*, *My Name Is Nobody* and *Il ricatto*.

Valerii and Stefanelli got along well. Theirs was a professional relationship and a friendship as well: the experienced stuntman did not disdain valuable advices to the young filmmaker, as an older brother would do, and helped him overcome the small and large daily mishaps. "One day we have to shoot the scene where the three hitmen arrive to kill Van Cleef, and one of them, with whom we filmed the day before, does not show up. I call Benito and ask him what happened. He is truly pissed off: 'Don't mention it, when I see him again I'm gonna kill him!' 'Come on, stay cool, tell me what happened!' 'Well, he's gone to the Naples racetrack, to drug a horse!' So we had to make do as best we could. That's what could happen back then, on the set."

Day of Anger

In the peaceful town of Clifton, the young Scott, the son of a prostitute and an unknown father, is assigned to humiliating tasks, like emptying the town's toilets, and is treated as a pariah by the other citizens. Scott, whose only friends are a half-blind tramp, Blind Bill, and the wise stableman Murph Allan, dreams of buying a gun and avenging the humiliations and insults he received. One day a stranger comes to town: aging gunslinger Frank Talby, who takes a liking to the boy. In turn, Scott sees Talby as a father figure. When Talby, after provoking and killing a man at the saloon, leaves Clifton, Scott follows him: the gunslinger imparts to him a series of life lessons, in the form of cynical commandments. Talby is looking for an old buddy, Wild Jack, who has just escaped from jail. Jack, who owes Talby 50,000 dollars, had robbed a train with the complicity of some notable Clifton citizens, who then betrayed him and had him convicted, so as to keep the stolen money to themselves. Talby has Wild Jack give him the names of his ex-accomplices, then kills him. Captured and tortured by Wild Jack's thugs, Frank is rescued by Scott. The two men return to Clifton, where Talby, via threats and blackmail, manages to hold the town in his grip, with the now-ruthless Scott acting as his right-hand man. Turner the banker, Judge Cutchell and the owner of the saloon, Murray, hire a hitman to dispatch him, but Talby has the upper hand. Determined to build a real empire, Talby sets fire to the saloon (killing Murray in the process), rebuilds a new one, and surrounds himself with a small army of gunmen; Murph tries to warn Scott, telling him that when Talby will no longer need him, he will get rid of him. Increasingly disillusioned with his mentor, Scott falls into a trap set up for him by Cutchell's daughter and is severely wounded; once recovered, he finds out that Murph has become sheriff. Scott fails to save his friend from Talby, but he then faces his old master in a duel with a gun which belonged to Doc Holliday, and prevails. Scott shows no mercy towards the wounded Talby, who begs to be spared, but then throws the gun away in disgust, and leaves the town with Blind Bill.

The idea for *Day of Anger* is not unprecedented: it was a contemporary of *Death Rides a Horse* (*Da uomo a uomo*, 1967, Giulio Petroni, starring Van Cleef and John Phillip Law), *Bandidos* (1967, Massimo Dallamano) and the delirious *Last of the Badmen* (*Il tempo degli avvoltoi*, 1967, Nando Cicero, starring Frank Wolff and George Hilton), all focused on a relationship between a mentor and a pupil of sorts. A similar motif would return in Giancarlo Santi's *The Grand Duel* (*Il grande duello*, 1972), also written by Gastaldi and starring Van Cleef. Even Talby's teachings have a singular antecedent in Gianni Puccini's *Fury of Johnny Kid* (*Dove si spara di più*, 1967), where the young protagonist (Peter Lee Lawrence) is told that "the Holy Colt has six commandments"—which include shoot to kill, finish off the wounded, and never turn your back on another man's gun. What is more, many American Westerns depicted the relationship between a younger gunman and an older one (yet sometimes reversing the prospect, and making the latter the hero, as in Robert Aldrich's *Vera Cruz*, 1954). An interesting antecedent to Valerii's film might also be Allen H. Miner's little-seen *Black Patch* (1957), an intriguing psychological Western starring George Montgomery as Clay Morgan, a one-eyed Sheriff in a New Mexico town who is forced to arrest his former best friend Hank (played by screenwriter Leo Gordon) after a bank robbery, and is framed for the latter's murder by the local seedy saloon owner (Sebastian Cabot, playing the spinet and dipping bullets in champagne so as to sabotage them). The analogies rely mostly in the character of a young apprentice, Carl "Flytrap" (Tom Pittman), humiliated and ridiculed by the townspeople and befriended by Hank, who becomes the fastest gun in town and swears vengeance against the Sheriff.[7]

Still, *Day of Anger* focuses with undeniable power on a theme that would become a recurrent one in Valerii's *oeuvre*, and which the director himself summarized as "the long search for the father": the naive Scott, born and raised in a brothel and used to the most menial jobs, selects the charismatic Frank Talby as a father figure, in lieu of that parent that he never met; Talby, for his part, baptizes him (Scott "Mary," with his mother's name to act as surname) and gives him a series of life lessons, ten "commandments" aimed at shaping Scott in his own image and likeness.

Never beg another man.
Never trust anyone.
Never get between a gun and its target.
Punches are like bullets. If you don't make the first ones count, you might just be finished.
If you wound a man, you better kill him. Because sooner or later he's gonna kill you.
The right bullet at the right time.
If you untie a man, take his gun before that.
Don't give a man any more bullets than what he's got use for.
A challenge shouldn't be refused, no matter what it might mean to you.
When you start killing you can't stop it.

An instinctive sympathy—the unconscious solidarity between outsiders—is immediately established between the two men. But Valerii ends the scene of their first encounter with a sinister gloss, by showing Talby heading left, to the saloon, while Scott goes to the right, bringing the gunslinger's horse with him: an image that prelsages the different directions the two men will eventually take.

Scott's "education" goes through rites of passage: the "father" tests his pent-up anger and desire for revenge right from the start[8]; then he welcomes Scott at his table, offers him a whisky, and demonstrates his own power, by provoking and killing another customer. The murder of Perkins (played by stuntman and character actor Romano Puppo, an inescapable presence in many films by Enzo G. Castellari, as well as Van Cleef's double in the scene where Talby is dragged by Wild Jack's men on horseback and in the duel with Owen) is Scott's first encounter with death. And when, after gulping down a shot of alcohol, the young man confesses it was the first whisky of his life, Talby's reply is: "You better have another drink to keep it company." The same goes for killing: the most difficult is the first one. Talby's tenth commandment, the one which he conceals to Scott up to the very last, says precisely that: When you start killing, you can't stop it.

All this leads to the film's core: the theme of generational conflicts, that is "the salt of the earth [...] concord and discord, the old and the new, wisdom and inexperience one against the other."[9] The development lends itself to a number of interpretations—literary, religious, mythological, psychoanalytic. Starting, of course, with the title's Biblical references and Talby's commandments, ten like those in the Old Testament, of which more than one are a reversal (the gunman must never pray, nor trust anyone, and not show mercy); if Gastaldi was drawing on the "Holy Colt commandments" of Puccini's film, he certainly improved upon them. The relationship between Talby and Scott, with the latter brainwashed by the mature gunslinger's personality to the point of undergoing an impressive psychological transformation himself, takes on Faustian shades ("You sold your life for very little," says the Marshall to Scott); Talby himself is a cruel Cronus-like figure, who devours his sons for fear of raising a rival. And when the time comes to buy Scott a gun, he deliberately discards three short-barrelled guns in favor of a long-barrelled one—apparently a more imposing weapon, with the implied phallic innuendo—so as to slow down Scott's draw.[10]

"Their encounter becomes a paradigm of Oedipus' tragedy," Valerii commented. "In order to grow up, the young man must kill his father, in Freud's old axiom: until you kill the father figure, of course not materially but inside you, you cannot emerge. This is what the film was trying to tell." It was a theme underlined by the renowned Italian film critic Tullio Kezich, who wrote: "The title draws from Salacrou,[11] the story from the tradition of psychological Western. We are indeed in the thread of the Oedipal Western…. The gruesome effects and the even too smart hesitations belong to the Leone recipe; but this time, on the thin bones of the Italian Western, there is a little psychological and sociological pulp."[12] Kezich was not the only one who noticed the Oedipus reference, as Valerii pointed out. "One day I invited Pepe Calvo to visit Siena, which he adored as a city of art, but where he had never been to. So, one Sunday morning, I went to his hotel to pick him up and drove him there. During the trip, my wife asked him if the part he was playing in my film seemed interesting to him: 'Señora, no se…' he replied, 'it's the first time I'm playing Tiresias in a movie…' and then he laughed out loud! Kezich never loved the Italian Western, but perhaps he understood it more than anyone else."

Italian lobby card for *Day of Anger*.

The Oedipal significance is related to the director's personal experiences. "I started shooting *Day of Anger* a few months after telling my analyst, Professor Stefano Fajrajzen, that I considered my training over. Kezich must have sensed something of my Freudian experience and developed it in his review of the film." Valerii had been in analysis for three years with Fajrajzen, the brother of stage director Alessandro Fersen, for a depression with deep roots.

> My mother lost two daughters at a very early age. Elvira, the first, whom I never knew, but about whom all in the family spoke of as a little angel: sweet, affectionate, obedient. The only image I have of her is her photo on her deathbed. With the second, Anna, I spent my childhood. She was an adorable little girl, my playmate. But one day we argued, over one of those silly things kids fight for, and I, with one of those hysterical gestures typical of childhood, threw at her the first thing that came to hand. It was a pair of scissors that sank into her thigh. I was upset by the episode, and to this day I still cannot forgive myself. I believe my gesture had a great influence on my situation. When Anna died, my mother fell into a depression: she kept the windows and the shutters constantly closed, because the death of her daughters urged her to live in the dark, as if to deny herself the light that had gone with them. The three years of analysis benefited a lot, and I learned to understand that with time the analysis is tempered. At the beginning it gives you a potent charge, helps you grow up, motivates you; then it wears out. Just as feelings do.

The final duel, in which the student backfires on the master the commandments the latter had given him, has the flavor of a ritual parricide, even more so as the weapon itself is surrounded by a mythical halo, being the gun Doc Holliday had used in the Tombstone shootout, "endowed with the tricks of three generations of gunmen," as a character points out. In the end, Talby is on the ground, wounded, and Scott towers over him. "Find me a horse, Scotty—I'll get out of your way," he begs, breaking his own first commandment, with a line that desperately echoes a famous one from *Richard III*. Scott, almost in tears, shakes his head: "I learned your lessons like a good boy. When a man has been wounded, you've gotta end it. Or it might be that later he'll try to kill you...." But once he has accomplished his cathartic mission, Scott/Oedipus throws away his gun and walks away towards an uncertain future with his Tiresias. A conclusion that strips the typical climactic showdown of any spectacular artifice: when Scott shoots Talby point blank in the head—and Valerii chooses to show the act in a single shot, without the relief of the shot-counter-shot routine to ease the brutality of the gesture—what is left is not adrenaline, masterfully urged by *The Good, the Bad and the Ugly*'s three-way duel, but a sense of void and desolation.

Day of Anger represents a symbolic parricide for Valerii as well: the director repudiates the irony of *Taste of Killing* and the postmodern winks of the Italian Western, and shakes off the bulky shadow of Sergio Leone. What is left of the father-cum-master of the trend are merely the vestiges: the colorful opening credits (by Iginio Lardani), accompanied by Riz Ortolani's beautiful score,[13] and the iconic power of close-ups in the sequence of the duel—but in this dark, desperate, plumbeous Western yarn, Leone's discourse on the genre's mythology (either homage or critical re-reading) gives way to an introspective, problematic approach. "After the boom of Italian Western," Valerii stated just before the film's release, "we have witnessed an inflation of movies full of violence and deaths, where it was quite clear that no one was afraid of guns anymore. Why did we come to this? In my opinion, because of the disappearance of the American Western. ... I, who do not like violence, have felt the need to downsize a bit all that the Italian Western emphasized in recent times." All this is served by a direction more attentive to details than to effects, and often elegant in its visual solutions: the opening dolly shot which starts next to Clifton's sign and descends on the main street to introduce Scott; the editing cut from Talby, who, after killing Perkins in the saloon, beats the glass on the table asking for whisky, to the judge who beats his hammer before pronouncing sentence; the use of mirrors (as in the effective sequence of Scott's entrance in the saloon) within the frame to avoid the shot-reverse shot routine. Gastaldi was not stingy with compliments about the way Valerii developed his material, stating that the movie was "superbly shot."[14]

Day of Anger is an adult genre film that makes few concessions to the audience, and depicts two interesting multi-faceted main characters. Talby is a further evolution of the neocapitalist gunman seen in *Taste of Killing*: Instead of asking to be paid in cash the 50,000 dollars that he's owed, he obtains a small cash advance and works his way up, alternating his Colt with official papers ("What's done inside the law is sometimes safer than what's done outside the law," he claims), thus building a business empire and becoming the owner of the whole town, in a narrative turn perhaps inspired by Edward Dmytryk's *Warlock* (1959). It is no longer the time when "a good pistol was worth more than money in the bank," and Talby has realized that the spring of capitalism is expansion, through economical investment; for his business he chooses a small town whose immaculate façade hides a den of snakes, and where order is maintained by the ruling oligarchy through rigid class relations that the aging self-made man systematically overturns. Talby's is a distorted reinterpretation of the American Dream, as well as the last chance to carve himself respectability after a whole life wandering, before someone younger and faster settles the score with him. "Pretty soon, I'll be opening up a new saloon," he announces. It is called "The Forty-Five" in honor of the Colt that helped building it—and which becomes, literally, its pillar.

Scott's American Dream hinges on violence as well, embodied by the Colt that he dreams of purchasing, laboriously putting aside his savings for the purpose. Scott is an angry young man who harbors class revenge, and it is no wonder that Valerii had initially thought of Lou Castel, the symbol of protest in Italian cinema from *Fists in the Pocket* onwards; in such regard, a significant moment is the exchange between the doctor and Talby, about Scott's nature and the deterministic environment in which he grew up: "What did you do to him? He's acting like some rabid wolf!" "He was born a wolf—you made it rabid, not me." For Gemma, after the "light" characterizations of the two *Ringo* films, it was the opportunity to test his skills in drama, already glimpsed in *Long Days of Vengeance* (*I lunghi giorni della vendetta*, 1967, Florestano Vancini), in a more challenging and ambiguous role, far from the all-round hero in Tessari and Ferroni's films, as well as from Leone's vulgar imitators. The actor emphasized the film's moral qualities: "*Day of Anger* is a Western on personal and social injustice, and on the hardship endured by the individual who suffers it. And it contains a high level of compromise, it says that you can't be rude to anyone, and to do so it employs the Italian Western's characteristic violence. My character undergoes a transformation caused by external forces and that no one would have guessed possible in someone like him."[15]

Even though the screenplay suffers from a certain episodic nature in the second half, and some supporting characters are not fully fleshed out, *Day of Anger* displays remarkable sociological awareness and dramatic firmness. Moreover, it features one of the Italian Western's very best action sequences: the duel on horseback with muzzle-loading rifles between Talby and Owen White, with the two contenders galloping towards each other as they load their weapons, and which Talby wins by way of trickery, by spitting the bullet he holds

U.S. poster for *Day of Anger*: note how Lee Van Cleef's name is top-billed and Gemma's appears in tiny characters.

between his teeth right into the barrel, thus gaining that edge necessary to beat the rival on time and dispatch him.

Day of Anger came out to theaters in Italy just before Christmas 1967. Initially the board of censors rated it V.M.14 (forbidden to audiences under 14 years old), a decision not uncommon with Westerns, and here motivated by the "cold homicidal determination with which the various characters act and which, in the case of the main character, has him even trained to kill through the enunciation of a kind of catechism of the perfect 'gunslinger'; by the realistic climate of continuous and ruthless violence; and, finally, by the presence of sequences (Scott's beating on the part of Wild Jack; Talby tormentedly trained by horses) and lines ('If you wound a man, you better kill him'; 'Now you are a man' after the first massacre carried out by Scott) that, exasperating the aspects of revenge and hatred, make the film counterpoint to the particular sensitivity and the peaceful educational requirements of the minors"—although the board acknowledged the hero's final repudiation of violence. The censors did not mention foul language, an ever-growing occurrence in the genre which had had critics grimace (Tullio Kezich had deplored the frequency with which the characters uttered the insult "Son of a bitch" in *The Good, the Bad and the Ugly*), although Valerii recalled an amusing anecdote that took place during a screening: "After the third four-letter-word, a viewer in Terni yelled: 'They speak with finesse in this film!'"[16] The producers appealed, but to no avail: the decision was confirmed, and the motivation stressed between the lines that the censors were not only disturbed by the "exaltation of violence with utter contempt for human life," but precisely by the way the message was transmitted, that is through Talby's "commandments," and further condemned the film's "suggestive power." Even though vaguely intimated, the parallels with Christian religion were nevertheless annoying for the board.

In February 1968, Sansone and Chrosicki submitted another version of the film, with cuts amounting to a total of 113 meters (resulting in a total running time of 111 minutes and 11 seconds, against the original 115 minutes and 18 seconds) which toned down the aforementioned violent excesses; the censors agreed to give *Day of Anger* a "Per tutti" (all audiences allowed) rating. At the end of the season, the film was the second-highest-grossing Italian release at the box office, with almost two billion *lire*, after Giuseppe Colizzi's *God Forgives... I Don't!* (*Dio perdona... io no!*) starring Bud Spencer and Terence Hill. In the Italian and Spanish versions, Giuliano Gemma was top-billed, whereas in the U.S. market Lee Van Cleef's name came first (and the opening sequence was altered accordingly).

Day of Anger was released in the States in 1969 (opening November 5, in Houston), in two different versions: the longer one, rated M, and another shortened to just 85 minutes (known as *The Days of Wrath* and *Gunlaw*), which left the opening and ending untouched, but cut many important scenes, including Talby's arrival in the village of Bowie; Scott and Talby's visit to the gunsmith; the target practice with the barber sign; the scenes between Scott and the Judge's daughter; the ambush and Scott's convalescence in the brothel; and the arrival of Talby's four thugs. Even the duel between Owen and Talby was shortened, as was Scott's beating by Wild Jack. The result was an awkward hodgepodge of action sequences with a thin logical thread.

Chapter Five

Death of a President

"No bullet can stop an idea."
—President Garfield, *The Price of Power*

Day of Anger had not yet arrived in theaters when Valerii announced new projects. "In April [1968] I will start filming a great motion picture, which will be shot in Italy, Bulgaria, Yugoslavia, Finland and Russia, and will cost about 700 milion. Then I will make a Western in the States, with American actors, and then, at the end of the year, *Un mercenario per tutte le guerre* (A Mercenary for All Wars), a story I particularly like," he revealed in an interview.[1] None of these projects would ever see light. "The picture I was supposed to make after *Day of Anger* was part of a two-film package that Titanus would produce on the basis of a contract that Goffredo Lombardo had made me sign after watching *Taste of Killing*," the director explained. "However, during that period Titanus was sailing in troubled waters, and difficulties arose, so eventually the contract was terminated. So I met Carlo Ponti and tried to convince him to produce the film. But Ponti had a script in his drawer, *Un mercenario per tutte le guerre*, and offered it to me." The script, written by Ugo Liberatore, tells the story of the kidnapping of a German industrialist's two little sons. The industrialist pays the demanded ransom without batting an eyelid, but the children are found dead; he then hires a mercenary to find and kill the murderer. "It was a beautiful story that perfectly fit in the atmosphere of those days, sinister and unfortunate. Van Cleef was to be the lead. We did location scouting in Germany and Holland, but upon my return I learned that Ponti intended to leave Italy because he felt threatened—a friend of his, an oilman, had been shot in the leg by criminals, and badly wounded—and therefore he gave up on the project." The year 1968 did not bring any new film, but it did bring a second son: On December 10, Rita gave birth to Luca. The couple's third son, Andrea, would come eight years later, on May 26, 1976.

The reading of a script signed by Massimo Patrizi, which adapted the story of John Fitzgerald Kennedy's assassination as a Western, would help the director come out of his momentary impasse. "Patrizi was Luigi Comencini's brother-in-law; everyone called him 'Marquis Patrizi' because he was of noble origins. He had been an associate of Alfredo Mirabile in a production company called Emmepi, and after it disbanded he leaned on his brother-in-law to keep working in the movies. Comencini had him work as production manager. Taking inspiration from Kennedy's assassination, Patrizi had the idea of making a film out of it, by dating the episode back and superimposing it on another true story, President James A. Garfield's murder attempt in 1881." Finally, all this was somehow liberally retrodated to the Reconstruction era, with the ashes of the Civil War still burning.

Although the opening titles credit the story and screenplay solely to Patrizi, the project was in fact thoroughly rewritten by Valerii and Ernesto Gastaldi. "I don't remember Patrizi's treatment word for word, but it was extremely basic, whereas Gastaldi and I deepened it. We established the essential themes to develop, introduced the character played by Fernando Rey, the banker who is also the assassination's mandator, and so on." Gastaldi is even more tranchent: "Patrizi's treatment was simply thrown in the bin, but the producer had signed a contract with him which stated that he was to be credited as the sole author of the script. Since I didn't care about my name in the titles, I had no problem writing the script and not signing it."[2] Valerii and Gastaldi did some research to come up with a believable historical context:

> We tried to depict the preposterous reasons that led to the Civil War, and make the deeper ones emerge. Because it is true that in the South there was slavery and slaves were kept like animals, but it must be said that the South had made considerable progress with the administration of slavery, while the North had economical and financial interests to end the exploitation of cotton fields. It was a confrontation between the old and the new in which not everything old is really old, and not everything new is really new.

The Price of Power was once again co-produced with Iberian money: Valerii returned to shoot in Almería, and re-used the sets of Flagstone City and Sweetwater seen in *Once Upon a Time in the West*,[3] for a total of nine weeks. Again, Giuliano Gemma played the lead,[4] heading a diverse cast that included a glorious "has-been" such as Van Johnson, the great Spanish actor Fernando Rey, and Warren Vanders (real name Warren John Vanderschuit, 1930–2009), a character actor who had mainly worked in television, in series such as *Empire*, *Daniel Boone* and *Bonanza*. That's how Giuliano Gemma recalled his first meeting with Johnson: "He was [dressed like] a lady in her sixties, a little clumsy but very nice! When I saw him for the first time I was a little upset as I did not expect him to be so blatant [in his effeminate behavior]. I asked where he was to welcome him and was told that he

Spanish poster for *The Price of Power*.

was at the bar, and there I saw him, wearing a large straw hat with a handkerchief serving as a ribbon, and large shades—in short, he looked like Garbo!"⁵ Gemma also recalled his co-star's preoccupation with the role: "Van Johnson was a little worried because he knew the Kennedy family and said, 'I don't know about this film, what will they think about it when they see it?' To which I replied, 'I wouldn't worry if I were you.' 'Why not?' he asked me. 'Do you actually think the Kennedy family is ever going to see this film?' I answered."⁶

The Price of Power

Dallas. While people in the streets burn Lincoln's effiges, the visit of President Garfield is imminent. Willer, a former Confederate soldier, meets Sheriff Jefferson to inform him that some men are preparing an ambush against the President: the bridge over which the presidential train will pass has been packed with explosives. But Jefferson, who is part of the conspiracy, has Willer murdered by one of his men, the fanatic Wallace. A black man, Jack Donovan, escapes from prison to warn Willer's son, Bill, who fought in the war with the North. After discovering his father's body, Bill—who even served four years in prison by order of Garfield, his Colonel during the war, for treason—manages to foil the attack. In Dallas, the conspirators (among whom is the powerful Pinkerton) decide to turn Willer into a scapegoat. After a conference at which he promises an increase in taxes for the wealthiest, clashing with a hostile audience, Garfield meets Willer, who tells him the truth about the incident that cost him his conviction for high treason: He found himself facing his own father, in Confederate uniform, and did not have the courage to shoot him, a hesitation which caused the massacre of his platoon. When Garfield crosses Dallas' main street in a carriage, he is shot by some snipers hired by Jefferson. Jack, who attended the parade, is arrested on suspicion of being the author of the attack. Garfield dies, and Pinkerton is quick to appoint the Vice President as his successor. Willer investigates to prove Donovan's innocence: along with a journalist, Nick, he collects evidence that the shooting started from a different place than where Jack was, and he captures one of Jefferson's men and makes him confess. Meanwhile, McDonald, Garfield's counselor, finds out that the new President is being blackmailed by Pinkerton, who is in possession of incriminating documents. To recover them, McDonald pretends to be on the side of the conspirators, and releases Willer's prisoner. Willer faces Jefferson and makes him sign a confession. However, he fails to rescue Jack, who is slain by Wallace and his men on the way to Fort Worth prison. At the inquest, McDonald exposes the network of complicity and lies, and Bill delivers to the judge the sheriff's confession. Jefferson escapes and Willer pursues him, but he is captured by Wallace's gang and held captive in an abandoned village. Wallace meets Pinkerton, has the latter hand him over the incriminating documents and kills him: his intention is to spark a new civil war. Meanwhile Nick has released Bill, who kills the sheriff in a duel. Back in Dallas, where anarchy reigns, Willer faces Wallace and kills him. After getting the documents back, Bill initially meditates on whether to make them public, then he capitulates before the nation's greater good, and delivers the envelope to McDonald, who is leaving for Washington.

The Price of Power tells of a conflict that is not fought on the battlefield, but among the papers of politics, in a South that has just emerged from the Civil War, and whose actual and ideological wounds have not yet healed. The setting in the period immediately following the Reconstruction Era was not new—Sergio Corbucci's powerful *The Hellbenders* (*I crudeli*, 1967) being an antecedent—but the film's winning idea was to overlap the situation of 19th century Texas, characterized by slavery and landlordism, and the one that matured a century later, during Kennedy's presidency, and which led to the Dallas assassination. Valerii and Gastaldi manipulated history, blending fact and fiction: On July 2, 1881, about four months after his election as President of the United States, James A. Garfield was seriously wounded by a fanatic, a certain Charles J. Guiteau, who fired two shots at him at the Washington station. One of the bullets embedded itself in the abdomen and could not be extracted; infection and blood poisoning ensued. Garfield died on September 19, after eleven weeks of agony.

In Valerii's film, the assassination is imagined to be not the work of a fanatic but the result of a conspiracy among the elders of the state of Texas, and carried out in the same manner as JFK's: the presidential cortege is targeted from a flyover by a group of snipers, a Lee Harvey Oswald–like figure—moreover, a black man—is turned into a scapegoat, a superficial investigation ensues, with complacent doctors who invent ballistic trajectories and non-existent wounds. If one thinks that the first film produced in Hollywood that dealt with the Dallas events, David Miller's *Executive Action*, came out only four years later, in 1973, it is enough to consider *The Price of Power* as a one-of-a-kind item in the realm of the Italian Western. Whereas the political inspiration usually leads to an openly leftist, populist discourse, as in the Franco Solinas-scripted Mexican westerns, *The Price of Power* ends with the triumph of the raison d'État, personified by the head of the President's security, McDonald—who, during the film, does not hesitate to pose as if he is in cahoots with the conspirators ("Don't think we're all fools in Washington") and plays a double-cross in order to avoid having compromising documents end up in the wrong hands and causing a scandal that would destroy the new President, whose corrupt past cannot interfere with the country's greater good. Bill Willer's utopian idealism crashes against this raison d'État, and his thirst for justice is destined to remain unfulfilled.

Torn between ideals and disenchantment, instinct and pride, Willer—a surname which openly quotes Italy's most famous comic-strip Western hero, Tex Willer—is the most complex of Valerii's anti-heroes; the director reprises the theme of the generational conflict, already at the core of *Day of Anger*, with the reference to Ambrose Bierce's marvelous short story *A Horseman in the Sky* (1889), whence comes the image of father and son fighting in hostile camps and facing one another in battle. Willer and his father

Giuliano Gemma as Bill Willer in a German lobby card for *The Price of Power*.

served different flags, and it was to avoid killing his parent that Bill faced jail and the ignominity of an accusation of treason; likewise, it is the urgency of vengeance that pushed the young man to take sides with those who once humiliated him. But what is left in the end is the awareness of being just a pawn in the game: those pulling the strings that make history do so from far away, and act in ways and with consequences that are often incomprehensible. Eventually, an idealistic bent is overcome by the knowledge of the impossibility of changing the world single-handedly. "I thought about it, you know? You need these papers more than I do. A gun is enough for me," Bill tells McDonald before leaving (in the English language version, the line is shortened and somehow softened in significance: "You need these more than I do.")

Although there were critics who labeled *The Price of Power* as "a post-'68 film, with its evil capitalists, its stuffy citizens who don't talk, the latent racism of American society,"[7] the message—lucid and detailed—is hardly in line with the revolutionary spirit that prevailed at the time, as far away from the nihilism of Giulio Petroni's *Tepepa* (1968) as from the Mao quotation in the opening of *Duck, You Sucker* (*Giù la testa*, 1971), and devoid of certain demagogic and populist excesses of the so-called "*tortilla* western." President Garfield, as depicted by Valerii and Gastaldi, is a dreamer, ready to take unpopular measures to pursue his idealistic vision of America and doomed to pay for that. "Some people look at things and ask 'Why?,' I dream of things to come and ask 'Why not?'" he proclaims in front of a hostile audience of bankers and cotton farmers, only to have them reply, "You don't make politics with dreams," a sort of bitter endnote to Martin Luther King's famous "I have a dream" speech, given that his own staff is involved in the conspiracy to kill him. (Again, the English translation changes the reply to a less significant "We had the answer to that for some time.")

Overall, the political content and worldview of the film can be more easily understood by putting the film against the background of Italian history. *The Price of Power* was released just one week after the infamous Piazza Fontana bombing in Milan, which killed seventeen people and injured eighty-eight. Initially ascribed to anarchists, it was eventually proved to be perpetrated by extreme right-wing terrorist groups with the complicity of secret service members, and marked the beginning of the so-called "strategy of tension," which resulted in a number of bloody bombings and terrorist attacks in the following decade. No wonder the theme of conspiracy and a diffuse distrust towards the institutions would soon imbibe the crime genre as well, with a distinct and widespread pessimism.

The theme of racism, although closely linked to the film's discourse, sounds less effective in comparison, and a bit overwritten. "Fundamental is the premise that a white man's a man, and a negro is a negro!" Pinkerton (Fernando Rey) says at a certain point. One year after the assassination of Martin Luther King, *The Price of Power* depicts a black martyr whose suffering at times take on Christ-like characteristics. Jack is beaten, insulted, wounded, betrayed, accused of a crime he did not commit, imprisoned and finally killed like a dog; we see him drag himself from scene to scene, humiliated and offended, a bloody mask and an emblem of the abuses endured by African Americans, up to an unfair and terrible death, and one last look behind the bars of a prison wagon.

But *The Price of Power* is still a genre film, not a pamphlet. The fistfights and the shootouts take a back seat, but leave their mark: that is especially the case with the duel between Willer and the corrupt Sheriff Jefferson (Benito Stefanelli), which takes place in

German lobby card for *The Price of Power*, featuring one of the film's most dramatic scenes, the aftermath of the shooting of President Garfield. From left to right: Giuliano Gemma, José Calvo, María Cuadra, Van Johnson.

a pitch black room lit only by the opponents' cigars—a showpiece similar in concept to *Day of Anger*'s duel on horseback. Overall, the film is solid and well-shot: the sequence of Garfield's assassination, with the camera accompanying the wounded president's carriage, and capturing quick flashes of faces in the crowd, gives the idea of the urgency and chaos following the event, and Valerii finds the time for a stylistic refinement even during the final shootout, filming Willer's figure reflected in a window pane, which will then be shattered by a gun that suddenly turns up in the frame. What impress the most are the taste for frame composition and the felicitous use of the panoramic aspect ratio and depth-of-field, with the juxtaposition of details in the foreground and full figures in the distance—all perfectly sharp—within the same shot thanks to the use of diopters, as in the beautiful sequence of the murder of Willer's father. "It was Stelvio Massi's merit, as he employed additional lenses. For instance, there were three characters in a shot, one in the foreground, in close-up, and the others in the background. Keeping all three in focus was impossible, and we had to use 'pan-focus' technique plus an additional lens. To avoid it being visible, we had to have the light 'fall' on a vertical element, a wall or a column. I wanted to recreate Gregg Toland's use of the depth-of-field in *Citizen Kane*, his idea to bring out the depth by leaving the character in foreground in the shadows, while increasing the light in the background—the farther, the brighter. But it was Stelvio who found the way to implement my idea."

The Price of Power is more flawed when it comes to production values: the director's intention to stage a South teeming with black slaves and cotton fields clashed against the stingy producers' lack of commitment. "I had though of a Dallas packed full with negroes, slave merchants, cotton fields, echoing spirituals and heroic exploits to save black men from their desperate condition. Well, in the whole movie I only had five—I say five—black extras, whom I had to recruit personally. In fact, despite our agreement, the producer refused to pay several hundred extras that would come from Madrid to Almería."[8] And if Van Johnson is well-cast as the noble-hearted president, his wife María Cuadra is an anonymous presence, while the horselike Warren Vanders does not have the charisma suitable to play such an important role as the shrewd McDonald. Valerii cast the American-born Michael Harvey, who played one of Henry Fonda's henchmen in *Once Upon a Time in the West* and would turn up again as a coach driver in *Duck, You Sucker*, as the hateful racist Wallace; incredibly, despite playing one of the major roles, the actor is not even credited.

With a higher budget (or a more careful Spanish co-producer), *The Price of Power* could have been a minor classic of Italian genre cinema. As it is, it nevertheless remains an interesting work within the realm of Euro Western, and an important step in Valerii's filmography.[9] Commercially, it was a success, grossing over 1,273 million lire and ending at 11th place among the most popular Italian films of the season, right after Gillo Pontecorvo's *Burn!* (*Queimada*). It was also the year's top grossing Western, beating Tessari's *Alive or Preferably Dead* (*Vivi o preferibilmente morti*, 1969), also starring Gemma alongside ex-prizefighter Nino Benvenuti, Gianfranco Parolini's *Sabata* (*Ehi amico... c'è Sabata. Hai chiuso!*, 1969), with Lee Van Cleef, and Giuseppe Colizzi's *Boot Hill* (*La collina degli stivali*, 1969), which paired Bud Spencer and Terence Hill.

CHAPTER SIX

The Anomalous Venetian

> "Curiosity is evil, it is sin!"
> —Father Dario, *A Girl Called Jules*

After three films of the same genre, Valerii began to feel uncomfortable with the label of "Spaghetti Western director." The billions grossed at the box-office by *Day of Anger* and *The Price of Power* were an insurance for the future, but also a golden cage that limited the aspirations and whittled away the dreams of a filmmaker who, before his meeting with Leone, had dealt with the lower depths of commercial moviemaking, but had also breathed the heady air of *auteur* cinema, with the post-production jobs on works by Pabst, Lang and Autant-Lara, and whose authorial ambitions were supported by a refined cinephile culture.

The opportunity for change might have been Livia De Stefani's *Black Grapes* (*La vigna di uve nere*), a novel which Valerii loved very much. "*Black Grapes*, which was written in the early '50s, was about the irruption of Greek tragedy in the story of a small-time mafioso who marries a prostitute he is madly in love with. He locks her in their house and has her give birth to five children, whom he separates from their mother; when he becomes a '*capobastone*'[1] he decides to reunite the family, and goes around the countryside, to recover the children grown with different families; but two of them, brother and sister, who never knew each other as such, begin an incestuous relationship, and the girl becomes pregnant."

As with the original project for his film debut, *Una volta sola nella vita*, Valerii had chosen a powerful melodrama, deeply imbibed in Italian culture and mores: Sicily and the Mafia—whose existence was still minimized or ignored by politicians—had become a commercial topic after the success of Damiano Damiani's *The Day of the Owl* (*Il giorno della civetta*, 1968). It was as if a taboo had been broken. Valerii's approach to the theme was not sensationalist, but anthropological. "I had set the story in the fetid atmosphere of Sicily and its secular traditions, still populated by the '*campieri*',[2] who murdered those that dared take a carboy of water from the wells of the rich landowners, but with a very topical background, Mafia." Once again, however, things did not go as the director had hoped. "Maestro Riz Ortolani introduced me to this producer, Francesco Mazzei, and I showed up at the appointment with my *Black Grapes* treatment. In response, Mazzei pulled out of the drawer another book and said, 'I want you to do *this*.' It was *La ragazza di nome Giulio*."[3]

Published in April 1964, the novel written by Milena Milani, a journalist, writer and painter from Savona, soon became a literary event in the prudish, itchy Italy of the 1960s. In March 1966 Milani and the head of the Longanesi company, Mario Monti, were put on trial for obscene publications and sentenced to six months' imprisonment; in appeal, though, Milani managed to overturn the first-instance verdict, calling upon several personalities of the literary world to testify, all of whom attested to the novel's artistic value. "I remember that morning when the poet Ungaretti arrived in Milan and showed up to testify in my favor," Milani would later write. "I, on the dock, wore a skirt too short, and my lawyer kept gesturing that I cover my knees. [...] Ungaretti was asked how I was, morally. The old poet answered that, as far as he knew, I did not even like jokes."[4]

Next to the escalating violence, eroticism made strides in Italian cinema since the mid-'60s, as a consequence of the changing cultural and sociological climate, the relaxation of censorship, and a wider freedom on the part of the moviemaking industry, resulting in "the intersection between an expanding demand and an offer that proposed to satisfy the emerging needs in excess," as film historian Gian Piero Brunetta glossed.[5] In 1968, the year in which Italy was swept by the winds of rebellion of the culture of dissent, and the acceptance of cultural, economic and religious patterns (work, progress, family) crumbled, movie screens were invaded by films focusing on eroticism: arthouse efforts (*Teorema*), exotic fantasies (*Bora Bora*, *Le salamandre*), allusive, morbid *gialli* (*The Sweet Body of Deborah*, *Orgasmo*). Then, 1969 marked a leap in the representation of sexuality on the screen and in the media, with the release of many genre films that were blatantly oriented towards eroticism, while *auteurs* such as Fellini and Visconti displayed a more problematic approach to the subject matter within the historical frescos of *Fellini—Satyricon* and *The Damned*. As film critic Callisto Cosulich noted, "The sexualization of film is nothing but an aspect of the sexualization of mores, which in turn is strictly connected with the gradual emergence of the society of well-being."[6] This was evident when looking at other medias: the first issue of the photonovel *Cinesex* came out, which displayed complete films in photonovel form and—as the title suggested—gave ample room to the erotic interludes. The erotic component ballooned and took over the entire film, rising to a genre in itself and resulting in a selection of the audience differentiating and skimming as a consequence. Valerii's film ideally related to those morbid dramas which mixed high ambitions and blatant concessions to the public.

A Girl Called Jules

Venice. On the eve of her wedding with Lorenzo, the beautiful and restless Jules recalls episodes from her life that marked her sexuality. The earliest memories are those of childhood as a little girl, in Perugia, neglected by her mother and morbidly linked to the memory of her deceased father (whose name she bears). Jules is initiated into homosexuality by her lesbian housekeeper Lia, who teaches her to be wary of men; she is courted by the shy Lorenzo, and watches her mother's turbulent liaisons. During adolescence in Caorle, the 13-year-old Jules spies on her maid Serafina and the latter's boyfriend Amerigo during their sexual encounters. Jules chooses to lose her virginity to Amerigo; however, she discovers she is not able to have complete intercourse. Meanwhile, she becomes the object of attention from mature men, like her confessor and her philosophy professor, who asks her to marry him. When Jules tells this to her mother, she immediately takes her away to another destination. In Cortina d'Ampezzo, Jules flirts with 16-year-old Camillo, and goes to bed with the owner of the hotel, Luciano, but the experience is disastrous; moreover, Camillo dies in a skiing accident. In Venice, Jules is harassed by a maniac in a phone booth, then ends up in bed with the mature Marco. Finally, she meets Lia again, now the secretary of a painter named Franco, with whom Jules falls in love. The young woman finds the courage to tell Lorenzo that it is over between them; then she goes to a gynecologist, who diagnoses a vaginal malformation (an excessive thickening of the hymen) and surgically corrects the problem. Jules and Franco make love, but she cannot achieve orgasm. Desperate, the woman returns to the place where she and the painter had sworn love. The caretaker of a nearby factory persuades her to have sex with him, but Jules stabs the man repeatedly in the groin and leaves.

The opening titles credit five screenwriters: Valerii, plus four more names: Marcello Coscia, Bruno Di Geronimo, Mauro Di Nardo, Francesco Mazzei—"Who, however, did not actually write the film!" the director sneered: "*A Girl Called Jules* was written by Pier Giuseppe Murgia, and Beppe Bellecca." Pier Giuseppe Murgia was a novelist who enjoyed a certain notoriety with his novel *Il ragazzo di fuoco* (1960), about the erotic adventures of an adolescent boy in Vipiteno, in the Alto-Adige region, which caused a sensation and, as with Milani's novel, underwent a trial for obscenity. Murgia would eventually step behind the camera to direct the scandalous teenage erotic drama *Maladolescenza* (1977), starring Eva Ionesco and Lara Wendel, then moved to television. "He was quite good, I was sorry to see him so lost," Valerii commented. "He was a man of value, and ended up doing *Chi l'ha visto?*"[7] Giuseppe Bellecca, Valerii's assistant on *The Price of Power*, took part in a number of thought-provoking short documentaries and reportages—including Cesare Zavattini's "Cinegiornali liberi" (Free Newsreels) and the 1969 television documentary *La traversata*—and contributed to a number of forgettable scripts in the early 1970s, before abandoning cinema for television and journalism. He eventually teamed up again with Murgia in the aforementioned television program *Chi l'ha visto?*, where he made several remarkable journalistic scoops. As for the "official" screenwriters, Valerii bluntly explained: "Mazzei attended a club, whose members were precisely this Marcello Coscia, who had a certain experience as a scriptwriter, and Bruno Di Geronimo, who was close to the Socialist Party. Whereas Di Nardo was a man of the Vatican, with whose money he went on to produce *The Jeweller's Shop* (*La bottega dell'orefice*, 1989, Michael Anderson)."

For the role of Jules, Mazzei suggested Taryn Power, Romina's younger sister; Valerii, on the other hand, would have preferred an insignificant-looking, even rather ugly lead: "This way, the men's sexual obstinacy towards her would have become something horrible." Another name considered and immediately discarded was that of the 24-year-old Haydée Politoff, fresh from the success in *Bora Bora*: too old. Eventually the role went to Silvia Dionisio, who was certainly not ugly-looking—actually quite the opposite. Moreover, she was not even 18, and Valerii had to wait for her to reach legal age to shoot the more daring scenes. "Silvia was a rather helpful girl, but to be honest she was not totally suitable for the role, as she did not have that depth of look nor the understanding of the psychological nuances that the film needed." As Lorenzo, Jules' lifelong sweetheart, the "quiet, solid, elegant" young man who passively accepts his role as cavalier servant ("He will be quite a good husband, with that stupid look of a purebred puppy dog!" is Jules' mother's sharp judgment in the film), Valerii cast Maurizio Degli Esposti, the revelation of Salvatore Samperi's *Kill the Fatted Calf and Roast It* (*Uccidete il vitello grasso e arrostitelo*, 1970), while soprano Anna Moffo played Lia.

The most curious presence in the movie is that of Gianni Macchia, who starred in a couple of interesting erotic dramas directed by Fernando di Leo, *A Woman on Fire*, a.k.a.

Italian poster for *A Girl Called Jules* (1970).

Burn, Boy, Burn (*Brucia ragazzo, brucia*, 1969) and *A Wrong Way to Love* (*Amarsi male*, 1969), as Franco, the painter who finally seems to give Jules the happiness that always eluded her. "Macchia was a kind of icon of ambiguity. I cast him just because of that: in the context of the film I did not mind the ambiguity of a bisexual man, because ultimately the relationship between Jules and Franco is the best thing in the movie. We wanted the encounter with him to put Jules before her own bisexuality. That is why she feels very close to Franco: she seems happy, but she is destined not to be. And the only man she relates to is a bisexual." The sequences in the painter's Venetian study, filmed at the Guggenheim foundation, have an intensity that the rest of the film lacks somehow. Macchia, a painter in real life as well, recalled with great satisfaction his participation on the film, especially the sequence where Franco paints a nude portrait of Jules, where he was left free to improvise, identifying with the character's creative urgency, and the elegant scenes filmed at the isle of Burano.[8]

As the frivolous and distant mother, Valerii managed to cast Joan Fontaine, close to retirement but still a prestigious name to sell the film in the U.S. market. Unfortunately, the former star of Hitchcock's *Suspicion* quit the film when she only had one day of shooting left. "We were filming in Cortina; one morning I went out of my hotel room and saw four or five waiters come out of Fontaine's, which was opposite mine, carrying trunks and suitcases. I learned that there had been an absurd argument with the producer because of 5,000 dollars that she had been promised but never bestowed. Thing is, Fontaine and her sister were related to the founder of the De Havilland Aircraft Company—I mean, she did not really *need* those 5,000 dollars, but viewed it as a matter of principle." After vainly attempting a tug-of-war with the actress, having her luggage seized at the Fiumicino airport, the producer announced that Maria Schell was going to take over her role.[9] Eventually, though, Jules' mother was played by the 42-year-old Esmeralda Ruspoli (1928–1988), previously seen in Michelangelo Antonioni's *L'avventura* (1960) and Vittorio De Sica's *A Place for Lovers* (*Amanti*, 1968), among others. "Esmeralda did what she could, but had nothing to do with Fontaine, nor with the film." Among the scenes played by the British-American actress that had to be reshot, Valerii remembered with greater regret one in which Jules' mother consoles her adolescent daughter, who has just had her first period and refuses to get out of bed as she is completely unaware of her new condition. "I appealed to Fontaine's talent and asked her to lead the scene with Dionisio. She told me to trust her ... she approached the bed, disclosed the sheets and said, 'You've become a woman,' with such a grace and ease, cutting short a dialogue passage that was embarassing to say the least...."

Fontaine's walk-off was not the only mistake that the director blamed on the producer. "Even though he had lots of money available, and huge ambitions, Mazzei made grievous errors. For instance, he was convinced that films cost too much because of pre-production! So he did not want to make any pre-production shooting schedule. In the morning we woke up and said, 'What are we going to shoot today?' In a sense he was right, because *A Girl Called Jules* did not cost much, but with a precise schedule it would have cost even less. It did not exceed 180 million: almost nothing."

The film updates the setting from the 1940s to the present, and eliminates the first-person narration of the novel, but respects its structure, and distributes the tale of Jules' experiences since childhood in four long flashbacks set respectively in Perugia, Caorle, Cortina and Venice. The latter town also provides the framing narrative, with Jules' journey to the church for the wedding rehearsal, the definitive break-up with Lorenzo and the tragic ending. After the last hope to reach the "normality" that since the beginning has been denied to her—undergoing surgery to get rid of the thick hymen that caused her inability to have sexual intercourse—has proved illusory, Jules wanders through the countryside; she is approached by the caretaker of a nearby factory (played by John Steiner, in a brief cameo role) who convinces her to go off with him, but when they are alone, Jules stabs the man repeatedly in the groin (similarly to what she had done at the film's beginning with her immaculate wedding dress) and leaves, by now engulfed by madness. "Basically, Jules is scared by her own ambiguity, by her own desire of transgression: in the end, by stabbing the man in the groin, she stabs herself and her own sexual identity which she so poorly relates to," Valerii commented.

Jules' story, morbidly linked to her late father's memory and ignored by a mother who goes from one lover to the next, is at the same time the story of a Freudian Oedipal complex that was never removed, and of a paradoxical inability to love. Initiated to Sapphic love in pre-teen age, Jules soon starts collecting escapades, unconsciously imitating her mother's behavior while at the same time being attracted to mature men, paternal surrogates that provide security (and possibly a less menacing sexual appetite): the priest confessor who rather ambiguously offers to assist her ("You need a spiritual guidance, you must remain pure, in body and in thought…"), the philosophy professor who awkwardly asks her to marry him, the mature salesman with whom she has a fleeting, and obviously disastrous, adventure, and who tells Jules he is a family man. And yet Jules is unable to love, apparently because of a vaginal malformation, but in fact because of the impossibility of being able to cope with her bisexual nature in a patriarchal society that represses sexual impulses ("Curiosity is evil, it is sin!" the priest warns her) and where for a woman it is impossible to escape the duality between sexual object and family mother, advocated by the *bourgeois* orthodoxy.

Unlike *Day of Anger*, the psychoanalytic content is overall more cumbersome, stressed, and demonstrative. In a curious anticipation of *Once Upon a Time in America* (*C'era una volta in America*, 1984), the flow of memory is accompanied by the insistent ringing of a telephone that Jules is determined not to pick up; and to suggest the close connection between the past and the present, Valerii resorts to theatrical gimmicks, such as the sudden change of lighting that introduces the first flashback. Jules is in front of the mirror, the background turns black, the camera zooms in on the girl's face; a cut suddenly shows her much younger, still a child; a zoom back reveals Jules' figure framed in the same mirror, where her mother is putting on her makeup. The symbolic use of the color red as a recurring element in the flashback is equally emphasized, starting with Jules' scarlet dresses: a memorable sequence has the confessor (Umberto Raho) blaming the girl for the short dress she wears, walking around her in circles like some sort of rapacious predator. Elsewhere, red returns in the frame in the shape of a scarf, a dress, the lining of a swing on which the girl is sitting, a bow in the hair, a pair of trousers (in the Cortina episode), a poncho. We associate the color with passion, but also with the menstrual blood the first appearance of which shocks the girl, and with the violent episodes that turn up unexpectedly, inextricably accompanying Jules' sexual experiences, from young Camillo's deadly accident to the tragic ending. In Jules' meeting with Franco, though, it is the latter who is dressed in red, thus symbolizing his nature as the protagonist's mirror image. As Lee van Cleef's character did in *Day of Anger*, Franco "baptizes" Jules, calling her with a woman's name, Giulia, thus imposing upon her to finally give up to the unwieldy paternal memory and at the same time to fully accept her womanhood. Franco's workshop is also filled with sexual symbols and motifs, from an erotic bronze statue that first welcomes Jules in the building's courtyard, to Paul Delvaux's surrealist painting, *Women-Trees*, on the wall of Franco's bedroom, to which the camera pans after he and Jules have made one last failed attempt at mutually satisfying sexual intercourse.

Despite the story's roughness, Valerii never underlines the more morbid moments. The tête-à-têtes between Dionisio and Anna Moffo are portrayed with taste and measure, and the director favors a less intrusive, voyeuristic dimension: take the scene where Lia, after Jules' desertion, undresses before a mirror; the sexual encounter between the maid (Malisa Longo) and her fiancé (Roberto Chevalier), peeked on by Jules hiding behind a motorbike; and the scene at Franco's home, when Lia asks Jules if she is happy to marry Lorenzo and the camera frames Silvia Dionisio's face through a slit between two paintings, as if to suggest a glimmer of awareness in the wall that the girl built around herself, choosing the path of compliance to society's unwritten rules. Valerii has always been adamant about his approach to eroticism: "I did not want to film vulgar scenes. Even in the making of *Unscrupulous* I was not embarassed in filming sex scenes, but in my opinion it takes measure in all things, otherwise you reach the opposite effect. I always deeply despised porn movies, and I could have never made one. Do you know how many sex flicks I was offered to shoot, years later? I would have become a millionaire, by making one a week.... Let people say I'm a moralist, but I never wanted to get involved in that kind of stuff. I would not have been able to look my wife in the eye, when I came home from the set."

Nevertheless, *A Girl Called Jules* underwent some censorship trouble. On May 29, the 7th section of the board of censors initially rejected it a visa, as it unanimously recognized "both in the concept behind the film and in many scenes, elements of great offense to the 'good mores' [...] that is in the sense of an attack on public morality. Its theme, substantially centered on the disturbing frustrations and inhibitions of a young woman haunted by the fear of her physical and mental inability of an intimate relationship, reveals an obscene content and constantly recurring sexual situations and acts, lesbianism, masturbation, etc., in a context of nudity and unequivocally lewd attitudes, up to the final murder." Several years after Milani's trial, it seemed it was the film's turn to suffer the darts of the right-thinking.

Together with Bernardo Bertolucci's *The Conformist (Il conformista)* and Tinto Brass' *The Howl (L'urlo)*, *A Girl Called Jules* was selected to represent Italy at the 1970 Berlin Film Festival, to be held from June 26 to July 7. Valerii liked to tell a funny anecdote about the film having not yet been given the visa just days before the festival. "I personally went to the Ministry, in an attempt to talk with someone from the board of censors. There was an unattended secondary entrance: I sneaked in, climbed the stairs to the seventh floor, opened a window-paneled door and ... found myself face to face with a scared-looking official: 'Who are you? What are you doing in here?' Those were dangerous times, you know—at first he probably took me for a political protester or something. So, I tell him who I am and what I'm asking for, and I add: 'If tomorrow my film is not leaving for Berlin with the visa, I will file a complaint against the Ministry, hold a big press conference and tell the journalists that you are not allowing me to send my film to Berlin for moralistic reasons!' The next morning I got a phone call: 'Come and get your visa!'"

Valerii's amusing story is likely a fabrication. According to the ministerial papers, *A Girl Called Jules* was resubmitted in appeal just 5 days after the first verdict, on June 3, 1970. With a majority voting, the appeal commission suspended judgment and invited the producers to perform some cuts to the film, namely: "Lia, alone in the room, turning in front of the mirror (13 frames[10]); Lia standing up, in the same scene, after leaning on the table (19 frames[11]); Luciano sliding his hand under the protagonist's poncho (4 meters[12]); Eliminating from the dialogue the following lines (from Jules): "You hurt me" (and from Amerigo): "Because it's the first time." The producer agreed to make the cuts on the spot, and the board granted the film the visa, accompanied by a V.M.18 rating "because of the theme which illustrates the protagonist's inhibitions, impulses and sexual experiences and because of the connected erotic sequences." The next day, June 4, *A Girl Called Jules* had its official visa.

In Berlin, however, all hell broke loose. Among the films in competition in 1970 there was *o.k.* by the German-born director Michael Verhoeven, the story of the rape and murder of a girl by a group of soldiers. Although set in Central Europe, it was a blatant reconstruction of a notorious authentic episode which had occurred in Vietnam, and perpetrated by U.S. soldiers against a young Vietnamese woman. The President of the International jury, George Stevens, was not pleased with it; having served during World War II, he claimed *o.k.* to be "Anti-American." Following the premiere, the jury "neutralized" Verhoeven's pic and asked the selection committee for a re-appraisal. Amid charges of censorship and political interference, the jury were at loggerheads: another member, Dušan Makavejev, stood against Stevens' pressures and claimed that the jury had chosen "the path of censorship," abusing of its power. Eventually all the members resigned and on July 5 the competition was cancelled; the director of the festival, Alfred Bauer, and the head of Berliner Festspiele GmbH, Walther Schmiederer, announced their resignation as well. The screening of Valerii's film, scheduled for the last day of the competition, did not take place.

The bout of bad luck that accompanied *A Girl Called Jules* during the Berlin Film Festival did not bode well. At its release in Italy the pic was coldly received by critics, but it also garnered some illustrious praise: director Alberto Lattuada, a jury member at Berlin, called it "pure as a drop of water." Still, with over 542 million *lire* grossed at the box-office, it was a modest success, but a disappointment nonetheless if compared with the results of Valerii's previous works. It was released theatrically in some European countries, but failed to make it overseas: although some sources refer to an existing dubbed version released in the States as *Jet-Set Swingers*, this was actually the U.S. title of Michele Lupo's *Una storia d'amore* (1969), also starring Anna Moffo and Gianni Macchia—hence the confusion between the two pics.

All in all, *A Girl Called Jules* is an interesting but flawed picture, unresolved just like its heroine: the intention to portray "an anomalous being to whom society offers no way of salvation,"[13] collides with the schematic, uneven episodic structure, where well-developed characters (Jules' mother, her eternal boyfriend) co-exist with evanescent ones (as in the whole part set in Cortina); moreover, the need to explain and underline deprives the story of the ambiguity that would have helped it. Still, as film critic Morando Morandini wrote, there is an honesty behind the film that is a credit to Valerii's integrity as a filmmaker, and which elevates the director above what is essentially a commercial compromise of a movie.[14]

After *A Girl Called Jules*, Valerii worked on a couple of projects that did not see the light of day.[15] The first, *Molti, troppi amori*, was the adaptation of a successful American novel about the life of intercontinental aircrews, *Coffee, Tea or Me? The Unhibited Memoirs of Two Airline Stewardesses* by Donald Bain (masquerading behind a fictitious collective alias, "Trudy Baker and Rachel Jones"), published in 1967. "I was entertained by the idea of making a softcore comedy about the events narrated in the novel. I spoke with Goffredo Lombardo, who was enthusiastic about it. Anyway, he asked me to come up with an Italian title that might suggest the formidable erotic innuendo of the original one, just as effectively. I suggested *Molti, troppi amori* (Many, Too Many Loves), which he liked, but then the film was cancelled for productive reasons, as Titanus was administered by courts during that period." American director Norman Panama would loosely adapt the novel into a television movie, *Coffee, Tea or Me?* (1973), which was released theatrically in Italy as *Preferisci caffé, tè o me?*

Another ill-fated project, and one that Valerii cared very much about, was a period spy drama, *Una spia del regime* (A Spy of the Regime). The story was based on the memoir-cum-novel of the anti–Fascist intellectual Ernesto Rossi, published in 1955, and centered on the figure of Carlo Del Re, a Milanese lawyer who, in order to make up for a shortfall in the accounts of a bankruptcy proceedings of which he was the curator, in 1930 denounced to the OVRA (the secret Fascist police) all the members of "*Giustizia e Libertà*" (Justice and Freedom), the anti–Fascist clandestine movement in which he himself was involved. Del Re's role was uncovered only after the war, when the names of OVRA agents were made public. The release of Rossi's book caused Del Re's definitive expulsion for unworthiness from the register of lawyers (from which he had already been expelled in 1946 and later re-admitted). Understandably, the director was thrilled by the gripping true story. "That was perhaps the biggest disappointment I've had in my career. When I read the book, I got so thrilled about it that I did research at Rome's Archive of State and in tribunals, looking for whatever might be relevant to the story. I wrote a lengthy treatment and delivered it to RAI, but I never heard anything from them. Years later, though, *Una spia del regime* became a TV miniseries quite similar to my film.[16] I complained, but all were amazed and told me that the project had been in development for years…. I still suffer at the memory of it."

CHAPTER SEVEN

"There once was a little girl…"

"… and for every child that dies it is like the last flower in the world has died …"
—Commissioner Peretti, *My Dear Killer*

Valerii's next film would mark yet another change of pace for the director. It took shape in the Summer of 1971, when producer Manolo Bolognini (the financier of genre and *auteur* films alike, such as Corbucci's *Django*, Pasolini's *Teorema* and *Bubù*, directed by his brother Mauro) handed Valerii a treatment written by two young screenwriters, Franco Bucceri and Roberto Leoni. The delayed but phenomenal success of Dario Argento's debut, *The Bird with the Crystal Plumage* (*L'uccello dalle piume di cristallo*, 1970) paved the way for a bunch of films that, albeit with the necessary distinctions, drew—even if only with their bizarre animal-related titles—from the atmosphere of the prototype. The project Valerii got involved with, however, was something rather different than the usual *gialli*. "There was a very good idea to start with, the kidnapping of a little girl for a family blackmail plot, in a vipers' nest where everyone is ready to kill each other for money. But we had to work on it." During the months of July and August of the hot summer of 1971, Leoni and Valerii reshaped the script, with particular attention given to the psychological examination of the characters, such as little Stefania's mother, who sinks into madness after the loss of her girl, or the pedophile uncle, completely rewritten in the process. "It was a character that you could not tell what he was in the film for, so we told ourselves, 'Either we take it out of the film or we develop it.' And we had the idea of the naked little girl that appears at the door of his studio during the commissioner's visit…"

My Dear Killer was shot partly in Italy and partly in Spain, in the customary nine-week span, in October and November 1971.[1] For the Spanish scenes, there was the problem of creating a believable Italian setting, with plates, cars, posters and other assorted details; among the scenes shot in Spain were the one in which Patty Shepard's character is scared by her accountant neighbor (Sergio Mendizábal) and the cruel murder that follows, as well as the sequences in Beniamino's (Alfredo Mayo) house. The stalking and killing of Helga Liné's character were shot in Rome (in a post office near RAI's building), and so were the scenes at Villa Moroni and those set in the marsh, specifically created for the film by throwing several water tankers in a quarry just outside the city.

My Dear Killer

Commissioner Peretti investigates the murder of an insurance agent, Paradisi, decapitated with an excavator near a marsh that he wanted to dredge. The discovery of the body of the excavator operator, who apparently hanged himself out of remorse, seemingly solves the case, but a detail reveals to Perelli that the man has actually been murdered. The Commissioner meets an elderly man, Mattia, who lives in a shack near the marsh, and his companion, Adele, and learns that Paradisi was investigating an old case—the kidnapping of a little girl, Stefania, the daughter of the rich industrialist Massimiliano Moroni. At the moment of paying the ransom, Moroni had been kidnapped as well, and both father and daughter had been left to starve in a bunker right on the edge of the swamp. Paradisi's wife, who keeps the key to a particular mailbox, is lured to the post office and killed, but the murderer is not able to steal the box's contents: an old drawing by Stefania, depicting Mattia's house as seen from the marsh, which leads Peretti to deduct that the girl had already been on the site before the kidnapping. Meanwhile, the murderer is dispatching other potential threats: Stefania's elementary teacher is horribly slain and the girl's notebooks are stolen. At Villa Moroni, Peretti meets Stefania's mother, Eleonora, who has gone crazy out of grief, and the other members of the family: Oliviero, Moroni's brother, maimed by a war wound (he has an artificial hand), who hired Paradisi; Beniamino, the other brother, a sculptor with pedophile tendencies; and the deceased's brother-in-law, Giorgio Canavese. After a visit to the bunker, the Commissioner discovers that the object Paradisi was looking for in the marsh was a mirror that the dying child had thrown out of the bunker. It was found by Mattia, who becomes the umpteenth victim, but now it is in Adele's possession. Peretti saves her from the murderer just in time, and summons a meeting to unmask the culprit. The solution to the mystery is in a drawing that the child has engraved on the back of the mirror...

With *My Dear Killer*, Valerii follows a different path from the usual beaten track of the Argento-inspired *gialli*. Of course, there is a black-gloved murderer, whose presence is suggested through POV shots while spying upon or stalking the next victim; and there is no shortage of brutal murder scenes, as gruesome as they are inventive in concept and effective in filming. Compared with the feverish, unreal atmosphere of the model, however, the whole affair remains fully anchored to a daily feel, and developed with meticulous realism: Witness, for instance, the attention to the police procedural details, and to Peretti's office routine with his assistants, his elderly vice Marò (Salvo Randone) and the young and naive brigadier Bozzi (Manuel Zarzo).

Even the characters that show up for just a few minutes become full-fledged figures, not mere pawns to be sent to the slaughter. And Peretti is a humane, intelligent protagonist, as well as the vehicle of a moral and dismayed look, unable as he is to accept the cruelty and violence which he has to face every day: he is almost a younger brother to the unforgettable Commissioner Ingravallo (Pietro Germi) in Germi's own *The Facts of Murder* (*Un maledetto imbroglio*, 1959). Like Ingravallo, Peretti is unable to separate work from his private life, has a lover (Marilù Tolo) whom he seldom meets ("We have nothing to say to each other," she complains) and with whom he is often forced to communicate only by phone, merely to find an answering machine at the other end of the line. And isn't the great Salvo Randone a twin brother of sorts to Saro Urzì's character in Germi's film—that is, a shoulder to lean on, a confessor and a sporadic scapegoat when things go wrong? As a result, the police procedural sequences, which would normally provide the film's soft underbelly, are surprisingly strong. Consider, for example, the sequence set in the warehouse where the body of the excavator operator (Remo De Angelis) has been found, apparently having committed suicide out of remorse; there, the use of depth-of-field in a long take filmed with a dolly—a technique Valerii had already employed on *The Price of Power*—gives life and movement to what would otherwise have been a standard expository dialogue scene.

My Dear Killer is, among Valerii's films, the one where the director's ability to guide actors stands out the most. The Uruguayan-born George Hilton is more convincing than in his other *gialli* of the period, in a role that asks a lot of his skills as an actor, imposing on him to be something more than the usual handsome devil. The supporting actors are also employed wisely: Manuel Zarzo (on his second film with Valerii, after playing the lame journalist in *The Price of Power*) is a willing and playful cop; the veteran Neapolitan actor Dante Maggio is a filthy and incredibly nice bum who looks like having been recruited directly off the streets; while the veteran Iberian actress Lola Gaos becomes a very believable Roman proletarian; and the aging Alfredo Mayo, a former idol of 1940s Spanish cinema, gives the necessary ambiguity to the character of the pedophile uncle. Little Stefania is played by the debuting Daniela Rachele Barnes, later known as Lara Wendel.

Valerii leaves out most of the gimmicks employed by Argento's epigones: There are no weird camera angles or frantic cuts, the pacing is fluid and long takes prevail. One surprising stylistic choice is the use of slow-motion, which is associated with a specific expressive function within the flashbacks, where it introduces almost fairy-like flashes, thanks also to the use of the *flou*. This happens with Stefania's disappearance, as the little girl's puppy is seen wandering in the villa's garden without its master, and with the mirror being thrown out of the bunker, which rolls down the hill, carrying upon itself the solution to

Italian poster for *My Dear Killer* (1972).

the mystery. The concessions to the typical thriller paraphernalia are few and sometimes forced (such as the murderer spying on Repetti at his lover's house so as to, presumably, forestall his moves), but are executed with first-rate technical mastery: that is the case with the elaborate POV shot of the killer inside the schoolteacher's apartment, which offers the director the opportunity for a remarkable set-piece. The murders often occur in broad daylight (and Helga Liné's dispatch in the crowded post office anticipated one of *Tenebrae*'s most famous scenes, John Saxon's murder in a square in full view), and are ferocious and savage in a way that is quite different from the aesthetics of death *à la manière de* Argento. When the circular saw mangles the back and the pale bare thigh of the unfortunate victim, it is difficult not to look away: the sadism of the act and the identification with the murderer guaranteed by the subjective point of view do not cancel the discomfort of the pain shown on the screen.

The film's two most powerful scenes, Paradisi's beheading and the schoolteacher's murder, are worth a close examination. The frightening opening scene, with the man being raised from the ground, his neck trapped in the metallic jaws of the excavator bucket, and struggling in mid-air, is worthy of an ideal "best of" of Italian *giallo*:

> It came out so well thanks to Remo De Angelis's courage: he had two steel longitudinal bars fixed inside the bucket, so that it could not close beyond a certain point, exactly the measure of his neck. And so De Angelis could remain hanging in the air, strapped to a steel cable and with the bucket closed around the head. If we had used a dummy hanging in mid-air, the sequence wouldn't have worked so well: this way, the effect was terrific. To increase its effectiveness, we also shot some footage from inside the bucket, which comes down towards the head of the victim, by placing a camera inside it. And here it was all the merit of a young and willing key grip, who built a sort of harness for the camera, so that it could be stuck inside in order for the bucket to open and the camera remain still. And all this in a matter of hours. The excavator was lent to the production by a firm which wanted to advertise it, but when we explained the operator what he had to do, he refused: he was too scared. De Angelis signed a release that exonerated the operator from any responsibility, but when it came to shoot the scene, the other guy was shaking like a leaf. It was really dangerous, even though Remo had taken all kinds of precautions: but who assured us that the "safety bucket" would work? Luckily everything went smoothly on the first take.

Patty Shepard's murder was another difficult sequence to achieve: it was shot in real interiors, in a Madrid apartment. The scene starts with a POV long take of the killer who is welcomed by the woman: she then turns and precedes him along the corridor. The camera, still acting as the killer's point of view, proceeds forward, and for a brief moment it pans leftward, showing another room where, on a table, there is a drill on which a circular saw blade has been mounted: the murderer will get hold of it and kill the woman. The use of a real apartment added authenticity to the scene, but when the time came to shoot, it turned out that the corridor was too narrow to mount the rails for the dolly. "The Spanish key grip was desperate, he literally banged his head against the wall. Then he approached me and asked, '*Señor diretór, puede usted hacer esta escena mañana?*' (Mr. director, could you shoot this scene tomorrow?). So I did. And the next day the dolly was ready. The key grip had been up all night to adapt the dolly, cutting off a few inches in order for it to move along the corridor! That was the magic of cinema! And now what's left? The golden hour..."[2]

The gore effects were also achieved through artisanal means. "The blade had been replaced by a blade made with aluminum paper and treated with glue that hardened it. The paper had been cut to shape with the real blade, and looked definitely real itself [...]. The robe that the woman wore had been previously sliced with a razor, and during the scene the edges stayed close thanks to tape that had been applied on the inside. A thread had been attached to the tape.... The person who struck the blow was not an actor, but the special effects technician [...]. The drill had been modified and a small pump added to it: when the special effects guy operated the fake blade, as soon as it touched the robe, another technician, lying on the floor, pulled the thread and the robe tore off ... simultaneously, fake blood was pumped out and the effect was complete. [...] During the first screening—which took place at Fono Roma [...] people screamed and looked away."[3]

The construction of the enigma is strictly classical, complete with a final meeting with all the suspects, where the Commissioner sums up the investigation for the benefit of those present, and little by little discloses the puzzle, with a use of *ars retorica* worthy of a consummate orator, and addressing directly to the culprit ("My dear killer...")—just like in an Agatha Christie mystery, according to some critics. But also, it is to be added, as in a psychoanalytic session, where the mirror that Peretti shows to each suspect, encouraging them to look at their own face, acts as a Freudian shortcut to the subconscious. After all, the story of little Stefania's kidnapping and murder, and the trail of horror and murders that ensues, only marginally belong to the thriller genre; in fact, the mechanics of fear are not Valerii's main concern.

"There once was a girl, and for every child that dies it is like the last flower in the world has died...." Thus begins—at least in the Italian version[4]—the final monologue of Commissioner Peretti, who pulls the strings of the story, by directly addressing the still-unnamed author of the ruthless murders that punctuated the film. Accompanied by Ennio Morricone's eerie, otherworldly nursery rhyme, it sounds literally like the beginning of a dark fairy tale. But *My Dear Killer* is not a fairy tale, although it shares the same soul and heart. Valerii's film is the most profoundly and relentlessly moral—*not* moralistic, mind you—among Italian *gialli* of the 1970s, just like *Day of Anger* and *The Price of Power* were rare examples of ethical Westerns. The police investigation proceeds accordingly, thanks to the flashback construction, with the descent into a family nest filled with hatred, grudges not appeased, betrayals and snakes in its bosom. Perhaps the idea of a movie centered on the kidnapping of a little girl (with vague references to the Lindbergh Baby case and, consequently, to Christie's *Murder on the Orient Express*) allowed Valerii to develop ideas that drew back to the unfilmed *Un mercenario per tutte le guerre*; moreover, as a fervent Akira Kurosawa admirer, the director seems at times to be building a ruthless variation on *High and Low* (*Tengoku to jigoku*, 1963). Consider the importance of the geographical location of the bunker on the edge of the marsh, whereas in Kurosawa's masterpiece Toshirô Mifune's villa dominated the city suburbs from the top of a hill. In both films, what leaks out behind the cold lucidity of the narration is the vision of a sick daily world where monsters thrive; the mephitic swamp on which *My Dear Killer* opens thus becomes its central metaphor, a metaphysical *non-place* which hides and reveals upsetting truths, and which ineluctably draws to itself, soiling it, the solitary and miserable humanity that populates the picture.

In the end, when the truth is revealed and the murderer unmasked, there is neither catharsis nor redemption, and what remains is a feeling of waste and defeat. Whoever committed the killings did it all unnecessarily, because the destiny they hoped to change was fixed from the very beginning. Those who survive will never be the same after looking at their own image reflected in the mirror which also provides the solution to the mystery, unveiled only in the very last frame. It is a mirror with two faces: on one side, the inane mask of normality, on the other, the unbearable knowledge of what hides behind.

Chapter Eight

Once We're Dead…

"Gentlemen, I can't promise you nothing, except a chance to die honorably, and possibly live. In any case, freedom at the end."
—Colonel Pembroke, *A Reason to Live, a Reason to Die!*

My Dear Killer performed rather disappointingly at the Italian box-office: only 250 million *lire*, less than other *gialli* of the period. It might be understandable in the case of Sergio Martino's *All the Colors of the Dark* (*Tutti i colori del buio*, 1972) which boasted the radiant presence of Edwige Fenech; on the other hand, Valerii's powerful film was outgrossed even by such dreck as *The French Sex Murders* (*Casa d'appuntamento*, 1972, Ferdinando Merighi)—quite a disappointing result for a filmmaker who had been on top of the box-office just a few years earlier. Valerii blamed an inadequate distribution: "We had found a deal with Rizzoli's Cineriz, which at that time was the best option […]. They would give us 450 million *lire* as a guaranteed minimum, which was an enormous sum by then. Unfortunately things went differently, because the producers […] chose to give the film to another distributor which then went bankrupt a short time later."[1] The director refers to Jumbo Cinematografica, a minor company specialized in genre films, which also distributed, among others, Mario Bava's *Baron Blood* (*Gli orrori del castello di Norimberga*, 1972), Mario Caiano's chop-suey Western *The Fighting Fists of Shanghai Joe* (*Il mio nome è Shangai Joe*, 1973), Antonio Margheriti's *Seven Deaths in the Cat's Eye* (*La morte negli occhi del gatto*, 1973) and Corrado Farina's *Baba Yaga* (*Id.*, 1973)—the latter plagued by the same distribution problems as Valerii's film. Jumbo Cinematografica ceased activity in 1974. *Mio caro assassino* came out in Spain as *Sumario sangriento de la pequeña Stefania*, but found its way in English-speaking countries only years later, on home video.

Valerii's next film seemed at first to fall again into the crime genre, as his name was initially attached to another script written by Leoni and Bucceri, the crepuscular film noir *The Master Touch* (*Un uomo da rispettare*, 1972), starring Kirk Douglas, Giuliano Gemma and Florinda Bolkan. It was a project that reversed the father/son relationship at the core of *Day of Anger*, juxtaposing an aging master safecracker and his young, angelic-looking protegé, who work together on a risky jewel heist in Hamburg. This time, though, the script openly took sides with the elderly, more experienced character, and turned the confrontation between the two protagonists into a symbol of the clash between the "old school" criminals who followed the rules and the "new school" ones who did not mind breaking them, in typical *film noir* fashion. Eventually, however, *The Master Touch* was directed by Michele Lupo.

It was time for Valerii to get back to basics—that is, the Western. It was a return characterized by a gloomy, funereal tone: the original title of the treatment that became *A Reason to Live, a Reason to Die!* was *Morti noi, morto il mondo …* (Once We're Dead, the Whole World's Dead…). "The film held this view: Revenge alone cannot be the goal of a whole life, and therefore cannot be a reason to live. If whoever pursues it and consumes it eventually realizes that basically revenge was not enough to justify his life, then it becomes a reason to die."[2] The basic idea came from Ernesto Gastaldi, who openly admits the inspi-

U.S. poster for *A Reason to Live, a Reason to Die!* (1972).

ration being Robert Aldrich's *The Dirty Dozen* (1967),[3] but Valerii claimed he once again added elements from Ambrose Bierce's work, namely the 1891 collection of short stories *Tales of Soldiers and Civilians*. "One of these stories had set in motion the narrative mechanism which then resulted in *A Reason to Live, a Reason to Die!*, and I think it was *Parker Adderson, Philosopher*. Everything can be said about it, but not that Bierce's short story and the treatment it inspired were ironic, sly, good-natured."[4]

Actually, the connection with Bierce's story—the tale of a Union spy captured by the Confederates, who is waiting to be executed at dawn and faces his fate first with contemptuous irony, then with fear and anguish—is weak, and concerns the overall atmosphere rather than the narrative development, almost non-existent in the short story. The treatment focused on two main characters: Confederate Colonel Van Dooren and Mortalito, a deaf-and-mute vagabond who follows the protagonist in the hope that the latter takes him somewhere where he could feel accepted. "It was basically the story of a double delusion; Van Dooren is grimly absorbed in pursuing his revenge to the point of abjection, until he realizes that only suicide would have taken him away from the existential despair caused by having chosen the wrong side—the ultimate reason for his son's death. On the other hand, Mortalito eventually realizes that the man he always admired, and who commits suicide before his very eyes, was much weaker and cowardly than him."[5] However, the story's desperate mood was not appreciated by the producers: rather than massacre time, in Italian Western now it was the time of eating beans and getting slaps in the face, and the distributor was not happy at all with Valerii's planned ruminations on honor, vengeance and suicide. A compromise had to be reached.

In that period, Rafael Azcona, a friend and collaborator of Marco Ferreri since *El Pisito* and *El Cochecito*, was in Rome. According to Valerii, producer Alfonso Sansone, who had worked with the Spanish screenwriter on *The Conjugal Bed* and *The Wedding March*, suggested that he hire Azcona, so as to dampen the harsher tones and add a note of irony to the script. Azcona dedicated himself to defining the character of the tramp who links his own fate to the avenger's: in addition to being rebaptised Eli, he was given the capacity to speak, as well as a picaresque verve previously unknown

> Rafael and I had long talks in order to establish the vagabond's habits (he's going to move like this, talk like that, etc.), but in short the scenes that were invented by him from scratch are as follows: the arrival of the Confederate squad while our heroes are about to reach the fort and risk to be intercepted and captured, Eli's invention to get out of it, the square dance with the announcement "War is over!" and the Confederate soldier being replaced by Eli; then, the arrival at the fort, and the reversal of roles between the guard and the vagabond. It is the latter who orders the soldier inside the fort to give him the password, and the other obliges; and finally, Eli's attempt to open the locked door of the room where he is held prisoner, frustrated by the blast that blows up the whole door ... except for the lock. And the vagabond, risking his life, lingers to open it even if now he no longer has to.

On the other hand, Gastaldi is adamant that Azcona's name was credited for co-production reasons only, and that he never even met him.

A Reason to Live, a Reason to Die!

New Mexico, 1862. In the town of Buck Store, about to be conquered by the Confederate army, a tramp named Eli is arrested by the Unionists for looting, and thrown into jail with another stranger. The latter is revealed to be Union Colonel Pembroke, wanted for high treason for having handed over to the enemy without resistance Fort Holman, a vital strategic outpost perched on the mountains. Pembroke proposes to Major Ballard an agreement: He will take Fort Holman again and disappear, leaving all the merit to the Major. Pembroke chooses six men to accompany him in his mission; all are convicts waiting to be hanged, including Eli. The group is joined by the despicable Sergeant Brent. Along the journey to Fort Holman, the men repeatedly threaten mutiny; to keep them together, Pembroke reveals to them that half a million dollars in gold is buried inside the fort. More incidents ensue: the arrival at a farmhouse whose occupants, apparently charitable, have the habit of killing and robbing the passersby, and the encounter with a Confederate patrol which stops Pembroke and Brent while they are purchasing supplies. It is up to Eli to save them, by spreading the false news that the war is over and fleeing with his companions amid the general euphoria. Eli then sneaks into the fort, disguised as a Confederate soldier, and finds out that Pembroke is actually seeking revenge against Major Ward, who forced him to surrender by threatening to kill his son, whom he had taken hostage, and whom he slaughtered anyway once the fort was taken. Eli manages to have his companions climb the cliff overlooking the "pulpit," a rock which leads to the back of Fort Holman, but he is arrested. Pembroke and the others attack the fort. A massacre follows, and in the end Ward is the only Confederate left alive. He surrenders, but Pembroke kills him in cold blood with his sword. Then he leaves with Eli, the only other survivor from the carnage.

A vital element in the toning down of the film's grim content was the casting of the actor who would play the role of the tramp. Valerii's first choice was Eli Wallach, who read the script and accepted—only to pull back after receiving an offer for a stage tour in the States, most likely in *Waltz of the Toreadors*. His place was taken, for obvious box-office reasons, by Bud Spencer (real name Carlo Pedersoli), who had to harden the character of good-natured ogre which he specialized in since his first starring roles in 1960s Westerns. Valerii asked him to blunt his usual exuberance and physicality, and the actor obliged, although retaining some sporadic and unrequested relapses into triviality, such as the raspberry that marks Eli's release from Fort Holman's prison, after the providential explosion that eradicates the wall of his cell, an out of tune and avoidable gloss to a funny surreal aside. "Why didn't I reshoot it?" Valerii commented. "I'd lose half a day, whereas I had a hundred extras waiting for me outside to do a long shot which I absolutely could not postpone!"

In fact, even though Sansone claimed that the budget was no less than the by-then-huge sum of one billion *lire*,[6] the final massacre was shot in just five days, in the imposing set of the (real) fort built for the filming of *El Condor* (1970, John Guillermin)—whose plot has marginal similarities with *A Reason to Live, a Reason to Die!*, namely the MacGuffin of the hidden gold, which is central to Guillermin's film—and which appears in other Westerns of the period shot in Spain. Located in Gérgal, it is one of the few sets that survive to this day. The result is partially affected by such haste, with a few awkwardly filmed bits (such as a "brute" lamp reflected in the fort's window during a tracking shot, for instance).[7] Pedersoli had only a few weeks available for the shooting, and yet the relationship between the actor and the director was a happy one, cemented by gargantuan plates of spaghetti devoured together during lunch breaks.[8] Overall, filming lasted eight weeks: three in Rome and five in Spain.

To Valerii, the real problems had the face and grin of James Coburn, the Hollywood star who gave prestige to the production (after Lee Van Cleef had been initially considered for the role), but who turned out to be a real pain in the ass throughout the shooting.

> He was the only actor with whom I ever had an argument in my life on the set: duplicitous to the point of falsehood, narrow-minded and obtuse. When I first met him, I noticed that he did not really look anyone in the eyes, but looked away instead. I did not trust him right from the start, and I asked the producer to have him sign the script, page by page. Sansone did not want to do that. I insisted, and it was our salvation. After a week of shooting, Coburn began to act impatient, and said the script did not work. So he demanded that a writer from Hollywood fly over. The producer consulted with me; I told him to send him to hell, but Lloyds, that had insured the movie with a "warranty and control" policy, advised us to oblige. A certain Cirriacione came: he read the script and claimed it was perfect, with all due respect to Coburn. He said goodbye, cashed his 10,000 dollars fee, and left. It took me a week to have Coburn hit that dance step in the square dance scene ... enough said.

Another clue that the American actor was listless is that he did not even dub himself in the English version. Still, he managed to suggest his character's stark, obsessive determination with sparse details. Coburn's measured acting is finely counterbalanced by Telly Savalas' consummate hamming (although he does not even try to come up with a Southern accent): It was the Greek actor who added the grotesque touches in the characterization of the Confederate Major as a sadistic homosexual, who in his headquarters lights a match against the pubic parts of a statue portraying a male nude, and who apparently shares with his attendant (Fabrizio Moresco) something more than a mere camaraderie. On his part, Valerii was definitely pleased with Savalas' additions to the character.

> When the time came to cast the actor playing the attendant, Cineriz (the distributor) sent over an effeminate young man with large dark circles around the eyes. I got angry: it seemed absurd to me to have him act alongside Savalas. But Telly, who was nearby, motioned his eyes as if to say: "It's okay! Take him ..." and then, without saying a word, he approached the statue and lighted the match on its balls. I immediately understood and sent the young man to dress up for the scene. Elio Micheli, the costume designer, added a master touch: a hat that maybe only Gary Cooper could wear without looking ridiculous. And the character was ready to shoot.

The rest of the cast featured among others José Suárez, in his second film with Valerii, the great French actor Georges Géret (seen among others in Luis Buñuel's *Diary of a Chambermaid* and Riccardo Freda's *Roger la Honte*) and a number of reliable character actors: the slimy René Kolldehoff, Guy Mairesse, the inevitable Benito Stefanelli and, in an unusual dramatic role, comedian Ugo Fangareggi.[9]

In spite of the (alleged) Azcona cure, *A Reason to Live, a Reason to Die!* is patently in contrast with the degrading paths of Euro Western: it is a cruel and barbaric existential adventure whose grim view of the Civil War is closer to the mean digression in *The Good, the Bad and the Ugly* than to the cheerfully cynical recreation of *A Bullet for Sandoval* (*Quei disperati che puzzano di sudore e di morte*, 1969, Julio Buchs). Even though the Biblical references and quotes, often delivered in a grotesque mode, are a staple of Italian Western, in Valerii's film they take on a much more bitter significance, and hint at a world where, in the wild chaos of war, all things human—pity, the comfort of religion, common sense—are wiped out. Take the many Biblical quotes on the part of both Eli and Pembroke: Their opening encounter takes place inside a church, where the tramp improvises a mocking act of atonement ("Oh God, my God, how could I? How could I even think of stealing from the church? When I think what a saint my mother was...") after noticing that he is not alone in the church he is looting; then he repeatedly asks Pembroke to repent, claiming

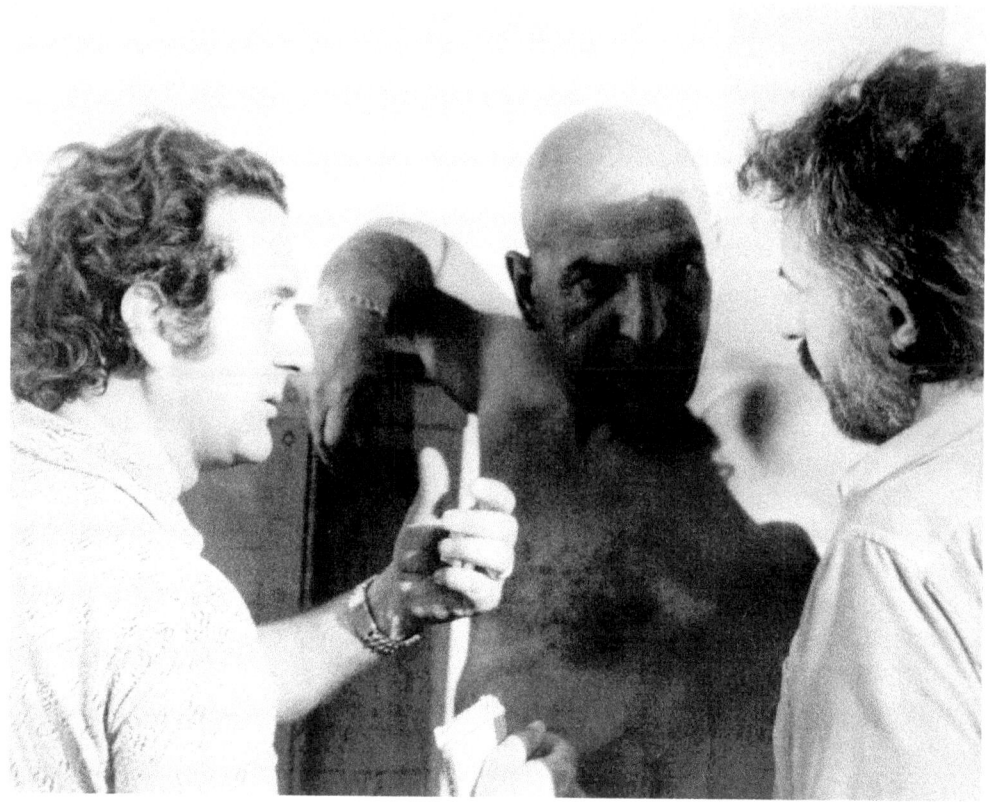

Valerii (left) and Telly Savalas (center) on the set of *A Reason to Live, a Reason to Die!*

that "The Lord has guided me to you!" before unsuccessfully attempting to pass himself off as a sexton when the army arrives in town. The Colonel—who carries a cross that belonged to his dead wife—is a loner without peace, who, after losing everything (honor, family, dignity), pursues a vengeance that has become an obsession with an almost Puritan determination, envisaging himself as an exterminating angel of sorts. Significantly, the only convict who refuses to take part in the mission is a priest ("The worst of the bunch, a religious fanatic" an officer calls him) arrested for inciting desertion, who urges his executioners to repent, and replies to Pembroke's Biblical quote ("Vengeance is mine") that vengeance is the Lord's, not men's. And while the handful of *desperados* leave the fort, the priest is seen hanging from the gallows. On the other hand, the good samaritan who offers a bowl of soup to the hungry travelers ("Who comes from afar, comes from God" he says) and recites a prayer to the Lord before the meal is actually a jackal who robs passers-by, whereas the young soldier who throws away his gun in horror and flees during the massacre at Fort Holman is executed on the spot by the cruel Ward. In this context, Pembroke's ascent to the mountain where his nemesis is barricaded (on a rock called "the pulpit"...) has the flavor of an existential journey[10] which leads him from *cupio dissolvi* to a painful awareness.

A Reason to Live, a Reason to Die! suffers from a barely cohesive structure: the scape-gallows who accompany Pembroke are only summarily characterized, and the digression about the farmers who kill and rob travelers, a homage to Kurosawa's *The Seven Samurai* (1954), is a superflous appendage. According to general manager Pietro Innocenzi, the film "was built [...] American-style, packaged for a certain audience that does not get the whole story, so you have to do it all very simple."[11] What is more, the music score composed by Riz Ortolani, which recycles themes from *Day of Anger* and *Beyond the Law* (*Al di là della legge*, 1968, by Giorgio Stegani), is disappointing. Nevertheless, Valerii effectively builds suspense during the second half, from Eli's entrance in the fort to his attempts at sabotage, from the climbing of the rock wall to the final machine gun and dynamite massacre. The climax leaves aside the sad elegy of Peckinpah's *The Wild Bunch* (1969) and is only partly mitigated by the dialogue exchange between the two survivors which seals the film. "I've killed for the first time in my life..." Eli murmurs, "And it's the last for me" Pembroke replies, having just cut Ward's throat—after the major had surrendered—with the latter's own sword. It is "a haul down the flag of military honor for a barbaric, liberating ritual" which according to Valerii juxtaposes "the military school ethics to the codes of the samurai's *bushidō*," and which is impressively topped by Savalas' final gesture: the dying Ward, his throat punctured by the sword and a dip of blood coming out of his neck and mouth, takes his head in his hands, as if he was crying in despair. It is a moment that sticks in one's mind long after the end credits have rolled.

A Reason to Live, a Reason to Die! draws from the core of cinema itself to depict the story's main elements. Despite the obvious similarities with *The Dirty Dozen*—an oft-quoted reference by reviewers of the time[12]—and the reminiscences of Leone's films (the opening sequence in a town devastated by bombings recalls the Civil War episode in *The Good, the Bad and the Ugly*, and Coburn's character handles dynamite with the same expertise as *Duck, You Sucker*'s Sean), Valerii himself pointed out other, less obvious models. One such was Gordon Douglas' *Only the Valiant* (1951), starring Gregory Peck and Lon Chaney, Jr., in which a group of army misfits redeem themselves by accomplishing a dangerous mission, defending a mountain pass against the Indians; the most surprising reference, however, was the Fascist war film *L'assedio dell'Alcazar* (1940, Augusto Genina), set during the Spanish civil war, from which the director and Gastaldi drew the theme of Pembroke's revenge, paying homage to the great Italian adventure cinema of the Fascist era but depriving it of its reactionary essence. "*L'assedio dell'Alcazar* told the story of a commander of a fort—the Alcázar in Toledo, in fact—faithful to Francisco Franco, who was submitted to a hateful blackmail by the Republican army: 'Either the fort surrenders or we will shoot your son, who's our prisoner....' The father appeared in the stands with a megaphone and told his son: 'Die a hero! *Viva* Spain!' I had seen *L'assedio dell'Alcazar* as a kid and was truly impressed by it. To me, paying homage to Genina's film meant the recovery of a childlike enthusiasm without having to reproach myself for feeling it."

The box-office grossings were up to expectations: almost two billion *lire*. If they seem dwarfed by Terence Hill's lone venture without his usual partner in Enzo Barboni's *Man of the East* (*...E poi lo chiamarono il Magnifico*, 1972–3,367 million *lire*), nevertheless *A Reason to Live, a Reason to Die!* managed to beat Bud Spencer's other solitary effort of the year, *It Can Be Done Amigo* (*Si può fare ... amigo*, 1972, Maurizio Lucidi) which stopped short of 1,600 million *lire*; Valerii's film even out-grossed *Execution Squad* (*La polizia ringrazia*, 1972, Stefano Vanzina), which announced the boom of the so-called *poliziotteschi*, as well as Luigi Comencini's black comedy *The Scopone Game* (*Lo scopone scientifico*, 1972), starring a quartet of aces in Alberto Sordi, Silvana Mangano, Bette Davis and Joseph Cotten. Valerii proved again he was one of the Italian Western's top directors: the next step would be a return to his roots, and the reunion with one of the two great mentors of his career.

The film was distributed abroad, albeit after ill-fated manipulations. The U.S. version (released in 1974 by Heritage Entertainment, as *Massacre at Fort Holman*) messed around with the editing with ill-fated results to say the least, turning the epilogue with Eli and Pembroke alone in the fort after the carnage into a prologue, replete with a spurious, awkward text (allegedly taken from a period newspaper, possibly in order to fit in with the daguerrotypes underneath the opening credits) stitched over the final dolly shot, which didactically sums up the story and gives away from the start the juxtaposition between Pembroke and Ward.[13] The running time was severely trimmed to little more than 90 minutes. On top of that, in a curious move that aped what Italians used to do in the Sixties, the cast and crew are Anglicized with totally invented pseudonyms: the story is credited to "Howard Sandford" and the screenplay to "Jay Lynn," and only the three protagonists and Valerii are featured with their names.

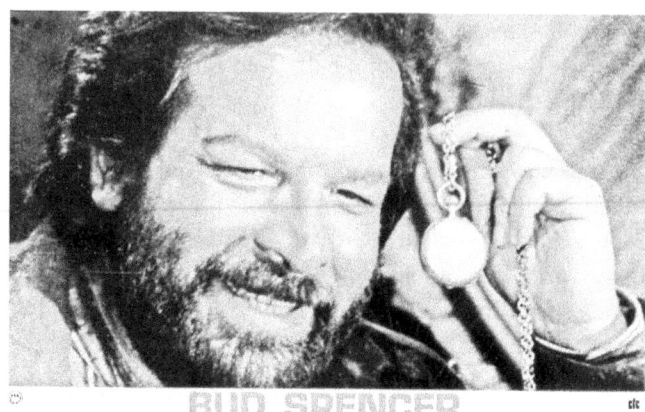

Bud Spencer in a German lobby card for the 1980 re-release of *A Reason to Live, A Reason to Die!*: the film was redubbed as a comedy, with totally made-up new dialogue.

A Reason to Live, a Reason to Die! met an even more bizarre fate in Germany. In the early 1980s, to cash in on the huge success of Spencer and Hill comedies, it was re-released in theaters in a severely truncated version (barely 79 minutes long!) and redubbed as a comedy, with totally made-up new dialogue, under the title *Der Dicke und das Warzenschwein* (The Fat and the Warthog). What is more, at the end of the film Ward remains alive. Another dub was made in 1985 on behalf of ZDF: the new version was close to the original one and avoided any kind of stupid jokes.

CHAPTER NINE

Nobody's Fool

"When I was a kid I used to make believe I was Jack Beauregard"
—Nobody, *My Name Is Nobody*

Sergio Leone definitely was not happy about it. With its 3,100 billion *lire* grossed in the 1970/'71 season, *They Call Me Trinity* had out-grossed *For a Few Dollars More* at the top spot of the most commercially successful films produced in Italy between 1956 and 1971. A Western, and a comic one to boot: the natural drift of a genre whose increasingly significant load of brutality had slipped into the unintentionally ridiculous. The Italian Western is, together with the Argento-style *giallo*—which in some respects (such as the fetishistic insistence on the murder weapons) can be considered its affiliate—the genre where the portrayal of death in all its variables touches sometimes paroxysmal levels. Yet, ritual and repetition favor the abstraction of violence. As noted by film historian Gian Piero Brunetta, "death—being present in an abnormal way—is, in a sense, stripped of its tragedy and uniqueness [...] to fall within the normal behavior of game and spectacle."[1]

The playful and spectacular portrayal of death, underlined by the sardonic distance that characterizes almost all the examples of the genre, announced the only possible step forward: parody, with the abandonment of political ambitions and the adherence to the picaresque, innocuous demystification of the *Trinity* films. Enzo Barboni's Western comedy seemed to trace what looked like a new, fruitful way for a genre that had reached unexpected sadistic and grotesque peaks. Actually, it announced its imminent end. And Leone realized that immediately. "When a title such as *Se incontri Sartana digli che è un uomo morto* (If You Meet Sartana Tell Him He's A Dead Man) is spoofed by its very audience and becomes *Se incontri Sartana digli che è uno stronzo* (If You Meet Sartana Tell Him He's an Asshole), it means that the author has been unmasked, and the genre has lost credibility. Hence the success of Trinity: the audience has felt vindicated."[2]

The original core for *My Name Is Nobody* dates back to 1970. As Sergio Donati explained, "*My Name Is Nobody* was born from an idea (of Leone's brother-in-law [Fulvio Morsella], bear in mind) to which I contributed too, at an early stage. It was, as is evident from the title, which never changed, a Western adaptation of Homer's *Odyssey*, where Ulysses was a Confederate prisoner escaped from a Union concentration camp who returned home after endless adventures, only to find his farmhouse invaded by Yankee carpetbaggers who courted Penelope. Massacre ensues, like in Homer. The End."[3] The many references to the *Odyssey* ("We had everything in there: Circe, the pigs, the Cyclops, even Penelope with the bad guys...") were then put aside and the project changed shape, becoming "essentially a productive-commercial operation because Sergio wanted to cast Terence

Hill, whose success in Barboni-Clucher's films he somehow wanted to patronize and suck into his own 'thread.'"

Donati passed on it due to other commitments, when location scouting in New Mexico had already been done. "The story changed, adapting to Hill's character, and I moved on to other things as I felt inadequate to the *Trinity* subgenre—after all, Leone always used to say about it: 'I don't get it, it doesn't make me laugh'" he admitted.[4] Leone then got in touch with other scriptwriters and eventually settled on Ernesto Gastaldi, who recalled his meeting with Leone as follows:

> When Piero Lazzari introduced me to Leone, he whispered to my ear that I wore jersey number 23, which means I was the *twenty-third* scriptwriter that Sergio "examined," and probably the count included those who uselessly worked on the Western version of the *Odyssey*. Sergio didn't even greet me. He looked at me and started telling, miming it, the film's opening scene, the way he had envisioned it: three riders arriving at sunset, a barber shop, a middle-aged man in need of a shave … he talked for ten minutes without saying anything practical, but only suggesting the atmosphere. Then he stared at me with an ironic look and said, "Ok. Now you go on. Bring me a story in one week." And so I did: therefore, the story of *My Name Is Nobody* is only and entirely mine, and the name Fulvio Morsella, which appears in the credits as co-author of the story, is there because Fulvio himself asked me to put it there "out of courtesy"—a courtesy you cannot refuse to someone with whom you have signed a lucrative deal.[5]

Leone, however, had no intention of directing the movie, and the choice of a director proved troublesome. According to Gastaldi, the first choice, Michele Lupo, was discarded just a couple of weeks before shooting began "because Sergio realized that he did not understand the project." Other sources mention Giuliano Carnimeo as another name considered by Leone at a certain point; however, Gastaldi explained: "It was I who suggested Tonino's name to Sergio, since he had been his assistant director, and Sergio immediately agreed enthusiastically." Benito Stefanelli too advocated Valerii's candidature, taking Leone to see *The Price of Power* at the Galleria theater in piazza Colonna, in Rome.[6] Therefore, the rumors reported by Marco Giusti, that Lupo was fired *after* two weeks of shooting, appear unsubstantiated, as proven by the notification of the start of production, where Valerii's name appears as the director.[7]

Eventually, at Morsella's insistence, Valerii decided to accept the offer when another project close to his heart went up in smoke: *Ostrowsky*, a story set in the U.S. which would have represented yet another change of course after the erotic drama *A Girl Called Jules* and the *giallo My Dear Killer*. Written by Sergio Donati, Massimo De Rita and Luisa Montagnana, *Ostrowsky* told the story of the eponymous innocent lifer convict, to whom the prison warden proposes a deal: he will have him out of jail in the trunk of his car, long enough for him to go kill a woman; once back, he will let Ostrowsky escape. But Ostrowsky falls for the designated victim…. "The interesting side of the story," Valerii reflected some time later, "is precisely in the ferocity of the institution that first condemns an innocent man, and then offers him, as a means of salvation, the chance to commit a murder."[8] The director got interested in the script through Nello Meniconi, the general manager on *La Dolce Vita*. Their plan was to cast Robert De Niro, who at the time was in Sicily, for the filming of *The Godfather—Part II*. "One morning we set off by car to Catania, got there in the evening, had dinner with De Niro and told him the story. But we were in for a big disappointment: he liked the story, but told us he was busy for another three years with Bertolucci to do *1900* (*Novecento*, 1976) and then with another American director, for who knows what other movie. Then, if we agreed to wait, he would gladly do *Ostrowsky*. Of course it ended there."

However, Valerii did not like the producer's idea of a film made out of spite. "If Terence Hill had ridiculed the Italian Western, he would face a retaliation [...] and come to recognize his own nullity, hence the relevancy of the title, *My Name Is Nobody*. [...] In short, it was all about putting to death the Trinity character."[9] It was also because of this, to distance himself from something he did not feel his own, that Leone did not want to get behind the camera. Instead of a jester, however, Valerii saw Nobody as a Peter Pan, "a child who refuses to grow up, attached as he is to the mythology of childhood. The inventor of an imaginary world, ready to welcome all the imaginative kids."[10]

In the scriptwriting stage, the original confrontation between Polyphemus and Ulysses, the fierce and powerful yet obtuse giant and the little man, weak but clever, changed shape and turned into a generational conflict: an encounter/clash between father and son where the former—Jack Beauregard, played by Henry Fonda—is also a patent embodiment of the Hollywood Western, whereas Terence Hill's Nobody is there to represent its Italian equivalent, both a filiation and a betrayal of the "father." If at first Leone could not make up his mind whether to make him a sympathetic character or not, with the casting of Terence Hill—to the benefit of whom a number of comic scenes were written, so as not to disappoint those who loved *They Call Me Trinity*—Nobody became "just a good boy who dreams of meeting the hero of his childhood, and when he does meet him finds that he is in something of a personal crisis and helps him bow out of his career in a way that is fitting."[11]

Writing the screenplay was a long and elaborate process, as was Leone's custom. "It lasted eight months, day after day, twelve hours a day at Sergio's house, reading the scenes written the night before, discussing the new ones, and re-reading the finished scenes to half of Italian cinema's professionals, whom Sergio summoned and to whom he then painstakingly told the film in the slightest details, spying their faces and their reactions to the story," Gastaldi explained.

I went to a well-deserved vacation in the Sicilian waters, after eight months of intense work: I had bought a sailboat and put my whole family aboard it. The radio telephone rang: it was Sergio, who yelled that he had been told from the U.S. set that the opening scene, where a fake barber is about to cut Henry Fonda's throat but cannot do it because the latter has a gun pointed at his balls, could not be shot because barbers, when shaving a customer, turn around him. Good grief! I started the engine and headed to Cefalù, to a barber shop: shave! And he shaved me with compunction, without imagining the importance of the act, and without ever moving from my right side, but turning my face toward his razor. I grabbed the phone and called Sergio in Rome to yell at him that barbers do not turn around customers at all![12]

My Name Is Nobody

Three gunmen set up an ambush in a barber shop on the famous gunslinger Jack Beauregard, who gets rid of them easily. "Pa, ain't nobody faster on the draw than him?" asks a boy to his father. "Faster than him? Nobody!" Nobody happens to be the name of an easygoing young and skilled gunman, who idolizes Beauregard and knows his deeds by heart. Beauregard, tired of the violence of the Wild West, would leave for Europe with a ship that will sail within a fortnight, but he needs $500 to pay for the trip. After following him to a

Indian burial ground, to the grave of Beauregard's brother, Nevada, Nobody proposes to his hero one last challenge that will make history: to face the legendary "Wild Bunch," 150 outlaws who terrorize the West with their raids. We meet Nobody again at a town festival, with visitors and circus attractions; at the local saloon, after winning a challenge of skill with the gun (drinking four glasses of whiskey, throwing them in the air and shooting them before they touch the ground), he is hired by the wealthy Sullivan to kill Beauregard. But rather than face him in a duel, Nobody helps him get rid of Sullivan's men. Beauregard, whose brother was killed by Sullivan, learns that his enemy is really a straw man of the Wild Bunch, and recycles the stolen gold by pretending to extract it from a now-exhausted mine. Beauregard saves Sullivan's life in exchange for a large sum and leaves to embark from New Orleans, but he finds himself in front of the Wild Bunch. Nobody, who stole a locomotive, witnesses the confrontation. Beauregard shoots the dynamite that his adversaries carry with them on horseback and blows up a large number of the bandits, then flees with Nobody on the train. The aging gunman now has to bow out; he and his disciple set up a duel in the main street of New Orleans, which ends with Beauregard's fake death. Now it is up to Nobody to take on the title of "Fastest Gun in the West"...

Shooting for *My Name Is Nobody* started on April 30, 1973. As Donati pointed out, it was "the only Western somehow related to Leone for which 80 percent of the outdoor scenes were actually shot in the United States." But the nine-week shoot in America was marked by difficulties of all kinds, from the choice of locations to the mounting expense. Filming took place at Acoma Pueblo and at the mission of San Esteban Del Rey in New Mexico (for the scene at the Navajo cemetery, recreated next to the pueblo's real burial site), and amid the chalk dunes at White Sands (the opening shots of the Wild Bunch riding in the desert); the early sequence in the barber shop was also shot in New Mexico, with Cabezón Peak (already seen in the final scenes of Peter Fonda's remarkable *The Hired Hand*) in the background, while the semi-ghost town of Mogollón, at the bottom of the Silver Creek Canyon, was used for the scene in Leo Gordon's shack and in the saloon where the first encounter between Nobody and Beauregard takes place.[13]

Leone stayed in Rome. He joined the crew for five days in New Orleans—where the climactic duel (in Royal Street, in the French district) and the final scene at the dock were filmed—and replaced Valerii, who was suffering from an ear infection, for one day. The relationship between the director and the two leads was good. Fonda was malleable, and asked to be directed as if he was an unknown actor; Hill, who practiced daily yoga for two hours, was over the moon about the idea of working with such a myth as the man who had played Tom Joad, Abraham Lincoln and Wyatt Earp. On the other hand, issues arose with the director of photography, Armando Nannuzzi. Valerii recalled:

> I had been out, location scouting [...], I needed a place where to shoot the scene with Henry Fonda and that old man who says that there's a telegram for him.... Back in the barber shop for that scene [...] I found Henry Fonda very angry... [...] Well, Fonda told me: "Sorry Tonino, there's one thing I don't understand: do I have to do what you tell me or what this man tells me?," pointing at Nannuzzi. "You kidding me?"—I replied— "You must do what I say." And Fonda: "You told me to pick the 10 dollar-bill this way, but he says to do it another way!" At that point I addressed the cinematographer, and told him: "Armando, please, don't do such a thing anymore, the actor must do what the director says, and that's it."[14]

But the relationship with Nannuzzi got even tenser, and after yet another argument the director of photography was ousted from the movie. The same fate occurred to production

Nine. Nobody's Fool

U.S. poster for *My Name Is Nobody* (1973).

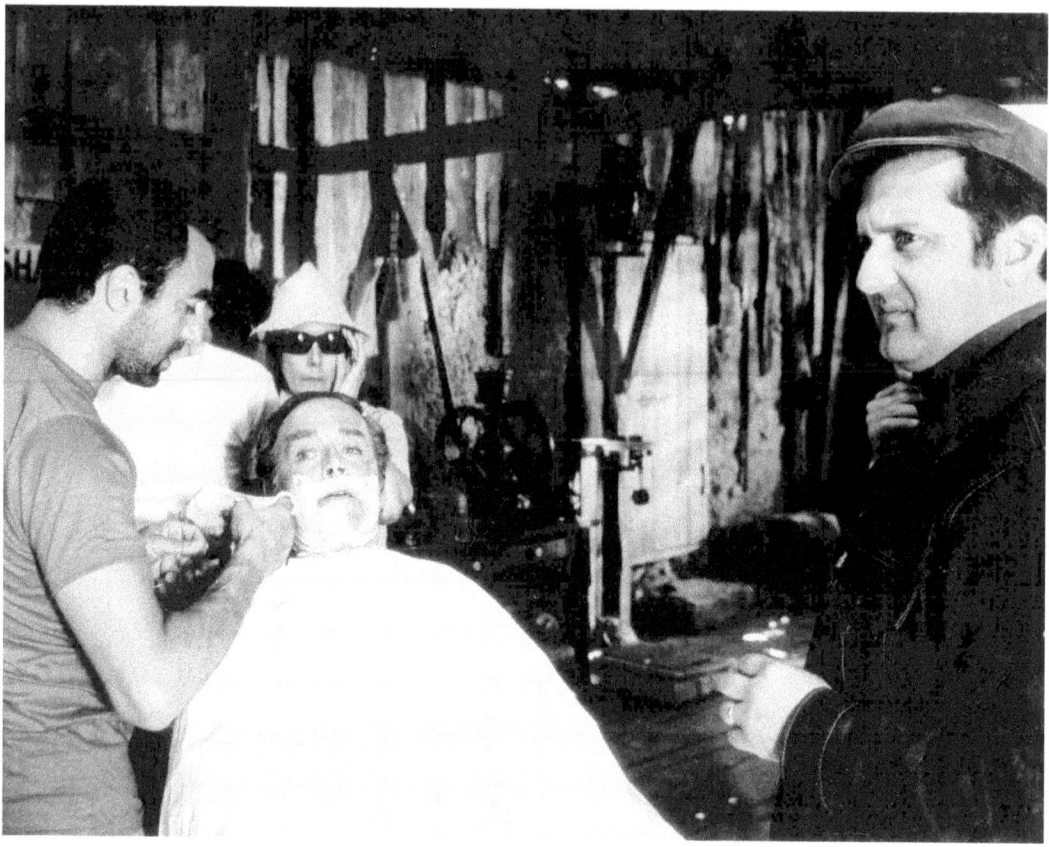

Henry Fonda (center) and Valerii (right) during the preparation of the opening barber scene, shot in New Mexico.

manager Piero Lazzari, who, as Fulvio Morsella recalled, "started talking over Tonino's head all the time. And they quarrelled."[15] According to Donati,

> Valerii is an introverted type, but very tough, and found himself having to fight alone against all, until the most fatal thing that may occur during the shooting of a motion picture happened, when together with every setting sun tens or even hundreds of millions disappear: there was a terrible showdown, an "either him or me," between the director and [...] Piero Lazzari, another first-rate type. Sergio had been behind the scenes and always showed utter respect for the director, but he had seen the daily rushes, of course, and realized that, despite all the blood and tears, the movie was turning out very good. So he did not hesitate to intervene as a producer: he dismissed Lazzari and replaced him with his trusted and tough and stainless Claudio Mancini.[16]

On the other hand, there may be a possibility that Nannuzzi and Lazzari had actually received instructions from Leone to "help" Valerii. But it was back in Europe that the producer's interference became more direct.

For the shooting in Spain, in Almería and Guadix (Granada), Valerii had a new cinematographer available, Giuseppe Ruzzolini, who had already worked with Leone on *Duck, You Sucker*, and a new crew; a new member was Sergio Salvati, who acted as cameraman, uncredited, for the sequence of the duel among the mirrors and Nobody's meeting with Sullivan (Jean Martin) in the gambling room. But the sets were not ready yet, and another

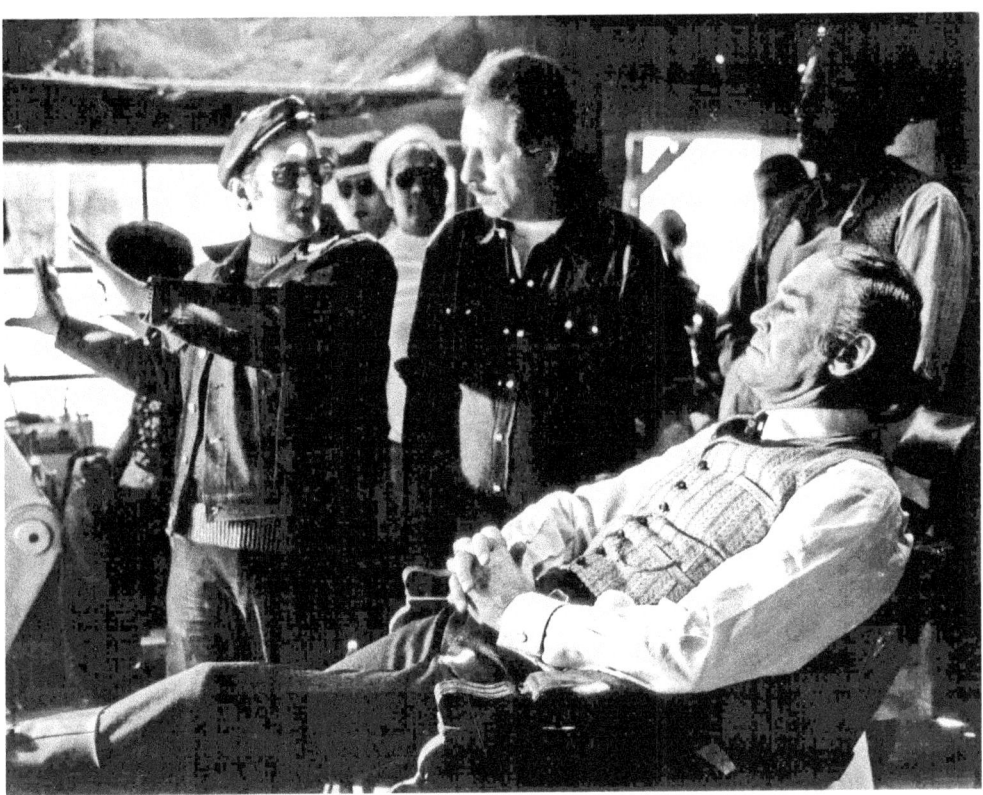

Valerii (left, with shades), Fulvio Morsella (center) and Henry Fonda, preparing a scene.

setback was likely to stretch out the shooting: A crate of costumes, almost all destined to Henry Fonda, disappeared, and the production was forced to a nine-day halt. Meanwhile the costumes were recovered, but another problem arose: Fonda had to absolutely finish his scenes within a precise stop day, for he was expected on the set of Larry Peerce's *Ash Wednesday*. To pay a high penalty (250,000 dollars) and keep Fonda, or postpone the rest of his scenes after the shooting of Peerce's film, was out of the question. There were only two solutions left: "Leone came to me, and in the presence of Fonda, told me about it. 'Tonino, what would you rather do,' he said, 'cut 30 or 40 pages of the script or put together a second unit?'"[17] Among the scenes to be shot, there were still those with Terence Hill at the village and Nobody getting drunk. Leone offered to take care of the second unit, and Valerii willingly accepted, without taking into account the words of Claudio Mancini, Rafran's executive producer, who warned him: "*Toni*, don't let this guy shoot not even a single frame, or else you'll see that when he gets back to Rome he'll say for sure that he's the one who made the entire movie."[18]

While Valerii took care of the scenes with Henry Fonda and the action sequences in the desert near Guadix, Leone directed the sequence in the saloon where Terence Hill displays his skills as a gunslinger (which took nine days instead of the two originally planned in the shooting schedule), part of the sequence of the village festival and, last but not least, the public urinal scene, not featured in the script and added at the very last minute.

The assumptions about the exact scope of Leone's contribution vary. According to Sir

Christopher Frayling, "the most likely scenario is that Leone helped out on a duel, then took charge of second-unit work on 'the battle' (in Almería) as well as directing the opening scene and the carnival section of the film."[19] The hypothesis of Leone's presence during the filming of the showdown between Beauregard and the "Wild Bunch scene" is proved by a set still depicting the producer on location with Fonda and Hill, and it seems to coincide with John Landis' statements about his participation to the scene as an extra: "We shot for a couple of weeks, among hundreds of extras on horseback, attacking and firing wildly. Fonda and Hill kept us all at bay. The film was produced by Leone, who directed that battle on horseback."[20] American actor Neil Summers (who played Squirrel, the gunfighter with chattering teeth, in the saloon sequence) recalled that "Sergio directed most of the scenes I was in…. On the first day I was on location there, we only rehearsed the action between Terence and myself, and we shot some of it the next day. It took over a week to shoot the fast-draw scenes with the glass shattering…. Sergio worked slowly and was constantly trying new angles with his camera and new innovative shots with his actors."[21] And yet the Roman director's intervention in the opening duel must be excluded, since Leone stayed in the U.S. for a very limited time in New Orleans, while the barber shop sequence—the first to be filmed, during the second half of May 1973—was set near Rio Puerco, in New Mexico, where Leone never set foot (see also Gastaldi's recollection above).

Italian film historian Marco Giusti states that some scenes with Hill were shot in Manziana by assistant director Marcello Crescenzi,[22] an occurrence which Valerii flatly denied. "Crescenzi, a good production manager and an ex-a.d., never shot one single frame in his life, let alone in my film!" Giusti also gathers a very diminishing statement of Valerii's work on the part of Rik Battaglia: according to the actor, Valerii had written in his contract that Leone was not present when shooting, "but when he saw the rushes, and saw it very soon, [Leone] said 'This guy shoots the way he thinks I would, but I would not shoot this way.' And so he took the film in his hands. He got very alarmed. Maybe he let [Valerii] shoot a little more, but then he said 'Enough.'"[23]

Giusti went as far as collecting rumors from people like Battaglia (who was not even involved in the production in the first place) but never even bothered to check and report Valerii and Gastaldi's version of the facts: not exactly the behavior of a scrupulous film historian—actually not a fair behavior at all, full stop.[24] For the record, Valerii's version as told to this writer is as follows:

> The scenes filmed by Leone are: Terence Hill getting drunk in the saloon (but not the close-ups of the shattering glasses, I shot those myself; and also the footage of the betting, with Piero Lulli taking the money, is mine); the part of the sequence at the fair which starts from the moment where Nobody steals the apple from the boy, to the episode of the pies thrown at the negroes' faces; the digression in the public urinal, not included in the script because Terence Hill had simply to steal the train while the machinist was taking a leak—a scene of such vulgarity that I'm surprised it received praise by a renowned critic such as Pietro Bianchi, and which I believe shows Leone's contempt towards the character—; and several close-ups of Nobody who, while Beauregard fights the Wild Bunch, takes note of the body count as if they were points at a game, another addition on the part of Leone, who thought it was a funny idea. The rest, starting with the barber shop scene, I shot myself, and I dare everyone to prove the contrary.

Gastaldi confirms Valerii's words: "Tonino shot the whole film, absolutely ON HIS OWN.[25] Sergio, when the shooting started going on for too long, organized a second unit crew and shot a couple of sequences, which in my opinion are among the weakest in the film: the urinal, stretched in an abnormal way, and the glass contest in the saloon. Nothing else."[26] Even Sergio Donati weighed in on the vexing question, pointing out the difficulties which the director underwent and the backstory of those set stills, taken during the shooting of the climactic duel in New Orleans, and in Almería, where Leone seems to be giving instructions to Terence Hill and Henry Fonda during the filming of the "Wild Bunch scene" as Valerii attends.

> To reassure the director, actors and crew, one day [Leone] turned up on the set. There were a couple of photographers sent over by the press office, who asked him to sit behind the Mitchell camera, in a director's pose. "If Tonino allows," said Leone. And Tonino not only declared himself honored, but suggested that Sergio shoot the next small scene which was programmed for the day. So, Leone looked through the camera eye, yelled lights, camera, action, and the scene was immortalized in many pictures, which then became famous and were published in magazines all around the world, as it is the duty and pride of every good press office. Shall I add that, inevitably, from that moment on, everyone, in and outside the movie business, started saying: "Yeah, actually the real director of the film was Leone, who saved it from the disaster of an incapable director"? Now, I am sure that Sergio did not shrewdly predict this effect. But it occurred, and afterwards he never, ever intervened to explicitly state that it was not true, even if poor Tonino was literally crushed by it, both as a professional and especially as a human being. But so was Leone, capable of incredible gestures of generosity and coldness almost within the same breath. All those who have worked for him, loving him to the point of devotion because it was difficult not to do otherwise, sooner or later have found these same scars on their skin: even Clint Eastwood, and Morricone, and Delli Colli...."

Was it therefore by chance or calculation that Leone's presence on the set became more active? The delays caused by the unfinished sets and costumes are the producer's responsibility; and Frayling conjectures the possibility that Leone had "deliberately created a situation where he would *have* to direct Terence Hill."[27] Which would coincide with Leone's feeling toward the eponymous hero of his first film as a producer: loved and hated, at the same time the object of mockery and (as played by Terence Hill) the likely trump card at the box-office, with all due respect to the producer's boundless ego. According to film historian Italo Moscati, over the years Leone developed an inferiority complex towards colleagues and friends, after the (relative) critical failure of *Once Upon a Time in the West*, the lower-than-expected grosses of *Duck, You Sucker*, and the weight of expectations of an audience that every time anticipated from him a bigger, more definitive movie than the previous one. On top of that, there were the temptation of an early retirement, the lulled idea of turning into a producer, the melancholy, the boredom in the isolation of his own personal Xanadu at Rome's EUR. "Leone found other reasons to be embittered. He knew what other people with whom he had had an intense relationship thought of him. Insights, fears, uncertainties. He sensed that Tonino Valerii, a Western director, a professional, a friend, had an unpleasant opinion on his cultural quality. Valerii then confirmed it. He considered him an amazing director, but an immature man, who started too early in the movie business, and was devoid of a solid, autonomous preparation."[28]

With over 3,600 billion *lire* grossed at the box-office, *My Name Is Nobody* reached the third spot among the most popular films of the year: it ended up behind the commercial phenomenon that was *Malicious* (*Malizia*, 1973, Salvatore Samperi—five-and-a half billion *lire* grossed) and Dino Risi's *Sessomatto* (1973), both starring sex bomb Laura Antonelli, but it out-grossed the unusual pairing of Giuliano Gemma and Bud Spencer in Enzo Barboni's *Even Angels Eat Beans* (*Anche gli angeli mangiano fagioli*, 1973). Trinity, however, was only partially defeated: Valerii's film collected more money than *They Call Me Trinity*, but less than *Trinity Is Still My Name*. It did very good in France and West Germany as well, whereas in the U.S. (where Universal distributed it in a shortened version: 111 minutes

Valerii and Fonda on the set.

instead of the original 117-minute version) it nearly flopped.²⁹ But to Valerii it became a curse. On one hand, it was the biggest hit of his career. On the other, it haunted him for years to come: Leone's long shadow ended up obscuring Valerii's directorial stature in the eyes of many, who labeled him as a copycat or, even worse, a straw man—to the point that several critics attributed the film solely to Leone, describing it as a necessary step in his *oeuvre*. With even more humiliating effect, *Variety* wrote that any way one looked at it, *My Name Is Nobody* was a Sergio Leone film.³⁰ Peter Bogdanovich liquidated Valerii as "an inexperienced Italian fellow,"³¹ as if he was talking about a debuting, er, nobody. Laurence Staig and Tony Williams, in the pioneering volume *Italian Western: The Opera of Violence*, wrote: "That the film is vastly successful is due less to its director Tonino Valerii, but more to Leone as its producer bearing the same general relation to the Hawks-Nyby *Thing from Another World* in the influence of a lesser by a greater talent. […] Though flawed in parts due no doubt to Valerii's direction, *My Name Is Nobody* is an enjoyable provisional film until the completion of *Once Upon a Time in America*."³²

In a 1997 interview published on *Video Watchdog*, Gastaldi conjectured that Leone had tried to diminish the film in some way, by inserting "a vulgar, useless scene in which Terence Hill sings a stupid popular song in a street of the village"—actually Gastaldi was mistakenly referring to the nursery rhyme which accompanies the action on the soundtrack—"only to make sure that this film wasn't one of the important serious films he had directed, because it was beginning to look every day, more and more, like it was going to be a very good Western indeed—maybe better than his Westerns! And he couldn't bear it."³³ The screenwriter later recalled another alleged low blow to Leone's self-esteem:

> *My Name Is Nobody* was a tremendous box-office hit, more than the films signed Sergio Leone, but the straw that broke the camel's back was Spielberg. One afternoon he called Sergio and offered him to direct *The Pirates*, but Sergio refused; since Sergio did not speak English, Spielberg's voice was amplified with a speakerphone while Morsella translated into Italian. Spielberg asked Sergio which, in his opinion, was his best film, and Sergio said *Duel* (which may be true, but it was not a nice answer since that was Spielberg's first film), and when Sergio asked the same question of Spielberg he replied, perhaps maliciously, that Sergio Leone's best film was *My Name Is Nobody*, that is, a movie he did not actually direct! Since that day, Sergio, who never said he did shoot the film, tried to make it clear that, yes, well, in fact behind Tonino there was him ... but it was not true, if not for the power of his directing style which Tonino had partly learned when he was his assistant, and for the psychological pressure that the movie had to please the producer Sergio Leone and had to be shot in Sergio Leone's style.³⁴

Over the years, Leone increasingly emphasized his contribution to the film, while minimizing Valerii's. In Nöel Simsolo's volume, *Conversations avec Sergio Leone*, which includes a 1986 interview, he declared: "This kid [Valerii] had never done anything in the movies before working with me. He was afraid of the sun. He could not run. Then, I told him he better become a filmmaker. After all, anyone did Westerns. Why not him? He was intelligent and cultured ... he became a good director. Not a genius, but with a lot of honesty. *My Name Is Nobody* is a fairly successful film. [...] I shot the opening, the battle and the final duel. I was forced to do so because Henry Fonda had a stop date." The contradiction is patent, since Leone mentions scenes that were filmed in different times and places (and even continents!) and could not have been shot in a hurry to oblige Fonda's stop date. Moreover, Leone added about the final result: "The film turned out a bit disappointing in the end. Valerii could not give a suitable poetic dimension to the encounter between the two characters."³⁵

Valerii on the set during the preparation of a scene involving the Wild Bunch (note the riders in the background).

Leone's words actually contradict what he himself had previously written about his role as the film's producer and his relationship with Valerii, in an article where nevertheless the evidence of a now-deteriorated human relationship clearly emerges:

> I decided to resume contact with the young Tonino Valerii. Upon our meeting I found myself facing a plump and placid 40-year-old. The only survivor from the past was his *scoppoletta* hat. But that plump and placid man had an enthusiasm that impressed me, a subterranean aggressiveness and a typically Abruzzi stubborness that brought us to a violent argument right on that first meeting. We quarrelled for three hours, quarrelled for another couple of afternoons, and in the end I said to myself that maybe I had found the right director [...] I'd explained my concept of producer to him. I only wanted to be his adviser, thanks to the experience accumulated over many years of moviemaking [...]. When I suggested I could also be his assistant director, he came out with the blackmail. "If you don't want me to ditch you—he said—you gotta promise that you will never show up on the set. I'll call you when I'll feel the absolute master of the film." And with such words he left for the States, leaving me back in Italy, wringing my hands waiting for a phone call. The phone call came seven weeks later, when Tonino had now really become the master of the film. I paid him a couple of visits in New Orleans and Spain, solving a couple of big production problems. Smug, self-confident, now he could also show himself to be generous, and before the end of the film he allowed me to shoot one scene. A humiliating concession [...], especially because—as I later found out—Henry Fonda had to leave at a certain unpostponable date, and Tonino absolutely needed a second unit.[36]

Here, Leone seems to diminish his own role in rather unbelievable terms, as it is highly unlikely that he learned only later about Fonda's stop date, whereas Valerii knew about it. But amid the grudge towards his former a.d. (and possibly vice versa) what emerges from Leone's words is Valerii's independence and responsability in the shooting, as well as the admission between the lines that Leone could not have possibly shot the opening barber scene in New Mexico, and the anecdote (which Donati also mentioned) of Valerii *allowing* Leone to shoot one single scene (the aforementioned bit in the confrontation with the Wild Bunch?). In the same article, another telling passage stands out, when Leone discusses his relationship with Valerii during post-production. "Only in the editing phase Tonino became more conciliatory. But now he was possessed by the neurotic anxiety of the author who doesn't know whether he has given birth to a normal child or a phocomelic. [...] However, how to edit that film *shot in a different way than I would have had*?" [Author's italics]

The final straw came after Leone's death, with the publishing of a booklet of the prestigious director series *Il Castoro cinema*, dedicated to Leone and written by film critic Francesco Mininni, which came out added as a supplement to the newspaper *L'Unità*, on March 22, 1995, reaching an enormous audience, much wider than the one to which the *Castoro* releases were usually destined. In an interview accompanying the text, and dating back to November 1988, Leone claimed that the choice of Valerii as a director "did not prove felicitous, because he found it quite hard to get in tune with what I wanted that film to be. Therefore the result is a bit uncertain, and certainly it lacks balance." Mininni asks Leone: "*My Name Is Nobody* contains several scenes that are 'Leone-esque' in every way. Did you shoot them?" Leone's reply, verbatim: "I admit it, it is my work. The whole opening, similar to that of *The Good, the Bad and the Ugly*; the duel with the hats in the Indian cemetery, a reminder of *For a Few Dollars More*; Beauregard's battle with the wild bunch and the fake final duel, are all scenes that I shot personally. And without false modesty, they are the ones that the public remembers most. For the rest, I find the film's burlesque aspect, the most directly related to the *Trinity* series, is too stressed."[37]

Valerii went on a rampage. He wrote a raging letter to *L'Unità*, and penned an article, *Il vero e il falso* (The True and the False), later included in a small volume published on

Valerii (left) and Terence Hill on the set.

the magazine *Nocturno Cinema* in November 2000, as an appendix to a long interview with film critic Tommaso La Selva. Incidentally, the vexed question of the relationship between Leone and Valerii came back to the fore, and gave way to a controversial tit-for-tat between Valerii and Fernando di Leo on the pages of *Nocturno*, about the genesis of Leone's first

Valerii gives instruction to the crew via walkie-talkie, on a particularly hot day on the set.

two Westerns.[38] Even Terence Hill gave his own contribution to the legend of Leone directing the movie: when interviewed during a popular prime time TV program (*Che tempo che fa*, hosted by Fabio Fazio), in March 2008, and asked—whether artfully or by sheer ignorance on the part of the host is open to anyone's guess—"How does it feel to be directed by Sergio Leone?," Hill launched in a long paean to the Roman director, without ever mentioning Tonino Valerii and thus implying that, yes, Leone had in fact directed *My Name Is Nobody*. Valerii did not comment on that, whereas Gastaldi was less diplomatic: "Too bad it's all a big lie! Terence Hill has never acted in a film directed by Sergio Leone!" and adding: "Indeed, there's more: when, a couple of weeks before the shooting for *My Name Is Nobody* started, we were left without a director, Terence begged Leone to direct it himself, and I advised Sergio to take on directing, but he answered with a disgusted air: "But do you really think that I'm going to direct.... Trinity!??"[39]

In a paradoxical, and bitter irony, a film about the construction and propagation of a myth has itself become, over the years, a source of endless myths and fabrications. The story behind *My Name Is Nobody* caused in the Abruzzi-born director a deep sense of bitterness. It put an end to a decade-long friendship, and left behind a long trail of recriminations, lies and grudges. Leone and Valerii never had the chance to set things straight, and the latter's resentment turned into a hood that surrounds the past as well: The memory of a former friend ended up being poisoned by the rancor for what happened next. Perhaps it was to exorcise the insult and vindicate his rights that Valerii, years later, vainly tried to

The duel between Jack Beauregard and Nobody, shot in New Orleans.

put in the pipeline with the Japanese producer Asao Kumada a sequel to *My Name Is Nobody*, to be shot in South Africa.

> I wrote the story and we went to Johannesburg to seek financings, but then, because of the mutual distrust between the producers, it all came to nothing. Too bad because it could have been fun. It started with Nobody in front of a poster which says that the Boers, who are about to start a war with the British, are looking for a huge quantity of mules and horses. Nobody converts all he has in horses, gets on a boat and sets off to South Africa. But as soon as he lands, he is attacked, robbed of everything and left for dead. He goes in search of those who ruined him: meanwhile the war starts. During his search, wounded, he comes across Beauregard, who takes him in the backlines and cures him. Nobody meets a girl, falls in love, marries her: Beauregard is the best man and after the war we see him cuddle a beautiful baby who looks just like Nobody.

It is patent—and inevitable, considering its genesis and productive vicissitudes—that *My Name Is Nobody* retains many points of contact with Sergio Leone's universe. The opening sequence, with the arrival of the three hitmen, pays homage both to *Once Upon a Time in the West* and Tuco's introductory barber shop scene in *The Good, the Bad and the Ugly*; the encounter at the Indian cemetery, where Beauregard shoots Nobody's hat away, refers to a celebrated moment in *For a Few Dollars More*; the duel between Nobody and Beauregard restages the one between Harmonica and Cheyenne in *Once Upon a Time in the West*. The metafilmic dimension that has always been the breeding ground to Leone's works here returns, amplified and veered into a good-natured self-celebration. Gastaldi replicates

Terence Hill (second from left) and Valerii (center) relaxing on the set of *My Name Is Nobody*.

Leone's typical taste for one-liners, with such dialogue as "Two things go straight to a man's heart: bullets and gold!" Ennio Morricone's score—which Leone personally supervised as customary, insisting on being present alongside Valerii on all discussions about the music[40]—is an anthology of references and self-references, from the theme of *Once Upon a Time in the West* (when Beauregard arrives at the *pueblo*) to *Like a Judgment* (from the same film) for the climactic duel, although the prettiest idea is the extract from Wagner's *Ride of the Valkyries*, which comments with ironic decontextualisation the apparitions of the Wild Bunch.[41]

What is more, homages to classic Hollywood Westerns abound: from *The Gunfighter* (1950, Henry King: like Gregory Peck's Johnny Ringo, Beauregard too wants only peace and quiet, but is a prisoner of his own legend) to *Warlock*, from *Forty Guns* (1957, Samuel Fuller: Barbara Stanwyck has at her service a "bunch" of hired guns), to the beautiful and underrated *The Fastest Gun Alive* (1956, Russell Rouse: see the final duel). Moreover, familiar faces pop up in minor supporting roles: a regular of Peckinpah's films, R.G. Armstrong; the villain of so many films and TV series, Leo Gordon; and one of the most characteristic faces of 1970s American Western, Geoffrey Lewis—sharing the screen with such Leone regulars as Mario Brega, Benito Stefanelli and Antonio Molino Rojo. It would be no wonder if Beauregard was called Henry Fonda instead: because it *is* Fonda, and not his celluloid counterpart, that we (and Nobody with us) see. And if the opening scene reprises a typical situation in Westerns—see Fritz Lang's *Western Union* (1941) and *Rancho Notorious* (1952) as well as the aforementioned *Warlock*—it is also a twisted homage to the amiable barber shop gag of *My Darling Clementine* (1946).[42] On top of that, the film as a whole is a reflection on the final line of John Ford's *The Man Who Shot Liberty Valance* (1962): "When legend becomes fact, print the legend."

About the sequence in the Indian burial ground where Nobody reads the name "Sam Peckinpah" on a tombstone (observing carefully the frame, one can see that the name is actually Sam *Pekinpek*) and comments "That's a beautiful name in Navajo," Gastaldi's version of the episode is definitely demistifying, though:

> Since I had to invent Apache names to be read on the tombs of an Indian cemetery, I wrote Peckinpah's name as an example, esclusively because of its exotic sound, then I told Tonino to get more names from the Navajos. I heard Peckinpah's name in the rushes and at the screening of the first rough cut, and Sergio told me that he would take it away in the dubbing, but he didn't: someone might have pointed out to him the "beauty" of that casual reference. To this regard, I sent a telegram to the late film critic Oreste Del Buono—who had begun his review of the film with this sentence "Not by chance, Sam Peckinpah is buried in Sergio Leone's cemetery..."—saying: "By chance, Oreste, by chance, and the cemetery is Tonino Valerii's unless you are referring to the one who pulled out from his pocket the money to build it!"[43]

The discourse on myth is typically Leone: to Christopher Frayling, the producer appropriated of the Homeric title "in order to show that the roots of the Western lay in the origins of the myth itself, and the function of myth—from storytelling around a campfire to big-budget movies; from a folk culture to an entrepreneurial one—had not really changed that much."[44] And, to quote Robert Cumbow, "Nobody is to Beauregard as Leone is to Ford. Literally a 'Nobody' in his use of a pseudonym on his first film, Leone is as concerned with the perpetuation of Ford's glory as he is with overhauling the Western mythos in terms of his own vision."[45] And so, the referential tone involves the story as well, so that each stage of Beauregard's route becomes a paraphrase of the trappings of the Western genre, of which he is the embodiment *par excellence*. Consider the opening ambush: "the" Western, the one made in Hollywood, with its ethical and mythical significance, faces Spaghetti Western, made of traps, disguises and betrayals, epitomized by the three thugs in disguise—one poses as a barber, the second curries a horse, the third milks a cow. To survive in the face of the growing disproportion of forces, the American Western—bled by television, by the critical broadsides of revisionist anti–Westerns, by the decline of the genre's main cantors; whereas the Italian one is constantly reinvigorated and fleshed out by new films, characters, antiheroes, subgenres—has to act clever. And aim below the belt.

Thematically, as a project born and developed under the aegis of a "creative" producer whose romantic model was the "Scott Fitzgerald–type tycoon"[46] or, better still, *Gone with the Wind*'s David O. Selznick, *My Name Is Nobody* reflects Leone's influence. But in terms of directing it is in every way a Tonino Valerii film. Compare, for instance, the use of depth-of-field with that exhibited in *The Price of Power*; moreover, as underlined by the director himself, *My Name Is Nobody* is an agile movie, with few close-ups, and devoid of the exasperated slow passages that are the trademark of Leone's cinema. The three hitmen's initial arrival, although it ideally quotes *Once Upon a Time in the West*, is built according to a very classical scheme, without that emphasis on details and extremely dilated timing that characterized the former film's opening. The final duel between Nobody and Beauregard is also lacking the exaggerated close-ups of faces; the camera moves a lot more, not only on the dolly as was customary with Leone, and often there are tracking shots paired with zoom outs; Valerii also employs hand-held cameras, and in a couple of scenes (the shooting at the barber shop, the battle with the Wild Bunch) he recurs to slow-motion, which Leone previously used only in a very different context—see Harmonica's recurring flashbacks in *Once Upon a Time in the West*. On top of that, the aforementioned battle, with the riders falling off horseback amid the explosions, recalls the sequence of the arrival of Kennebeck's gang in the village in *Taste of Killing*.[47]

My Name Is Nobody is not Valerii's best Western: It lacks *Day of Anger*'s emotional density and *The Price of Power*'s historical breath, and is penalized by the pretextuous subplot about Sullivan's fake gold mine; on top of that, the strident contrast between the elegiac tone and the comedy bits affects the film, to an even greater extent than Bud Spencer's sporadic buffoonery did to the dark barbaric universe of *A Reason to Live, a Reason to Die!*—especially since in *Man of the East* Terence Hill had shown he could play a more thoughtful character, less prone to parodic excesses. As Howard Hughes summed it up,

> there are some huge inconsistencies in the film's tone and style; it often appears to be three separate films stitched together. *Nobody* has three distinct tones: the lyrical "old man and boy" sequences; the more straightforward revenge subplot between Sullivan and Beauregard; and the broad, "Trinity"-inspired comedy scenes. The mood ranges from touching homage to cruel parody, but never within the same scene, which gives *Nobody* a juddering pace. This was down to a number of factors. Valerii directed most of *Nobody*, but Leone lent a hand and directed the second unit in Spain. Valerii is no Leone, but equally Leone is no Valerii—and neither of them have the comic timing of Enzo Barboni. Over the years the juxtapositions in *Nobody*'s style have been blamed on Valerii, but Leone was co-director, producer and general factotum—perhaps he was losing his touch.[48]

Donning Trinity's trademark uniform (a filthy shirt, suspenders, red socks with holes), Nobody/Hill is the hero of a film-within-a-film, a Peter Pan transplanted in a "serious" Western, who does not have the anarchic ruthlessness of certain grotesque Tomas Milian characterizations (such as the over-the-top Japanese samurai Sakura in Sergio Corbucci's *Shoot First... Ask Questions Later* [*Il bianco il giallo il nero*, 1975]) nor the lightness of the heroes played by Giuliano Gemma. It is hard to reconcile his cartoonish forays in the plot, often accompanied by a surreal Tex Avery-style humor—the bomb hidden in the basket, the sequence in the labyrinth of mirrors, the automaton which slaps people, inspired by the Saracen Joust, an ancient game of chivalry which takes place every year in the city of Arezzo, in Tuscany[49]—with the passages where the discourse on Myth comes to the fore. Even the battle against the Wild Bunch, with horses and riders being blown up in the air with dynamite, in freeze-frames which become illustrations of a book, is interspersed with shots of Nobody keeping note of the body count with a chalk on a railroad shovel, with a strident anticlimactic effect. And if the insistent use of farcical speedups (in the saloon scene, Hill draws his adversary's gun and repeatedly slaps him, a gag recycled from *Trinity Is Still My Name*) has aged badly, the digression in the public urinal is indeed a dispensable surplus, as Valerii pointed out. As a consequence, the generational conflict between Nobody and the "father" Beauregard does not reach the significance it had in Valerii's previous works, and—necessarily—the parricide is revealed to be only apparent, unlike what happened in *Day of Anger*, which perhaps Gastaldi remembered when writing certain scenes (Nobody follows Beauregard just like Scott did with Talby).

It is when he escapes from the uncomfortable cage built around him, that the character (and consequently the film) gains in sharpness and originality. With a beautiful intuition, Italian film critic Alberto Crespi underlined both Nobody's intratextual and extratextual nature: "Nobody is not a character [...]. Nobody is a spectator because, it is quite clear, he has seen a lot of Westerns [...] and his head is full of film references. Nobody is also a scriptwriter because it is he who, in essence, dictates the when and how of the film's story. Nobody even becomes a director when he literally 'stages' several sequences (the fight with the Wild Bunch, the fake final duel) and gives real indications to the other actors. But Nobody is also a creature of the collective subconscious, that penetrates in Beauregard's individual subconscious."[50]

In some moments, Nobody's childlike innocence takes on disturbing traits. With his saddle on his back drawing the shape of a pair of wings, surrounded by the smoke from an explosion, he appears to Beauregard as an angel of death ("my blue-eyed angel who protects me from harm," the elderly gunslinger says). And death is where his actions lead to: the massacre of the Wild Bunch, Beauregard's fake demise and the Wild West's real one. It is an epiphany that has an apocalyptic range: the story takes place in 1899, on the verge of a new century (even the ship Beauregard wants to get aboard has an openly symbolic name in this respect: the *Sundowner*), and Beauregard himself is the last, legendary survivor of a world that has already vanished; the advancing novelty has the face of the plutocrat Sullivan, a scoundrel in white gloves who covers skullduggery behind a façade of respectability (as did the notables of Clifton in *Day of Anger* and Mr. Pinkerton in *The Price of Power*) and who dominates the landscape from his office as from the penthouse of a skyscraper *avant la lettre*. But the "only hope for law and order in the West," as Nobody calls him, is a disenchanted hero who renounces avenging his dead brother in exchange for a large amount of gold (a homage to Joseph L. Mankiewicz's extraordinary *There Was a Crooked Man...*?) and who eventually moves to Europe, bringing with him the body of knowledge of an entire era. As it has been noted, Beauregard's path Eastward is also a way of "divesting himself of the moral and spiritual accoutrement of the Western hero. [...] He wants to behave as unlike a legend as possible. He's the Hollywood Western trying to be realistic, adult, contemporary, and anti-mythic."[51] Nobody succeeds him, and by embodying "both the romantic and businessman soul," he becomes "the perfect *trait d'union* between the two centuries: the social gap experienced with discomfort by Fonda's character [...] is not even sensed by Nobody, and certainly not because of his indifference or superficiality. Nobody is already the twentieth century's everyman."[52]

In this regard, Henry Fonda's final monologue is a real testament. Beauregard asks his successor to "preserve a little of that illusion that made my generation tick"; complains that the West "got small and crowded," paraphrasing Norma Desmond's words about cinema in Billy Wilder's *Sunset Blvd.* (1950) but alluding to the hundreds of Westerns produced between Almería and Tor Caldara; and takes his leave concluding that "it's your kind of times, not mine." A symbolic handover: From the New to the Old World and vice versa (Leone and Valerii had taken the opposite road, from Almería to the Monument Valley) the circle is over, and the Western changes domicile.

My Name Is Nobody is the final tombstone of the Italian Western, because, despite (or perhaps *thanks to*) its faults, it summarizes (unintentionally? It does not matter) *also* the process that gave birth to the postmodernist Western and would lead it to a quick end. "What did Sergio Leone and Tonino Valerii mean to say with *My Name Is Nobody*? That the West as it was conceived once is now empty of meaning: even a 'typical' hero such as Henry Fonda does not believe in the myth of the frontier anymore; in his place Terence Hill, the typical representative of the new times, takes over," film critic Dario Zanelli wrote. "Whatever you see, Valerii seems to say, is just fiction (the amusement park in the middle of the desert, the enchanted castle, the shooting in the sideshow of distorting mirrors instead of the traditional saloon) and the vast prairie is now empty."[53]

With the classic Hollywood Western fading away, the Italian one burns out within two hours' running time, characterized by accumulation and waste. Nobody enunciates the stages, in the scene where he recalls Beauregard's escalation as a gunslinger (a growing number of adversaries killed at one time), and reveals his absurd project: Beauregard will have to face a mammoth task—destroying the entire Wild Bunch—to become the stuff of legend. Therefore, with accumulation and waste come hyperbole and repetition—Valerii points out that Leone did not want to slim down the editing of the final part of the battle against the Wild Bunch—which subtract the wonder and pave the way for the ludicrous. Once all the enemies have been killed, and all the combinations have run out, all that is left to Beauregard is to "die": a fictitious death which in fact is a change of skin, just as the whole genre will do, by disguising as the 1970s *poliziottesco*.

"But if you're able to run around in the West peacefully, catching flies, it's only 'cause fellows like me were there first" the gunman writes to his disciple. "But you won't be able to have it your own way much longer … 'cause the country ain't the same anymore and I'm already feeling a stranger myself. But what's worse, violence has changed, too."[54] It is a theoretical endnote which implies an admission of defeat. Because, in spite of Leone's initial intentions, the one who wins is Trinity/Nobody: By ridiculing a genre already at the risk of saturation, it dealt a fatal blow to it, well hidden behind the princely grossings. It is, however, a short-term victory. In the final scene, "Nobody settles in for a shave just as Beauregard did in the film's opening, knowing full well that the 'barber' is out to kill him. But where Beauregard steadily held a pistol at the barber's crotch to ensure no slip of the razor, Nobody holds a stiffened finger at the barber's backside, just below the crotch. Indexing how the stylised whimsy of the comic Spaghetti Westerns had replaced the stylized drama of the mythic Spaghetti Westerns that went before it, Nobody's reputation and audacity have eliminated the need for the pistol."[55] Sooner or later, even though the barber wouldn't notice the trick, the audience would. And they got bored of it.

The Spaghetti Western's formalism, really ahead of its time, ran out in jest, only to no longer meet certain requirements on the part of the average viewer. Its heritage and its wealth of experiences had to be reinvested elsewhere, with an eye on the box-office, in an increasingly difficult everyday reality, and within a society that was struggling with the tragedies of modernity and the urgent needs and concerns that, partly because of an increasingly threatening criminality (both political and common), afflicted 1970s Italy. The postmodernist stylization adopted from the Western was then put at the citizen's service—citizens who, paraphrasing the title of Enzo Castellari's film and at least in the movies, rebelled (*Il cittadino si ribella*, 1974). The abstractions and stereotypes already metabolized during the days of the Italian Western benefitted from settings (Italian cities) and sadly familiar situations (the constant risk of being subjected to violence), and made up, thus reinforced, the backbone of (almost) all the Italian crime film genre. And it was there that Valerii came with his next movie.

CHAPTER TEN

Beware the Gorilla!

"If one acts as a coward once, he does so for a lifetime!"
—Marco Sartori, *Go Gorilla Go*

With over 1,800 million *lire* grossed in the 1974–75 season, Enzo G. Castellari's *Street Law* (*Il cittadino si ribella*) had launched a new and commercially fruitful subgenre within the already successful Italian crime film (or *poliziottesco*, as it was contemptuously called by the critics). On the other hand, Castellari's film—about a meek engineer (played by Franco Nero) who becomes a vigilante after facing the police's inability to protect him and his properties from the widespread crimewave—also called upon itself accusations of being Fascist. By placing the "ordinary man" at the center of the stories in place of police commissioners—as in the earlier examples of the genre, such as Stefano Vanzina's *Execution Squad* (*La polizia ringrazia*, 1972)—the vigilante subgenre tickled the viewers' indignation and their deepest fears: the police was powerless against the skyrocketing criminality, and the only solution was to take the weapons and do justice, by every means. The civil appeal of the so-called "civically-committed" films by Damiano Damiani and Elio Petri was therefore replaced (and in some cases, reversed) by a pitying and mildly populist vision: rather than sheer Fascist propaganda, this was often the result of a cynical commercial discourse, since Italian 1970s genre cinema was founded upon the pillars of sex and violence, sometimes the only way to keep afloat in a market considerably flooded with products characterized by a rush towards excess. In such a landscape, an ideological reading was misleading, as it applied a rigid scheme of meanings and purposes to a kind of cinema where ideology was an oscillating, unpredictable variable.

And so came the day when Valerii received a phone call on the part of a Florence-born producer. Quite a colorful character who had made his first steps in the movie biz as Dino De Laurentiis' and Vittorio De Sica's driver, Mario Cecchi Gori (1920–1993) had started business in the late 1950s, and made his name by producing mainly comedies, including Steno's *Uncle Was a Vampire* (*Tempi duri per i vampiri*, 1959), *Opiate '67*, a.k.a. *15 from Rome* (*I mostri*, 1963, Dino Risi) and *Brancaleone's Army* (*L'armata Brancaleone*, 1966, Mario Monicelli). By the early 1970s, Cecchi Gori had realized that crime films had a noticeable potential: after *La polizia è al servizio del cittadino?* (1973, Romolo Guerrieri) came *Street Law*. For his third crime film in a row, Cecchi Gori demanded another hit, and Valerii looked as the right filmmaker to guarantee that kind of solid, spectacular product he needed. "Cecchi Gori called me on advice of Luciano Luna, with whom I had already worked in the past—Luna had been the production manager on my first film, *Taste of Killing*, and it had been his first experience as well," Valerii recalled to this writer:

Our first meetings were interlocutory. Mario invited me to his home to play cards, or to have a cappuccino. He clearly wanted to know more about my temper and my political ideas. I openly told him that I didn't want to do a "revanchist" film. Cecchi Gori didn't take it too well, yet I think he liked my straightforwardness. Then came the first meetings with screenwriter Massimo De Rita to define our project more clearly, and we focused on three outlines: the first was about a police patrol car—a so-called "panther"—which comes out at night and ends the shift at dawn, structured in various episodes. It was the one I liked the least. The second was kind of like *Death Wish*, about a lawyer who, using his knowledge of the penal code, carried out a private revenge and, in spite of being identified, got away with it. Cecchi Gori and I liked this one, but De Rita saw in it the danger of a lengthy pre-production which might prejudice the making of the film which, at least in Cecchi Gori's idea, was to be an instant movie on the wave of a widespread resentment against criminal and/or terrorist actions. Finally, a movie about the hard life of a bodyguard, which seemed the most spot-on. I saw on the producer's desk a folded newspaper on which a five-column headline reported the invective of an Italian tanker—the president of API, I think—who claimed he was sick and tired of the anarchy that reigned in Italy and declared he wanted to move abroad: it immediately seemed to me the most emblematic situation of that historical period, and I warmly commended the project. I realised we got the movie as soon as De Rita got up, and with a threatrical gesture he raised one arm forward and proclaimed: "Go, gorilla!…" Cecchi Gori didn't hesitate for a second: "It's a deal! Once you have the title, you have the movie!" And he immediately called his secretary to pay De Rita and myself a sum in advance, without us having written even a line of the script![1]

As it often happened during that period, producers, scriptwriters and filmmakers alike drew the basic plots from newspaper headlines. In the mid-1970s a dizzying escalation of kidnappings occurred, and an emblematic figure of the period was that of the "gorilla," that is the bodyguard, imported from the States and soon adopted by the movies, as an exotic novelty worthy at least of a few laughs. Alberto Sordi, in an episode from the comic anthology *Di che segno sei?* (1975, Sergio Corbucci), released just one month before Valerii's film, reprised one of his most famous characters, Nando Moriconi—appearing first in *A Day in Court* (*Un giorno in pretura*, 1954), and most memorably in *An American in Rome* (*Un americano a Roma*, 1954)—in a biting sketch about an inept bodyguard who ends up involuntarily helping a gang of kidnappers. In spite of its immediately effective title, *Go Gorilla Go* sported a tagline which seemed to make clear to the viewers what the film was about. "Nowadays, violence in Italy has given birth to a new profession, that of the 'gorilla.'"

Go Gorilla Go

In order to get hired as a bodyguard by wealthy engineer Gaetano Sampioni, the ex-stuntman Marco Sartori stages a mock kidnapping with the help of his friend Ciro, which he then foils all by himself. Marco's plan is successful and he becomes Sampioni's "gorilla." But the two men don't get along at all because of the engineer's bad temper and Marco's own pride; what's more, Marco falls in love with Sampioni's daughter Vera, whom he has to watch over. The engineer is being threatened with anonymous phone calls and letters, which demand a huge amount of money, and the construction sites he is working at are sabotaged. Marco and his younger brother Piero investigate, and find out that one of the blackmailers is a biker with a precision shotgun and cowboy boots. To keep Sampioni from paying, Marco kidnaps the engineer, hides him in a safe place, and sets up a trap in alliance with the police, which unfortunately turns out a failure. Marco finds out that Ciro is involved with the racket, and persuades him to arrange a meeting with Berto, the biker, but falls into a trap in an abandoned apartment block, and miraculously escapes with his life. Yet he cannot save Ciro, who is mercilessly killed by his former accomplices. Berto's men attempt to kidnap Vera, but Marco saves her. *The gangsters then capture Piero, but Marco and the police come to his rescue. The racket is decimated, and Berto escapes aboard a train. After a breathtaking chase, Marco kills Berto in a duel.*

"Don't mention the rope in the hanged man's house!" the director joked about the film's noble ascendances.² In keeping with the many twists and turns that characterize Italian genre cinema, again the long shadow of Kurosawa's *Yojimbo*, which nurtured the Italian Western like a mother's womb since Sergio Leone took inspiration from it, towers on Valerii's film, as the stalwart Marco (Fabio Testi) who got himself hired as bodyguard by the irascible engineer Sampioni (Renzo Palmer), finds out that the same "gorillas" who are supposed to protect their employers are actually in cahoots with the kidnapping racket, and are double-crossing them. In a way, the Kurosawa reference was a compensation of sorts for Valerii, after the bizarre fate that

Italian poster for *Go Gorilla Go* (1975).

awaited a script he and Gastaldi had been working on circa 1973, and which in turn was based on another famous Japanese film (Masaki Kobayashi's extraordinary *Harakiri*, 1962), remade in a Western setting. The scriptwriter recalls:

> It was titled *Una buona giornata per morire*. It told the story of the revenge of a man against a group of landowners who had chased away small farmers from their land with violence and ferocity. In the Japanese film, the protagonist showed up at the shogun's castle and threw on the ground the topknots of those he had killed, and ours did something similar with his victims' scalps, in a one-against-all finale. But Tonino gave the script to somebody, I don't remember who, to read, without making a copy first, and never managed to get it back. I got a bit pissed off because I had told him to make several copies before passing it around.³

Valerii came from the Western, he had it in his blood, and it is no wonder that *Go Gorilla Go* features so many references to the genre, transposed into present-day Italy. Near the beginning Marco calls himself "the rider from the solitary valley" (quoting the Italian title of George Stevens' *Shane*, 1953), and in the end he tries his hand at a spectacular assault on a speeding train, which climaxes in a rousing duel with the hitman/biker Berto (Antonio

Marsina) who eventually gets a bullet in the eye through his gun's viewfinder. As Valerii noted, "The final duel was wholly expunged from *Taste of Killing*. There, the confrontation took place between the good guy, Craig Hill, and the bad one, George Martin: the result was identical, but just a few critics noticed it. Among them was Morando Morandini. Even the way Testi leaps from the police car onto the train was a homage to a classic Western movie cliché, such as the scene in *Stagecoach* where John Wayne jumps onto the stagecoach horses' backs to stop their run." *Go Gorilla Go* also took the characters, their conflicts and dynamics from the Western mythology—namely, from the aforementioned *Shane*. Marco is a younger and more impetuous version of the lone gunman played by Alan Ladd, who falls for his boss's daughter instead of his wife; Sampioni is a foul-mouthed version of Van Heflin's character—a self-made man who's ready to protect his family and possessions at all costs; and the villain, Berto, a mean-looking, black-dressed biker with Texas boots, is a contemporary variation on Jack Palance's Jack Wilson in Stevens' film.

When it came to casting the lead, Cecchi Gori sent Valerii to Fulvio Frizzi, the commercial director of the powerful distributor Cineriz, which had the last word on the protagonist's choice. Frizzi suggested Fabio Testi, with whom the company had a three-picture contract. The first film, *Cormack of the Mounties* (*Giubbe rosse*, 1974, Aristide Massaccesi) did not do well at the box office, and the second one, *Four of the Apocalypse* (*I quattro dell'Apocalisse*, 1975, Lucio Fulci), would not be a success either. "That was an attempt, on the part of Frizzi, to see if he could give Cecchi Gori the guaranteed minimum for the film, but I didn't know anything about that." Even though Testi's box-office appeal was not irresistible, Valerii accepted; if Testi seemed unlikely as a Canadian "Red Serge," he might work as a bodyguard. And he did.

Alongside Testi, the director cast a debuting 27-year-old stage actor who looked like he just stepped out of a Pasolini film, Saverio Marconi, and a recurring face of the crime genre, the reliable character and voice actor Renzo Palmer, who was perfect for the role of the enriched proletarian with rough manners and even rougher language ("I made myself with my own hands, you cannot even use yours to jerk off!"). The Italian-American actor Al Lettieri, who had played Virgil "The Turk" Sollozzo in Coppola's *The Godfather* (1972) and Steve McQueen's nemesis Rudy Butler in *The Getaway* (1972), had a small yet incisive role as Testi's colleague and best friend who double-crosses him and later pays for his betrayal. Antonio Marsina, on the other hand, was cast almost by chance; after a few bit roles in '60s Westerns, he had given up acting and became a professional photographer. "He showed up at our office accompanying his girlfriend, an actress whom we auditioned. She wasn't cast, but I thought Antonio had an interesting face. I asked him to do a screen test and in the end he got the role." Principal shooting started May 12, 1975.

Set among construction sites, barracks and fences which look like frontier forts and outposts, *Go Gorilla Go* makes the outskirts of the Capital look like a wild and dangerous plain, and has the merit of capturing the leaden and uneasy atmosphere of a country in full economic expansion yet on the edge of an abyss, shaken by anarchic spasms and submitted to the law of the fittest—here the mysterious mandators who pull the strings of the kidnapping racket and employ a gang of ruthless thugs, an idea developed further the following year by Enzo G. Castellari's outstanding *The Big Racket* (*Il grande racket*, 1976), again starring Testi and Renzo Palmer. It is a contemporary frontier, where family and friendship look as if they are about to collapse, depicted in a much more successful way

Valerii (second from right) on the set of *Go Gorilla Go* (courtesy Pasquale Rachini).

than Stelvio Massi's *The Last Round* (*Il conto è chiuso*, 1976), yet another riff on *A Fistful of Dollars* as well as another crime film which used the Italian suburbs like a modern Wild West, as Valerii's film did.

Go Gorilla Go's main theme is self-determination, which pushes Marco to show that he is up to the task, despite hating his job and having to endure taunts at the hand of Sampioni's site workers. "There's only one choice you have to make: Decide what kind of man you want to be" Marco says to his brother, while later on he tells Sampioni, "Even though you are paying me, you didn't buy me. I am and I want to remain a free man." Freedom, however, does not become the retaliatory urge of a private citizen who takes the law into his own hands; it is the possibility of choosing one's own future. Once again Valerii depicts a man at a crossroads: Can he be content with the illusory social status he has reached (well-dressed, impeccable in suit and tie, but in fact a slave, forced to follow his employer or the latter's wife like a puppy dog, and having to bear their reprimands) or must he start from scratch, and build his own future based on the values he believes in?

As in *Day of Anger* and *The Price of Power*, generational conflicts have a central role: Once again, the director stages a father/son relationship, with the former's death "seen as the portrayal of a destiny which one cannot escape."[4] Here, again, the father figure is split in two: on one side, the "father and master" Sampioni, a role model but also a suffocating authority; on the other, Marco's older friend Ciro, more comprehensive and supportive, whose betrayal is even more painful because of the two men's affinity. As Murph Allan did with Scott in *Day of Anger*, at a certain point Ciro tries to give Marco a moral lesson, and make him understand what their life is about: In a sense, he dictates him his own epitaph. "I'm not here to judge you" Marco tells him when he finds out that Ciro has double-crossed him for money. "But I do want you to judge me" Ciro replies, "because you are still young, and you can afford the luxury of being honest." It is a singularly touching moment, in a film filled with half-baked dialogue and barely sketched characters, often trapped within the genre's clichés. "We must not suffer, we must rebel, we can not always say "Not me!" Testi proclaims in one scene: a line which could belong to any crime film of the period—say, Marino Girolami's *Violent Rome* (*Roma violenta*, 1975), starring Maurizio Merli—in its generic demagoguery.

The director himself admitted that he had to make do with a rather hastily written screenplay, and adjust several dialogue exchanges at post-production stage, like he used to do in his beginnings at Jolly Film. "Since we were doing an instant movie, De Rita had to write at great speed, and I had to remedy some flaws by rewriting the dialogue at the moviola: that was the case with the scene in the car between Marco and Vera Sampioni (the insipid Claudia Marsani[5]), where he reveals to her with disenchantment the fraudulent way he got the job. Whereas for the other scene in the car between Testi and Al Lettieri, since I wasn't satisfied with the dialogue, I asked Lettieri to improvise on the theme of aging. And Al did it so well that I think it was one of his best performances." It was an unusual role indeed for Lettieri, who usually played heavies. Similarly, in his other Italian foray of

Fabio Testi performing a spectacular stunt in the climax of *Go Gorilla Go*.

the period, Pupi Avati's grotesque farce *Bordella* (1975), he showed himself adept at comedy too. Unfortunately these were to be his last screen roles, as the actor died of a heart attack on October 18th, 1975, a month before the film's release.

However, *Go Gorilla Go* is technically first-rate, starting with the photography by Mario Vulpiani (the director of photography on Marco Ferreri's best films, such as *Dillinger Is Dead* and *La Grande Bouffe*), and its action sequences linger in the memory. The one where Fabio Testi is trapped inside an elevator car in an abandoned building, and the bad guys remove the floor under his feet, leaving him dangling in the void, is simply breathtaking, and features a pioneering use of blue-back technology in Italian cinema:

> To shoot the elevator scene we had to improvise, because it was the first time blue-back was used in Italy, and there were many difficulties. We had to rebuild three flights of stairs inside an abandoned apartment block about to be demolished near the Colosseum, and used two real lift cabins operated by hand through ropes and counterweights. The scene cost a lot of money, and Cecchi Gori forgave me only when he saw the final result. To shoot the train chase I burnt no less than three motors of the Mitchell camera, very costly. But the cyclist's death, shot backwards and at eight frames a second, came out exactly the way I wanted it.

Violence is conspicuous, as was customary in *poliziotteschi*: the aforementioned scene in which a man on a bike is run over by the train, Testi brutally beating the seedy owner of a shooting range (played by character actor Luciano Catenacci), the harrowing sequence where Ciro's accomplices run over his legs with their bikes, mangling them, and the gruesome final showdown between Marco and Berto are all punches below the belt which leave their mark, as well as tangible signs of an "average" commercial film which still can still grab and shake the viewers. No wonder that, when it was submitted to the board of censors,

Pasquale Rachini (left) and Valerii (center, with shades and walkie-talkie) filming the assault on the speeding train (courtesy Pasquale Rachini).

the latter commented that "in the second part, the film features a succession of scenes of violence, in some places even repugnant and cruel," and gave the film a V.M.18 rating. "When *Go Gorilla Go* was classified by the board of censors as forbidden to minors, Cecchi Gori insisted that I cut the most violent scenes as requested by the commission of revision. I didn't accept and no cuts were made. When I said 'No!' producer Fulvio Lucisano, who was a member of the commission, looked at Cecchi Gori as if to say, 'And you're allowing him that?' Note that Cecchi Gori was not a sweet guy, but on that occasion he supported me. And the movie came out with the V.M.18 rating." Which did not stop *Go Gorilla Go* from grossing a significant sum at the box-office: almost 1,850 million *lire*.

Chapter Eleven

A Sting in the Desert

"Sorry, but I get a kick out of fooling people!"
—Jean Bellard, *Sahara Cross*

Valerii's next working commitments after *Go Gorilla Go* marked a definite change of pace for the director, and allowed him to return to the places of his childhood. "In 1976 the region Abruzzi commissioned me to make a documentary about the mores of my land, thanks to a friend, Vittorio di Sabatino, then the director of the Teramo Savings Bank. While location scouting, I discovered a small abbey, lost in the vast mountainous territory of my region: the abbey of Bominaco, a holy place which had been long forgotten, but was well-known in ancient art chronicles. So, the documentaries became two: one on Abruzzi in general, *L'Abruzzo? Prendilo è tuo!...*, and the other, on the small Romano-Byzantine abbey, *Bominaco: una scoperta*, which I'm truly proud of." Valerii also mentioned a third documentary, *La città e la memoria*, which he considered the most heartfelt and personal of the three. "The city was Teramo. The memory, mine. On Easter Sunday there was a custom, which I remembered since I was a child, that when the bells rang (after a fasting that lasted since Good Friday), we met with other friends to 'de-fast.' Since I was in the area for my documentary on Abruzzi, I was invited by an old schoolmate who, after treating us to lunch, took us to see the places where as kids we kept apart with our female classmates. That's how I got the idea of making a documentary. It's a small thing which even now I am very fond of." However, it must be noted that there is no trace of the latter documentary in the MIBAC archives.

After *Go Gorilla Go*'s urban violence, the African setting of Valerii's next feature film looked like an escape of sorts, like the one engineer Sampioni dreamed about in the previous film. *Sahara Cross* was born following an agreement with a Tunisian company (one of whose members was a young Tarak Ben Ammar), which provided the technical equipment for the realization of a co-production feature.

> The script was written by Adriano Belli and the title was *Arissa Ballerina*; it was a strange story which I don't even recall quite well, but very inconclusive. It was about a heist, but with no reference to the motivations of what the characters were doing, and with the aggravating circumstance of a cryptic dialogue that hinted at something big that they would do, but taking care not to make this known to the audience, who therefore had no reason to follow the developments of the narrative. In short, everything was the opposite of what Hitchcock recommended, that is the characters must ignore what is revealed to the viewer. I told the producers I would never make a film out of that script, because it just made no sense!

So, Valerii completely rewrote the script with his old friend Ernesto Gastaldi, trying to salvage it. "The attempt to overthrow the story kind of failed; since the Tunisian company had signed the co-production deal on Belli's screenplay, we had to work around it, even though it was anodyne and shapeless. Gastaldi's contribution concerned the invention of new motivations for the characters and a few scenes such as the battle between the two bulldozers, and the initial setting on *gorfas*, the pre–Christian granaries."

It is impossible to judge the extent of the rewriting, given that Belli's original script is nowhere to be found. The screenplay kept at Rome's CSC, and credited solely to Gastaldi, is basically identical to the movie. The sole exception is the opening sequence in Tunis, which is absent from the screenplay, and looks like a last-minute attempt at warning the viewer about the film's deceptive nature, while giving a stronger backup to the protagonists' unlikely plan.

Sahara Cross

Sunday, June 5, 10:45 a.m. At the Tunis airport, George Kentoff and Hamida meet Jean Bellard and Karl Mank; all four are oil engineers working for the powerful International Petroleum Company. In the casbah they meet a fifth colleague, Louis, and George reveals to his colleagues a mysterious plan to make lots of money. A line reads: "Then, it all happened in a few days." The engineers are being targeted by terrorists; their jeep is blown up in the desert and they have to get back to their base on foot. When a group of terrorists, stopped by the police at a gas station, blast the station and flee, George is killed in the explosion. His colleagues, led by Jean, set out to chase the terrorists and avenge him. The chase is full of pitfalls. One of the terrorists, dying and abandoned by his companions, blocks the pursuers with a grenade. Karl decides to use an old World War II trail to regain lost time, but the trail is mined. The engineers kill one of the terrorists and capture the other two, Kemal and Nicole, then set out for the city, but get lost in the Chott, a barren salt lake. During an overnight pause in a cave, Jean promises to release Nicole if she makes love to him, only to renege on that promise. The group arrives at another camp, where Kemal breaks free and engages in a duel with Jean aboard two excavators. The Frenchman has the upper hand again, but after the arrival of the police helicopter, Nicole grabs a gun and takes control of the situation. The two terrorists and three technicians depart by helicopter, but Jean reveals to Nicole that the weapon is not loaded, and the situation is reversed again. It is now clear that Jean and his colleagues—whom the Tunisian police still consider to be hostages—have a plan, and that they are using the terrorists as cover. Nicole and Kemal hijack a plane, demanding a ransom of three million dollars from IPC. The authorities and company cannot help but meet their demands. The terrorists release the hostages, among whom are Jean and Karl, and depart. The four engineers gather at a hotel. "Let me introduce you to Mr. Washington" Jean says. The plan is finally revealed: Jean and his comrades used the situation to pocket the three million dollars' ransom. Jean and Karl undress frantically; hidden under their clothes, in the shoes and in their underwear, they carry rolls of banknotes. Rich and happy, they make a toast to the memory of George, the unfortunate mastermind behind the plan.

Valerii's perplexities concerned the plot's construction, which leans on an unrelenting disguise, a bluff played again and again with unashamed straight face. Even the less involved in the audience eventually realize that something is wrong with the story of four oil engineers in pursuit of a terrorist commando who killed their colleague, and that perhaps the quartet do not act for the sake of revenge, but for money. Behind the façade of an exotic action film, *Sahara Cross* plays its well-camouflaged cards as a con flick in the vein of George Roy Hill's *The Sting* (1973), with better luck compared to other Italian epigones—such as Fernando di Leo's *Nick the Sting* (*Gli amici di Nick Hezard*, 1976)—that are more explicit and therefore more vulnerable in comparison with the American film's perfectly oiled plot. The apparently incongruous sequence of Jean (Franco Nero) playing card tricks at the bar (the hands actually belong to illusionist Tony Binarelli) is revealing; the viewer experiences a similar feel of being deceived, while watching a story whose sense will become clear only at the end. Everything is happening before our very eyes, Valerii implies, even though we are not noticing it. The cards that Jean carries with him throughout the film hint at his role in the story: He is ultimately a cheat, who is carrying out his plan under our noses. Take, for instance, the puzzling lack of interest on behalf of Karl and friends when the radio gives the news of them being supposedly held captive by the terrorists, or Jean's apparent carelessness which allows Nicole (Pamela Villoresi) to get hold of a gun and escape capture. *Sahara Cross* is full of such enigmatic moments, the meaning of which eventually become clear in the end.

It is all part of the game, including the fulsome accumulation of plot twists and turns that lead Jean and his colleagues to share three million dollars paid by a powerful multinational oil company. The film's essence as a *divertissement* is disclosed right from the opening sequence, with the date and hour superimposed on the screen like in a standard heist movie, accompanying the protagonists' walks in Tunis' casbah, across the ruins of Carthago and in other typical tourist locations, followed by the mocking caption "and then everything happened in a few days"… which *de facto* makes the previous ones useless. It is a tongue-in-cheek moment that borders on parody—and which perhaps is a last-minute invention on the part of Gastaldi, as it echoes the demistifying approach of his spy comedy *Cin … cin … cianuro* (1968)—as does the ending, with Franco Nero's speeded up striptease to reveal the money he has hidden on himself, and Jean sipping champagne in his underwear and socks.

Unfortunately several of the director's most intriguing ideas did not materialize. One regarded a spectacular opening, *Touch of Evil*-style, which was eventually aborted during shooting. Valerii described it as follows:

> We see a man inside a hotel room (it should have been George, played by Antonio Cantafora), looking at his watch. From the close-up of the quadrant the camera zooms back on his face, then to a long shot, comes back out of the window, follows the man getting out of the room, going downstairs, and leaving the hotel. When Cantafora gets on a jeep, the camera lifts off and follows him across the city streets to the airport, when a plane is landing. Franco Nero comes out of the plane, and boards the jeep. All of this in one long take, which should have lasted ten minutes—that is, one reel. Because since the opening detail, the camera would be positioned on a helicopter, with a balancing system that would allow us to avoid shakes and jerks. We had an agreement with TunisAir (the pilot would alert us of the exact time he would land, and Franco would be the first to descend from the aircraft), we had hired a helicopter pilot, and asked permission of the airport's directors. The helicopter was a French Alouette, with that function called hovering which allowed it, with a good pilot that is, to stay perfectly still at whatever height. But when it came to rehearse the shot, we discovered that due to the presence of sand we had to change the air filter, which cost 10,000 dollars in addition to the agreed price, which was another 10,000. So, of course, it all came to nothing.

The cast was heterogeneous to say the least. Aside from Franco Nero, the other main roles were played by Frenchman Michel Constantin, an ex-volleyball player launched by

French poster for *Sahara Cross* (1977). Note how Michel Cosntantin's character is featured prominently, instead of the film's real protagonist, Franco Nero (courtesy Lucas Balbo; copyright 1977, Cinevera SPA).

Jacques Becker's *Le trou* (1960), and Pamela Villoresi, a young stage actress who had just appeared in Miklos Jancsó's scandalous *Private Vices, Public Pleasures* (*Vizi privati, pubbliche virtù*, 1976). "Sometimes you have to make do with compromises or economical limitations," Valerii explained.

Villoresi is a very good actress, but I wouldn't have cast her as a terrorist, if it weren't for a pre-signed agreement. Another issue that we had after shooting was that she insisted on doing her own dubbing, in spite of her very strong Tuscan accent. Consider that she played a terrorist, I don't remember of which nation. I told her, 'Pamela, it can't be done!' but she insisted … and eventually I let her do that. Then, when she heard herself, she realized that the character was not believable. Fact is, usually actors think they are damaged by dubbing, but they haven't understood that very often dubbing is not something less, but something more….

Shooting lasted nine weeks, one in Rome and the rest in Tunisia. Filming in the desert involved many technical difficulties: the camera often risked collapsing in the sand, or, even worse, in the *chott*, a salt lake whose surface evaporates, leaving an even layer of salt, beneath which in some places there is quicksand (and to shoot there the crew had to hire a guide). For the same reason, the use of tracking shots was out of the question: it would be impossible to employ several feet-long tracks in such conditions. To overcome the issue, Valerii resorted to a new kind of camera, which by then had been used only in several big-budget American productions: the Steadicam. "Shooting was about to start, when I came across an article, on the mag *Il giornale dello spettacolo*, dedicated to that novelty. I told the producers that with the Steadicam we would save on the equipment and on the transportation costs, because there would be no need for tracks or other material, and we would avoid wasting time and inconveniences."

The producers got in touch with Mole & Richardson, the company specialized in movie equipment which imported and rented the Steadicam in Italy, but to no avail: the new camera had not been introduced in Italy, due to lack of requests. Valerii eventually got in touch with a Viennese dealer, and managed to get hold of one Steadicam. It was the very first model that came out on the market, very heavy and without a video output. "Since the director did not have the possibility of checking the shot, I asked the dealer to make a change, and add a video output so that I could see all that the camera operator saw. And so I followed all the Steadicam shots through this derivation, a solution that Ed Di Giulio adopted for all the Steadicam units from then on." To cut costs and avoid hiring a specialized cameraman, whose daily wage was equal to an ordinary cameraman's weekly one, the producer sent the camera operator Gianfranco Transunto and the director of photography Franco Di Giacomo to Vienna, to learn how to use the device. "I remember that the dealer asked me, 'What does the cameraman look like?' 'What do you mean?' 'Is he hefty? Because, you know, to operate a Steadicam you need a tall, strong man. And most of all, trained, otherwise he won't resist for long.' 'Well, he is tall and strong, he is young too … but trained, well, I don't know…' 'No problem, I'm gonna train him then!'"[1] Transunto recalled on his part: "I went there with Franco Di Giacomo, who, firstly, wanted to personally try the tool; the cameraman was not there […] and the Steadicam was to be completely calibrated, it was unbalanced and uncontrollable. So, when Di Giacomo put it on, he started to shout: 'But you're crazy! This is a piece of lead! Take it off of me! Take it off of me!' […] I stayed there for ten days. All the tests were recorded: there was none of today's equipment, and somebody had to run behind me all the time carrying a tape recorder connected with the camera via a cable. Valerii was thrilled by the results."[2]

For the director, Garrett Brown's invention was also the chance to experiment with looser, more fluid camera movements, like those he noticed in the most recent American films, such as *Marathon Man* (1976, John Schlesinger), and which were still unthinkable in Italian productions. Valerii recalls that "when Ed Di Giulio, who produced the Steadicam, knew that an Italian film crew was using his device, he came over from Hollywood to see the results, and said that ours was the most beautiful footage shot with his camera outside America; he even sent me a certificate from Cinema Products." According to film director and essayist David Ballerini, the author of an in-depth book study on the subject, *Sahara Cross* "displays such a technical and artistic maturity in the use of the Steadicam" that it makes the film "a rare gem, for its earliness and the maturity of the stylistic solutions adopted by the director, among the entire film productions prior to 1980."[3] Ballerini dedicates an in-depth analysis to several sequences: the one on the *chott*, quite difficult to shoot and entirely filmed with the special camera[4]; the gas station scene, consisting of two sinuous, elaborate long takes, which contain two 360-degree panoramic shots; and the bus theft, the occasion for yet another long sequence shot across a crowded square.

The use of the Steadicam in *Sahara Cross* is complex and innovative; through it, Valerii emancipated long takes from their basic form, "substantially linear, and derived, in a small evolution, from the stalking-type shot," and employed them outdoors, building a tridimensional space to be explored circularly,

> where the Steadicam's great opportunities of mobility and mise-en-scène are put to the test in a sort of overturned narrow space, which does not lock it up or constrains it, like a small room or a corridor (the Steadicam's typical places of use) would, but excludes it, rejects it, "encloses it" out in the open: an obstacle, an already occupied space [...] which always prevents the shortest path, and forces the eyes and the action [...] to revolve around it, like satellites around a planet, and explore the surrounding space in all its 360 degrees. An attitude to be found only in Brian De Palma's (much later) masterpieces.[5]

The biggest issues, paradoxically, came at the moment of filming in the studio the scene in which the helicopter with Franco Nero and the others aboard malfunctions, makes an emergency landing and explodes, right after its occupants have fled.

> We had to build a mock helicopter, hang it to a crane, and do a number of rehearsals to make it slide and stop on the ground, which was a patch of land at Cinecittà with a layer of sand sprayed on top of it. The helicopter, which cost us lots of money, was identical to the real one; once we did the first take, we sent the footage to the printing lab and when watching the rushes we realized that you couldn't see a thing. On film, the plastic-made windshield hid the sight of the actors inside the cabin. And so we had to rebuild the windshield, and lost two or three days of trial and error: it was a difficult moment, because we were near the end of shooting ... and of the money as well.

Despite the odd bursts of violence—such as George's death scene, as the man is horribly burned in the explosion of the gas pump, or Michel Constantin's character shooting a terrorist in the temple—Valerii did not emphasize the gruesome details, unlike in *Go Gorilla Go*, but he relieved the tension with picaresque diversions (such as the scene with Franco Nero and the anti-tank mine) and male bonding typical of old-style adventure films, as proven by the reference to the ice cold beer that the friends will drink together once all is finished, a cinephile homage to J. Lee Thompson's *Ice Cold In Alex*, a.k.a. *Desert Attack* (1958). The pacing is fast, aided by Riz Ortolani's pounding, percussion-driven score and occasionally the director gives the viewer some nice over-the-top bits. The sensational duel between the two excavators, which launch one against the other like two mechanical Japanese monsters, is a true *pièce de résistance* that borders on the surreal, and conceived with such a straight face that it solicits applause—what is more, it proves Valerii's prowess and his creativity when it came to use film technique to obtain the results he wanted on screen. "When it was time to shoot that scene, everyone was looking at me, as if to say: and now, how are we gonna do *that*? 'Well, gentlemen, we're gonna use one of cinema's

Franco Nero in one of *Sahara Cross*' most spectacular scenes (courtesy Lucas Balbo; copyright 1977, Cinevera SPA).

oldest tricks: we're putting the two excavators in the final position of the shot, and then film them backwards, having them make the opposite movements as the ones that they are supposed to, and speed it all up a bit, by filming at 20 frames per second instead of 24.' Then, during editing, we reversed the film, so that it looked like the two excavators were hurling one against the other, rather than moving away as they actually did. And it seems to me that the result is good."

Every now and then, Valerii's past in Westerns comes out in *Sahara Cross*: the director filmed the Tunisian deserts and canyons as if they were those of Almería, capturing on camera a number of suggestive images at the Chott el-Jerid salt lake, as the protagonists' jeep is isolated in a bright, blinding landscape; what is more, he even staged a scene where the protagonists hop on a train, like desperadoes heading West. And the Western—namely his first feature film, *Taste of Killing*—is where the overall cynicism draws from. The "heroes" of *Sahara Cross* are certainly not the typical good guys of classic adventure movies: rather, they are like Japanese *ronin*, amoral mercenaries who only care about money, nice scoundrels who are even ready to dispatch the terrorists to avoid that the police suspect them. And, as bounty hunter Hank Fellows did, they are betting on themselves and their own ability to survive and reverse an adverse situation in their favor. "Genius is the art of making the most of one's opportunities," one says, quoting Napoleon—and luck, it should be added. A billionaire sum is at stake: in *Taste of Killing*, Fellows claimed that "You can never have too much money," while in this film Michel Constantin says "Money's never enough."

On the other hand, the two terrorists, Nicole and Kemal, retain a moral integrity that their adversaries lack ("To each his own vocation," Bellard says). Consider the scene where Jean persuades Nicole to have sex with him, flaunting a facade of pacifist sensitiveness which sounds very much like a mockery of the 1968 ideals,[6] and promising to set her free afterwards ("That's my only defect.... I always keep my promises") only to go back on his word, with a line that sums up the whole film: "Sorry, but I get a kick out of fooling people!"

CHAPTER TWELVE

The Long Silence

"Those were difficult years. For all of us."
—Tonino Valerii

Sahara Cross did not prove the box-office success the producers had envisaged. It reached 64th among that year's most popular Italian films, grossing just over 706 million lire. A trifle, compared to the over six billion-and-a-half grossed by the Bud Spencer–Terence Hill vehicle *Crime Busters* (*I due superpiedi quasi piatti*, 1977, Sergio Corbucci). "We hoped for something more, sure. But inside my head I did think: 'Why would people go see a movie starring Franco Nero and Pamela Villoresi?'" Perhaps, part of the film's lack of appeal at the box-office was due to its wildly uneven tone: a mixture of adventure, thriller, and black comedy, and on top of that a story featuring a group of terrorists. In 1977, terrorism was a difficult topic to touch, even if, like in Valerii's film, the story was set outside Italy. Terrorism was the elephant in the room of Italian cinema; the films that ventured into such a taboo topic—such as *Could It Happen Here?* (*Italia: ultimo atto?*, 1977, Massimo Pirri), *I Am Afraid* (*Io ho paura*, 1977, Damiano Damiani), *Kleinhoff Hotel* (1977, Carlo Lizzani)—were mostly destined for failure or misunderstanding. *Sahara Cross* ultimately seemed to imply that, for all their violence and fanaticism, the film's terrorists were ultimately preferable to the Moloch—the multinational oil company—they were fighting, not to mention that they were substantially more honest and adherent to their ideals compared with the smart, scoundrel-like engineers led by Franco Nero's character, and that their Third Worldist fight was not unjustified. What is more, it implied that terrorists were always liable to be exploited and manipulated by someone smarter, and used as scapegoats—a thought-provoking thesis that was not explicitly enunciated, but cunningly alluded to. All things considered, *Sahara Cross* was not exactly the most pleasant of time-killing *divertissements*, or at least not the kind the average viewer was expecting to see.

What is more, the film was penalized by bad distribution, much to Valerii's dismay:

> I had gotten in touch with Cineriz's Frizzi, who, after the success of *Go Gorilla Go* and Fabio Testi's box-office relaunch, was ready to distribute the film, but the producer, Donatella Senatore (the sister of Daniele, who produced *Investigation of a Citizen Above Suspicion*) would not listen to me and entrusted *Sahara Cross* to Elephant Film—a newly funded distribution company, with no experience—which went bankrupt after a few months. When a company declares bankruptcy, all assets are frozen until a curator is appointed, who redistributes everything to remedy the deficit. Such was the fate of *Sahara Cross*: withdrawn from the distribution circuit, it was shelved in a warehouse and there it stayed.

These were hard times, indeed, for the national film industry: within a couple of years, from 1975 to 1977, viewers per year dropped from 513 million to 373 million units. At the rate of one hundred million spectators per year, the hemorrhage was uncontrollable. Ticket prices increased, but more and more people would rather spend the evening at home, in slippers, explorers with the remote control, scouting the free and wild program schedules of the newly liberalized private television channels.

In retrospect, though, the tepid box-office performance of *Sahara Cross* was only marginally the cause of the hiatus in Valerii's output that proved to be decisive in the filmmaker's subsequent career. According to Ernesto Gastaldi, who suffered a similar if decidedly less dramatic period, "the slowdown in our career, both Tonino's and mine, was caused, paradoxically, by having worked with Leone. Minor producers, perhaps thinking that by then we were asking for exorbitant fees, did not call us anymore. And of course, in Tonino's case, Leone's behavior regarding the paternity of *My Name Is Nobody* was highly damaging."[1]

Valerii did not like to recall that period. "Those were difficult years. For all of us." In 1979, on the yearly *Almanacco del cinema* (Film Almanac) published by Il Formichiere, a long article-interview appeared which collected the answers by several Italian film directors to questions about the crisis of cinema, the difficulty of carrying out new projects, the hopes for the future. Among the names interviewed, were Alessandro Blasetti, Carlo Lizzani, Fernando di Leo, Luciano Salce, Giuliano Montaldo, and Valerii—a further demonstration of the filmmaker's prominence in the realm of commercial Italian cinema.

The director discussed in detail a series of projects abandoned in the making, or put aside in the hope of better times. "I had to make a movie inspired by a popular character of Italian Western comics. But after over a year's worth of negotiations the project was shelved because of differences with the rights holder." The project Valerii referred to was a motion picture based on *Tex*. Created in 1948 by Gian Luigi Bonelli and Aurelio Galeppini, *Tex* remains Italy's most durable comic book to date, still being published after almost 70 years. The titular hero, Tex Willer, was a Texas ranger with the features of a young Gary Cooper and a staunchly moral code of honor, and the series was characterized by a revisionist approach towards Native Americans, often seen as more sympathetic and wiser than the cynical and violent "white people." *Tex* soon experienced incredible success, and it was translated and published in many other European countries, such as France (as *Texas Boy*), Spain (as *Texas Bill*), Finland, Norway, Sweden, Yugoslavia and Greece. It became immensely popular in Turkey (as *Teks*) and landed in such exotic markets as India, Indonesia, South America (especially Brazil) and Israel. Its only appearance in the United States, on the other hand, was in a special issue drawn by the great Joe Kubert and published in the U.S. by Dark Horse Comics in the early 2000s.

The idea of bringing *Tex* to the screen had been floating around for years. Gian Luigi Bonelli started working on a film adaptation in the late 1960s; he founded a production company named "Condor Cinematografica," based in Milan, and concocted a script inspired by the 1969 story *Fort Defiance*. Among the actors considered for the main roles were Charlton Heston (as Tex) and Jack Palance (as the hero's sidekick, Kit Carson). In the early 1970s, Bonelli summoned Valerii to verify the possibility of bringing Italy's popular comic to the screen.

> I had never read *Tex* in my whole life. I bought a few issues to see what it was all about, and I liked *Sangue Navajo* very much. I told Bonelli that we could make a good film out of it, and he was glad to hear that—it was one of the stories he loved the most. He even showed me how he worked: he sketched a drawing with the characters' dialogue and sent it over to the drawing artist. However, then it emerged that Bonelli wanted

to take care personally of all the costumes and sets; what is more, he put aside the idea of *Sangue Navajo* and chose another story instead, about a stampeding herd of cattle which destroys a whole Western village, with all the stories of the main characters intertwined. Which meant we would have to shoot scenes featuring 400 cows ... besides, the costume thing was impractical. On paper, it is perfectly fine to have a character wear a yellow scarf, red shirt and black trousers, but on a screen it looks ridiculous. Eventually the project fell apart. Tessari eventually made a film based on *Tex*, years later, and we know how it went.[2]

In the same period as his negotiations with Bonelli, Valerii was contacted by Franco Cristaldi, who, together with Nicola Carraro, wanted to set up a big Western with the help of U.S. money: Warner Bros. was in talks, and the budget was one million and a half dollars. Valerii worked on the screenplay with Alberto Ongaro, but the project ended up in smoke. Other scripts languished in the drawer, starting with *Ostrowsky*, to be filmed not in the States but between Berlin and Zagreb ("I would still be happy. But in the end will they ask me to set the film in an 'imaginary' country? Foreign sales have their weight, as everybody knows..." he complained on *Almanacco del cinema*[3]). *Piccolo Sam*, an original script written in 1978, whose idea dated back to the pre-production of *My Name Is Nobody*, was the story of a travelling salesman who abandons everything to become a gold digger in South Dakota, and its anti-capitalist theme echoed certain intuitions of the director's previous Westerns ("It is a fierce apologue on the capitalist myth of accumulation and the dreams that money can buy, to quote Richter"), transposed to the present day, amid mobile houses and new nomads, to tell the neurotic need for uprooting and the constant impulse to reposition, which brought to the continuous displacement of families and entire communities.

Inspired by a short story by Giuseppe D'Agata (two columns published in *Il Corriere della Sera*) and written for the screen together with D'Agata and Lucio Battistrada, *La pistola che spara un colpo solo* (The Gun That Fires a Single Shot) was a spy story—the title refers to the unreliable spies, hired for one job (for instance, killing someone) and then in turn immediately dispatched—placed in the context of terrorism. "The film was supposed to start with riots in Rome, seen from inside the police superintendent's car, as he received news and gave orders." It was the story of a man obsessed with the world of espionage and with the idea of becoming a secret agent, who one day notices a common newspaper advertisement, which he thinks hides a coded message. He is actually right, but ends up entangled in an intrigue much bigger than he imagined. "This project was the umpteenth victim of terrorism. I remember when we talked about it with the producers, they touched their balls and said: 'In these days, a story like that?' Today, to think of it, it might be developed and be successful. But, today, would they make me do it?"[4]

Closer to the Western, on the other hand, was *La prateria di San Jacinto* (The Prairie on the San Jacinto River), based on the novel *Die Prairie am Jacinto* by Charles Sealsfield (that is, the Austrian Karl Anton Postl), and adapted together with the renowned scriptwriter Sergio Amidei.[5]

> It was an anomalous Western. It told the story of the harsh conflict that arose between the United States and Mexico about the annexation of Texas by the States. From Baltimore, on a stagecoach which must cross a vast Indian territory, a journalist is traveling: he must go to the border between the two states, which are about to start the war that will result in the battle of the Alamo. On the stagecoach there is also a Texan girl returning to her family, disguised in male clothes. The story of these and other characters intersect: patriots, criminals, traitors and Mexican generals. In short, an epic period fresco, between history and anecdote. The title's prairie is the one at the border between Texas and Mexico. It was a challenging, expensive story.

Valerii learned of the project from an ad on *Il giornale dello spettacolo*, got in touch with Amidei and proposed himself as the director. "I went to Amidei's house and stayed there a whole summer, writing this story with a very fast Sardinian typist to whom Amidei dictated the script. And when once he had a say about what we were writing, Amidei destroyed his typewriter with a golf club!" Rounding out the list are *A che serve la laurea?...* (What's a Degree For?...), written with Marino Moretti, and another long-lulled project, *La terra rossa*, based on William Henry Hudson's novel *The Purple Land*, adapted by Amidei. Needless to say, none of these would ever see the light of day.

Years would pass before Tonino Valerii returned to his place behind the camera.[6] When one considers the directors at work in popular genre filmmaking, his eight-year absence from the big screen is all the more painful and at the same time significant. Valerii's struggle to mount film projects he believed in, and on which he painstakingly worked while trying to maintain control until they eventually fell apart, whereas other filmmakers continued to regularly churn out one movie after another, gives the measure of Valerii's distance from the average genre film. Despite being identified with movies destined for large consumption, in his heart and mind Valerii was an *auteur* of sorts, a film director who considered his role as central and unassailable in the making of a film: The producer would put up the money, and the director would make the movie, with little or no influence whatsoever on the part of the former. This may seem a paradox, given that during the course of his career Valerii often had to undergo compromises and take work-for-hire jobs, but it was a clear example of his conception of the filmmaker as a creator, especially regarding the genesis of the script and its development. To him, the main point was telling a story, and one that would offer food for thought; entertainment was a primary value, but it would never suffice alone. Such a concept was proving to be more and more irreconcilable with what cinema was evolving into, and it was all the more painful for such a stubborn and proud filmmaker as Valerii.

While attempting to put together film projects, the director was forced to accept other jobs which no doubt sounded humiliating to someone who just a few years earlier had been directing Hollywood stars and grossed big money at the box-office. "I did some TV ads in France, for a brand of decaffeinated coffee.[7] They wanted a Western-type ad, and called me." Another work-for-hire job of the period was the documentary short *INAIL: 100 anni e non sentirli* (INAIL: 100 Years and Not Feeling Them), commissioned by Italy's National Institute for Insurance against Accidents at Work. Around the early 1980s, finally, Valerii resumed working steadily—not for the big screen, though. In the summer of 1982[8] the director was involved by producer Gianni Hecht Lucari in the making of another TV series, *Caccia al ladro d'autore* (To Catch an Art Thief). The idea was to make an action series, American-style, but set in Italy's major art cities, and focused on crimes set in the world of art—that is to say, almost a marketing operation commissioned by the tourist office. Even the protagonist was a hybrid in a way: Captain Maffei, a nomad yet cultured cop, as effective in dismantling trafficking rings and forgers as he is unable to resist the charms of a beautiful woman, was a dynamic and Gascon character, devoid of the gloomy air of the *poliziotteschi*'s "iron commissioners." Although the plots featured criminals and murders, the scripts held away from the news stories' material, and did not really try to portray actual, contemporary Italy. In this sense, the reassuring choice of Giuliano Gemma as Maffei was perfect, whereas the lackluster Vanni Corbellini was a forgettable sidekick.

The two recurring characters were sided by other familiar faces in supporting roles, such as Fabrizio Bentivoglio, Ennio Fantastichini, Isabel Russinova (who also appeared alongside Gemma in Tessari's *Tex and the Lord of the Deep*) and Caterina Boratto.[9]

The pilot, "Il ratto di Proserpina," directed by Duccio Tessari, was shown at a television festival, in 1983, to poor reception.[10] After an 18-month halt, RAI gave the green light to *Caccia al ladro d'autore*, even though the 13 episodes initially programmed were reduced to seven (including Tessari's pilot) because of budget cuts. The Abruzzi-born director took care of three episodes, scripted with Ugo Liberatore and, uncredited, Ottavio Alessi, and set in Venice, Florence and Siena; the remaining three were directed by Sergio Martino. The setting, of course, was essential to the atmosphere: "Cartografia sacra" (Sacred Cartography) takes place during the Palio di Siena, the Venetian episode "La foresta che vola" (The Flying Forest) ends with images of the re-enactment of the election of the first Doge and the traditional regatta, a sequence of "Addio Raffaello" (Goodbye Raffaello) is set during the historical football match in Piazza Santa Croce. Moreover, the art cities' landscapes act as a proven corollary to the most adrenalin-filled moments. The Venice episode, for example, features a fistfight on the roofs of Piazza San Marco, next to the Moors, and a motorboat chase in the canals. What does not work so well are the stories, predictable and not very exciting in terms of detection; despite the inclusion of technical details (reflectography identifies the fake painting in "Addio Raffaello") and several Hitchcock-like flashes, such as the telephoto lens through which the villains spy on the building across the street in the Florence episode, the overall result is anodyne, with red herrings scattered without conviction throughout and banal fistfights as filler—not to mention the overdose of regional dialects: In each episode there seems to be the need to cram the dialogue with the cadences of the city in which the story takes place, so that in Venice everyone speaks as if they just came out of a Goldoni comedy (and the solution of the mystery in "La foresta che vola" is indeed entrusted to the double meaning of a dialectal term, a plot twist lifted off *The Sunday Woman*), in Florence there is a proliferation of aspired "c"s, and so on. That is not Valerii's fault: he was a mere executor, and his skills are the same as always, although the impact of television and its tight schedule can be sensed.

> The most terrible thing about working in television is the time you are provided with. For *Sahara Cross*, which was an average film, I had a nine weeks' shoot, whereas for *Caccia al ladro d'autore* I had an average of four-and-a-half weeks per episode, that is half the time. And in such cases you have to make up for the lack of time with cunning, with inventions, since you have to structure the story in a different way. When you start working in television, to do a 100 minute thing you have to use half of the shots; for a film, you shoot an average of 600 to 700 shots, for a TV movie you can do up to 400, 450, and you must always be able to cut, and adjust the pacing. It takes lots of skills, and you don't always get the desired results.

"My friend Paolo Valmarana asked me to work on a project handed to him by the producer Luciano Perugia, previously a great general organizer for Visconti. There was a thin and confused outline, and a tiny screenplay by none other than Luigi Malerba"[11] Valerii commented about his other assignment of the period. It was a series for RAI originally titled *T.I.R.*, which would then become *Due assi per un turbo* (Two Aces For One Turbo), created by Perugia and centered around the adventures of a pair of truck drivers around Europe, aboard an Iveco 190.42 Turbostar. *Due assi per un turbo* was filmed in co-production with Hungary; the 13 episodes, one hour each, aired in 1987. Over the years, the series acquired a certain cult status—thanks also to its catchy theme song, written by Detto Mariano—and was rebroadcast several times, albeit usually late at night. A second season was initially scheduled, but never produced.

On the two episodes he directed (the others were helmed by Stelvio Massi, Giovanni Fago and Sándor Mihályfy), Valerii recalled:

> I wrote the story of a couple of truck drivers who often had to compete with very aggressive colleagues, because of the need to arrive early in the markets that supplied stuff, since who comes there first decrees the price and sells the goods at the best conditions. It was titled "Chi primo arriva" (Whoever Comes First), with Adolfo Celi as a special guest star. I made another episode about the smuggling of works of art, *L'uomo dal turbante rosso* (The Man with the Red Turban). For the two truck drivers, we had the idea of somatically reproducing my friends Bud Spencer and Terence Hill.

The chosen ones were Renato D'Amore, a stevedore at Rome's general markets who had acted in bit parts in such films as *Grunt!* (1983, Andy Luotto), *Eccezziunale... veramente* (1982, Carlo Vanzina) and *Il ragazzo di campagna* (1984, Castellano and Pipolo), and Christian Fremont, another *sui generis* actor with a past as the chef on the yacht of Saudi Arabian billionaire Adnan Khasoggi. The shooting schedules were narrower compared with those the director was used to: four weeks for each episode, and little time for technically difficult sequences, such as a fistfight on the flatbed of a truck that carries cement pipes, shot from a helicopter, in "Chi primo arriva."

With respect to "L'uomo dal turbante rosso," which is divided into two parts because of its complex story, is related a nice anecdote that the director often liked to tell:

> It was the story of an old lady who went to museums and copied the paintings on display, and who one day put the one she just copied—Van Eyck's *Portrait of a Man in a Red Turban*—in place of the real one. For the role, we needed a lovely elderly woman, who would inspire sympathy, but we just could not find her. We filmed in Locarno, and when the Saturday before the beginning of the shooting came, the production manager and I were eating in a luxury restaurant in Lugano, downhearted and dispirited. At a certain point, I look around and down the hall I see not an old lady but *the* old lady! Exactly the person we were looking for! An elderly woman who was dining alone at a table down the hall. I turn to my diner and say, "Do not turn suddenly, but on your left, back there, there's the old lady we've been looking for..." The production manager pales, then politely turns, sees her and says: "It's impossible—it's *her*!" Said and done: he calls the waiter and first inquires about that elegant and classy old lady—because she is a true *grande dame*, that is. The waiter collects the lavish tip we offered and talks. The lady is alone; the lady is wealthy; the lady will surely not accept. The production manager asks the lady to be treated *tout de suite* a bottle of Philipponat *pas dosè* with our business cards and the request to be able to approach her after the meal. The waiter earns the highest tip he has ever taken, lavishes exaggerated bows [upon her] and looks at our table; eventually he gets her consent. We take a long breath and wait. After a few minutes I turn to my friend and say: "She's ours!" And I was right. How did I realize it? From the corner of my eye I noticed she was checking on her makeup....

CHAPTER THIRTEEN

The Naked Charm of the Bourgeoisie

"A husband can be boring, but even boredom sometimes has its merits."
—Clara, *Unscrupulous*

Caccia al ladro d'autore was broadcast on Sunday's prime time, on RaiUno, starting in November 1985. That same month, Italy's most popular film magazine *Ciak* published an interview with the director on the set of his new film, *Unscrupulous* (*Senza scrupoli*), accompanied by rather risqué stills of the shoot. Eight years after *Sahara Cross*, Valerii's comeback on the big screen left most people bewildered: what was the director of *My Name Is Nobody* doing with a story that openly nodded to the then-prevailing soft-porn thread, revived by the success of Tinto Brass's *The Key* (*La chiave*, 1983)?

In the mid–Eighties many filmmakers tried their hands at eroticism. The map of 1980s Italian softcore is a cross-section of an industry which, as had occurred during the previous decades, followed the wave of the trailblazing hit, intensively exploiting a thread before moving to the next. And it is right here, amid the modest transgressions and the naive morbidities of the erotic genre, that Italian genre cinema's last gleamings burned out, just one step away from the production-distribution monopolies and the TV destination that would mark the industry's final hour. Brass led the way, relaunching the sex cougar *par excellence* Stefania Sandrelli and offering to the paying public a new erotic dream in flesh, the mightily buxom Serena Grandi; in tow came the legion of imitators, such as Joe D'Amato/Aristide Massaccesi, with his fake Dannunzian softcores starring Lilli Carati—*The Alcove* (*L'alcova*, 1985), *The Pleasure* (*Il piacere*, 1985), *A Lustful Mind* (*Lussuria*, 1986), *Midnight Gigolo* a.k.a. *Peepshow* (*Voglia di guardare*, 1986)—and Bruno Gaburro, with *Erotic Games* (*Malombra*, 1984), *Maladonna* (1984) and *Penombra* (1986), all starring the declining sexy starlet Paola Senatore, one step from the hardcore abyss. In between were those filmmakers with good skills and an illustrious past, who were making a virtue of necessity, such as Piero Schivazappa, who directed Serena Grandi in a softcore present-day adaptation of Italo Svevo's 1898 novel *Senilità*—*Lady of the Night* (*La signora della notte*, 1986)—and Valerii himself.

The director took on an existing project set up by producer Enzo Gallo: "A well-known distributor from Campania asked Gallo to provide him with an erotic softcore *giallo* in which to cast an ex–Miss Italy very close to a well-known politician's heart. Gallo activated and focused on a story written by Mino Roli, entrusting the script to Riccardo Ghione. I intervened at this stage." Ghione is a *sui generis* figure of Italian cinema: the son of the famous orchestra conductor Franco Ghione, a scriptwriter (often as a ghost writer) for Marco Ferreri, he directed a few unusual films to say the least, such as *La rivoluzione sessuale* (1968, starring Laura Antonelli, inspired by the figure and theories of Wilhelm Reich) and *Il prato macchiato di rosso* (filmed in 1970, but released in 1973), a delirious psychedelic socio-political horror film featuring in the cast the popular singer Lucio Dalla.

Unscrupulous was shot in seven weeks, between Turin and Rome. The female lead, the French Sandra Wey, who had starred in the forgettable *The Story of O 2* (*Histoire d'O: Chapitre 2*, 1984, Éric Rochat), was no Bette Davis, but was eager to take her clothes off; the cast also featured the Neapolitan stage actor Marzio Honorato—already seen alongside (and, well, on) Sandrelli in *Una donna allo specchio*, 1984, also produced by Gallo, and with whom Valerii would work again several years later in *Shatterer*—and an old acquaintance of the director, Antonio Marsina, whom one reviewer labeled as "Italy's most inexpressive actor."[1] Valerii stated: "My film is a metaphor on violence and eroticism, and so cinematically I portrayed a harsh reality, in an aberrant social context, where human relationships are unstable and difficult. To make all this clear, it was necessary on my part to depict realistically certain scenes of sex and eroticism."[2] In fact, despite the bait thrown to the fans of the genre, *Unscrupulous*—which was released in January 1986 and did rather well at the box-office, increasing the revenues in the home video market and even inspiring an apocryphal sequel, Carlo Ausino's abysmal *Senza scrupoli 2* (1991)—did not maintain the promises hinted at by a lurid title, a sensationalist poster and a cunning trailer.

Sandra Wey and Marzio Honorato in *Unscrupulous* (1986).

Unscrupulous

Turin. The petty thief Diego Campus breaks into the house of jeweler Antonio Combi. Silvia, Combi's beautiful and bored wife, is home alone; Campus brutally rapes her and steals a valuable drawing. Silvia, upset, wants to go to the police, but Massimo dis-

suades her; he is afraid of bad publicity, and believes it is better to forget everything. Silvia does not give up, and scours the city in search of the rapist: but behind the anger and humiliation, in her dreams she nurtures a strong attraction to the man. And when she finally finds Campus, Silvia becomes first his lover, then his accomplice, urging him to rob in her friend Clara's villa. Massimo uncovers the affair, follows the lovers, but seems to passively accept the betrayal. Meanwhile, the passion between Silvia and Diego is becoming more rampant and ambiguous: he takes her to a strip club and makes her undress in front of an audience of voyeurs, then makes her exhibit herself in a public place; finally, he involves her in a robbery which ends in bloodshed. Silvia, frightened, decides to leave him, and return to the tranquility of a bourgeois life. But after he learns that Combi purchased a load of diamonds, Diego returns to Silvia's house, gun in hand. His plans go up in smoke with the arrival of the police, who kept an eye on him; in the ensuing shootout, Campus is killed. Silvia and Massimo leave for a holiday; the husband asks her how she's going to live from then on, and Silvia replies, "Unscrupulous."

Unscrupulous inaugurates the second phase of Valerii's career, a series of genre films of decidedly minor value, both historically and artistically, compared to his output of the previous decades. Each of them is marked by some compromises and displays the director's personality and talent only in bits and pieces, and yet, for all their flaws, these works show the changing face of Italian cinema and its increasingly suffocating practices.

At the times of its release, Marco Giusti dismissed the film as the perfect "link between A-grade porn[3] with ideas and the most facile one, leaving room for lower products [...] to come to the fore," judging the *mise-en-scène* "dignified and professional" but definitely "not interested in the subject and in the human material it deals with."[4] In fact, although in Silvia's dream Marzio Honorato shows off a phallic prothesis *à la manière de* Tinto Brass, the erotic scenes never transcend certain limits. During Silvia's rape, for instance, the camera abandons the actors and rises to frame a drawing on the wall, only to return to them (with no cuts) just when the intercourse is over, with a calligraphic ellipsis destined to disappoint most viewers.

During the shooting, Gallo showed up on the set right on the day when the rape scene was scheduled, and asked Valerii to emphasize the more titillating details. "I told him: 'I'm going to shoot the scene the way I want, if you want to put together your personal cut of the film for your friends, you're going to shoot it on your own…' and in the end he admitted that the way I shot it, the scene was much more erotic, so much so that in the end we even cut it a little bit. When Honorato sneaks into the house and rapes Wey, I had shot the scene this way: he puts her prone, and penetrates her from behind; she is leaning on a straw-backed chair, and when he penetrates her, he does it with such violence that she breaks through the straw with her head; you could see her head that suddenly breaks the straw and comes out, getting stuck…. I was the first to say that we could not leave that, and we cut it." However, the board of censors asked for a couple of cuts to be made, in order to grant the film a V.M.18 rating: a moment, just after the rape, when Silvia reaches out to her private parts and her hand emerges covered in blood (about 4 seconds), and the nightmare scene (with 9 seconds excised).

Elsewhere, Valerii pushed the pedal of the grotesque, as in the strip scene in the club, with some clumsy and a little overweight housewives performing for an audience of lonely men. The mood recalls Marco Ferreri's films, and the sequence summarizes the desire for transgression in a country that dreams of America but is still prisoner of a seedy provincialism; the comparison with Kim Basinger's famous, glossy striptease scene in 9½ Weeks (1986), which would arrive on Italian screens within a few months, was inevitable. Other moments feature a more banal symbolism: When Silvia confesses the rape to her husband, the not-so-happy couple is reflected in a heart-shaped mirror, whereas in the end Silvia burns the phallic-shaped mask that Campus wore during the rape and emerges to a new life/light.

The theme is not unusual, as it is not the relationship between the two protagonists, with the proletarian Campus trying to shape his upper-class lover in his own image ("You must be like me!"), to the point of making her his accomplice.[5] However, despite the film being a work-for-hire, the style is the same as always. Film critic Oreste De Fornari called it "soft," and it is the adjective that best fits Silvia's wanderings—accompanied by James Senese's saxophone-driven score—in the city streets, with all the men's eyes on her, or the long take that illustrates the woman's arrival on the bank of the river Po, as the camera goes down, backs off and finally reveals a lovemaking couple, a counterpoint to the woman's sexual restlessness— proof that Valerii cared about the movie's visuals, and a moment that underlines the similarities with *A Girl Called Jules*, another story of a woman torn between norm and transgression. A line of dialogue such as "A husband can be boring, but even boredom sometimes has its merits" explicitly draws back to the 1970 film, where Jules' betrothed was likened to a faithful puppy dog, guaranteeing protection, tranquility, routine, while here Antonio Marsina's character is more interested in his rare drawings than in the trauma suffered by his wife.

But ultimately the director cared less about the story of the "progressive loss of identity and the search of an impossible regeneration through eroticism," than the context in which it takes place. "I realized that if I wanted to get a decent result I had to push the pedal so as to thicken around Silvia a selfish environment, incapable even of simply listening to what had happened to her." An arid and bored *bourgeois* background, all games of bridge and empty conversations whose recurring topic is that of the next holidays. This is 1980s Italy: the opulence, the pursuit of appearance, the cultural lethargy that produces monsters.

CHAPTER FOURTEEN

Too Late the Hero?

"We don't want any unauthorized heroes lying around!"
—Major Briggs, *Brothers in Blood*

In the mid–Eighties, the Italian film industry was a sinking ship, abandoned by the passengers (between 1980 and 1985 the number of filmgoers fell from 241.8 to 123.1 million) and the crew alike. More and more, the technicians, writers and directors were settling down into television. The breakdown involved the so-called "in-depth market," consisting of second- and third-run theaters; for some, it meant a sad conversion to "red light" cinemas devoted to hardcore porn, to others it resulted in closing down, making room for banks or shopping malls. The U.S. companies recovered a dominating position on the market, and television networks got involved in production; if in previous decades it was the distributors who called the shots, with the guaranteed minimum to the producer, now it was RAI and Silvio Berlusconi's Fininvest that shared the cake. With the 1984 decree and the 1990 Mammì law, which regulated the broadcasting system, the television networks' financial power affected the modes of production and the content of the products, conceived according to television airing, and nipped in the bud any potentially indigestible or transgressive element.

Small producers made a virtue of necessity, turning out flicks concocted and filmed for export in less demanding markets, such as Central America, or destined for home video. The blueprint changed from time to time: *First Blood*'s muscular action, *Miami Vice*'s urban cop film, the war or adventure movie…. What mattered was that the products were marketable, which, in a nutshell, meant a more or less slavish imitation of the Anglophone filmic and television universe, to the benefit of foreign buyers. *Brothers in Blood* (*La sporca insegna del coraggio*) was born like that, as a subsidiary of a successful war movie, *Uncommon Valor* (1983, Ted Kotcheff), the antecedent of other Italian flicks of the period destined for foreign markets. After more than a decade, Valerii teamed up again with Roberto Leoni, whose career as a scriptwriter had taken off with such works as the bizarre *Giro girotondo… con il sesso è bello il mondo* (1975, Oscar Brazzi), a sci-fi/erotic version of *Little Red Riding Hood* starring Rossano Brazzi, the comedy *Pure as a Lily* (*Come una rosa al naso*, 1976, Franco Rossi) with Vittorio Gassman and Ornella Muti, the crime film *Street People* (*Gli esecutori*, 1976, Maurizio Lucidi), which paired Roger Moore and Stacy Keach, the crepuscular Western *California* (1977, Michele Lupo), starring Giuliano Gemma, and Luciano Salce's cult comedy *Vieni avanti cretino* (1982) with Lino Banfi. In addition to writing the script, Leoni also acted as assistant director during the shooting.

Brothers in Blood starred the Swedish-born tough guy Bo Svenson, a former athlete and a recurring presence of Italian genre cinema since the mid-to-late 1970s, besides his stints in supporting roles in A-grade American productions such as *North Dallas Forty* (1979) and *Heartbreak Ridge* (1986), just to name a couple. He was paired with another American actor with working experience in Italy: Peter Hooten (Dr. Strange in the 1978 television movie), who had played alongside Svenson in Enzo G. Castellari's cult war film *The Inglorious Bastards* (*Quel maledetto treno blindato*, 1978), and also co-starred in Duccio Tessari's period drama *The Fifth Commandment* (*L'alba dei falsi dei*, 1978) and Aristide Massaccesi's post-atomic sci-fi *2020 Freedom Fighters* (*Anno 2020—I gladiatori del futuro*, 1982). The cast also featured the Italian Carlo Mucari (seen in Tessari's *Tex and the Lord of the Deep*) plus a number of experienced stuntmen (Pietro Torrisi, Rocco Lerro, Sergio Testori), and the invariable Hollywood has-been, Martin Balsam. Among them, Nat Kelly Cole (Nat King Cole's adopted son, in his only film role) looked like a fish out of water.

Filming started in late 1985 and took place mostly in the Dominican Republic, plus a few days in New York where the opening scenes were shot, and was plagued by budget problems. In his biography of Pulitzer Prize-winning poet James Merrill (1926–1995), Hooten's partner from 1983 to his death, author Langdon Hammer recalls the experience as seen through the perspective of the author of *Divine Comedies*: "For two years, Peter had tried and failed to find film work, and it weighed on him and Jimmy both. A break came when he was hired to work alongside 'a hulking actor named Bo Svenson' in 'a Grade B jungle thriller,' 'a sort of cheapo Rambo,' as Jimmy put it. Filming began in the Dominican Republic in December. Peter was at first 'thrilled,' but then puzzled to find himself paid 'on the spot in stage money' (satchels of Italian *lire*)." Much about this production was dubious. When Svenson walked off the set in a pique and filming collapsed, "Jimmy flew south on a 'rescue mission' and brought Peter back to Key West."[1]

Inevitably, this also affected the results. In many ways, *Brothers in Blood* was a bitter comedown for a filmmaker who in the previous decade had been working on A-grade productions. A number of scenes were obviously made on a shoestring budget, production values are threadbare, and the performances are unmemorable. Svenson soldiered on out of respect for the director, whereas Balsam looks visibly tired and uninterested. Both, incidentally, are dubbed.

Brothers in Blood

Vietnam 1974: Six American soldiers attack a Vietcong post. On the way back two are killed, and the third, Danny, is wounded while climbing the helicopter that will take them to safety, and is abandoned by his companions. New York 1987. Steel, the commander of the team, is a violent and alcoholic veteran, tormented by the remorse for not saving his comrade. But when television spreads the news that the plane on which Danny—returning from Vietnam after years of captivity—and other former POWs were traveling back home has been hijacked to the Caribbean by terrorists of the Anti-imperialist Guerrilla Group, Steel decides to save his old buddy. For the mission, he recruits his ex-companions: the helicopter pilot Richard, married and with a son suffering from leukemia (a legacy of the toxins absorbed by his father in Vietnam); Mark, the manager of a casino in Santo Domingo in trouble with the Mafia; Travis, a cross-dresser who performs in a club and is blackmailed by his lover, General Ortega.

And it is from Ortega's arsenal that the four men take the necessary artillery. Meanwhile Major Briggs, a ringleader of the CIA who follows the trail of Steel and his men, makes a deal with the country's military authorities: Whatever happens, the four will be eliminated once the task is completed. The terrorists are hiding in an abandoned sugar refinery; Steel and company arrive at their destination in a shabby truck "borrowed" from a farmer. Richard waits on the river with a getaway boat, while Steel sneaks into the complex alone. But once inside, a bitter surprise awaits him: Danny is not a hostage, but is part of the terrorist commando group. Captured and tortured, Steel is saved by Travis, and Mark releases the hostages. The group reaches the boat and is rescued; they are joined by Danny, who, after the shock of an explosion, believes he is still in Vietnam, but Briggs' helicopter, which has followed the action, kills him. Steel and his men set up an ambush for Briggs, and take pictures that prove his responsibility in the death of the soldier, buying their safety with blackmail.

The story does not reserve too many surprises in the unfolding of the plot and characterizations, but there is room for a sharp commentary on Reagan-era interventionism and America's long arm in the Central American affairs which sums up with the distrust toward power, typical of so many genre films. A case in point is the duplicitous CIA major (a bored-looking Balsam) who does not hesitate to use Steel and his men as bait to flush out the enemy, only to dispatch them as well afterwards ("We don't want any unauthorized heroes lying around!"), and as a character says, "You *americanos* are happy to suggest too many solutions, but let me say this: they're not always suitable to us." There is also room to hint at the plight of veterans and their difficult reintegration into society, although sometimes with didactic excesses: Steel continually ends up in jail for fighting, and is released from prison with the help of his ex-wife ("You can't spend the rest of your life in bars, beating up all the cowards that stayed home while you were in the army! It's been ten years, and most of us have forgotten about Vietnam..." "I haven't"), Richard has infected his son with the effects of Agent Orange (a theme explored also in Buddy Giovinazzo's exceptionally grim *Combat Shock*, 1986), the other fellow soldiers are involved in seedy businesses. And there are allusions to the economical difficulties caused by Reaganomics—a confirmation of the political implications in Leoni's script: "Here's where you gotta fight a war, Steele ... for your family, money, for your job ... if you don't look out you'll lose this war too!" says Steel's ex-wife, who then discovers that her husband has taken a mortgage on her house to raise the money needed to go and save his comrade.

Forced to work under humiliating conditions, Valerii tried to stick to the themes that were dear to him: male bonding, coherence, self-respect, betrayal. In this sense, the central twist, which has the "brother in blood" turning out to be in cahoots with the enemies, is suitably effective, and introduces a much-welcome ambiguity into the tiresome good guys-versus-bad guys routine, as well as a bitter note in line with the director's poetry. Presumably forced to tone down violence because of the lack of money (the torture with pins to which Steel is subjected, which would provide material for some cringe-inducing moments, is not even shown), the director attempted to at least develop the characters' psychologies, and their essence of out-of-time survivors, which he certainly felt close to himself.

Still, despite the fairly obvious budget issues, the style is not sloppy as one might expect. The title sequence, with the camera flowing gently on the surface of a tropical river, is an impressive introduction to the raid in the Vietnamese camp, which in spite of the limited production values has the right pacing, sound and shots (such as Bo Svenson's initial close-up, his motionless face partially painted black like that of a warrior, his eyes closed in concentration before the attack); what is more, the use of hand-held camera adds immediacy to the action. Valerii even manages to come up with some elegant, effective long takes, such as in Steel and Richard's entrance in the casino, Mark's escape attempt at the Santo Domingo airport and, later on, the scene in the refinery where Steel knocks out a sentinel with a sling.

Overall, though, the film is routine at best, and is not aided by Riz Ortolani's below-average synth-driven score. The most curious moments are those concerning the character played by the Austrian-born Werner Pochath, a familiar face for genre film buffs thanks to his apparitions in works by Riccardo Freda (*The Iguana with the Tongue of Fire*, 1971), Dario Argento (*The Cat O'Nine Tails*, 1971), Enzo G. Castellari (*The Shark Hunter*, 1979) and Jess Franco (*Devil Hunter*, 1980), here playing a homosexual soldier, the lover of a corrupt general and forced to perform in drag on stage in a dingy nightclub (incidentally, Pochath would die of AIDS in 1993, as did Cole two years later). In the embarrassing meeting with his old comrades, among calls to duty and ill-concealed irony ("There comes a time when a man has to be a man," says the African-American Mark to his friend), one can find that original attitude towards clichés, somewhere between their reproposition and their reconstruction, typical of Italian genre cinema in its heyday—the same that surfaces in such delicious impromptu moments as Steel asking for directions in the slums of Santo Domingo from an elderly woman in a rocking chair, who just can't stop laughing (presumably from the thrill of being recruited for a movie).

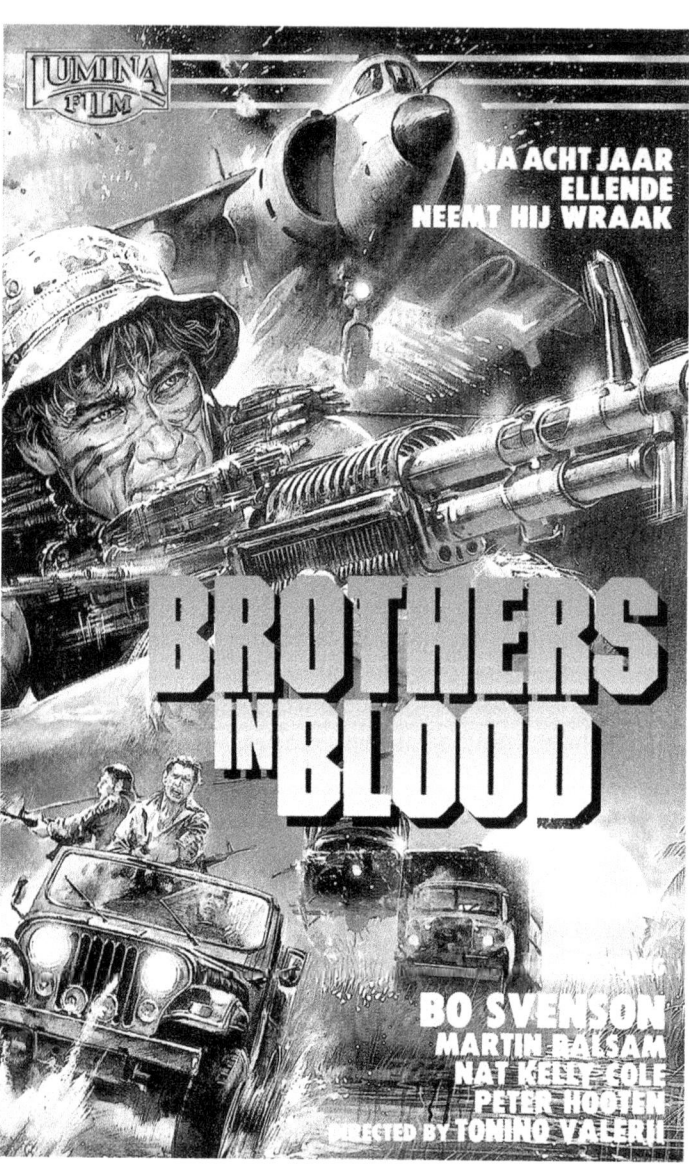

The war film *Brothers in Blood* (1987) surfaced only on home video. This is the cover sleeve for a Dutch VHS release.

However, lots of water has passed under the bridge. Overall, *Brothers in Blood* is not dissimilar to the many direct-to-video flicks, professionally made but without any particular merits, helmed during the decade—that is, a dignified and not despicable product which nevertheless did not have any reason to exist in the Italian market. And in fact the fate of Valerii's film was invisibility: Never released theatrically in the country, it was destined to home video and late-night showings on television. It surfaced abroad on video as well; it came out in the U.S. as *Savage Attack*.

Chapter Fifteen

Yojimbo vs. Cosa Nostra

No better luck awaited Valerii's following film, *Shatterer*, produced with Japanese money, which disappeared from circulation in the director's home country after a fleeting television appearance with the title *Sicilian Connection*, let down by terrible dubbing. The producer Asao Kumada got in touch with Valerii at the suggestion of Peter Shepherd, whom the director had known on the set of *The Best of Enemies* and who had been Giuliano Gemma's dialogue coach on *Day of Anger*. The director did not like Kumada's story, though. According to Valerii, Kumada

> had read, in one of those magazines you find on planes, the story of a huge steel mill in Taranto about to go bankrupt: and he thought of making a movie in which an Italian steel mill, about to be taken over by the Mafia, is saved by the intervention of a Japanese team. I pointed out that it was absurd that the Mafia aim to take possession of a company at a loss. But I read that an innovative porcelain car engine which would work at optimum temperature, consume less fuel and so on, was being tested, so I suggested Kumada a story based on that. It was an unlikely story, but it worked well in Japan.

Shatterer

> The specialized Japanese personnel working at SCD, a pioneering car factory based in Sicily and the result of a joint venture between Italy and Japan, are the targets of incessant attacks. The person responsible is Mafia boss Don Turi Catalano, who acts on behalf of Cosa Nostra, determined to stop the Japanese commercial escalation in the market. In London, the representative of SCD's insurance company, Murai, instructs the private eye Victor Bridges to protect SCD employees, among whom is the engineer Yanagida, who is perfecting a revolutionary porcelain car engine. Things get worse when Catalano entrusts his right-hand man, Silvio, to kill a technician and his wife and kidnap Yanagida; in order to convince the Japanese employees to leave, the Mafia men cut off the prisoner's ear. With the help of a journalist friend, Salvatore, Victor discovers Don Catalano's plan. After saving test pilot Koichi from Silvio's men, Victor ends up in turn targeted by mobsters, and with Koichi's help narrowly escapes death. Whoever tries to help Victor is killed: first the elderly Marco, then Salvatore. When Silvio kidnaps Adriana, the secretary of SCD's CEO De Majo, the latter decides to close down the factory, but Victor does not give up: he and Koichi release Adriana, and Silvio dies in a car explosion. As an ultimatum, the kidnappers cut off Yanagida's hand; Murai, who came from London to meet Catalano, sets up a plan together with Victor and Koichi to release the engineer. By way of a trick, the three men take the Mafia boss as hostage and arrange an exchange of prisoners. The showdown ends with the death of Catalano and his men.

Shooting took place in early 1987, at Rome's Empire Studios (formerly Dinocittà) and then in Sicily.[1] Co-production requirements demanded a Japanese protagonist, played by the singer Kôji Kikkawa, for whom *Shatterer* was meant serve as a stepping stone on the Western market—which eventually did not happen.[2] Needless to say, the Japanese actor—who in the film is also saddled with a preposterous romantic subplot with the beautiful Beatrice Ring, replete with a romantic slow-motion scene on a sunny Sicilian beach—is a fish out of water in a cast that's heterogeneous to say the least. The male lead Andy J. Forest, a blues harmonicist who ended up in movies under Tinto Brass' protective wing (*Miranda*, 1985; *Capriccio*, a.k.a. *Love & Passion*, 1987), is joined by familiar faces in more or less impromptu cameos (Marina Suma, Orazio Orlando, Dalila Di Lazzaro) and by a newcomer with a bright future, the Italian-Irish Lorenzo Flaherty, who will become one of the most popular faces of Italian television, thanks to his participation in many television movies and series. According to Japanese sources, Kikkawa was originally cast as the film's hero, but his role was drastically reduced during filming, after the death of executive producer Shin Watanabe, as Valerii changed the story in order to make it more Italian, and gave more screen time to Forest as the hard-boiled private eye (of the self-appointed "Top Secret Agency," no less!) with license to kill. However, Forest himself denied that. Nevertheless, *Shatterer* was released in Japan (as *Shataraa*), with the dialogue tracks dubbed into English and presented with Japanese subtitles.[3]

Always a lover of Japanese cinema, thanks to the weekly screenings of Kurosawa and Mizoguchi's films by the Institute of Japanese Culture in Rome, and passionate about the country's culture, Valerii had the opportunity to work with a legend such as Toshirô Mifune:

Kôji Kikkawa, Beatrice Ring and Andy J. Forest in a promotional picture for *Shatterer* (1987) (courtesy Beatrice Ring).

He brought his own wardrobe over from Japan: jackets with gold cuff links, embossed buttons.... I explained to him that he could not dress that way, as he would have been too showy and unlikely a character. His dedication to the role impressed me: throughout the film his character carries a stick, from which in the final scene he extracts a sword and cuts one of the villains' throat. Well, a couple of days before shooting started, he suddenly got a sciatica and began to limp. A psychosomatic illness, so as to make good use of the stick in his scenes ... unbelievable! Yet, every time I said that Mifune was a great actor, the late Kon Ichikawa burst out laughing, and then told me that Kurosawa used a stick to direct him, as Gillo Pontecorvo did with Evaristo Márquez in *Burn!* (*Queimada*, 1969).

Despite Forest's character mentioning at one point the murder of General Dalla Chiesa,[4] the Mafia as seen in *Shatterer* is certainly not the one that filled the headlines of the period, and not even the one seen in Damiano Damiani's television series *The Octopus* (*La Piovra*, 1984). Valerii and Gastaldi had no other claims but to put together an action movie for the foreign market, with the right dose of killings, car chases and some tourist views to act as an accompaniment to a hearty dose of stereotypes. Since the mobsters have the all-too-familiar faces of some of genre cinema's most recurring bit actors—such as Tommaso Palladino, Salvatore Billa, Nello Pazzafini and Tano Cimarosa—the result was even nostalgic, worthy of the golden age of the Italian B-movie, but it takes a lot of goodwill to overlook the improbabilities of the script, sometimes so blatant as to border on the grotesque. Unlike *Brothers in Blood*, Valerii added some over-the-top gruesomeness for the International market (such as the ear cut off in close-up, with no cuts or Tarantino-like ellipses—perhaps a nod to a notorious scene in *Django*) and focused on the action bits: a suspenseful scene follows two Mafia killers (Pazzafini and Elio Bonadonna), disguised as orchestra musicians, as they infiltrate Victor's hotel and break into his room, armed with machine guns, only to find out that their target is much smarter than they thought. As he did in *Go Gorilla Go*, the director sets up a well-made car chase on a narrow countryside road (a helicopter–bike chase fares less impressively), and makes the most out of the evocative Sicilian setting in the scene where Andy J. Forest enters the labyrinth of Donnafugata Castle near Ragusa, where the use of Steadicam pays homage to one of *The Shining*'s most celebrated sequences. However, the final showdown, set in Agrigento's Valley of the Temples, was actually filmed in Paestum, in the region of Campania, because of logistical issues.

Shatterer's climactic rendezvous is possibly one of Italian genre cinema's very last, finest hours, the umpteenth out-of-time evocation of the over-the-top final duels in the golden age of Westerns. Still, it is also significant for reasons that go beyond the mere spectacular values. When Toshirô Mifune pulls out a katana sword from his walking stick, chopping off hands and cutting throats with the same unexpected elegance as in *Yojimbo*, it is not just a naive reference to the samurai soul that every Japanese carries within himself, and an homage to the unforgettable protagonist of Kurosawa's films. It is also some sort of unconscious compensation, or perhaps a retaliation: After stealing one of its movie heroes, and reshaping it at will in what would be the start of a golden age, Italian cinema once again turned to the Japanese for help, to regain one last time, thanks to Toshirô Mifune's totemic presence, that mythical dimension that it no longer had. And the millenary ruins that frame the scene take on an allegorical significance: the vestiges of a past splendor, which is not that of Magna Graecia, but the one—much closer yet irretrievably lost—of the cardboard rocks and columns of the *pepla* shot at Cinecittà—which that same year was attacked and set on fire by Indians armed with television antennas in Fellini's requiem to the Italian film industry, *Intervista* (1987).

CHAPTER SIXTEEN

His Master's Voice

"No one cares about the finished result anymore..."
—Tonino Valerii

The extraordinary success of Damiano Damiani's *The Octopus*, sold to 80 foreign countries, paved the way for television series related to real events and topical social issues; Damiani's work indicated the possibility of merging the language of film with that of television, linked to the need of splitting the story into several parts, to be broadcast separately. With the development of *The Octopus*'s second season, Italian television was introduced to the North American practice of serial production. In this context television series bloomed, focusing on the Mafia, Camorra and 'Ndrangheta. And it was on one of these that Valerii ended up working at Silvio Berlusconi's network Mediaset, as a number of his colleagues had done, cut off from an increasingly feeble market. The occasion was tempting, the production means (by Berlusconi's production company Reteitalia) consistent. Just one month after the ending of *The Octopus*'s fourth season, in April 1989, RAI's main competitor Canale 5 aired *Il ricatto*.

Il ricatto

Naples. Commissioner Fedeli of the postal police is asked by his priest brother, Vito, to investigate a massacre that took place in the Sant'Agnello municipality: the investigations lead to the name of Angelo Rasmo, a powerful property developer linked to local politicians. The only one who supports Fedeli is a journalist, Grossi, who came over from Milan to write a report on the Camorra. The Commissioner has to cope with silence, false leads and warnings, and when Vito is killed, he decides to leave Naples. But he changes his mind when Rasmo's daughter, Giovanna, is kidnapped. With the help of a mature transvestite, "Carla," Fedeli investigates among sex workers, while his relationship with his son Luca becomes more and more tense. The Commissioner's inquiries lead him to a drug and prostitution ring: Fedeli finds the kidnapped girl, but he also discovers new evidence of collusion between the authorities and the Camorra, whose men get rid of any potential witness. Fedeli decides to make Rasmo talk, but he finds the latter dead at home. Rasmo's wife, Leonetta, is put behind bars, but Fedeli manages to prove her innocence; the two then become lovers. The investigation leads to a round of arrests, which involve the Mayor of Pozzuoli, who disappears and will later be found dead. The underworld is linked to the Church as well: heroin trafficking is taking place, with the drug hidden inside sacred satues. Meanwhile, Fedeli becomes increasingly isolated...

Ennio De Concini's script reprises from its model the theme of the solitary hero and the mixture of public and private, pairing police investigations and painful personal stories, yet with less political implications and a more robust melodramatic vein. Critic Aldo Grasso noted that "compared with *The Octopus*, this TV series assumes a more folksy connotation, evident also in the dialectal acting, but especially in the choice of portraying the more visible and brutal level of Camorra violence, that of the criminal laborers, instead of the high places where the connivance between the underworld and the political power takes place."[1] As with his celluloid predecessors of 1970s Italian cinema, Commissioner Fedeli (played by the Neapolitan singer-cum-actor Massimo Ranieri) has a conflicting relationship with the authorities, from the superintendent who puts a spoke in its wheels to the ambiguous magistrate (Fernando Rey) too loyal to the letter of the law: the latter character brings to mind a classic of Italian crime film, Damiani's *Confessions of a Police Captain* (*Confessione di un commissario di polizia al Procuratore della Repubblica*, 1971) starring Franco Nero and Martin Balsam.

Fedeli is a young-looking cop, a single father who dresses casually, reads James Hadley Chase novels and listens to Bruce Springsteen. A character tailor-made for the charismatic Ranieri, one of Italy's most popular thesps since his film debut in 1970, in Mauro Bolognini's *Metello*, and a versatile actor who could play drama—as in Antonio Margheriti's crime film *Death Rage* (*Con la rabbia agli occhi*, 1976) co-starring Yul Brynner and Barbara Bouchet—and comedy—as in Steno's cult hit *La patata bollente* (1979), alongside Renato Pozzetto and Edwige Fenech—with the same ease and believability.

> *Il ricatto* was born from the request of a production company, owned by Massimo Ranieri, to make a TV miniseries with him in the lead. Initially there were to be just four episodes, but then De Concini, who knocked out the script with several ghost writers, said we had to blow it up to five episodes, otherwise we would not have the necessary sum to cover the budget. Therefore the story was watered down: to make the extra episode they came up with every trick in the book, for instance phone conversations where with every line you had to turn page. "Hello?" "Yes, it's me…" "Where are you calling from?" Each line, a scene change, so that the script looked like a huge thing whereas there were just a few lines…

The Mafia in Damiani's series is replaced in *Il ricatto* by the Neapolitan underworld; the Camorra is seen as a cancer which infiltrates the institutions, infecting them—from family to Church to the State itself. The story is about rigged contracts, money laundering, drug trafficking, and the dialogue even mentions the Rognoni-Latorre law, promulgated after Dalla Chiesa's killing. It is a didactic and spectacular drive, inherited from the committed "civil" cinema on one hand, and the *poliziotteschi* on the other. It is an attempt to approach rules of the small screen by still talking about reality, explaining it, and reinventing it in a poetic and spectacular key. An approach not yet reduced to an empty celebration, hypocritical self-censorship and cheap emphasis—an all-too-common commodity to many TV series to come.

But whereas *The Octopus*'s Commissioner Cattani was a full-fledged hero, and the ideal heir of the "iron commissioners" played by Maurizio Merli and the other stars of the *poliziottesco*, Fedeli—a slacker and a womanizer, with a restless son in college to take care of—is a cop with no particular avenging ideals. "Every time I pick up a newspaper it seems to me I'm reading that of the day before," he resignedly comments at the beginning, after coming across the umpteenth front page littered with murders, robberies and so on. Accustomed to the office routine, Fedeli is forced to become a hero unwillingly, after a series of

Valerii (left) during the filming of *Il ricatto* (1989): the director of photography Pasquale Rachini is the second from right, with the striped shirt (courtesy Pasquale Rachini).

events awaken his civic sense. *Il ricatto* is the story of the blossoming of a civic conscience, exemplified by the scene where, after the murder of his priest brother (Luca De Filippo), Fedeli looks out the window to watch the sea, and notices for the first time the garbage floating on the water, a moment which symbolically represents the awareness of Naples' sad and tormented reality.

But when it comes to pulling the strings of the plot, the detective story mechanism jams and misfires. "In the end there was also a whodunnit twist, quite bad in my opinion, which I did my best to take off the film, but with no success," Valerii explained: "It turned out that the priest's murderer was actually the commissioner's son, who eventually killed himself out of remorse. A bad melodrama, in short." Fedeli's son is played by Kim Rossi Stuart, Giacomo's son, who is very good in one of his first important roles. "I learned later that Ranieri resented that I had cast Rossi Stuart—young, handsome—without asking his opinion. And these are things you pay for. I was not used to this way of working, and in a sense it was a great school."

Despite a substantial budget, filming did not proceed smoothly. "One day I had to shoot a scene set in a photographer's studio, and found myself in a barren set, with no floor, no furniture, no window, to which I said, 'I'm not shooting here!' And these as well are things you eventually pay for, because in the new way of making television that was establishing itself, this kind of stance could not be taken anymore. At the time of serious filmmaking, yes. But those were other times."

Valerii did not finish *Il ricatto*: he was fired during the filming of the fourth episode and replaced by Ruggero Deodato. Here is how the director recounts the events that led to his sacking:

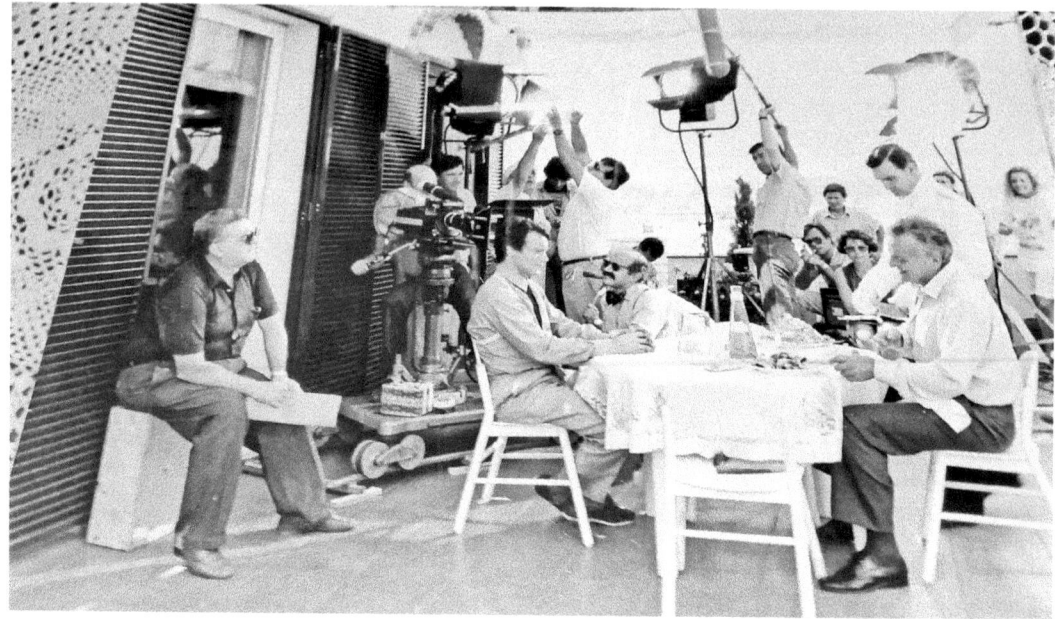

Shooting the TV movie *Il ricatto*: Valerii (left), director of photography, Pasquale Rachini (behind the camera) and protagonist Massimo Ranieri (center) (courtesy Pasquale Rachini).

One day, while we were moving from Rome to Naples to finish shooting a few things, I saw Ranieri's Porsche car parked in front of the printing and developing lab: I was told he had been watching the filmed footage since early morning. I had not been informed, so I got really angry, since it was footage that I had not yet seen or approved, so it did not seem right to me. I found Ranieri and the production manager in the projection room: in the beginning they denied ("You see, we did not want to disturb you…"), citing as an excuse the fact that we had been filming the night before and we were about to move on location. But the editor let out a phrase that unravelled their game: "I told you Tonino would get pissed…" I realized that the whole thing had been set up to allow the production manager—who had every right to it, mind you, but I would want to be informed too since I was the director!—to see a rough cut, summarily put together by the assistant editor. There was an argument, harsh words flew, and eventually there was a breakup. My lawyer advised me to show up on the set regardless, and so I did: as soon as I yelled "Lights, camera, action!" the phone rang: "Don't let Valerii shoot." They had to pay me the entire salary, nevertheless. And of course I never approved the final cut.

Il ricatto was a considerable success; later on a new edition was prepared, with the five episodes reduced to two, with imaginable consequences. The breakup between Valerii and Ranieri was so harsh that, to this day, on the Neapolitan actor's website, *Il ricatto* is credited to Deodato and Vittorio De Sisti (who would direct its sequel, *Il ricatto 2—Bambini nell'ombra*, 1991). Valerii is never mentioned.

The director's next project for television was *Due madri* (Two Mothers, 1989); initially programmed for a 1990 broadcasting, it was hastily rescheduled after a successful run on France's Antenne 2 and broadcast in the prime time slot on RaiUno on April 30, 1989. *Due madri* was a decidedly happier experience from a professional standpoint, and the most successful among Valerii's works for the small screen. A proper film (only 95 minutes long: quite a different pacing and narrative structure compared with *Il ricatto*) which addressed issues that were apparently far removed from one another—such as the problem of adoption, a child's acceptance in a stranger's household and the traumas that may arise, and the drama of the Argentinian *desaparecidos*—and did so with measure and modesty, along the lines of a script that largely avoided the pitfalls of the typical tearjerking dramas as well as the didactic excesses that the theme might have allowed for. It gained Barbara De Rossi an award as the year's best television actress.

Due madri

Pinuccia, six years old, is staying in provisional custody of a middle-class couple, Ester and Oscar Stasi. She is a problem child. At school she does not speak, does not bind with the other classmates, is aggressive, refuses food but eats ants. Dolores, Pinuccia's natural mother, arrives in Italy from Buenos Aires. She has survived the horrors of the military regime, and her intention is to take back the girl, whose real name is Pilar, and whom she has not seen in three years. The hearing at the juvenile court confirms the adoption, but Dolores manages to get hired as a maid by the Stasi family. Her presence is good for Pinuccia, who begins to behave normally, but the little girl's affection towards Dolores makes Ester jealous. The relationship between her and Oscar, who was never convinced of the adoption, is tense; during a stay at the beach house in Fregene, Pinuccia starts to eat ants again, to spite Ester. Oscar is suspicious about Dolores, and after glimpsing torture marks on the body, he realizes the truth. A few days later, Dolores kidnaps the child and hides, preparing to leave the country. Ester asks her husband to fly to Buenos Aires, and at the boarding gate she and Oscar come across Dolores, who was about to leave too. The juvenile court's pronounciation is in favor of the Stasi family, but the judge recommends that they find a solution in their own conscience. Upon leaving prison, Dolores finds Ester and the girl waiting for her; while Dolores embraces her daughter, Ester walks away.

The script, originally titled *Cronaca di un amore materno* (Chronicle of a Motherly Love), was the work of Ugo Pirro, who took inspiration from a story by the child psychologist Marta Prandi, based on true events, and added the context of Argentina's military dictatorship. Valerii contributed with an episode told him during the filming of *Brothers in Blood*, by Nat Kelly Cole. "He was Nat King Cole's adopted son, and one night he dreamed of meeting his real mother again. The next morning, he found in the mailbox a letter from a woman who claimed she was his mother, and asked just to see him. I told the episode to Pirro, who put it in the script, during the adoptive mother's speech in court."

The result is convincing and engrossing right from the very beginning, in which the camera discovers little Pinuccia, secluded from the other children in the school yard and intent on eating ants ("It was inspired by the case of a little girl whom Prandi had cured, who in fact ate worms, scorpions and beetles. For obvious reasons we had to soften it a little bit, in order to make it acceptable for the viewers"). Such an opening introduces an upsetting note in an otherwise apparently happy *bourgeois* family portrait, which in fact is plagued by misunderstandings, as shown by the next, specular sequence of the Stasi family meal, where Pinuccia does not touch food, her adoptive mother Ester (Sonia Petrovna) tries to rely on the weight of her authority, and her husband Oscar (the capable Gianni Garko) assists, discouraged by his wife's unsuccessful attempts at proving a good mother.

It is in this household that Dolores shows up, persecuted by the military regime and arriving in Italy to take her daughter back: she gets hired as a maid and starts a struggle of sorts with Ester to win the child's affection. "We Argentinians have all lost half of our lives" Dolores says, recalling the bleak times of the dictatorship, whose physical and psychological injuries she is still carrying. The theme is also addressed specifically in the courtroom scene, when Dolores's laywer shows the court *Nunca mas*—the book published by the Minister of Interiors, novelist Ernesto Sabàto, after the fall of Jorge Rafael Videla, which tells the terrible story of the *desaparecidos* during the Videlista regime—and asks it to be put on record. "It was one of our sources of inspiration: Ugo Pirro brought it in, and it was the basis of the film." The anger of denunciation is paired with the pain for the loss of one's cultural and family roots, in the scene where Dolores tells Pilar a fairytale in her own language, and especially in the sequence of Oscar's arrival at the recreation center where the Argentinians gather: It is the film's most intense moment, as the camera accompanies the character in the discovery of a world of exiles uprooted from their homeland, seeking mutual comfort in the music of a soft tango.

In his following work for the small screen, *Una prova d'innocenza* (A Proof of Innocence, 1991), Valerii directed comedy actor Enrico Montesano in an unusual dramatic role. "It was an original screenplay by Valerio Zurlini, who should have made the movie with Goffredo Lombardo, but then fell ill and died. The script was then reshaped by me and Franco Verucci in order to make it more topical, but also a bit more popular, so to speak. The basic idea was the same: we had to make it less personal because of TV requirements." The price to pay to said requirements was the inevitable dilution of a story that could have been half as long, plus a schematic happy ending that clashed with the dark and pessimistic tones of the film ("You have to stay underground like a rat so as not to see the disgust of this vile world," a character says.)

Una prova d'innocenza

A petty thief, Franco Cruciani, sneaks in a villa at night, steals documents and asks a two billion lire ransom. The man sent to negotiate, a certain Guido Marino, kills Cruciani. Two years later, Marino has a car accident: on his deathbed he confesses the murder to the priest that is assisting him, Don Alessio. An innocent man, Marco Tessitore, has been wrongly convicted for the homicide, and the evidence that might save him, a gun, is hidden in an attic. Don Alessio, bound to the secrecy of confession, cannot reveal anything to the Police. He recovers the weapon and decides to investigate on his own: he mingles with the homeless at Rome's Termini station and becomes friends with one of them, Amleto; he then locates Cruciani's ex-girlfriend, a prostitute named Rita, and two old associates of the deceased, Nando and Alvaro, who perjured themselves at the time of the trial so as to have Tessitore convicted. The two men beat Don Alessio and try to kill him. The priest takes refuge at Rita's, who tells him that Cruciani was working for a powerful man, and planned to blackmail him. Through the seedy counselor Filippelli, Don Alessio meets Cremonese, the head of an arms trafficking ring in which Marino—an ex-secret agent—was involved, together with Filippelli as well as a powerful politician, Ponziani. The priest faces Cremonese and threatens to kill him, but cannot do it. Desperate, he gives in, accusing himself of the murder. At the trial, Rita—bound on a wheelchair after being seriously injured by Cremonese's men—delivers the tape with the evidence that exonerates Don Alessio.

The original idea had blatant Hitchcockian reminiscences, recalling *I Confess* (1953), whereas the character of Don Alessio, who mingles with homeless and tramps, crooks and prostitutes in his search for truth and justice, has distinct Christ-like traits, and if Rita (Corinne Dacla), the high-class prostitute who falls for the priest and sacrifices herself in order to help him, is a modern-day Magdalene with license to strip, the powerful Cremonese (Gianni Garko) is a Lucifer-like tempter. *Una prova d'innocenza* is primarily a vehicle for Enrico Montesano, in his first dramatic role *tout court*. "When Lombardo called me," Valerii explained, "he asked me who I wanted for the role of the priest. And I: 'But, can I choose?' 'Of course, in absolute freedom!' 'Well, I think Jeremy Irons would be perfect'" And Lombardo, in reply: 'But I can only give you Enrico Montesano!' I restrained myself: 'Well, why not? Let's try ... let's see....' And in the end we succeeded, of course adapting the character to Montesano's characteristics and needs. Sometimes, though, he asked me: 'But couldn't we put a joke in here?' 'Enrico, we're making a serious movie!' 'What do you mean by that, there are many serious movies where sometimes someone tells a joke....'"

Indeed, Montesano is often awkward, uncomfortable, and it shows: as a result, his character is muffled, not very believable, rarely engaging. However, the director's skills are as good as ever, as proven by several effective sequences: the opening murder, with the suggestive image of a door in which a hole appears after the shot; Don Alessio, looking for a gun in Cruciani's attic and being forced to hide after the arrival of several thugs, whose shoes are the only part of their body we get to see; the scenes at the Termini station, with Luigi Pistilli as a tramp who recites *Hamlet*. "When Pistilli's agent, Fausto Ferzetti, Gabriele's brother, offered him for the role of the homeless man, at first I was puzzled, because I remembered Luigi from the days of *For a Few Dollars More*, and did not really see him fit for the role. But Pistilli showed up with a long beard as the one you see in the film, and was just perfect. He was already very depressed, and killed himself just a few years later..."

Una prova d'innocenza was broadcast on RaiDue on February 12 and 14, 1991, with reasonable success: seven to eight million viewers per episode, a remarkable result for Rai's second channel. "To think that at first the network's director-in-chief did not want to make the film!" Valerii commented. "He said, 'How come I, a socialist, am appointed as head of RaiDue,[2] and the first thing I'm producing is the story of a priest?' Then, after a number of political interventions, to which Montesano himself (who back then was a Socialist) was not extraneous, *Una prova d'innocenza* was finally made. And when the director-in-chief saw it, he claimed it was the best thing RaiDue had produced that year."

For all its technical proficiency, Valerii's output for the small screen underlined the core of the problem: the director was becoming an increasingly marginal figure, an executor, so to speak, having to reshape his vision according to what the producer, the star, the television executives demanded. Other filmmakers made the best out of such an unfavorable situation, and adapted to the new role, even if that meant giving up their considerable talents (think of Michele Soavi, and the string of mostly unmemorable TV films he made since the late 1990s) to keep on working; Valerii refused to do so, as proven by the unpleasant experience on *Il ricatto* and the half-hearted job on *Una prova d'innocenza*. As such, his days as a television director were numbered. Unlike Lorenzo, Jules' betrothed, he would never, ever be satisfied of being just a "loyal purebred puppy dog."

Il cielo non cade mai (1992), starring Kim Rossi Stuart, from a story by Maria Venturi, was an experience aborted in the bud: Valerii was fired after just three days of shooting.

The film was then directed by my assistant, Gianni Ricci. I did location scouting, and shot a couple of scenes in all, but I think that my footage is not even in the finished film. The story wasn't bad, but the movie was awful. For instance, there was a scene with nine people talking in a room. These are the most difficult ones to shoot, because you have to have a precise timing scan to maintain the right pacing, without messing up. And in that scene the actors were standing in a semicircle. One finished talking, the other started—static camera set up, and on and on. I wonder how the actors felt.... Fact is, Berlusconi's entry in TV production has totally upset both the working rhythms and the quality of the products. No one cares about the finished result anymore, but rather about the minimum required to get a certain share and the guaranteed advertising revenue.

CHAPTER SEVENTEEN

Twilight's Last Gleamings

"You don't age with the passing of years, but by betraying your ideals."
—Emilio, *Un bel dì vedremo*

Ten years after *Shatterer*, Valerii and Kumada reunited for another production: *Un bel dì vedremo* (One Fine Day We Will See), based on an idea by Kon Ichikawa, who conceived the story with the producer and was supposed to direct the picture, but had to give up due to health problems. Kumada called on his compatriot Yasushi Tanabe to write the script; Valerii took care of the revision with Enzo Azzolina and Arturo Orsini. The protagonists were the Bulgarian soprano Raina Kabaivanska, by then in her sixties, and the 78-year-old Massimo Girotti, the unforgettable protagonist of Luchino Visconti's *Obsession* (*Ossessione*, 1943), with a special appearance by Giuliano Gemma, on his fourth film with the director.

Un bel dì vedremo was aimed at the Japanese market, and shot in high definition, back then at a still pioneering stage (the photography was by Mario Vulpiani, on his second collaboration with Valerii after *Go Gorilla Go*). Valerii went on to illustrate the technical difficulties at length:

> Working with HD meant a number of limitations, and not insignificant ones. If you use two or three cameras at once, shooting in 35mm you have complete freedom: the cameraman can shoot one thing, then move on, so as to have various cuts on a same scene, etc. With high def, no way. The main problem is the cable, a sort of umbilical cord, which connects the camera to the equipment positioned off the set, on a truck with the monitors. For *Un bel dì vedremo*, I had two cameras and two monitors, whose interaction was severely limited by these cables: no way of using quick traveling shots and the like, because the cables were like leashes: it just wasn't possible to move the camera beyond a certain point. On top of that, the tapes we were using were very costly: I called "Cut" but the tapes went on filming. They explained that they did so to avoid the risk of breaking the tape when restarting it. It was definitely not a practical system!

Un bel dì vedremo

The death of a pianist, Teresa, in a retirement home for opera singers, provides Emilio and his old flame, Isabella, the opportunity to meet again. Emilio, a former orchestra conductor of international renown, is spending his last days there; Isabella is a famous opera singer, and was once Teresa's favorite student. Emilio involves Isabella and the other guests in the fulfillment of his ultimate dream: the staging of "Madama Butterfly." He will conduct it, Isabella will play the main role and the proceeds of the show will be used to save the nursing home, on the brink of financial collapse. With the support of the manager, Gianfranco, Emilio begins to work on the show, and to finance it he runs into debt personally: however, he is unaware that he is seriously ill. Despite the problems, fatigue and despair, comes the day of the play, at the Giuseppe Verdi theater in Salerno. In spite of Emilio's illness, the opera is a great success. Emilio and Isabella separate again, perhaps forever, and the former leaves to undergo the difficult surgery that awaits him.

"Youth is not a time of life, it is a state of mind," the elderly Emilio says, "you don't age with the passing of years, but by betraying your ideals." *Un bel dì vedremo* could have been a memorable film on senility: a gentle, rhapsodic version of *La casa del sorriso* (1991, Marco Ferreri), with passion erupting again in the existence of the aging protagonists, anticipated by the opening dream in which Emilio sees again the woman who stole his heart decades earlier. Too bad the script chooses the safest and most innocuous path, and merely sketches the most interesting ideas (such as the wealth of knowledge to pass on to the next generations) to take refuge in a banal feel-good dialectic typical of TV fiction. A case in point are the scenes dedicated to the family *ménage* of Emilio's daughter, Claudia (Antonella Fattori) and her husband (Massimo Wertmüller). The result slips away without being boring, nor exciting either. The exceptions are a couple of intense monologues by Massimo Girotti: the scene where Emilio, lost in discomfort, suddenly feels the weight of years upon himself and desperately takes refuge in a church, and the final goodbye between Emilio and Isabella. Girotti's character has indeed several things in common with the one he would later play in his final film, *Facing Windows* (*La finestra di fronte*, 2003, Ferzan Ozpetek), and the actor is, as always, remarkable. On the other hand, Kabaivanska is certainly not there to act, but to sing: and the last part, with the *mise-en-scène* of Puccini's opera, offers her ample room to do that. The result was nevertheless satisfying for the Japanese public: Valerii claimed that the film was screened in Tokyo in a theater reserved for high definition movies, and stayed on the bill for several weeks. Unfortunately it did not have the same luck in Italy: *Un bel dì vedremo* was acquired by RaiTre but never distributed theatrically nor broadcast on television. As Valerii disenchantedly put it, "Besides, in Italy, who do you think would go and see a movie about two old lovers who meet again?"

Twelve years after *Unscrupulous*, Valerii and Enzo Gallo teamed up again in 1997 for a project inspired by the investigative book *Bangkwang: Tre anni per droga nelle carceri thailandesi* (Bangkwang: Three Years for Drugs in Thai Prisons) by journalist Fabrizio Paladini, the true story of a young man arrested in Thailand for drug smuggling and imprisoned in the notorious Bangkwang prison, in the province of Nonthaburi. "Inside the prison, which was a real fortress, a real village of sorts had been created, where illegality and the law of the strongest ruled," the director explained. "Everything was marketable, even escape, even the fetters which the detainees had at their feet. Anything was being traded, including drugs; the guards were corrupt, the warden did not have any influence, and the power was *de facto* in the hands of some kind of internal mafia. Not even the prison's records reflected the truth: prisoners escaped and yet their names were still written in the registers. It was utter, wild anarchy. This was what the film was to be about, and this was to be the place where we'd shoot, despite the dangerous location."

Negotiations were initiated with the local authorities: Valerii asked to be able to film at least several long shots of the prison-village, "so as to show the inmates wandering around the alleys, amid the stalls run by the prisoners themselves, and then we would come up with something for the medium shots and close-ups. But eventually I had to give up. I never knew the real reason why. Gallo left all alone for Thailand, and upon his return he told me that in the end we were not given permission." At this point, with filming in Rome already in progress, the producer was forced to fall back on the Philippines. The exteriors were shot in Manila, and the filmmaker had to jump through hoops to get a passable imitation of Thailand, "starting from the fact that there were Catholic churches instead of pagodas, and we could not find anything that could recall a Thai setting, so I continually had to avoid framing crosses, steeples and so on." However, some revealing details slipped the makers' eyes, such as a supposedly Bangkok car with "Manila's Finest" emblazoned across its doors. The genuine Bangkok city exteriors, shot on 16mm, were poorly integrated with the Philippines footage—a return of sorts to the days of *A 001: Operazione Giamaica*...

The prison interiors were built inside an abandoned maximum security penitentiary in Frosinone, a feat not unlike Kubrick's recreation of 'Nam in *Full Metal Jacket* (1987), but done on the cheap. "We rebuilt the gates, repainted the place according to the pics of the real prison, threw soil over the floors, and so on. And only at the end of shooting I learned that the whole building was unsafe, and might have collapsed at any moment." Valerii's script was originally entitled *Bangkwang*, whereas the working title was *Una vita spezzata* (A Broken Life),[1] but the film was eventually released as *Una vacanza all'inferno* (Vacation in Hell).

Una vacanza all'inferno

Angelo, a young taxi driver with economic problems, agrees to accompany an acquaintance, Luciano, in Bangkok, on a business trip. He does not know that Luciano wants to use him as a courier to smuggle half a kilo of heroin to Italy, hiding the drugs in Angelo's camera. But the two are stopped and searched at the airport, and Angelo is arrested, while his friend leaves for Italy. In jail, Angelo is approached by a lawyer, Ortega, who offers him his services; the lawyer is actually a shady character who extorts money from the relatives of the Italian prisoners, by promising them to bribe the judge. Angelo's case is also followed by Michela Montini, of the Italian embassy; in trial the young man pleads guilty in the hope of a lenient verdict, but is sentenced to 16 years. Transferred to the prison of Chiang Mai, Angelo finds himself in a living hell, amidst abuse, violence and atrocities of all kinds, run by the cruel lieutenant Prang. However, the mature lifer Belisario takes him under his wing, and protects him from the attentions of another inmate, John. Belisario, however, can not do anything to save his own wife, Gabriella, who has relied on Ortega and promised him a large sum: Ortega kills the woman, simulating an overdose, and steals the money. In agreement with the lawyer, Prang hires John to dispatch Belisario, without success. Meanwhile Michela continues to fight for a retrial, but when Angelo learns that Luciano—the only one that could clear him—has died, he realizes that his only hope is to escape. The attempt, through the sewers of the prison, seems to be successful, but the boat carrying the prisoners to safety is intercepted by the police. Angelo is captured, but Belisario manages to flee and kills Ortega, before being captured again. New violence ensues in the prison, until the authorities depose Prang. In the new trial for the escape attempt, Angelo is again sentenced, this time to life imprisonment. An inscription informs us that five years later, in response to the pressure of the Italian government, he will be pardoned.

Despite the credits boasting the line "*film di interesse culturale nazionale*" (Film of national cultural interest), *Una vacanza all'inferno* is in fact a genre product: a prison movie in the wake of such classics as *Papillon* (1973, Franklin J. Schaffner) or *Midnight Express* (1978, Alan Parker), to name the most evident models.[2] As such, it features the usual inventory of atrocities and abominations: sadistic guards, rapes, tortures, public floggings, rats strolling over the prisoners' bodies, an escape attempt in the prison sewers. Certainly not an unprecedented repertoire, but staged with the director's customary grit and stylistic polish (as proven by the use of the Steadicam in the escape sequence), although at the risk of falling into cheap folklore, such as in the sequence of the spaghetti cooked in the cell. Overall, the result is a rare commodity in such a barren and devastated landscape as late 1990s Italian cinema, dominated by blockbusters and intimate comedies set between a bedroom and a kitchen, with few products that still relied on the desire to simply tell a story. Therefore, for its solid and no-frills structure and technical solidity, *Una vacanza all'inferno* is a honest and decent film, and deserves respect.

The problem, if anything, is that such a product, in the era of monopoly of television dramas, characterized by self-censorship and a vaunted civil committment which often masquerades didactic banalities, ends up belonging in a no man's land; in fact, despite being distributed in Italy by Giovanni Di Clemente's company C.D.I., then associated with Buena Vista, *Una vacanza all'inferno* passed almost unnoticed at the time of its theatrical release.[3] And it is from the dreaded television cancer that Valerii's film clearly inherited its weakest passages: that is the case with the sequences set in Italy, with a good guy (Marco Leonardi, already seen among others in *Cinema Paradiso* and Argento's *The Stendhal Syndrome*) who ekes out a living as best he can, dreams of leaving the country as Renzo Palmer's character did in *Go Gorilla Go*, and has the responsibility of maintaining a family worthy of a sugary soap opera. One senses that Valerii wanted to get rid of them as soon as he can, as an indispensible but unwanted burden, and get to the point. Which, luckily for the viewer, occurs pretty quickly: the sequence at the airport, in which Angelo and his "friend" Luciano, who hid half a kilo of heroin inside Angelo's videocamera, are arrested just before departure, mistreated and searched by the local police, openly nods to one of *Midnight Express*'s most celebrated scenes. It is a moment which illustrates the merits and limitations of the film. In spite of the descendance from an investigative book, though, social indignation is overshadowed by the narrative and spectacular needs. Unlike Brad Davis' character in Alan Parker's film, Angelo is an unwitting courier: and his resistance, his protests at the humiliating anal inspection, his nervousness that ends up being pernicious, are all elements that heighten the suspense, which Valerii handles quite skillfully. Yet, at the same time they end up alienating the viewer's sympathy, since we are called to identify with a character whose naivety borders at times on downright idiocy.

Angelo's drama, generating from a substantially one-dimensional character, is not enough to carry the weight of an entire movie. The same can be said about the scenes with the Italian embassy attache (former Miss Italy Mirca Viola, beautiful but wooden in her film debut) attempting to have her compatriot released. Valerii puts remedy to it by diverting the focus of the story from an individual to a choral narrative, and allowing room for a deuteragonist who attracts upon himself the viewers' interest: Angelo's fellow inmate Belisario (a convincing F. Murray Abraham, who basically draws on the same role he played in Peter Yates' *An Innocent Man*, 1989, although the actor claimed he took inspiration from Malcolm X[4]), a father figure—the umpteenth in Valerii's cinema—that takes him under his wing, protects him from the inevitable sexual attentions on the part of another inmate (Bobby Rhodes, a recurring presence in Italian genre cinema of the 1980s), but who cannot save his wife from the clutches of the slimy Ortega.

In Giancarlo Giannini's sly characterization, Ortega becomes the film's true villain: an insidious figure, much more ominous and disturbing that the stereotyped Thai guards who bark threats and impart corporal punishments: he is a duplicitous vermin who crawls between legality and illegality, deceiving the inmates' families into handing him large sums of money, and alternating mellifluous promises and fake solidarity. Ortega eventually takes on Mephistophelean traits in the sequence of the meeting with Belisario's wife, who has been warned by her husband of the lawyer's dirty tricks: the woman awkwardly fumbles for excuses, Ortega realizes this and plays it wily, making the best of a bad situation while coldly planning how to dispatch her and get the money. Through the characters of Ortega and Luciano, Valerii once again explores the theme of betrayal: Angelo's alleged friend, who exploits and abandons him, and dies before he can clear him from the accusations, is a sneaky Judas on which perhaps the director focuses his own bitterness for the memory of a poisoned friendship.

The Thai setting does not go beyond a stereotyped portrayal, from Angelo and Luciano's pilgrimages in alluring strip bars to the sweaty atmosphere of the indoor scenes. More significant are Ortega's words after the sadistic warden's xenophobic rant ("You foreigners must forget that Thailand exists. We have a saying here: the dung of foreigners has never fertilized!"), which well summarize the reality of a country with two faces: "Thailand is a strange country. There is something contagious here, the feeling that everything is allowed."

Unlike other examples of the men-in-prison genre, the overall gloominess does not dim even in the ending. As with *Due madri*, *Una vacanza all'inferno* ends in a courtroom, with the characters demanding a justice higher than that of the individual, which yet does not arrive: The judge sentences Angelo to 30 years in prison, and the film ends on the young man's desperate scream. A caption then informs us of his fate, and of the coveted freedom which he will eventually regain; but the final epigraph is, significantly, a quote credited to Schopenhauer but actually from Italian philosopher Anacleto Verrecchia: "The world is a condominium between evil and madness: one prevails and the other controls."[5]

Epilogue

Like Jack Beauregard, Tonino Valerii was a survivor, one of the last remaining stalwarts of a type of cinema that no longer existed. After *Una vacanza per l'inferno* he never resumed his place behind the camera, although he kept trying; in August 1999 he deposited at the CSC library a script, co-written with Lucio Battistrada, entitled *Colpi di pistola* (Gun Shots). Set right before World War I, it is centered on a mysterious young man, Aristide Dorn, who works as tutor in a Rich family in the Venetian countryside, and turns out to be one of the Serbian conspirators belonging to the Crna Ruka (Black Hand), the secret military society that plotted to kill the Archduke Franz Ferdinand in Sarajevo. Blending mystery, historical notations and melodrama, through the subplot of Aristide's unhappy love for the noble Daniela, *Colpi di pistola* was an interesting attempt at a respectable comeback that nonetheless failed to raise any interest on the part of potential financers.

Valerii found solace in writing. He penned essays for the film magazine *Cabiria* and wrote a textbook for aspiring directors, *Fare l'aiuto regista* (Being an Assistant Director) which anyone taking his first steps in the movie business would do well to read. In 2003 he announced he was at work on another book, entitled *Caro Sergio*, about "the whole story between me and Sergio Leone. I already have a 64-page draft and now I'm at the point that gives me great pain to write, because everyone has been telling me, 'No, you have to write it, not because of your relationship with Sergio Leone, but because you have to make things clear,'" he explained, referring to *My Name Is Nobody*; "I have been trying to write it for a whole year, but this arm of mine does not obey me [...] but now I have made up my mind and I'm going to write it. I hope to finish it by the end of the year, [...] I promise you that the book will definitely come out."[1] It didn't; the wound was still open and sore.

From 1996 to 2013 Valerii was the curator and director of the Roseto Opera Prima Film Festival, which takes place in Roseto degli Abruzzi: a Proustian return to the land of the ancestors. He enjoyed the attention of a new generation of film buffs, including Quentin Tarantino, who paid homage to Riz Ortolani's theme for *Day of Anger* in *Kill Bill vol. 1* (in the scene where the Bride gouges out the eye of a member of the Crazy 88 gang) and *Kill Bill vol. 2* (where the Bride and Elle Driver face one another in Budd's trailer) as well as in *Django Unchained* (in the gun training scene, when Django uses a snowman as target practice, and when he and Dr. Schultz ambush a bandit gang). He even fulfilled his dream of being an actor—he who as a kid used to send his pics to agencies before realizing he did not have the *physique du rôle*—playing a moving role in a small low-budget movie, *All'amore assente* (To the Absent Love, 2007, Andrea Adriatico), alongside other special guests such as Milena Vukotic, Corso Salani and Eva Robin's. *A Reason to Live, a Reason to Die!* was screened at the Venice Film Festival during the retrospective on Italian Western, and the

Spanish Diputación de Almería paid homage to the director at the annual film festival, "Almería en corto," which celebrates the most important names of Euro-Western. In 2007 Valerii returned to the United States for a directing course at Middlebury College in Vermont, alongside other illustrious guests such as the philosopher Gianni Vattimo. He appeared among the interviewees (other names involved were Enzo G. Castellari, Mario Caiano, Ruggero Deodato, Lamberto Bava…) in *I Tarantiniani* (2013), a documentary that paid a long-due tribute to filmmakers, producers and actors of the golden age of Italian film industry. Early 2015 saw the much-awaited Blu-Ray release of one of his best films, *Day of Anger*, allowing cinephiles to appreciate one of the best genre directors Italy has ever produced.

Tonino Valerii's career is a piece of history of Italian and European cinema, and his memories are the glimpse into an era that now seems mythical, populated by characters who seem like they came out of a film themselves. His voice still trembled with anger when speaking on the subject of the authorship of *My Name Is Nobody*, his pale blue eyes filled with tears when remembering his late friends. "When I look at the cast and credits of my old films, most are dead, there's almost no one left. One day I met Giovanni Corridori by the post office next to my home. 'Giovanni, they're all gone…' And we hugged each other for a long time." One of the last to go, and in a tragic, unexpected way, was Giuliano Gemma, who died in a car accident near Rome, on October 1, 2013. To Tonino, it was like losing a brother.

As one becomes old and tired, all he is left with are memories, and Tonino Valerii's are the core of this book. To this writer, one of the most moving recollections was of an old friend and companion in many battles on the set, Benito Stefanelli. "We came across each other after many years at the presentation of a book on Italian stuntmen,[2] and it was good to see him again. One day the phone rings, it's Benito. He invites me to a dinner, where he has gathered his relatives from Libya, his ex-wife, his friends. 'Look, you're going to be the only one from the movie biz, hope you don't mind,' he says." The dinner was at Sacrofano, a small village outside Rome. There were many people, the atmosphere was that of a big party—and yet there was something strange in the air. Certain looks, certain faces. "I got the impression that it was some kind of departure, and felt my heart sink. At dinner, Benito wants me by his side. At a certain point, out of the blue, he tells me that he's been diagnosed with liver cancer, and is undergoing medical care. And I realize that for him this is a goodbye dinner. I call him back a month later, to check how he's doing. His companion answers the phone. 'Hello, is Benito there? I just wanted to say "hi" …' Silence. 'Tonino, nobody told you…? Benito is gone.'" He continued,

> With Benito it has come full circle. His death really gave me the feeling of the end of a season. Leone was gone, Tessari was gone, and so are Corbucci, Tonino Delli Colli, Enzo Barboni. They are all gone. A whole era is truly over—not just the era of Italian Western, but a golden age of Italian cinema, because for a long time the Western *was* Italian cinema. We should not be ashamed. For over a decade, the Western has absorbed and molded energies and ideas, creative and brute forces: directors, screenwriters, cameramen, but also technicians, grips, stuntmen. This was Italian cinema. People like Aristide Spila, key grip: a true craftsman who did what he did with conviction, because he was paid for it and therefore had to give his best; and who not only cared about the dignity of work, but also had the sense of history. He always carried a binder, made like photo books, with all the incredible things he had done: set props, tracks, devices— it was the historical record of his work, and he wanted to pass it on—not out of pride, but because he felt it was worth it. He knew that it might be useful, if only there were someone able to pick it up. Or Sesto Salino, Blasetti's chief cameraman. Seven feet tall, a giant with Mongoloid traits and a face like Primo Carnera, who only ever

spoke in Roman dialect. The only one who was authorised to call Blasetti by name on the set. "Sandro, can I speak to ya for a moment...?" he said; he took Blasetti aside and: "Whadda fuck are ya doin'?!? Don't ya see that if this dolly moves from left to right the scene a-gonna work much better?" And Blasetti thanked him, hugged him, kissed him. Because Sesto didn't know a thing about directing, but he understood what the director wanted, and was doing his best to give it to him. Such things, such people are the true soul of filmmaking.

Afterword

Ernesto Gastaldi

When you reach 80, you walk through life with your head looking backwards, to see the faces of those friends who departed before you—or are about to.

Tonino, my dearest friend in that movie industry which had its golden age in the years between 1960 and 1980, is one such person.

I am talking about the great director Tonino Valerii, whom I first met in 1955 at the Centro Sperimentale di Cinematografia in Rome; he was thin as a pin, with pale blue eyes, fond of *auteur* movies and psychoanalysis, but destined to become a great director of Westerns.

CSC celebrated its 80 years since its foundation a few days ago. I was invited to the event, but did not show up; nowadays, the only reference points for me in that school where nothing has changed, and where I spent with Tonino and the other classmates the two most exciting years of my life, are the plaques on the classrooms' doors, with our teachers' names on them: Prosperi room, Verdone room, Blasetti room....

In 1957, having graduated from CSC, Valerii, myself and our colleagues started running all around Rome from one producer to the next, looking for work. It was a good period for the national economy, and yet all the doors were shut in our face: They said there was a cinema crisis, because there was always a "cinema crisis," even when they churned out 300 movies a year.

With CSC, the mid-day refectory where we used to make a supply of sandwiches was also gone, but Tonino was not starving because he lodged at the house of a fat Roman lady, in San Giovanni, and each Sunday he invited me over to lunch. Only one real meal a week, with all the hunger of a 6-foot 6-inch-tall 20-year-old: I devoured record amounts of food, with *Sora*[1] Giggia standing behind my back, muttering every now and then in amazement: "You eat so much, my little son!"

Tonino and I used to keep in touch almost every day by phone, but after a few months *Sora* Giggia started telling me that I had to call after 3 p.m. I suspected that Tonino had started working somewhere but did not want to confess it: in fact I found out that his father had forced him to get a *real* job at the "Cassa del Mezzogiorno" bank, putting his accounting degree to use. There, his superior, accountant Pipitone, tormented him with Aristotelian syllogisms: "Accountant Valerii, if 10 percent makes 10, then 20 percent makes twenty…"

Forced to confess the ignomiy of a job as a government employee, poor Tonino had a breakdown, and his knees started to swell. His psychoanalyst listened to him and did not say a word. One night Tonino dreamed of a black-and-white movie set that turned into color, and the psychiatrist pointed to the solution: resign.

So Tonino did, and his swollen knees returned to normal again.

If being a director was too hard, one could always try being an assistant director. I tried; with director Carlo Veo I lasted only one day, while with Emilio Marsili I became the director because he fell ill—only to find myself atop the chimney in the port of Genoa, shooting landscapes for the documentary *Un giorno in Europa*.

Tonino was luckier than me, as he managed to be the assistant director for movies that we had written together, since having a work to show offers better opportunities than does turning up at producers' offices with nothing in hand. And so Tonino passed from Camillo Mastrocinque to none other than Sergio Leone, and became his assistant on *For a Few Dollars More*. And so began his career in the Italian film industry, upon which he would leave an indelible mark.

But here is where the romantic memories of youth give way to career, marriage, children and life's routine; one lives under the illusion that it will never end, but inevitably it does. Somewhere, sometime, when I still had black hair on my head, I wrote that there are no happy endings, because if one keeps telling the story, you'll find out that Prince Charming dies of prostate cancer and Sleeping Beauty succumbs to Alzheimers.

So I'll just stop here.

Ernesto Gastaldi (born 1934) is one of Italy's most eclectic and prolific screenwriters, with more than 120 scripts in a career spanning four decades, as well as the director of five feature films and author of a number of science fiction and crime novels. He collaborated with many of Italy's finest genre filmmakers, such as Mario Bava, Riccardo Freda, Antonio Margheriti, Sergio Martino and Lucio Fulci, and is a specialist on the Gothic horror film, the giallo and the Spaghetti Western. He wrote several of Tonino Valerii's films, including My Name Is Nobody.

Appendix: Interviews

Andy J. Forest
(actor, *Shatterer*)

By the time you starred in Shatterer, *you had already been working as a musician and actor in Italy for quite a few years, after you had moved there in the late 1970s. It was right after Tinto Brass' Capriccio if I'm not wrong...*

I think that Mario Di Biase who worked as *Capo Gruppo* with Tinto Brass got me the screen test and vouched for me.... But I don't remember. Also my agent at the time was Cinzia De Curtis. I'm sure she was instrumental in getting me the part—and I remember being happy with my fee as well.

How long did it take to film Shatterer?

If I remember correctly about 5 or 6 weeks. It was interrupted for about a week because the producer in Japan died so Kôji Kikkawa and the director of photography (maybe), anyway several members of the Japanese crew returned to Japan for the funeral. It went pretty smoothly. Some of the more complex action scenes were removed due to a budget cut—like the motorcycle chase on a mountain road in Sicily. Later when producers saw the rushes or "dailies" they complained about wanting more action—so a scene was shot with myself (and a stunt double) hanging off of a rope ladder from a moving a helicopter while chasing a motorcycle. It was shot just outside Rome instead of Sicily.

The film was a Japanese/Italian co-production, with the participation of the great Toshirô Mifune. What was he like to work with?

Mr. Mifune had an interpreter and I had several conversations with him. At one point while we were shooting at DeLaurentiis studios—there was a scene which basically explained the entire situation—before rehearsal he said: "Give all of my lines to him," and he pointed at me. "My English isn't good enough." We had to come back the next day to finish it while the script was re-written.

And what about the ladies?

Marina Suma was (and is) a wonderful and radiant person and we became friends. We had Chinese food and went to the movies a couple of times. Great actress and a fun lady. Dalila Di Lazzaro was a very kind and humble person. And good company. One short story: the way I first met Dalila. I was in the dressing room at De Laurentiis studio and I went to the bathroom just when we were called to the set. Somehow I got locked in and started to panic, thinking everyone had left, I yelled "*Aiutooo!*" (Heeelp!) And I pounded on the door with both hands. Then, "click," the door opened and standing in front of me was this stunning woman. Dalila. *Brutta figura!* (Bad impression) We both had a laugh over it.

Japanese sources state that the script was significantly altered during filming, after the death of executive producer Shin Watanabe, and that your role (initially smaller) was enlarged, compared to Kôji Kikkawa's, as he was to be originally the lead. Is that correct?

I was under the impression that the re-writing only added or subtracted action scenes. I don't remember getting any new lines or scenes ... except the one I just mentioned with Toshirô Mifune. I was told when I got the part that I had the lead role, and on the set I quickly understood that they had said the same thing to Kôji. Producers and directors do that sometimes to make actors happy. That's my experience. It happened to me more than once. I didn't mind, or care who was the lead. Also I thought that maybe Kôji would be billed as the lead in Japan and myself in Europe...

Definitely, he was (still is) a big name in Japan. And, like you, he had a musical career as well...
I heard that Kôji trashed his hotel room at one point. I thought either he's unhappy with the film ... or he was just trying to get extra publicity on his rock star status in Japan. He was cordial and pleasant but never confided in me. He had an assistant who asked a lot of pointed questions about the choreography of the scenes we had together. Maybe he was trying to make sure Kôji looked more like the lead.... I don't know. The only sign that he may have felt competitive, or envious was that one day he told me that I "looked more like a model than an actor," and he asked me if that offended me. I laughed and said "No."

What was it like working with Valerii? Did he care about the actors' performances, guide you, etc., or was he mostly interested in the technical side when filming a scene?
Tonino was a very calm and patient person. He was comfortable in his own skin and seemed to have good control of the set without resorting to histrionics—like I've seen with some other directors. I couldn't think of one single negative thing to say about him. Also, he did care about acting. I feel like a few times I wasn't able to give him the subtleties in my performance that he was asking for. And I hated the hair cut and clothes they gave me—I thought my "look" was way too "Yuppie." At the time *Miami Vice* was new and I said "Give me that look!" The costume designer said "*Magari...*" (You wish...) Due to that I never felt completely comfortable in the role. I later discovered that Marina Suma had refused to wear what they gave her and demanded what she deemed stylish. I didn't know an actor could do that! But for me it was too late...

The film has a number of fluid long takes, such as the ones in the Donnafugata labyrinth. Were these scenes rehearsed, or was there room for improvisation?
They were rehearsed once or twice.... I think.

What about the action scenes, such as the gory ending with Toshirô Mifune cutting the Mafioso's hand and throat...?
I don't remember. Except that I was present for the "Samurai" scene and it was beautiful to see Mifune work.

Why was the final showdown shot in Paestum, Campania, and not in Agrigento's Valley of the Temples (where it is supposed to be set)?
That was part of the budget cut, I think.... It was closer to Rome and the cost was less.

How would you define Valerii, compared with the other directors you worked with, such as Brass, Lenzi or Deodato...?
A true gentleman. I'll always remember his smile which reflected his true good nature and intelligent sense of humor. The others.... All of them are steps in a ladder. All irreplaceable with their own qualities and defects. But Tonino and Peter Shepherd were the most calm and considerate. I like calm. Yelling and screaming makes it hard for me to concentrate.

What is your opinion of Shatterer?
I think it would have been better if they had left Mr. Valerii alone and not messed with the constant budget and location fussing. However I only saw it once on video cassette and I don't remember much—except I (selfishly) hated my hair and clothes!

It's funny because during the shooting the movie gained quite a bit of attention from the press, as there were news articles on Italian newspapers, mentioning Toshirô Mifune's first film in Italy, but then it practically disappeared...

At the big press conference arranged by Lucherini—which was mostly about the excitement around the arrival in Italy after 20 years of Mr. Mifune—a journalist asked him: "After working with so many great directors, Kurosawa, Spielberg, Huston, etc. etc. ... and making 142 films (more or less)... Which film was your favorite?" The interpreter took a long time to translate then listened to his answer in Japanese. There was silence in the room even though there were probably about 100 people there. (Incredible for Italy!) I don't remember the exact words, so I will paraphrase. He said "Each film is like one step in a very long staircase. Each one as important as all the others. If you take one away, they will all fall down. Each one is just as important as the others." I thought that was so beautiful, so Zen! Then the same journalist said ... "YES ... but which was your favorite?"!! Another long conversation with the interpreter ensued. The interpreter then repeated the exact same response but a little more slowly, obviously treating the journalist like a child who had not understood the first time. In the press release packages there were no photos of me. One promo picture which had been taken of Kôji and I had been ripped in half—by hand—and my half had been thrown away. I asked Lucherini about it. He seemed to get angry that I asked about it and said *"A nessuno frega di te"* (No one cares about you). He later said to me: "I'll never be interested in you or promote you because you're not gay." I swear he actually said that! I was so shocked that I was left speechless. I had no response. Not even anger. It made me glad that I had a music career as well.

(Email interview, October 2015)

Gianni Garko

(actor, *Due madri, Una prova d'innocenza*)

Due madri, written by Ugo Pirro, dealt with two themes seemingly distant from one another: adoption and the drama of the Argentinian desaparecidos. What do you recall about it?

Upon re-reading the script (which I fished out from a dusty box in the garage) I perceived the plot of the film as a direct emanation of the feelings, values and vital needs of the individual characters. As far as I can judge, it is screenwriting done to perfection: nothing artificial, mechanical, forced. Whereas the dialogue sounds *literary*, a language written rather than spoken, which the director corrected on time. There are traces of Valerii's interventions in the script; on the sidelines of my character's lines, you can see many corrections in pencil, offering other words and turns of phrase. These corrections, I remember, were suggested by Valerii, who wanted a conversational language, simple and fast. The same happened on *Una prova d'innocenza*.

Did shooting go smoothly?

I recall some difficulties in my relationship with actress Sonia Petrovna. Having seen Valerio Zurlini's film *Indian Summer* (*La prima notte di quiete*, 1972), in which she co-starred alongside Alain Delon, I was fascinated by her type, a brunette with pale eyes, and with delicate but determined features. I expected a great feeling between us, whereas the relationship on the set with her was not relaxing, due to the difficulties in the use of two different languages—she spoke French and I spoke Italian. Such a problem turned up often on Italian movie sets, which were a real Babel. In many films the dialogue was delivered simultaneously in three different languages, sometimes four, so I should have been trained, and indeed I was, but with the beautiful Petrovna, for some reason, it was not that easy. Many parts of the film were redubbed in post-production, of course—I think all those featuring the adoptive mother.

Were you happy with your performance? Did Valerii make any particular suggestions regarding your character?

I remember that he intervened very little in my acting, and devoted more time to the two female characters, who were more complex. Having not seen the movie since, I could not say anything about how I played that role. I was close enough to Oscar's character, though. In those years, since I divorced and remarried, the relationship between father and stepdaughter, and between ex-wife and ex-husband, were my bread and butter, so I knew thoroughly the dramatic aspects and the psychological nuances of the role. I know that Tonino Valerii considers the film, originally titled *Cronaca di un amore materno*, as one of his most valuable efforts, perhaps the one that he is most fond of. If this piece of information is reliable, definitely it must be a beautiful movie and still strong today, because of its thematic issues, and especially the excellent direction.

One year later Valerii called you back to work on the two-part TV movie, Una prova d'innocenza...

Initially I was supposed to make a cameo, but the producer, Goffredo Lombardo, suggested he use me for a more interesting role, that of Commendatore Cremonese. I later worked again with Lombardo on *Edera*, the first soap opera produced in Italy.

Were there any differences compared with your experience on Due madri*?*

Una prova d'innocenza was all shot with live sound. This time, Valerii gave me the right coordinates for the role of Cremonese, and guided me with precise tips on the nature of my character, an industrialist who deals with prefabricated buildings and moonlights as an arms trafficker with the complicity of corrupt politicians. When dealing with the actor, Valerii was aseptic, detached, and the relationship remained strictly professional—at least it was like that with me.

What was Valerii's approach to television, in your recollection?

I remember that he was uncomfortable with the timing of TV production schedules, which were too tight for him. He considered them a serious obstacle to the quality of the shooting, and he was right. The crisis of our film industry had long been an accepted fact by then, and the new methods of producing television material were being imposed on everyone. It was not easy for a master of cinema as Valerii to accept that revolution—or better, that involution.

Do you think something has changed in recent years?

Today, quality has surfaced again on the small screen—an example for all, *Romanzo Criminale—La Serie*, by Stefano Sollima. How has television changed in recent years, compared to then? Let's say that today, for a film like *Due madri*, there would be a Spanish language actress playing the character of Dolores, the real Argentinian mother, and an Italian actress playing Ester, Oscar's wife and Pilar's adoptive mother. And the child would be a real South American child. The director would not have difficulty finding good actors linguistically suitable for each role.

(Email interview, October 2015)

Giuliano Gemma

(actor, *Day of Anger, The Price of Power, Caccia al ladro d'autore, Un bel dì vedremo*)

You and Tonino Valerii have worked together several times, starting with Day of Anger. *Your first meeting occurred in rather unusual circumstances...*

We met in a strange way, indeed. I was riding my bicycle in Rome, in the Ostiense area, near Porta Portese, when I noticed that a car was following me. Then, at a certain point, the driver stopped me. "I'm Valerii, Sergio Leone's assistant, I am going to direct a Western and I wanted to know if you've been contacted for the role." Actually, no one had gotten in touch with me. So, Tonino engineered to have me as the lead, and we did our first film together. It was a beautiful and important collaboration: a lot of work, and hard too, but also a lot of satisfaction, because *Day of Anger* was a huge success.

What are Valerii's best qualities as a director, in your opinion?

The thing that I immediately liked in Tonino was that before the film he talked about the story and explained my character, but then on the set he let me do what I wanted with it: he intervened a few times, mostly at the beginning of a scene, and then if there was something that could be changed or improved upon, he pointed it out, but this rarely happened. He never prevaricated an actor's job. Also because I think I immediately understood how he conceived the character, and we found ourselves on the same wavelength; the role spoke for itself, anyway.

What is your view on Scott "Mary," the character you played in Day of Anger?

From a social point of view, Scott is a reject, with no family, grown up amid people's contempt, raised in a kind of brothel. He wants to climb the ladder, socially speaking, by any means, and is fascinated by determined men, like the one who will become his mentor, the gunslinger played by Lee Van Cleef. I must say I prefer to work with directors like Valerii, who tell you about the character but when it comes to shoot leave you a certain freedom to express yourself, giving you the chance to go your own way, and show you understood the role and "feel" it. On top of that, one must say that it is very easy to work with Tonino: he doesn't waste time, is very prepared technically, and always knows where to place the camera and what type of shot he wants.

German lobby card for *The Price of Power*, featuring (from left to right) Antonio Casas, Benito Stefanelli, Ray Saunders and Carlos Bravo.

How was your relationship with Lee Van Cleef like?

On set, it was a great relationship, as is often the case with American actors, who are very serious professionally. I would have liked to have a more in-depth relationship with him, because I held him in high esteem as an actor and admired his escalation: he had always played small roles in Hollywood, and he showed his skills thanks to Leone. I say "I would have liked" because the problem with Lee was that after shooting he started to drink, and became another person: unfriendly, sometimes sad, sometimes obnoxious. And if you didn't drink with him there was no reason to spend the evening together, because he isolated himself in his own world. Alcohol was his ruin.

In your opinion, what distinguished Valerii's films from other Italian Westerns of the period?

There was a very strong initial idea, which stood out from the average products, and we know that to make a good film you have to have a strong starting point. And I think *Day of Anger* represents a special case for the Italian Western, because of the characters' psychological accuracy. The second film I did with Valerii, *The Price of Power*, also had quite a strong basic idea, telling Kennedy's assassination in a Western key. I saw it again recently, and I find it a movie that still holds up great, intelligent and very well-made.

Benito Stefanelli was the master of arms and played a rather important role in The Price of Power, *as he had done in* Day of Anger...

I did a number of films with Benito, although I mainly worked with Nazzareno Zamperla. As master of arms, Stefanelli was very good with violent scenes, perhaps the best; he also played

German lobby card for *The Price of Power*, **featuring Giuliano Gemma and Manuel Zarzo (right).**

small roles, like in *For a Few Extra Dollars*. And even as an actor he was very laid-back, whereas the thing that perhaps he lacked—but in the case of the pics we did together there was no need, because those were very hard movies, based on violent situations—was a sense of humor, the irony that would break the tension in a scene, which on the other hand was Zamperla's forte. But in real life Benito did have this irony, mind you, as he was an amiable and witty person.

How did you prepare these scenes with the master of arms?

We set them up together, right before shooting, on the set. There was no time to rehearse beforehand; we took ourselves aside half an hour, or one hour at most, and rehearse the scene so the director would see immediately how it worked. It would have been useless to rehearse everything in advance when then, at the last moment, it would be necessary to shoot it in a totally different way. Moreover, since we were working with good stuntmen and I did not use doubles, it was possible to hurry up and adapt different situations to the necessity of the moment, or to impromptu ideas.

The Price of Power *was also a rather important production. With a good cast...*

Certainly. Van Johnson, Fernando Rey, the brilliant Manolo Zarzo. It was a medium budget production, with nine weeks of shooting. Actually, we did have a few problems with budget, although eventually we managed to get all we needed … almost. I had some problems with my salary, in the sense that I still have to see some money, but never mind … (laughs).

It took more than fifteen years for you and Valerii to work again, on the 1985 TV series Caccia al ladro d'autore.

That was truly a beautiful series, especially if we compare it with those TV series about the *Carabinieri* that are being made nowadays…. And it's not clear why RAI did not renew it for a second season. It was a clever production, with an international feel, crammed with action, it had everything…

The idea of valorizing art cities was apt.

It was an intelligent approach, all right, because each city has its own treasures, and offers many historical, cultural, and landscape suggestions. What is more, the idea of setting the episodes in the world of art opened the way to endless possibilities. We might have broadened the discourse abroad, because still today we can still see how the recovery of stolen works of art is significant. And since I always loved sculpting and nowadays I collect paintings, these kind of stories particularly captivated me.

It was rather successful at the time of its broadcasting, wasn't it?

Caccia al ladro d'autore could have gone on for a long time. And it is not clear why it ended so quickly instead. I remember that back then the General Commander of the *Carabinieri* Force, Bisogniero, used to call me: "Gemma, but why are you not making *Caccia al ladro d'autore* anymore?" "Commander, ask the big shots at RAI, I don't really know…" "I've been told that maybe it's you who don't want to play Captain Maffei anymore…" "Me? Absolutely not, if it were for me I'd have Maffei become a Colonel! (laughs). I don't think I'm so stupid as to give up something that has been so successful and which I have done with passion, I would go against my own interests!" Bisogniero even invited me to dinner together with Rai's director-in-chief Milani, who could not maintain in front of me that it was I who did not want to play Maffei. It was a matter of internal interests, probably, but I never found out the reason why.

Your last collaboration with Valerii was 1997's Un bel dì vedremo, *a very little-seen film…*

In fact, not seen at all! This also was as unusual story, centered on a group of elderly artists in retirement; an idea that came from the Japanese producer, then Tonino worked on it, and rewrote the script. We shot it in the "Eleonora Duse" center in Bologna.

You worked with a great opera singer such as Raina Kabaivanska, who however had little experience in film…

Kabaivanska was very helpful and attentive: of course, having to delve into a medium that requires another type of professional attitude, she often asked for advice. I remember telling her: "You are a great artist, but you are used to getting to the back rows in enormous theater houses. Here you are in close-up, and everything is played on interiority. Because on screen your close-up becomes twenty times bigger than your face: think of what you have to express and don't worry about getting to the back rows." And she did it well. She was an intelligent and very modest person.

What was it like to shoot in high definition? From a directorial standpoint, according to Valerii, it introduced several limitations. And for the actors?

As far as I'm concerned, I mostly remember its advantages. For instance, the focusing: when shooting with film, when two actors are standing several feet from each other, one is in focus and the other is out-of-focus, whereas with high-def they are both in focus. What is more, we were amazed by the sharpness of the image: normally in video you have about 600 lines to form the image, whereas with high-def it is over 1000 lines, and the effect is stunning. I remember the director of photography, Mario Vulpiani, told me: "Look, I'm using just a few lights, but this lense is so bright..." And so he used just small spots, otherwise there would have been too much light.

What was the importance of filmmakers like Valerii in Italian cinema in your opinion?

When we speak of Valerii and his peers, we speak of professionals with great experience, we speak of masters. And Italian cinema would better continue to employ them to train new generations of filmmakers who are learning their craft. Unfortunately, Italy is a country with no memory, and I'm not referring only to directors. Actors and directors who gave something for the good of the film industry are now totally forgotten. These are things that don't happen abroad, where such a wealth of experience and knowledge is retained and carried forward. I think that a huge problem is that, since at least 70 to 80 percent of film production is in the hands of television, there is no commitment to make world-class products instead of buying material from abroad. Whereas we buy, and buy, while we should produce in order to sell, and offer products that have a more acceptable, international language, and can be sold to other countries. The foreign market is like a big cake, we had to grab a large slice of it, and didn't make it.

Often it is also a matter of political alliances...

In the arts, politics should be put aside. People's talents don't emerge with phone calls. We need to focus on things that are for the common good, regardless of the "with us or against us" juxtapositions.

Still, there has been a reappreciation of Italian genre films in recent years...

To revive the interest in the Italian Western here in Italy, it took someone like Quentin Tarantino, citing films, names.... The Venice retrospective was meritorious. But the fact that it took Tarantino to re-evaluate those movies is significant. Here in Italy there has always been distrust, and detachment, toward this kind of film, because when they were produced Italian cinema was still a healthy body, with Petri, Rosi, Germi...

Tarantino often takes inspiration from Italian cinema, even the Western. As in Kill Bill...

Indeed, but he does so in a honest way, as he openly declared his influences. But take *Reservoir Dogs*: if you analyze the story, that's basically the same as *Blood for a Silver Dollar*, the story of a guy who infiltrates a gang of thugs. Of course, mixed with many other influences. But for better or worse the core of the story draws from there...

But perhaps now is it too late to open many people's eyes, don't you think?

The eyes are closed now, and not just cinema's. This is a country that has turned a blind eye on everything.

(Phone interview, April 2008)

George Hilton
(actor, *My Dear Killer*)

How did you become involved in the making of My Dear Killer? *It was quite a change from your usual roles in the gialli you starred in that period, by Sergio Martino and Giuliano Carnimeo...*

I was called by Tonino Valerii in person. He told me, "Look, this is a difficult role, and I've been told by many people that it does not suit you..."—you know, I was doing these films where I played the hero who killed all the bad guys in the end in Westerns, such as he was not a hero like the ones I used to play—like Alleluja[1] or Tresette,[2] or those *gialli* where I was the dark and handsome, beautiful and damned type, whereas this was a totally passive role. I remember that Tonino explained that this commissioner, this Luca Peretti, was a loser of sorts. But he said he believed in me, thought I could handle the role. And he wanted to physically reshape me for the part, so to speak. Hence the mustache ... and he even put some cotton in my nostrils so as to make my nose a little larger, as he wanted me to look slightly different from my usual characters...

How did it go, then?

It was quite a challenging task, let me tell you. Tonino is a very demanding director, and the movie was filmed in English. I remember that every now and then he changed my lines. And for the final scene, where I had this very long and intense monologue, at one point he came over and said, "Look, George, here's the new dialogue, I'm changing Peretti's final monologue, but I can give you only half a hour to learn it in English." So I said, "Well, ok..." but I was a bit nervous actually! Luckily I had a very good memory, as I had done my share of stage acting. So I learned that whole monologue in quite a short time and when it was time to shoot it came out really great.

My Dear Killer *was Valerii's only giallo. Was he comfortable with the material?*

He definitely knew his stuff. Very good with the camera, and he knew how to move the actors in a scene. I have quite a good memory of him...

What was he like working with, compared to other directors, such as Fulci, who notoriously had quite a temper on the set?

With Valerii there was a very good feeling, unlike with Fulci. Fulci was a difficult man. And I think Tonino was very happy with my performance too. Personally, I think *My Dear Killer* is one of the few films I'd save in my filmography. Of all the movies I've done, I'd save four, actually. The first, *Massacre Time*, which was the one that launched me, I had very favorable criticism as Franco Nero's drunken brother and that was the film that gave me everything, professionally speaking. Even though I did not have a good relationship with Fulci, I owe him that success. Then Giorgio Capitani's *The Ruthless Four*, Sergio Martino's *The Case of the Scorpion's Tail*, as I liked my role in it very much, and Tonino Valerii's *My Dear Killer*. These are my very best performances. Valerii's film allowed me to show that I was eclectic, and I could play different roles.

Did he allow you to add things to the character as well?

He trusted me, and I trusted him. During our very first meeting he told me, "Look, I'm going to bet on you in this film!" and he was very satisfied in the end. We discussed the scenes together, decided which way I would play them. Never had a single problem with him.

And from a human standpoint, what is your recollection of him?

Well, he was not overly communicative, perhaps a bit distant—I mean, we did not have the occasion of becoming friends outside the set, ours was a merely professional relationship, but it was impeccable.

As it often happened in the period, My Dear Killer *was shot partly in Spain...*
It was a Spanish co-production, yes. The Italian producer was Manolo Bolognini, who's a wonderful producer—I love Manolo, together we also did *The Two Faces of Fear*[3] with Fernando Rey and Anita Strindberg ... with Manolo you worked wonderfully.

So it was a high-level production...
Definitely. The budget was good, we were royally paid...

Compared to other gialli, what was the strength of My Dear Killer*?*
Well, it was rather different from the other films of that type that came out in those years. It was a thriller, a crime film, and quite violent indeed, but it was definitely one of the best. You know, perhaps because of the story, centered on this little girl, which really affected the viewers deeply. It wasn't like those by Dario Argento, or *The Case of the Scorpion's Tail* ... and the central character, the commissioner, was a loser, who always arrived too late and couldn't save the victims, had problems with his girlfriend ... and I think it added depth to the story.

The cast was great, too...
Wonderful cast! There was the great Salvo Randone, who to me was Italy's greatest stage actor together with Vittorio Gassman and Enrico Maria Salerno. Then there was Marilù Tolo, whom I liked very much both as an actress and as a woman (laughs), an exquisite person. And then William Berger, and several Spanish actors, Manolo Zarzo, Patty Shepard, who got that nasty scene with the circular saw, my beautiful friend Helga Liné.... It was an idyllic shooting. Too bad it didn't have the success it deserved...

Do you think it was a matter of distribution?
Indeed. Jumbo Distribuzione, which was the Italian distributor, well, I don't know what happened, but they just did not promote the film well. I remember going to Pescara for the film's premiere, under the snow, it was early February I think ... and there was not much advertising around. It was quite disappointing. So, it did not have the success we hoped for, it did not do nearly as good as *The Case of the Scorpion's Tail*, which was a big hit, or *The Strange Vice of Mrs. Wardh*, to name two ... which was a shame. And let me tell you: if it was re-released today, I think it would be successful, because it is a worthwhile film, and also because of this renewed interest toward Italian cinema. And I mean, it's incredible, people write to me on Facebook, and you can see their affection and love for those movies ... it's amazing. They have become cult films.... To think that back then they were dismissed as B-flicks.... A movie like *The Ruthless Four*, now it's in the Cinémathèque Française, and it's considered one of the very best. And Giorgio Capitani was a great director. And what a cast.... Van Heflin, Klaus Kinski, Gilbert Roland ... fantastic movie.... It's a good thing. Time heals all wounds.

It was a great time, as long as it lasted.
Absolutely. Nowadays there are not the producers as back then. Once they used to take money off of their own pockets—people like Manolo Bolognini, Luciano Martino, Italo Zingarelli ... nowadays it's all in the hands of television executives. A totally different world.

Still, you're looking forward to working on new projects...
Recently I have received no less than three offers. Let me tell you about one which I think is amazing. A great, great western, written by John J. Greenflowers [the pseudonym of Antonio Scutari, the author of the sci-fi novel *Badroots—Cattive radici*] and with Enzo G. Castellari directing. It is about the old guys of the Italian Western, and the cast will be something extraordinary: there is me, Claudia Cardinale, Antonio Banderas, and others ... the story begins in the 19th century and ends in 2015, with our grandchildren. An epic concept. If we do manage to make this movie, it'll be something worth remembering!

So it's not time to hang the gun on a nail yet...
Not at all, even though celebrations have already started. By the way, life is funny: tomorrow

I'm going to be in Teramo to receive a career award, and Tonino Valerii is from Teramo. And when I'll be there I'll talk about my films and I'll be glad to say that one of my best films was directed by their fellow citizen!
(Phone interview, October 2015)

Peter Hooten
(actor, *Brothers in Blood*)

At a certain point in your career, during the late 1970s, you found yourself acting in Italian productions. How's your recollection of that period?

With a remnant warm glow I loved working in Italy. From my time on *Orca*, a DeLaurentiis production, with Dino's brother Alfredo as production manager and the master designer Mario Garbuglia (working his magic creating the Arctic and a killer-whale in a Malta pond on the sea in hot weather), on to later projects, I found your countrymen's craftsmen to have gratitude for working at what they love and a zest with their enjoyment, having been chosen to partake in creative challenges, crossing disciplines readily to help one another, and knowing to be "sympathetic" in team spirit.

Surely the tone of the set was due greatly to its director…

Only once did I work with a director who I will not name, who was a "screamer," and the set's mood tended to be grim and robotic—he must have been raised fascistically. But in the evening his personal graces would return and he'd make the rounds to his actors and crew with charming warmth—Jekyll and Hyde. Whole-heartedly I enjoyed working with Enzo Castellari (on *The Inglorious Bastards*, 1978), Duccio Tessari (on *The Fifth Commandment*, 1978), and Tonino Valerii, on *Brothers in Blood*.

What are your memories of Valerii, compared with the other directors you mentioned?

Tonino was a very sympathetic man, kindly and solid, consistent in temperament, with a most sensitive visage. As for Enzo Castellari, I believe his family had some athletic or circus background [Castellari had been a prizefighter in his youth, just like his father Marino Girolami]. I know he was a champion of stunt persons. A great friend of his was the excellent stuntman and coordinator Rocco Lerro, and Rocco achieved some wonderful feats. This background also explained Enzo's ever-exuberant presence, his twinkle-in-the-eye persona, not unlike a performer entering before his act in the Big Top. He was always quick to respond excitedly when a scene went the way we hoped. That type of spirit is contagious, and there was oftentimes a gleeful and well-paced energy to the military and athletic proceedings.

Interestingly, The Inglorious Bastards *was one of the first Italian productions to employ the Steadicam, which Valerii had introduced to Italy with* Sahara Cross, *one year earlier…*

Indeed. I recall a rather longish master shot using a Steadicam; it was the first time in anyone's experience with the device; luckily, I was the focus of the shot (steps through a mud puddle into a German's eye) with tall, agile, quick-paced, backward-stepping cinematographer performing wonderfully, so all I had to do was follow. Enzo hugged us both afterwards. The filming was filled with all sorts of "highs" like that, and I think that energy comes through in the movie.

During filming in The Inglorious Bastards, *there were issues regarding the use of weapons…*

In the midst of shooting, the Italian government passed a law benning on-screen fire from guns—what to do? After a failed attempt to rig a gun with a gas pump, perplexity was prevailing, until actress Debra Berger, the partner of Prince Dado Ruspoli, invited a group of us to sup at his country palazzo, and Enzo Castellari, seeing the medieval armor and weaponry hung upon the castle walls, had the idea of hiring the castle at Bracciano, scaling its walls, using sling-shots and cross-bows, etc. Challenge met.

...and what about Tessari?

Duccio Tessari, with his accomplishments as a writer and director, was a clear-spoken and elegant personage, amusing raconteur, precise. He liked to listen to stories too, and liked being with his actors. His wife Lorella De Luca was lovely too. I remember his bespoke attire—in rough, winter location, his Battistoni suit, with a tie, a Loden coat and sensible hat. He liked the outdoors, on location. At lunch, picnicking, he would pull out his silver Napoleonic camp service. Subtly stylish man, pulling out his rare mess utensils, he didn't say a word.

Your co-star on The Fifth Commandment *was Helmut Berger...*

During filming Helmut would declare that "All the Germans hate me!" This was 1978 and the German public schoolers were first learning of the bad Nazi past. Visconti's *The Damned* was having its first release there on television, and everybody would see Helmut playing Marlene in drag. One night, the producers, Duccio, Helmut and I went to a cabaret in Essen, in the countryside. Entering this club, Helmut is reserved, unassuming, but the MC spots him and swirls at him the feather boa; it's well caught. Anyway, he was mostly amusing, easy to be with, teasingly (we played brothers), kindly. As a pro, he knew his stuff.

Let's move on to Brothers in Blood. *Everybody who's been involved in it tells me this was a mess of a production!*

Scene: Hotel *El Embajador*, Santo Domingo. Stacks of cash being paid out at the improvised office counter (secure but observable), the production manager is making a late payment to the hotel and vendors (per diems later, more discreet). Eagle-eyed Bo Svenson says aloud that a lot of that funny stuff is his. James Merrill, in the lobby, in his handy notebook, dashed "Funny money—A lot of *Lire*." But they were Pesos, not *Lire*.

So you all had lots of trouble getting paid, which resulted in delays, etc...

It was an off-and-on-again production, times three. Wire transactions were slower internationally, pre–Internet. Bo and his agent, one Mr. Gaines, were vociferous often about timeliness of their monies received and it caused a lot of delays and ill will. We were delayed up to two weeks at one time, executive production-wise. We broke production homeward-bound once, to re-meet in the Dominican Republic. There was an added day's shoot near NYC for Bo and me, wintertime. Needless to say Bo and I didn't hang out.

What was working with Bo Svenson like?

He's a strong, effective actor, but ensemble-playing social skills he lacked in our two projects together. Yes, he was a Marine; you never forgot it. But he would forget his chain of command. During *The Inglorious Bastards*, I remembered that Jackie Basehart's waxing courtly about the social season upcoming in Milan and Venice, and his looking forward to it with a certain drawing room effeteness, set off the he-man Bo onto a Drill Instructor streak of teasing, insinuating, bullying. One day the nice producer Roberto Sbarigia was showing to actors contact sheets from the set photographer for us to order the ones we liked, and Bo had punched out the small frames that he didn't want of himself, obliterating whoever else might have been in the frame. All about Bo. When I'd first arrived in Santo Domingo, he pulled me aside to apologize for his behavior in Italy 7 years prior. But it didn't take long for him to relapse. The syndrome: I'm not being paid; I'm not sleeping, I need pain pills, but I'm off them.

Svenson told me that during filming he unfairly blamed Valerii for the production difficulties, and found out too late that the director was not really responsible for that.

Indeed, Tonino is innocent of Bo's blame. Anyway, on that set I think Bo was being vindictive—you know, he played a Captain, and Tonino was the General. One night filming, setting up a complicated master shot was going too slow for him. He was ready. He shot off from his revolver some blanks into the air. Everyone was taken aback, he beamed and added something about real, live action. Kelly Cole and I were reading aloud to each other from Geoffrey Madan's *Notebooks* and there was the aphorism about beware the man whose wife has ulcers; Kelly glanced to me knowingly, smilingly, "Bo's wife." Bo became so often without company that at one point he had a "trainer" friend fly in from L.A. to be his confidant (at war).

How did Valerii react to all these setbacks?
In those hostage-taking delays of waiting for Bo and his agent's monies to reach Beverly Hills, or in actual production delays because of it, there wouldn't be a day that Tonino wasn't out in the field scouting with design and photography, trying to imagine what could be done for less, etc. Bo would bump heads with Tonino; Tonino would try to transcend, endure, and let him be. He finished the film with what footage he had. On a visit to Rome I had dinner at his home. Carlo Mucari was there as well. And Tonino spoke about a great lesson he'd learned in life: Finish the project you've started.

What about the other cast members, Carlo Mucari and Werner Pochath?
I worked twice with Carlo, who was so great to be with; I miss him; I hope he's doing well. Werner and I worked on a couple movies too. As he lived in L.A. and spoke several languages, Italian productions would hire him to cast American actors, so he called on me for several productions over the years.

So, are you into any film projects currently?
Primarily I'm retired, sometimes quasi, mostly all, since I moved to Sarasota in 1998. I'm from Florida originally, so the "provincial" was familiar. I'm ever so thankful I traveled a lot when younger in the film biz, gallivanting around a safer world it seemed, less crowded, cleaner, less war-torn.
(Private correspondence with the author, October 2015—March 2016)

Marco Leonardi
(actor, *Una vacanza all'inferno*)

When you shot Una vacanza all'inferno *you were already quite a popular actor in Italy, after appearing in such movies as Giuseppe Tornatore's* Cinema Paradiso, *Francesco Rosi's* The Palermo Connection *(*Dimenticare Palermo, *1990), Alfonso Arau's* Like Water for Chocolate *(1992), Dario Argento's* The Stendhal Syndrome *(*La sindrome di Stendhal, *1996). What do you remember about Valerii's film?*
A great experience. We filmed for several weeks—I think six—in an abandoned prison at Frosinone. We managed to shoot there all the scenes where my character is imprisoned in Thailand, instead of the real one in Bangkwang. Then we did one week in the Philippines, several outdoor scenes, a few bits outside the entrance of a penitentiary.

Why wasn't it possible to shoot on location?
I don't know, really. I heard there were problems and that was that—perhaps they failed to obtain permissions, or the authorities did not like the story we were filming … of course, shooting inside Bankwang was out of the question. Anyway, the Philippines are not that different from Thailand, so we managed to make do with them.

Did you get along well with Valerii?
Absolutely. We had a very good relationship from the start, since Tonino is a very easygoing, witty fellow. So there was a mutual good feeling. And we also agreed on how to develop the character, as we trusted each other reciprocally. And one thing I'll never forget, is the impression I had when watching him on the set—I mean, you felt that he breathed cinema, and important cinema. You could tell that he came from a mythical era, so to speak. Every now and then he used to tell us anecdotes about working with Sergio Leone. He knew how to do his job, professionally but with a touch of irony, because without irony, without having a bit of fun, it becomes more difficult to make good movies … or at least it is not so pleasant. It adds a twist when

shooting a scene, especially if you're making such a downbeat, harsh film as the one we were making. A smile always helps, you know. What is more, shooting in English was challenging, even though back then I lived in L.A. and was rather fluent in the language. But, you know Tonino: whenever I needed some advice, or I was unsure of something, he was there to help. In short, I have wonderful memories of the film. There was a good harmony on he set, and when this happens it is very much the director's merit. I mean, if there is an arrogant director, or someone who raises his voice often, then the consequences affect everyone on the set. There's tension, and you don't work well. And all this ultimately affects the picture.

Still, it was not an easy film to make, even if just on a physical level...
Yes, quite a difficult movie. The story, you know, openly recalled that of *Midnight Express*, it was one of those pictures—I wouldn't say a remake, but of course there were a number of similarities—that are very risky, because of the model you are emulating. But for an Italian movie, and one made in that period, I think we made a pretty good job.

Did you feel intimidated, working with such actors as Giancarlo Giannini and F. Murray Abraham?
Well, it taught me a lot! I was very young back then, and perhaps in a way my relationship with Abraham—since we had many scenes together—became a sort of uncle/nephew one. He was protective in the movie, but also on the set: he probably felt indulgent toward a young lad trying to make a career in the movies. For my part, I tried not to ask too many questions, not to sound too harassing. I kept my mouth shut, watched and tried to learn from him, to rob as much as I could from him, the way he moved, his gestures, his delivery of the dialogue. I was a *sponge*.

Technically, Una vacanza all'inferno *features a number of rather complex and fluid sequences made with the Steadicam. Did you spend much time rehearsing them?*
Before calling "Action," Tonino wanted to be absolutely sure of how a sequence would work. So, whenever there was one of those Steadicam shots, the set was cleared except for him, the cameraman and us actors, and we rehearsed several times in order to find the best way to film it. Since those were long takes, he wanted to make sure to have as much usable material as possible. It was on occasions like that that you could feel his mastery of directing. You could tell from the way he worked on some shots, the choices he made on some scenes, the way to work out issues.... I think the fact that he started as assistant director showed, he didn't miss anything.

Still, the film did not do well at the box-office...
Well, it was a period when Italian cinema was already limping on its legs, so to speak. Sometimes a good film can be killed by a bad distribution.... Not Valerii's fault, definitely. You see, cinema has no rules when it comes to being a box-office hit or not. I remember an American film, a big-budget production, starring Jeremy Irons, Antonio Banderas, Glenn Close [*The House of the Spirits*, 1993, by Bille August] ... You see these names and I think, "This is going to be a hit" ... whereas it barely made a dime over here. It happens.

Was Una vacanza all'inferno *too harsh and downbeat for the public, perhaps? There are a number of crude sequences...*
One good thing about Italian cinema is that, when it comes to be harsh, it is harsh. It does not oblige to the typical Hollywood compromises—you know, the hero must triumph over all. And while making the movie we tried to portray the reality of Thai prisons as it was, ditto for drug smuggling, and so on. By sheer coincidence, the other day I was watching a documentary about drug smuggling in Mexico, and the method these drug dealers use to smuggle drugs across the border with the United States is just like the one we described in the movie—putting the drugs inside objects carried by unwitting people who travel daily to go to work, without them noticing. And of course, using an innocent, naive courier is a strong dramatic hook...

Perhaps one of the film's strong points is the theme of betrayal, as well as the loss of innocence and hope...

Yes, the central conflict is quite strong. Not merely the humiliation of going to jail, but the fact that he is exploited and betrayed by his friend, no less. With Tonino we worked especially on this. And let me tell you, Tonino not only respected, but loved actors, and believe me, this does not always happen. I had the luck of making pictures since the 1980s [Leonardi debuted in 1987], and directors had more respect for actors. Nowadays this has faded, cinema has been—I'm using a strong term here—"soiled," and maybe it was television that did it, because it was accessible to everyone. Nowadays, everybody is a director, everybody is a producer ... but it's not like that. Real producers were people like Franco Cristaldi, whom I had the fortune to know while doing *Cinema Paradiso*. Today it is quite a different thing. It still is a fascinating job, and it still makes me proud ... lately my film *Anime nere* by Francesco Munzi won nine "David di Donatello" awards [Italy's most prestigious prize] and was sold all over the world. So I can say I am still being kissed by Lady Luck. But, generally speaking, it is not the same as it used to be. Even the crew members ... once they used to work on big Hollywood pictures shot in Rome, and used to have a big respect for their job and for the people around them. Today this is lost, and it's a bad thing. It is not by chance if ten years ago Giancarlo Giannini told me, "Well, this job is finished." Back then, I didn't understand, but now I realize he was right. I mean, it's the feeling that is lost. Creativity is lost. For instance, once make up artists spent whole weeks with the director and the leading actor, working on the character, the way he would look on film ... whereas now comes a young girl who's just finished school, has no experience at all and doesn't care a bit about what she's doing. Same for assistant directors. It almost seems they are bored, and care only about their wage. And it's bad. I mean, everybody just wants to make more money, and save on the budget. Quality is not a valuable option anymore.

(Phone interview, October 2015)

Roberto Leoni

(scriptwriter, assistant director: *My Dear Killer, Brothers in Blood*)

Author's note: the interview gives away
major spoilers about *My Dear Killer*

So, Roberto, let's start talking about My Dear Killer...

Do you know I almost ate a film critic alive because of that movie? (*laughs*)

No I didn't! What happened?

Well, I took a train to Bologna and went straight to the headquarters of a local newspaper that labeled the movie as "moral profiteering"...

Really?!

Yeah. There had been the case of that little girl, Milena Sutter, who had been kidnapped and killed,[1] and the reviewer claimed *My Dear Killer* was an instant movie that exploited the popular grief—in short, it implied we were jackals. So I took the train, went there, waited for the titular film critic, and when he showed up I grabbed him by the jacket and told him "You're an idiot! Anyone who knows about movies is aware that it takes months between the initial idea for a movie, the shooting and its release—sometimes a whole year or more!" Gee, I was so mad at him! So, since *My Dear Killer* came out two months after the murder of that poor girl[2] it was impossible that it exploited those events, but just like the best authors—which I'm not, but on that occasion it was an exception—I felt in the air the things that might happen.

Indeed, that was a dark and very violent period, with kidnappings, murders, terrorism, bombs...
Exactly, and you could feel that in the movies made in those years. Violence and ruthlessness were in the air...

So, could it be that this affinity with the Sutter case was one of the reasons why My Dear Killer *did not have the success you'd hoped for?*
Absolutely. The posters were covered with spray writings, *Sciacalli!* (Jackals!) Many people thought we were exploiting poor Milena Sutter ... which could not have been since we wrote the script many months earlier. And let me elaborate on this: if you remember *Santa Sangre* (1989, Alejandro Jodorowsky) and *California* (1977, Michele Lupo) as well, in my scripts I always deal with this relationship between cruelty and innocence. There is always an innocent who must fight, and who is sided by a violent individual who nevertheless becomes a mentor for him, and tries to save him from the horrors of the world. So, that is a constant in my work—even in *The Final Executioner* (*L'ultimo guerriero*, 1984, Romolo Guerrieri), where the poor become game for the rich—the theme of innocence preyed on by cruelty, and the horror that ensues...

Which incidentally makes the film very different from Argento's own gialli, as well as from the other rip-offs that were being produced at that time...
Indeed! Dario does not advocate innocence—on the contrary: the more it is preyed upon, the more it becomes cinematically beautiful, for him. That's one of the reasons why I didn't work with Argento, since I was against the slaughter of innocents. I mean, I knew there had to be a strong beginning in which cruelty rages on innocence, but then I wanted innocence to have the upper hand in the end. Take the little girl in *My Dear Killer*, it is she who draws the kidnapper's picture behind the mirror and thus condemns her own murderer...

That's an outstanding idea. It stays in your mind long after the credits...
That was Tonino's merit! As you know, after the first two weeks, usually producers start to cut corners and rush you, "Let's move on to the end," that's the way things go. Manolo [Bolognini] was putting us in a hurry, then. We were shooting in a villa—Villa Parodi Delfino in the Monte Mario district, which was often used in movies of the period—that has a striking-looking living room with that hole in the middle, which reminded me almost of a Greek amphiteater, or better still, an Anatomy theater. It was perfect for the final rendezvous, and I insisted with the art director that we use it, because I liked the affinity with a Renaissance-time Anatomy theater, where truth is dissected instead of a body. So, we both insisted with Manolo to rent the villa, and he obliged, but since it cost a lot he wanted us to finish shooting in a very short time—say, two days or so. But all the details—the mirror, the drawing, the killer hiding behind the armchair—required some more time to film. On that occasion, Tonino jibbed, refused to rush through the shoot and obtained from Manolo the necessary extra time to make things the way he wanted. And by the way, I did the drawing on the mirror—which had to be the "scream of the innocent," so to speak, rough but at the same time very expressive...

A striking image, which conveys the sense of the film and works as a perfect twist ending...
Moreover, if you listen to the killer's final monologue ... this always happens with my villains, they have always a very human motive. And the murderer, at the end of *My Dear Killer*, almost makes you sorry for him, because he's not some genius of evil or a complete nutcase, but a frustrated man, who nurtured hatred within himself for years. You know what I mean? I'm not justifying him, of course, but I tried to show that his motivations are complex. I think this was a result of my experience as a librarian at a mental hospital during university: it affected me deeply, and allowed me to grow a clinical approach to deviance. I realized that a villain is never just a dumb, banal villain, but he's got a deep reason for being like that. He wasn't born a villain! And you can find that especially in *Santa Sangre*...

So, back to the film's genesis…

I came up with this story about violated innocence. This little girl trusts her uncle, and what could there be more reassuring than your own uncle? Instead, he turns out to be a ruthless individual. The basic idea was that the blood of the innocent cries vengeance, and in the end the victim condemns her own murderer. So, what better than a little girl who leaves a drawing that accuses her killer? She cannot tell anyone, cannot write, but she can draw. I discussed the idea with Franco Bucceri and we built the movie around it. The mirror came later…

The mirror rolling down the hillside in slow-motion is another great image…

It rolls, and it shines … and the tramp notices it. Tonino loved the idea of the tramp. We characterized him like a thieving magpie, and that's why we chose the mirror. Besides being an emblematic, symbolic object in which the murderer sees his own reflection, what does a mirror do? It shines. It is a valueless object that nonetheless in the distance looks like a precious one, it calls for attention. And it *is* precious in the end, it is *invaluable*, because it contains the key to the mystery—the drawing!

How did you and Bucceri work together?

Franco had been an actor, and he had the sense of spectacle. We ran down the scenes together, and he had a sixth sense. If a scene convinced him, then it worked. He had the typical average taste, so to speak. I wrote *Santa Sangre* without him, because he would never "get" that kind of story. Had it been for him, he'd go on writing Lino Banfi flicks for the rest of his life, whereas I wanted to make other types of movies. What is more, soon after I started writing with Franco, my wife died, leaving me with my two young kids, five and nine years old, and I had to take care of them. So, Franco, who was single, did all that work—talking with producers, taking care of public relations, meeting people, and so on—that was needed in order to stay afloat in the movie biz. He weaved the network that served us to sell our scripts, while in the evening I had to go back home and stay with the kids. He also took care of all the prep work, discussing the contracts, and so on. I stayed home, wrote stuff, then we met once a week and discussed it. Then, when my kids grew up, I thought it was time for me to move on alone.

Was the script titled My Dear Killer *from the beginning?*

Yes. Franco and I used to do a cool thing for the period. We wrote a basic scenario, three or four pages long, something like a short story, with a cover I designed that was basically the film's poster. Since I'd done copywriting, I still liked to come up with ideas for movie posters. So, it looked like a book—let's say a digest—and we sent it to producers, sometimes with a tentative cast list. And usually it worked. We did the same with *My Dear Killer*, and sold it to Manolo Bolognini.

Did you go straight to Bolognini with the script then? Therefore you didn't need to look around for a producer…

Yes, because we had already worked with Manolo, and got along well. He used to say, "Guys, whenever you have something, bring your stuff to me first." He had an office in via Guido Reni, in the Trastevere district, on the first floor, and used to brag about not having any debts, because his office's window was at street level, and if he had had creditors, they could have jumped in—and actually when we paid visit to him, we used to knock at the window and come in, bypassing the secretary! "Hi Manolo, we brought you this!" Everyone used to do that way, Gigi Kuveiller [cinematographer Luigi Kuveiller], Franco Nero…. I remember once, we were chatting with Manolo, and Kuveiller showed up on his scooter just out of the window to say hello: "Hey, Gigi, what're you doin'?" "What do I know, we're shooting at the ghetto, the Professor's shootin' a movie…" The Professor was Elio Petri, Gigi used to call him like that. "What movie?" And Gigi, in Roman dialect, with his usual nonchalant, demistifying air, "What do I know, I don't understand a thing 'bout it, they're shootin' up and down this gate with Gian Maria…" The movie was *Investigation of a Citizen Above Suspicion* (*Indagine su un cittadino al di sopra di ogni sospetto*, 1970), and the scene was the famous gate scene, shot at Rome's synagogue…

So, how did Valerii come on board?

Tonino's was one of the names that came up and I immediately said ok. Because he didn't cost too much, and he was a cultured man, worth much more than his working fee. And Manolo asked me to be his assistant director—something which he usually did not want me to do because he said that I sided with the director instead than with the producer, since I was an *intellectual* (and imagine Manolo uttering the term with a openly disgusted tone…). "So you two'll understand each other…" he said. With Tonino, you could talk. And on *My Dear Killer* he immediately liked the story and took it to heart, didn't do any shilly-shallying. He immediately said it was a good story and he definitely wanted to make the movie.

Do you think it was the best choice? After all, for him it was quite a change of direction, after his first Westerns…

Yes, I think he wanted to try something different. He probably sensed that the Western was waning. Moreover, he'd been away from making movies for over a year I think, he'd made *A Girl Called Jules* which hadn't been a success, even though it got some good reviews. I recall he had to struggle quite hard with the book's author and the producer as well…. Anyway, he immediately understood the point of the story, the psychoanalytical references, and so on. He was not someone like, say, Ferdinando Baldi, who did understand those things but ultimately did not care about them since he only thought about moving on as fast as he could. If the producer told Baldi, "Make the movie in one week less than scheduled and I'll give you ten million," Baldi—or many other directors, for that matter—would do it. Tonino wouldn't. Because what he cared about was making a good movie.

Were there any changes in the finished film compared with the original script?

Actually there were a few things we had to leave out. We had tried to show how society was getting more and more corrupted by the need for money, wealth and so on…. What is more, there were also references to '68. In a scene, the commissioner goes to save his fiancée, played in the film by Marilù Tolo, who is doing a protest sit-in on the university roof. The scene was cut and she became a "normal" fiancée. By the way, the commissioner was to be played by Giancarlo Giannini, who accepted the role. But Manolo did not want him!

Why? Did he ask too much?

No. Manolo said he was a "thespian," and said it in his own contemptuous manner.

Were there any other changes to the script?

Yes, mostly concerning the commissioner, who has this ridiculous name, Peretti, which actually was a reference to Poirot … and he was constantly bullied by his superior. That was Salvo Randone's role, as Randone originally had to play the Chief of Police, then we turned him into his assistant…

Was it because the casting of a different lead in Giannini's place?

Indeed. When Manolo cast George Hilton, we realized that we had to characterize the commissioner a little differently. Originally he was a non-aligned, unconventional type. There was this scene about him photographed on the roof with his fiancée, ridiculed by the press, scolded by his chief … all this, Manolo demanded to be cut, saying, "Better not foster these things…" He was worried, you know, that the movie might come off as too political. So, the script was drained of all the references to the present day, in the name of a more traditional iconography.

How did George Hilton end up being cast in the lead?

It was Alfieri's distribution company Jumbo that was betting on Hilton. Jumbo had distributed some Western starring him that had done well at the box-office. So Alfieri persuaded Manolo to cast Hilton instead of Giannini, who was not that famous back then, at least among moviegoers. And Giannini was disappointed, because he really liked the character. Some years later—he just got nominated for Best Actor for *Seven Beauties* (*Pasqualino Settebellezze*, 1975, Lina Wertmüller)—I met him to discuss another movie, and he mentioned Peretti...

It was an unusual role for Hilton, playing the commissioner...
Yeah, an obvious case of miscasting! But he adapted well to the role, mind you—only, this dude wandering around, elegantly dressed, was not the Peretti we had conceived at first. With Giancarlo, we'd planned to make him ruffled, a bit slovenly—a type of detective that only came out later, think of Columbo, or better still, Elliot Gould's Marlowe in *The Long Goodbye* ... a loser, in short.

The character of Peretti reminded me of Ingravallo, as played by Pietro Germi in The Facts of Murder *(Un maledetto imbroglio, 1959), from Carlo Emilio Gadda's novel "Quer pasticciaccio brutto de Via Merulana"...*
Bravo! That was my literary reference, which unfortunately I made the serious mistake of mentioning. Everyone looked at me suspiciously, since it was too ... *intellectual*, you know. I vainly appealed to Germi's film as a precedent, but since *The Facts of Murder* didn't do well at all at the time, and Germi himself was mistreated, labeled as a Fascist and so on...

Anyway, Hilton was good in the movie, don't you think?
Yeah, he got away with it. And Tonino "curated" him a lot. At first he was a bit perplexed, because he thought George was too "cute-looking," but in the end it worked, and George was very helpful and committed to the role. We also helped him a little bit, having him wear mustache, you know, to make him a bit more believable...

Valerii cared about actors' performances, didn't he?
He did. Tonino's always been very good with actors, always cared about them a lot. He did lots of work with Dante Maggio, who played the dropout. He absolutely wanted him for the role, and the sister [Lola Gaos] as well. Tonino always spent quite some time with actors, speaking with them about the role.

Did Valerii contribute to the script?
Well, his name is in the credits, isn't it?

Yes it is. But there's also José Maesso, who didn't write a single line...
Of course, or else there would be no co-production deal, but Maesso didn't do absolutely anything! As for Tonino, he always took part in the writing, and wanted his name on it, having been a scriptwriter himself. Tonino gave us suggestions, tips, advices—good ones, I mean, so having his name on the script as well was also a sign of respect on our part.

You were also the assistant director on the film. How was that experience like?
Well, Tonino held me in high esteem as a scriptwriter, so I was a very privileged assistant director and he was always very nice towards me. Almost paternal, so to speak. Whereas the other assistant we had in Spain, Tonino bullied him!

Some scenes would be impossible to shoot nowadays. I mean, the ones involving the character of the uncle played by Alfredo Mayo...
Yes, the scene with that semi-naked child. Whereas at that time, the censors didn't object ... and it was very upsetting, because there was that hint of paedophilia, without actually saying anything, but just implying that the uncle liked little girls. Nowadays you couldn't do that.

And what about the Black & Decker murder scene?
Oh, that one with the cute Spanish actress [Patty Shepard, actually American-born]. The special effect is terrific—the final result on screen is the merit of the Spanish master of arms, whose name I don't recall, but I had the idea. You see, when playing soldiers and Indians with my two

kids, I used to make for them small knives out of tin foil, which looked like real blades, but of course when you stabbed someone the tin foil bent and did no harm. So, I remembered it while preparing the scene, and suggested that the master of arms build the Black & Decker blade out of tin foil. So, the blade is absolutely harmless, but while spinning it looks real—and behind it there was a small pump with stage blood. But at first we didn't tell the actress it was fake. And Tonino had lots of fun with that! (*laughs*)

Did he?

Yeah, he kept telling me, "Don't tell her, don't tell her!" (*laughs*) I wanted to reassure her, but he was right, because when we shot the close-ups of the fake blade near her face she looked *really* scared. And boy, was she! Tonino also wanted to do the whole sequence of the killer entering the girl's apartment and following her through the corridor in a long take. We did a lot of rehearsal because it was quite difficult, since we were shooting in a real apartment, an old Spanish house, which had a different planimetry compared to Italian houses, and at one point it was like the corridor forked—there she leans against the wall, runs to the other side, and so on. We tried with a hand-held camera, but it did not work, so we used a dolly.

On a totally different note, the sequence with the gloves at the window is a nice joke—was it in the script?

No, it came out impromptu, because there were those gloves hanging outside the kitchen window. I noticed them, "Hey, look at them, they look just like somebody's hands…" And so, *presto*! We shot it…

How long did it take to shoot the movie?

I think five, six weeks at most. But we didn't do location scouting beforehand, we did it when we arrived in Spain. Whereas the bunker scenes were filmed in Rome, at the De Paolis studios. It was a leftover set from a war movie, and we re-adapted it.

At one point, after My Dear Killer, *Valerii was attached to direct another movie you and Bucceri wrote,* The Master Touch, *starring Kirk Douglas, and also produced by Bolognini … eventually the film was made by Michele Lupo.*

Yes, it was Bolognini who wanted Michele Lupo, because he spoke English fluently, and Kirk Douglas needed an iron hand. With Lupo, not a leaf moved on the set. And he was a match for Manolo, which wasn't easy, believe me.

You and Valerii met again a dozen years later under very different circumstances. In retrospect, do you think that the experience with Sergio Leone on My Name Is Nobody *marked him?*

Absolutely, it was like a curse. The common voice was that he'd been ousted. Did you meet Sergio Leone?

No.

Sergio was a son-of-a-bitch like there are few, cinematically speaking I mean. He was a true movie animal, that is the best and worst thing you can have on a set. He knew everything there is to know about making movies. He was born on the set. You could not fuck up with Sergio. He could show up on the set and, with 150 people around him, spot the grip who was not doing his job well. "Hey, Richetti, what are ya doin' over there?" Know what I mean? He'd been second assistant, first assistant, he knew *everything*, and smelled a rat ten miles away. You didn't mess with Leone, no way. With Sergio, everyone on set ran like hell! And his right-hand man Claudio Mancini too, together they were two sons-of-bitches like you never heard of. Let me tell you about the first time I met Claudio Mancini. We were shooting a movie at Piazza Margana, in Rome, and all of a sudden this crazy drunk guy shows up, six-feet-six tall, bare-chested, full of tattoos, swirling a chain above his head, asking for money or else he's gonna kick our asses. So, all the crew stops, no one knows what to do. Then Claudio Mancini, who's just five-four , steps forward, picks up a stone and throws it right at the middle of the guy's forehead. Bam! Crazy guy goes down, knock out. And Claudio: "C'mon guys, back to work!" This was Sergio's production manager. To have someone like Claudio Mancini as your right-hand man, you must be really tough. Claudio would eat you alive, and Sergio ate him alive in turn. Claudio trembled before Sergio. Get the picture? So, Sergio put Claudio Mancini by Tonino's side to keep an eye on him on *My Name Is Nobody*. It was not a "soft" move. And the rumor spread, no one talked about it but everyone knew. And this is the kind of thing you don't recover from.

And yet after My Name Is Nobody *Valerii made* Go Gorilla Go, *which was a hit, then* Sahara Cross *which didn't do as well as expected, and then he spent several years without making a movie...*

Yeah, he had a contract with Cecchi Gori, then he tried different directions ... anyway, he had a reputation for being temperamental, which did not help. But Tonino was very good. He dedicated himself to the story, and did his best to make it stand out, whereas other directors simply bend the story to their capacities. Take Enzo Castellari: of course he's very good, but when you watch one of his films, the first thing you notice are Castellari's traits, his typical shots and camera angles, etc., whereas Valerii had the humility to adapt himself to the story. He understood the characters, the nuances of the script, and most of all he didn't resort to the genre's typical stylistic features.... Speaking of Castellari, he was the director initially attached to *Brothers in Blood*, did you know that?

Tell me more about it...

It was I who called Tonino, exactly because of his ability to adapt to the script, and to emphasize its nuances. For instance, the German actor, Werner Pochath, plays a transvestite, because in the story each of the main characters has to be humiliated and degraded—they're all Vietnam veterans who still carry the weight of the war upon themselves. So I said, "I'd like him to be a transvestite..." And Tonino: "Let's have him sing *Lili Marleen* and make a *Blue Angel*–type impersonation!" Because he was cultivated. Another director would simply have had Pochath play some nondescript slutty transvestite type...

So, let's step back to the project's genesis. Brothers in Blood *was made in the wake of the Vietnam war movies...*

Yes, but the core, if you think about it, is once again about innocence betrayed. A soldier is abandoned by his comrades, who carry the remorse with them for years ... so, ultimately it was about atonement. I was fascinated by the idea that each character lives his life until at one point they are all forced to come to terms with the skeleton in their closet. There is a famous Latin proverb, *Fortuna vitrea est; tum cum splendit, frangitur*, Fortune is like glass, as it shines, so it can smash. Which I think fits well with the theme of the film. And consider that the script was written before that American movie...

You mean Uncommon Valor, *starring Gene Hackman...*

That one, yes. The script underwent a long gestation, then I think it was eventually greenlighted after the success of the Hackman movie. Castellari was set to direct it. Actually, at first Enzo had been called to direct another movie I'd written, which started with an action scene he liked very much. A biker rides at full speed toward the American embassy in Rome, jumps over a barrier, runs across the stairs, enters the building and blows himself up!

Wow!

Enzo got crazy about the idea, and absolutely wanted to make the movie. Another scene had a bunch of kids play in a park, when a radio-controlled plane model turns up, circles around them and lands on the ground. The kids run around it ... and the plane explodes. Basically, it was about a bunch of terrorists blackmailing the city. The movie never got made, because it cost too much, and the production strayed into another picture directed by Sergio Martino, *Casablanca Express* (1989). So, Franco and I were asked to bring another script over, and we came up with *Brothers in Blood*, which Enzo didn't like as much as the previous one, moreover he had another commitment in the States. So the producer was looking for another director, and we said, "Why don't you call Tonino Valerii?"

You were also the assistant director, even though Franco Fantasia is credited in the movie...
Yes, but he was only the master of arms. Tonino hated Franco Fantasia from the moment he first saw him (*laughs*). When Franco showed up on the set wearing a scarf and shiny red dungarees, Tonino whispered, "Take him away from my sight! Does he think he's at the Olympic Games?" (*laughs*) What's more, Fantasia was fluent in English, he was agile, all things that got on Tonino's nerves. On top of that, he told Tonino, "I'd like to explain to you how I conceived the scene..." And Tonino, of course, would get pissed: "How *you* conceived the scene...?" You know, Fantasia was used to working with directors like Sergio Martino, who, when it came to shoot an action scene, let him have his way with it. Whereas Tonino wanted to know everything, and wanted to take part in it. Franco should have said, "Listen, what do you think if we do this scene this way?" and ask for his opinion. Tonino didn't like doing these stunt scenes very much in the first place.... Then, however, it was Rocco Lerro and Pietro Torrisi who practically took over from Fantasia as masters of arms, as they were more into that kind of war-action stuff.

Bo Svenson told me there were lots of money problems during the shooting...
Indeed. Actually, there had been some issues right at the beginning of the shoot, not because of money but because some idiot shipped the stage weapons to New York on a Lufthansa flight, and they were confiscated at the airport for a couple of days because at first the authorities thought those were real weapons. So, basically we spent the first week of shooting on the beach. Then, at a certain point the movie even halted since there was no money at all! The payments should have arrived by Friday, but didn't. The manager of the hotel *El Embajador* in Santo Domingo agreed to let us stay because I paid with my own credit card in advance for the whole crew, ditto for the plane tickets back to Italy. So, while we waited for the money to arrive, we survived that whole weekend with me gambling at the hotel's casino. The casino gave each customer a small free five-cigarette Marlboro packet: I corrupted the cigarette girl, stocked up the packages and distributed them to the crew so that at least we didn't have to spend money on cigarettes. And I gambled at *Rouge et Noir* with everyone's money, usually ending up with a twenty-dollar win that we used for small expenses. This, until the next Wednesday, when the money eventually arrived. Anyway, the producer had invented an absolutely brilliant cheat: the actors complained that the money had not been transferred to their bank accounts, but he sent over a telex with a copy of the wire transfer. So, apparently, the payment had been made. But if you checked the wire transfer in detail, you'd notice a slight mistake, say, in Martin Balsam's address, so that the payment had been delivered to his account, but the bank would not accept it and sent the money back because of that formal inaccuracy. It was brilliant, however after two or three weeks they uncovered the scam. And so the filming halted.

What happened then?
Eventually the producer had to fly to Santo Domingo, the next Wednesday, and carry the money personally, or else filming would stop for good. Thirty thousand dollars. We were filming in Santo Domingo with the help of the local secret service, but unfortunately someone overheard our general manager Maurizio Mattei mentioning that the producer would arrive the next day with a lot of money. And a hostess I'd become friends with warned me that some secret service guys were setting up a trap for him, to confiscate the money before the customs control. So, while Franco Fantasia was waiting in his hotel room, trembling with fear, me, Giancarlo Ferrando and some other crew member drove to the airport, and through this hostess friend we intercepted the producer. She went aboard and warned him to remain on the plane. Since the secret service people did not know his face, they stopped every single Italian tourist that came off that plane. Meanwhile we sneaked away from a back door and took him to the hotel. Then, once we

got to there safely, we decided to play a trick on Fantasia. We started running down the halls, yelling "They got the producer and all the money! They're coming to arrest us! Let's get away from here!" And Ferrando, that son of a bitch, started rolling his suitcase down the hall, as if he was on the run! (*laughs*) Poor Franco felt ill, he pictured all his money gone, pictured himself in jail ... in short, we had to take him to the E.R.! And on the ambulance, we were trying to make him feel better, "Franco, look! Here's the money..."

Did this hiatus in the filming affect the movie? I mean, were there scenes that had to be cut?
No, after all it was just a matter of a weekend.

What was Bo Svenson like?
He didn't sleep at all, did he tell you that? He claimed he'd been a Green Beret, and I must say that he gave us much advice during the shooting, about the gestures and techniques that soldiers employ. Anyway, I don't know whether it was for real or he just got too deep into the character, but he said that he'd developed PTSD, and stayed all night in the hotel lobby. And he ate only bananas, 10 or 15 a day, because he said potassium gave him energy ... and he used to do ambushes on Tonino...

What do you mean?
He wanted Tonino to discuss with him his character's motivations—in English. You know, Tonino spoke a little English, but wasn't fluent, and Bo Svenson—tall, musclebound, menacing-looking guy—used to stop him whenever he showed up in the lobby, "Toninooo, explain this to me, please!" So, Tonino used to send me on ahead when we came back to the hotel after dinner, to check if Bo Svenson was around. But after the third or fourth time, Bo realized our trick, and started doing ambushes on Tonino. I didn't find him in the hall, so I gave Tonino the green light, but Bo was waiting upstairs near his room, in the corridor, things like that! (*laughs*) So we came out of the elevator and, bang!, there was Bo Svenson waiting! (*laughs*)

What about the others? Martin Balsam, Peter Hooten, Werner Pochath...
Martin Balsam was a true gentleman. I met him again on a TV mini-series I did in Lanzarote with Ruggero Deodato, *Oceano* (1989), also starring Ernest Borgnine and Irene Papas. Werner was very nice. I first met him on the set of Umberto Lenzi's *Squadra selvaggia*, a.k.a. *I cinque del Condor* (1985). He was close friends with a German producer who paid one billion for each movie, which he then distributed and sold in Germany and other countries. And Werner put him in touch with people—he read scripts, and if he thought a script was good, he passed it on to his producer friend, who trusted him and put out the money. So I wrote a role specifically for him. Werner stayed six months in Italy and six in the States—he had an apartment in Corso Francia, in Rome, and sometimes he graciously let me stay in it. Anyway, through Werner I had put the Italian producer, Startari, in touch with the German one, who paid a generous advance for the movie, which meant an immediate profit for the Italian one since the actual budget was even lower than the advance. Anyway, the German guy got smarter, and at a certain point he just stopped sending the money. So, Startari had to collect the 30,000 dollars by himself to finish the picture. Anyway, in the end I don't know where the movie ended up, fact is it practically disappeared...

Indeed, it was not even released theatrically in Italy ... back to the cast, what can you tell me about Nat Kelly Cole?
He was Werner's friend. He, Werner and Peter were gay, all of them handsome, hefty, good-looking—did I tell you I used them as bait?

No you didn't! As bait?
Yeah! (*laughs*) After dinner we went dancing together, and since they were all great-looking guys, and in Santo Domingo's nightclubs there were plenty of female tourists from all over the world, they had all the women's eyes on them. I practically forced them to come with me, all

dressed smartly, Nat looking great in his all-white suit, and had them dance with the women I liked. They duly obliged, and were gallant but cold, since they couldn't care less about the lady. And then, when it was my turn to dance with her, I held her tight … and sometimes it worked! (*laughs*) Peter and Nat went, "Please Roberto, no dancing tonight…" And I, "Oh yes, dancing, or else you won't be shooting tomorrow!" (*laughs*)

There were some good action bits in the movie…
  Yeah, like the one where the truck is machine-gunned by helicopters and is blown up. By the way, we shot it with two cameras, one from the helicopter's point of view, shooting at the truck, and one placed on the road. I was in the truck with Elio Terribili, one of the special effects guys, and it was filled with nitroglycerine. We had to jump down from the truck, and at one point my sleeve got stuck in the handle—for a moment or two I thought I was going to blow up with the truck! I met Terribili again on the set of my own film *Dalla parte giusta* (2005). "Hey, Roberto, remember that time in Santo Domingo when we almost blew up?" And he almost blew us all up again, since for an explosion scene he put a load of napalm inside an apartment … the whole building almost collapsed!

Was it hard to find extras playing Vietcongs in Santo Domingo?
  Tonino sent me and cameraman Bruno Cascio, who then became a good cinematographer, to shoot the opening sequences in the jungle, but of course we needed to find Vietcong. I discovered that in Santo Domingo there was a huge fake passports business, and lots of Hong Kong citizens had taken on a new identity and residence in Santo Domingo in anticipation of the 1997 handover. So, we thought that if we had him wear Vietnamese cap and filmed him in medium shot, the average Chinese guy would look more or less like a Vietcong. So we took a trip to the Chinese neighborhood in Santo Domingo, and for five dollars a day we had our Vietcong extras. What is more, renting a helicopter in the U.S. cost 5,000 dollars a day or something like that, but luckily we found out that the Dominican Republic's army had purchased the helicopters employed by the U.S. army in Vietnam, after the war. They were perfect for the flashbacks, and cost us only 50 dollars an hour.

Do you think Valerii did a good job nonetheless, despite being saddled with a film he probably didn't care much about?
  He committed to it. He put his skills and his love of movies into it. Even at the beginning, when we were stuck waiting for the stage weapons, while everybody else was sunbathing at the hotel's pool or on the beach, Tonino and I went location scouting—I mean, it wasn't a holiday for him. And in the end shooting in Santo Domingo was a pleasant experience, despite those money problems. Surely more pleasant than on his following movies…

Especially on Il ricatto, *where he had an argument with Massimo Ranieri that cost him his job.*
  When Tonino loses his temper, it's easy to have the better of him. He just needed to have someone by his side on the set who made him reason. Someone who would tell him to calm down and think twice. Someone who cared about him and protected him. My impression is that whenever he got into trouble on the set, it was because he had somebody by his side who either couldn't stand him or wanted to put him into disrepute. I mean, what happened with *Il ricatto*, the fact that they did not call Tonino when they screened the rough edit—I mean, he was close friends with Sergio Montanari, the editor, did they really think he wouldn't get to know about it? What I mean is, the bad thing is that it seems there was a will to harm him as a professional. But in those moments, there needed to be someone who took him aside and allowed him to let off some steam. And he'd understand, and cool down immediately. But it didn't happen. And he did not deserve that.

So, Roberto, to end our conversation, you've been friends with him for over forty years now, what is your view on Tonino Valerii as a person?

You know, Tonino's always been a man of great grudges. If you behaved badly with him, you were marked … even after twenty years he'd say, "That asshole…!" Don't get me wrong—he's very generous, affectionate and all, but in this respect he's a very Abruzzi person. Tenacious in his loves and grudges alike, sometimes even bilious. For one thing, he never could stand people putting on airs—someone like him, cultured, well-read, could smell bullshitting one mile away. A very fond memory I have of him was when I did a scriptwriting course in Pescara, near his hometown, some years ago. Tonino attended all the lessons, but without telling me. I didn't spot him as he sat in the back row. He came for three days and just listened, and only at the end of the last lesson he came over and congratulated me, and it was a very generous, sincere and humble gesture, because he could have turned up earlier, and drawn all the attention to himself. And if I'd noticed him, I'd surely mention him and his work, and call him on stage. Others would have taken advantage of it, he didn't. And it's the kind of gesture that tells you more about the man than anything else.

(Phone interview, November 2015)

Saverio Marconi
(actor, *Go Gorilla Go*)

Go Gorilla Go was your feature film debut. What do you recall about the experience?

Well, the main problem is that so many years have passed (laughs). Being my first film, it was a never-ending emotion for me. It was my first time before the camera, as I had acted only on stage. I had just arrived in Rome—I lived in Florence, back then, worked with Turin's Teatro Stabile, and toured all over Italy—and decided to stay there, as of course there were many more working opportunities. It was May 1st, 1975. My agent immediately had me doing lots of auditions (which back then were simply called "meetings"), and after less than a month in Rome I ended up being cast in *Go Gorilla Go*. It was a turning point. I remember that back then there were no casting directors around, it was the director who examined portfolios, looked at actors' pictures and wanted to see them personally, immediately, and judge by himself if one had the right face or not. It was a good role, even though I was not the protagonist, so my agent scheduled a meeting with him, and within a matter of minutes he told me, "Yes, that's you!" And so it was—without any screen test or stuff like that. And of course I was very happy about that.

So it was an interesting character for you to play.

Yeah, I was Fabio Testi's reckless brother who wanted to help his brother but only managed to put himself into trouble.… Oh wait, there is a funny anecdote I recall about the meeting. Valerii chose me for the role exclusively for my face, which pleased me as it meant that my face would work on film. Then he asked me, "Do you have a car license?" "Of course!" "Can you drive a motorbike?" and I, without batting an eyelid, "Yes, sure!"—and neither did I have a license plate nor could I ride a bike. So, first thing I did after my meeting with Tonino, was to enroll at driving school! (laughs) That was my stab at method acting! (laughs) And then I showed up on the set on my cousin's bike, to show that I did indeed ride a bike. But then, in the movie, I didn't have any scenes on a bike, and you know why? I'd have to ride a Harley Davidson, which is an impossible bike to ride if you're not a big tall guy, which I'm definitely not (laughs) … I couldn't even keep the damn thing up on its wheels, as it was too heavy for me. And so they changed the scene on the spot: it was Fabio who drove the bike instead of me while I sat behind, as a passenger!

Were you familiar with Valerii's previous works?

Yes, he was already an established director. He had made very successful Westerns, box-office hits. So, being my first film, and being chosen on the spot by an important director, on a big production, meant having a great opportunity. A good way to start.

So, was Go Gorilla Go *a financially important production, budget-wise?*

It was a big movie. Many weeks of shooting, lots of locations, that incredible and complex scene on the train, masterfully shot.... I think it was a Cineriz movie, so we're talking about A-grade stuff. Cecchi Gori, the father, was the producer, he also showed up on the set one day...

How was it working with Testi and the other actors?

Well, most of my scenes were with Fabio, whereas I don't remember having scenes with Al Lettieri. In the final scene, where I was taken hostage there was the bad guy, the young one...

Antonio Marsina...

Yes! He played a weird character, black boots and, again, a motorbike...

How was it to work with Valerii?

He was a man who was absolutely in control of what he was doing. A filmmaker who knew his job to perfection. And I think *Go Gorilla Go* was Fabio Testi's most important film, notoriety-wise. He was at the peak of his fame—I mean, he had done beautiful films earlier, such as *The Garden of the Finzi-Continis*, but that was his big break, commercially speaking.

Then you and Testi worked together again on another movie, Lucio Fulci's Contraband...

Yes, after *Go Gorilla Go* there was a two-year hiatus as I worked mostly on stage, and then came my first big picture as a lead, the Taviani brothers' *Padre padrone*. Then I met Fabio again on the set of Fulci's film. A very nice person, and when we met again I had already done a number of films—the Tavianis' *Il prato*, Pontecorvo's *Ogro*, Comencini's *Voltati Eugenio*, Squitieri's *Razza selvaggia*—so I was less intimidated, so to speak.

Did you have a chance to know Valerii better outside the set as well?

Not really. But he was always very nice with me. There was a scene where I beat another guy in a shack, an actor who then committed suicide...

Ernesto Colli...

Him! He played a caretaker in cahoots with the bad guys. Anyway, it was a very violent scene, and since I was totally inexperienced and I was not used to fake a fistfight, Valerii had me replaced with a double. So it was another guy who ended up beating poor Colli...

It was a very violent movie. It even got a V.M. 18 rating...

There were rather gruesome scenes, for the period. Today, it would probably make people laugh, considering what we are used to see in movies, on television... (laughs) ... it is much, much, much worse!

What is your opinion of Go Gorilla Go, *compared to the other crime films that were produced in Italy in the 1970s?*

Well, this was an A-grade crime film, surely above average. In fact it did very well at the box-office. And Valerii was a valuable filmmaker, he made commercial films, but very good ones. You know, back then there was this distinction, on one side the commercial directors, and on the other side the artists, so to speak—the Tavianis, Fellini...

I know what you mean. And Valerii's films were commercial pictures, but quite good quality-wise, not despicable at all...

Indeed. A very good movie, especially if we compare it with those produced nowadays. The world's changed, there is another way of seeing things, especially in Italy. But take the Italian films shown at the Cannes Film Festival this year [Matteo Garrone's *The Tale of Tales*, Paolo Sorrentino's *Youth* and Nanni Moretti's *Mia madre*]. I've seen two, and didn't find anything special in them...

(Phone interview, October 2015)

Pasquale Rachini (left) and Tonino Valerii (right) on the set of *A Reason to Live, a Reason to Die!* (courtesy Pasquale Rachini).

Franco Nero
(actor, *Sahara Cross*)

What is your personal recollection of Tonino Valerii?

He immediately gave the impression of being a veracious, down-to-earth type. Maybe it was because of his heavy Abruzzo accent, but the first impression was such. Then, actually, he was a real gentleman, intelligent and sensible—I mean sensible also in the way he directed actors. He was never prevaricating; on the contrary, he was perfectly willing to follow other people's advice, which does not happen very often on the set. We shot *Sahara Cross* for a good part in the Tunisian desert, but we crossed the length and breadth of Tunisia, pushing up to Djierba. Very pleasant shooting. There had been created a certain atmosphere of complicity, and this is essential for the success of a movie.

And the cast helped, didn't it?

Of course. There was Michel Costantin, who at the time was often cast in Italian production; and Pamela Villoresi, who was very young but already divided herself between movie sets (she had just worked with Jancsó in *Private Vices, Public Pleasures*) and the stage, with Giorgio Strehler[1]; but the one I remember most fondly is the great Antonio Cantafora, a.k.a. Michael Coby, an incredibly nice Calabrian guy with whom I had lots of fun during the whole shooting. He is the one I immediately sympathized with the most on that set. And there was also Pietro Valsecchi, then just a boy who dreamed of having his big break as an actor. No one would ever imagine he would become Italy's most successful producer, thanks to Checco Zalone's films…[2]

Sahara Cross was the first Italian film where the Steadicam was employed...

And this is further proof of Valerii's open-mindedness. He just loved to experiment; the Steadicam allows an amazing freedom during shooting, you can literally stalk the actors with it, and he used it on many beautiful sequence shots that make the movie outstanding on a technical point of view.

Still, it did not do well at the box-office...

Yes, but it does not mean it wasn't a good film. Fact is, it was badly distributed: one thing is if you release a movie during Christmas holidays in 1500 copies, like with Zalone's last movie, another is if you put it out in late summer, where it's still too hot for people to lock themselves in smelly movie theaters with no air conditioning and wooden seats—because, remember, back then there were no multiplexes!—and in a ridiculous number of copies. And unfortunately that was the fate of *Sahara Cross*, which is puzzling since Valerii was a successful director, coming from two box-office hits in a row such as *My Name Is Nobody* and *Go Gorilla Go*. And it's a shame, because it was a top-notch action film, which works wonders still today.

(Phone interview, January 2016)

Pasquale Rachini
(cameraman, *A Reason to Live, a Reason to Die!*, *Go Gorilla Go*; director of photography, *Il ricatto*)

When and where did the shooting for A Reason to Live, a Reason to Die! *take place?*

It started in Rome, at Elios' Western village in via Tiburtina, in April 1972. Since it was a Spanish co-production, shooting took place for the first three weeks in Rome, and then five more weeks in Spain. I was the cameraman in Rome and Eduardo Noé was the cameraman in Spain. Valerii insisted a lot for me to shoot all the movie, but since I already had other working commitments I had to renounce.

Was it a difficult shooting?

Not particularly, even though Valerii was very demanding regarding both the technical part and the ending: the camera was placed on a dolly or on tracks in almost every shot.

What was your relationship with the cinematographer, Alejandro Ulloa?

Very collaborative and sympathetic, since he was a nice person and a great professional. He often worked in Italy on co-productions.

Valerii told me he had some issues on the set with James Coburn, whereas there was a very good feeling with Bud Spencer.

As for the filming in Rome, to which I was present, relationships were professional and quiet with both actors. As for the shooting in Spain, I honestly don't know.

What is your take on the film, compared to the Westerns made in Italy in the same period?

I saw it again recently on TV and found it quite a good movie with great action, great actors and a good story. Certainly above average compared to other Italian Westerns.

You and Valerii teamed up again in 1975 on Go Gorilla Go. *This was a challenging film, not least because of the complex action scenes...*

Indeed, from a technical standpoint it was a very demanding job, with lots of locations and plenty of action. The elevator scene was shot live, in a palace in Rome, in via Cola di Rienzo, by shooting the exterior of the booth against a "Blue Screen" and all the elevator bottom shots aside. Then we integrated them via special effects with the shots featuring actors. The assault on the train was all filmed live too, by shooting the train from the car driving at full speed and vice versa. I recall that while shooting the train scene, since I was the camera operator, I was tied outside the wagon on several wooden planks, and a rope that secured me to the train. At a certain point the production manager showed up, yelling: "If you fall off the train we're all going to jail!"

The director of photography on Go Gorilla Go *was Mario Vulpiani, with whom you worked on a number of important movies (*The Grand Duel, La chienne, La Grande Bouffe, How to Kill a Judge*…) …*

Mario Vulpiani was a great cinematographer. Very instinctive. He did not like to follow preordained settings. Likeable person, and a friend for all his collaborators.

As the director of photography on Il ricatto, *how did you deal with this TV miniseries? Did Valerii ask for a particular type of lighting?*

I approached *Il ricatto* as if I was making a very long movie. During location scouting Valerii and I discussed the kind of photography he wanted: it was going to be shot a bit like an English movie, with a careful choice of the exteriors in the Neapolitan setting and context. Despite the tighter schedule we managed to do a thorough job, I think. We were finishing shooting the second part when the management at Reteitalia sent us their congratulations, and the request to make a second series.

What happened during the shooting, which led to Valerii being replaced by Ruggero Deodato?

Valerii and the production broke the contract by mutual consent, he was not fired. The problem arose because the Neapolitan environments Tonino had chosen had to be changed because of logistic issues and lack of permits, and Tonino was not happy with several of the new ones. So, there were arguments between Valerii and the producers, and since they had two different visions, they eventually parted by mutual agreement, and Deodato took over directing.

Beatrice Ring and Tonino Valerii posing in front of the huge Japanese poster for *Shatterer*, during the promotional tour in Japan. The pic was taken by Beatrice's then fiancé, film director Deran Sarafian (courtesy Beatrice Ring).

What are Valerii's qualities as a filmmaker? And on the human side, what are his strengths and weaknesses in your opinion?

Valerii's best quality is preparation and the organization of work; in the morning he already had in mind the sequence he would shoot, shot by shot, and this was very helpful when working with the crew and the actors. His best qualities are the kindness and friendship with all the crew members and the actors. As for the weaknesses, he is very stubborn and obstinate, and if he set his mind on something it was extremely difficult to have him change it, and sometimes he turned out to be a bit touchy.

(Email interview, October 2015)

Beatrice Ring
(actress, *Shatterer*)

How did you get involved in Shatterer? *If I'm not wrong it was made around the same time as* Graveyard Disturbance *(a.k.a.* Una notte al cimitero*)?*

Around 1987, I started working as an actress and I had an agent, and I was very successful right away for a series of lucky meeting and interviews. I guess once you put your foot in the door everything happens. So, I worked for a movie with Deran Sarafian called *Interzone*, and right after that, I worked on *Sicilian Connection* (which was the script's original title) and Lamberto Bava's *Graveyard Disturbance*. It all happened really fast, back-to-back, one movie after the other. In fact, some people on one set worked on the other one, like make-up artists and directors of photography and crew. So, when I did the interview for Tonino Valerii, I just finished Bava's movie. I actually got some nice compliments from the crew for being a hard worker.

I understand you were not the first choice for the role, weren't you?

Yes, it's true. Originally, they were casting another actress, a French young woman working in Rome. Her and I were always competing when it came to parts and casting, we had similar looks and accents. My agent told me that after I signed the contract. He said, "you were the second pick because her agent made a mistake, negotiating her fees too much and it made them mad," so that they hired me. I was also at a time in my career where my fees were very decent, so I wasn't cheap either, but I guess the attitude of the actress and agent conflicted with what they were looking for. I can't thank them enough for the mistake because the opportunity to work on this movie, and later one the VIP journey to Japan and tour, was an experience that I will never forget for the rest of my life. It was extraordinary!

Shooting took place mostly in Sicily...

They did some of the filming in England with Toshirô Mifune, whom unfortunately I never met. But being a huge fan of Mifune, just the idea of him working on the same set as me was incredible. We then set tent in a hotel in Mondello, and I remember that hotel quite vividly because when we got there, the people working in the hotel told us that Tom Cruise had come to visit, and a lot of American movies had been shot there. Quite a beautiful little town to film in, and the site is absolutely in gorgeous, especially in winter—no tourism.

Did it go on smoothly?

Well, the owner of Uanchi Corporation passed while we were shooting the movie, and it interrupted somehow the schedule because Kôji Kikkawa had to fly back to Japan for the funerals, and he was very, very sad about it. I believe he was very close to this gentleman who had a terrible disease and died of a very painful death. I remember people cried on the set at the news. For the rest, the shooting went on smoothly. I remember one day, I got extremely sick with food poisoning, and I felt very bad about it since I didn't want to interrupt the shoot. I had slept two hours only, felt very nauseated, arrived at make-up, at 7 a.m., and told the make-up artist in tears that I couldn't breathe in the room. I remember he tried to accommodate me so much, he was very very nice, he put on a fan ... long story short, one by one different people on the set came and gave me advice on how to feel better, and so they ended up giving me so much emotional support, that I got myself together to make it all the way to the set, but I was very, very unhappy—I mean, food poisoning is extremely debilitating, let alone walking to the set, saying lines and working with other 50 people.... Well, within an hour that we started the shoot, the assistant director ran behind a bush and started being sick. Five minutes later the grips also started to get sick to his stomach, so following two or three people getting sick, the day was called off. We went back home and I was so relieved—we probably had water contamination in the hotel. Otherwise, I have to say, it was a very professional, very pleasant and organized shoot. Costume was super, make up people made me look beautiful in every scene...

The film was an Italian-Japanese production with a big budget. And the Japanese co-star was Kôji Kikkawa, who was very popular in his home country.

Kôji Kikkawa, well, he was not English proficient—he had a strong accent. He was a huge celebrity in Japan, and was treated like royalty, was extremely attended to. But he was having a hard time mixing up with the Italian crowd, both production and actors, and I saw that right away. I thought to myself, "This poor guy, he is miserable." No one spoke Japanese, and he had production people who visited him from Japan once in a while, who would assist him. Actually, the director's assistant, Mario [Mario Miyakawa] was half-Italian and half-Japanese, so he was able to communicate with him. I thought Kôji was a very nice fellow, and I would go up to him and chat up, and go over the scene, which was a bit complicated 'cause he wasn't really fluent in English, plus he wouldn't memorize his lines too well, so Tonino made us rehearse together many times, days prior to shooting our scenes together, and he warmed up to me, which made me very happy. I knew I could translate, and help him out any time he needed. The scenes we had together also required quite a level of—not intimacy, 'cause the scenes were very nice and not anything indecent, but...

You mean the romantic scene on the beach? I read Valerii shot it as a homage to a famous scene in Lelouch's A Man and a Woman *(1966)...*

Yes, that one, with the steadicam shot spinning around us, while we kiss. It was so cold, and I was in such great shape (*smiles*), how wonderful it is to be young and healthy...

What about the other actors?

I remember vividly one of the Mafia actors, very charming man, quite older than me—long black hair, charismatic, a chain smoker.. I don't remember his name, but one day he told me how he jump started his acting career. He was from Naples, and he was doing time in prison, and a celebrity actor came to see a play that the inmates put together. At the end of the play, he was picked him out and this celebrity told him, "when you're done doing time, come see me." And that's what he did. He went to see him, and that man was Vittorio De Sica's father, who generously gave his time to men in prison. Beautiful story, but it kind of made me nervous, because, (*laughs*) I never asked him why he was in jail for, but he played a Mafia guy really well—he was a natural (*laughs*).

Were you familiar with Valerii's films, such as My Name Is Nobody*?*

Yes, definitely, but I wasn't aware that he had directed the movie with Henry Fonda and Terence Hill. I mean, my understanding of his background was more of, he had worked with famous celebrities, and I didn't think *he* was a celebrity. Of course that's a terrible thing to say. I think he was a good director, and the shoot was pretty straightforward. Quite simple. I played a superficial character, this love interest of this Japanese young man visiting Sicily and fighting the Mafia. Our dialogues were not deep, there was nothing deep about our characters...

What was Valerii like on the set?

Tonino was a very kind, soft spoken man, he never lost his temper on the set like some directors. A sophisticated, educated intellectual. I understood from his wife that 48 hours prior to beginning the shoot, Tonino was having bad stomach cramps. She revealed in a heart to heart talk that it was always the case when he started a shoot, but that after a couple of days, he'd be just fine. He was a nervous wreck—he obviously had a lot of responsibility and was feeling quite nervous about filming with this huge crew. He was quite amicable and kind and we had room for our own artistic expression if we needed to change something.

Did he care about the actors' performances, or was he mostly interested on the technical side when filming a scene?

I don't remember him directing me much on the set. I think we were all quite comfortable with our parts. It wasn't a very complicated script. However, since *Sicilian Connection* was mainly an action film, a lot of the effort went into the action and the stuntmen. So, he was more interested in getting good footage, and being on time and budget, like most directors are. I was already carrying my camera with me then—I got a Pentax, which I was very attached to, and did lots of photography everywhere I went, including on set. I remember an episode when we arrived in this beautiful square in Mondello, with these fountains and statues in front of a big building, and the set was about to get organized. I pointed to the side of this place and said to Tonino, "Look, if you filmed from behind the small balcony columns, wouldn't that be beautiful, you could put a dolly there" and he looked at it and said "Yes, yes…" kind of distractingly. I had seen that shot on a previous documentary I worked on, Cortili di Roma, the photography was elaborated and magnificent. One hour later I came back on the set with the other actors, and they had a dolly behind the columns that were overseeing the scene, and the fountain. That's where one of the car chases was being filmed. And I was so happy because I'd suggested that angle. So I asked him later, "so you liked my idea?!" And he looked at me horrified: "What idea?" I felt betrayed that he had not acknowledged it at all, but I guess these things happen.

What are Valerii's qualities as a filmmaker, compared with the other directors you worked with?

Tonino Valerii is really a technical director. Of all the directors I worked with, starting with Nino Manfredi, who took over from Alberto Lattuada on *Nudo di donna*, Deran Sarafian is definitely the first person I would be grateful to for all his directing help. He was the one with which I had the deepest transformation as an actor, and also as a person, because he took me to America with him and I got involved in film-making. You know, 20 years ago my English was terrible and I could understand half of it, let alone have any training in film. I never thought I was going to become an actress when I was young, it all really happened by mistake. So, working with Deran Sarafian was a complete transformation, and a very quick fast-forward into acting method and meeting the right people and getting a lot of help. I think on the opposite end, Lucio Fulci was zero help with acting, as you probably heard from others. I really was not fond of him, and him of me, couldn't care less for his mean stunts on the set to actors, he was very abusive. Lamberto Bava was very correct, a very polite gentleman, and Aldo Lado, well, he was definitely interesting—a challenge to work with, because he would push you. And the movie we did, *Rito d'amore* (a.k.a. *Ritual of Love*, 1990) was very intellectual, philosophical, there was a psychological development—it went into obsession, OCD, masochism … he really worked with actors, we prepared the scenes for weeks and weeks…. It was definitely dark, and because it was a true story it affected me on a very deep level. I actually quit working on film after Lado's movie, as you may know. On Francesco Rosi's *The Palermo Connection* (*Dimenticare Palermo*, 1990) I had a very small part. He was very kind to give me a chance to work with him. I only had one line, and I took classes, and read a book on Frederick II of Swabia, because I wanted to be so prepared…! And I got Rosi very upset, without meaning to. I mentioned something about how he was breaking his reputation of being realist as a director, because we were working on a set, and the tomb of Federico II was actually somewhere else: he was using another tomb and I was wondering why he hadn't gone through the trouble of driving an hour from there and shoot in the right place. And he got very mad at me—he didn't even answer my question, and had me kicked out of the set! Anyway, Tonino was of all directors, the kindest one. A real gentleman. I have a lot of respect for director who work in tandem with their wives. It's a character quality.

Back to Shatterer, *are you happy with your performance in the film?*
Actually, I look back and I think that I could have done so much better. I'm quite embarrassed about my performance because you can see that I'm about to laugh with Kôji. We were good friends and laughed a lot together. In general, it's very hard for me to look at myself on the screen, I try to avoid it as much as possible.

And what is your opinion of Shatterer *overall?*
It is really hard to judge a movie 30 years later, because you have to consider what were the possibilities in the days that it was done, what was the audience like, what were the other kind of movies were done at the time. You know, obviously back then, action films were everything. People liked to see the Mafia, the kidnappings, those were the days of movies like *The Godfather* and *Once Upon a Time in America*, Henri Mancini and John Williams soundtracks ... it's hard to compare, you know. Nowadays film-making has become very difficult, there is a huge separation between what's being produced and made for TV and what's actually able to make it all the way to a theater distribution which lasts only a very few weeks across the States, and those are only big budgets. Everything else is for television nowadays, so it's mainly based on if you can hire big names, and the names will drive the sales and distribution to ensure the investment. So back then, this co-production between Italy and Japan was not a gamble as big as it would have been today. I think the Toshirô Mifune's name was pulling the distribution for it and the stunts and chase were making it suitable for TV distribution—my guess. But, sadly, the end the movie didn't do well at all.

Indeed, it was not even released theatrically in Italy, and went directly to TV...
...and when it came out in Japan there was a big disappointment from the audience, because the main actor of the movie, Andy Forest, had done such a fine job with his performance, that I think he took the movie over. That's how the response was in Japan, I heard.

Let's talk about the promotional tour in Japan with Deran Sarafian, Valerii and his wife—how was the experience like?
It was incredibly amazing to be invited, and when I look back at this trip I took in my early twenties, it was one of the most amazing experiences of my life. Uanchi Corporation graciously invited myself and Deran Sarafian, to whom I was engaged to, and we were staying in a suite at the Imperial Hotel in Tokyo. I was given an interpreter and a driver. Everything was taken care so beautifully, so I just can't express enough my gratitude at Uanchi Corporation. Dalila Di Lazzaro was actually playing a much bigger part than me, so when I got the invitation to go to Japan I was very surprised and happy, and also a little scared—I was 21, so the idea of going to the other side of the world was a little frightening but at the same time very exciting. I was greeted downstairs at the hotel lobby by a series of young fans who were neatly sitting by the side of the hallway, waiting for me. When I went to dinner and they spotted me, one young girl said—while everyone else lined up behind her, "Beatrice Ring?" and I thought she wanted me to sign an autograph, but instead she asked me if she could shake my hand. She looked very happy to do so—and everybody else did the same!

So I have the fondest memories of this trip, as I had a chance to live in an environment that was much ahead of us—the Japanese are so gracious and kind and respectful, we should only learn from them. Moreover, I attended Kôji Kikkawa's concert, and there were several TV stations in Japan that invited us for the promotion of the movie. The Japanese obviously adored Kôji Kikkawa and I remember that the public wanted to know if we had a real love affair in life because we smiled and giggled and were quite close—we were good friends by now—and Kôji smiled and said, "Almost boyfriend and girlfriend." And it made everybody very happy because for some reasons, that was something they would have liked.

The other fond memory that I have is that one day I ran into Gary Busey—whom I knew from working in the United States with Sarafian's family—in the Imperial's Hotel restaurant, and it was quite a shock because three weeks earlier, I was on his side on another set, in the United States. He gave me a big hug and said, "Beatrice, do you wanna meet this famous actor?," and he said the name. I said "Sure," and I thought that he wanted to introduce me to someone, because my posters were all over town. And he said, "But do you know who he is?" and I said, "No, no idea," and he goes, "He's really a famous American actor, actually he's Australian," "Yes, OK, I'll meet him,"—you know, I just wanted to make Gary happy. So he took me to his table at the restaurant, and he was sitting with…. Mel Gibson! And Mel Gibson was covered in freckles, with crazy long curly hair, and he gave me this giant smile, we shook hands—we compared movies and budgets right away. He asked me how long I was in Japan for, and I said two weeks, while they were staying there just four days, so I was coming across like this big star, and didn't realize that was Mel Gibson touring for *Lethal Weapon*! Was I impressed? No, because I had no idea who he was. Am I impressed today, 30 years later? No, because I think he's come across unpopular and produced movies that created a lot of problems for Jews around the world. You have to use talent and film prudently, and entertain and make believe, like Tonino Valerii's movies: labors of love.

(Audio interview, November 2015)

Bud Spencer

(actor, *A Reason to Live, a Reason to Die!*)

A Reason to Live, a Reason to Die! is a film that stands out quite considerably from the other works you starred in, in the early Seventies, and offered you the chance to play a character with dramatic implications, as was the case the same year with Carlo Lizzani's Black Turin *(Torino nera)…*

I have to thank Tonino for this. I am very attached to the character of the tramp, because it gave me the chance to do something different from the characters who allowed me to win the viewers' hearts. Not only for the dramatic implications, mind you, but also because of the way to use body language: think of the scene where the vagabond improvises a dance in the middle of the street, to save the character played by James Coburn, and yelling that the war is over. I think it is a beautiful scene. But the whole film was an exciting experience, even challenging because there was not much time for shooting, and we had to go all out to do well. On top of that, I had the opportunity to work with magnificent actors, such as James Coburn and Telly Savalas. *A Reason to Live, a Reason to Die!* is a beautiful film, and I am proud it has been chosen for the Venice Fim Festival retrospective on the Italian Western.

How was your relationship with your co-stars? I know that there flew some sparks between Coburn and Valerii…

Well, I don't know about that, but I can tell you that between us actors the atmosphere was idyllic. Coburn and Savalas were very nice to me. First of all, I must say that back then I spoke very little English, and so I had to learn my lines by heart according to their sound. I remember that Savalas and I had an extended dialogue scene together, and I had to say a rather long line, I don't remember which one. Well, I was pretty nervous, let me tell you! So, when my turn came, I rattled through the whole *spiel* I had learned, and thank God I made no mistakes, so at the end Telly says, "Thank you, Bud!" And I, "You're welcome!" Which was the only other phrase I knew in English (laughs).

Another memorable sequence is the final slaughter in the fort…

It was all true! I mean, if you remember the film, I had to run across the courtyard while all around me there were cannon shots, people killed each other, and so on. Well, you had to be pretty careful, because the explosive charges could really hurt you seriously, and I mean it! That was another way of making movies, and I must say I was lucky to work with real professionals.

What are your memories of Benito Stefanelli, who also played a role in the film?
An extraordinary stuntman, and an exquisite person. He was also an accomplished actor.

In a celebratory article which appeared in the catalogue published on the occasion of the retrospective dedicated to Bud Spencer and Terence Hill at the Assisi festival, in 2005, Valerii told an amusing anecdote about you cooking spaghetti on the set...
All true. Whenever I went to do a movie, I brought my own personal chef, Antonio, who was also my driver. And a huge supply of spaghetti! (laughs). So, when shooting the scenes in Almeria, we agreed that, just before lunch break, Tonino, Antonio and I exchange a coded signal, which meant something like: "We're almost done, start cooking the pasta!" (laughs). And when Tonino called the break we ran to my trailer, where a steaming plate of spaghetti was waiting for us...

What is your opinion on Valerii as a filmmaker?
Ah, Tonino is extraordinary, you write it down! He is one of those directors one no longer finds his like today. Just see the way he shoots, the way he moves the camera, the way he has his actors give their best. We have developed a beautiful friendship, and still see each other once in a while. I am and will always be grateful to him. It's men like Tonino that cinema needs.
(Phone interview, April 2008)

Bo Svenson
(actor, *Brothers in Blood*)

How did you get involved in Brothers in Blood?
My Italian agent Attilio de Santis (now deceased). I believe it was more or less in the same period as *Heartbreak Ridge*...

I heard it was a troubled production...
Filming went on much longer than expected because the producers didn't have enough money to make the movie. It was a nightmare, because my agent and the producers had lied to me about the money and I wasn't getting paid.

Was it hard to film the action scenes?
Everything was hard and difficult because of the lack of money. I had to pay for my own hotel and flights—I even paid for the rental of the North Vietnamese uniforms and Viet Cong clothes.

What was Valerii's attitude like on the set? And your working relationship with him?
Valerii was a most wonderful gentleman, a most wonderful man and director. The relationship was awful, though! I unfairly blamed him for the production difficulties. It wasn't until years later that I learned that he, too, had been lied to and that he wasn't responsible for the production.

Did he care about the actors' performances, guided you, etc.?
Absolutely! He was a consummate artist and a most wonderful person. It's too f-ing bad that he was in this situation that wasn't his fault and beyond his control—and that I wrongly held him responsible. I would have liked to have worked with him in a "real" film, not this "make it up as we go" situation. Tonino was an artist who cared equally about the emotional contents of the scenes and the film as he did the technical.

What are Valerii's qualities as a filmmaker, and as a person, in your recollection?
Tonino was a lovely person who, like some others in the group, myself included, would have been better off working on a film for which there was sufficient money and time with which to

tell the story. A lovely man, an artist who might have been better off if he had been living and able to make films in Italy's 1940s and 50s.

What was your view on the character you played, the embittered Vietnam veteran Steven Elliot Logan a.k.a. Steel?? Did you add any particular elements to it?
 I seem to recall that I didn't care for the character as written. I am a former U.S. Marine and war veteran and have a feel for the realities of being one, so the screenplay written in Italy by someone with zero combat experience needed work. I did what I could to make the scenes realistic. And I did what I could out of respect for Tonino and those who had put up the money for the film.

Was there any improvisation on the set?
 Oh, yes. The script was not very good so we did what we could to overcome it.

There is an amusing scene where you ask for direction to an elderly lady on a chair, in a Santo Domingo slum, and she just can't stop laughing. Was it an impromptu moment added on the spot, or simply the old lady could not keep a straight face and the scene was kept as it was?
 I don't remember this—and I was not drinking or high. Perhaps it was as you say—or perhaps there was no more film for the cameras…

The torture scene in the film is surprisingly tame—no grisly close-ups or stuff like that, it cuts to the aftermath with you having several pins stuck on your cheek…
 Again, probably a lack of resources like time or film for the camera. I actually don't remember whether we shot more footage of that one.

On Brothers in Blood *you worked again with Peter Hooten, and the cast also featured the German actor Werner Pochath, plus Nat King Cole's adoptive son, and Martin Balsam in a special participation. What are your memories about working with them?*
 Peter Hooten might be a nice person but also one of the weirdest. I remember meeting Marty on the set, shaking hands with him, after which we were shaking our heads, lamenting the situation we were in. Werner Pochath might have been a happier person if he had come out of the closet and been comfortable being accepted as gay. Kelly Cole, too, would have been a happier person if he had come out of the closet; his mother became a friend of my family and we shared her sadness when Kelly died.

What is your opinion of Brothers in Blood? *What are its strong and its weak points, in your view?*
 I haven't seen the film—even though I own the distribution rights to North America. The film's strong point is that it got made, one of the weaker points is that the voices of Martin Balsam and Bo Svenson are not their voices.
 (Email interview, October 2015)

Pamela Villoresi
(actress, *Sahara Cross*)

Around the same time as Sahara Cross *you worked with committed auteurs such as Miklós Jancsó and Marco Bellocchio, whereas Valerii's film did not have many artistic claims, but was rather demanding from a physical point of view, being shot all in exteriors in Tunisia…*
 Yes, it was a commercial film, but dignified and with good professionals. We shot a lot of scenes in the desert, and on location we stayed as guests at an oil field. It was a beautiful experience. We shot it in spring, and I was there for about three weeks. I remember the salt desert, the *chott*, and the optical illusions: a small clod of mud, raised by a jeep, in the distance looks like the wall of an old and mysterious city. And the more you come close by, the more it vanishes. In the desert you learn lots of things. Desert captures you, it forces you to keep a more objective

view compared to your ordinary life, invites you to silence. Desert is utter beauty. And fatigue never scared me: still today I practice sports at least one hour a day.

Your character in the film, Nicole, is an idealistic terrorist who fights against an oil corporation, and in the end turns out to be less cunning than her antagonists. What was your view on the character?

Nicole, like Antigone in the Greek tragedy, is the typical adolescent who is not yet able to combine her ideals with the sense of society and reality. She is clean—cleaner than the protagonists, actually—but she can be infinitely dangerous to herself and to others.

Did you get along with Valerii on the set?

Tonino was a kind and smiling man. He knew how to direct the actors with politeness and education. It is a rare gift.

And what about Franco Nero and the other actors…?

I went along very well with all of them. They were all extremely good professionals. There was also a very young Pietro Valsecchi, I think in his film debut. He later became an important producer, and did lots of important TV series: *R.I.S.—Delitti imperfetti,* *—Distretto di polizia,* *—Ultimo,* and Claudio Caligari's final film *Non essere cattivo…*

Were you following the script closely or were there any changes due to extra circumstances?

As far as I recall, the script was respected throughout. It may be that a few lines were adjusted on the spot, but we're talking minimal things.

Sahara Cross *is noteworthy for its pioneering use of the Steadicam, with many fluid long takes. Was it difficult for you actors to adapt to it?*

Not at all—actually, it was quite fun, and the locations and actions lent themselves to the use of the Steadicam. And then there were helicopters, people running and chasing each other amid the dunes … the dolly was certainly not the more apt instrument.

In your opinion, why didn't it have the expected commercial success?

I saw *Sahara Cross* when it came out, many years ago. I am always very critical toward my acting, and of course I thought that some parts of it I could have done better, even though now I don't remember exactly what. I really couldn't explain why it was not a box-office hit. Perhaps the subject matter was too serious. Terrorism was a new and scary topic. It caused many victims in Italy, put the world country in crisis. Terrorism has always been a bad bogeyman in movies.

(Email interview, October 2015)

Filmography

Abbreviations

The following abbreviations are used in the credits list for each entry

Crew
AC: Assistant camera
ACO: Costume assistant
ACON: Assistant continuity
AD: Assistant director
AE: Assistant editor
AMU: Assistant makeup
APD: Production design assistant
ArtD: Art director
B: Boom man
C: Camera
CC: Construction coordinator
CHOR: Choreographer
CO: Costumes
CON: Continuity
D: directed by
DialD: Dialogue coach / Dialogue director
DOP: Director of photography
DubD: Dubbing director

E: Editor
El: Electrician
ES: Editing supervisor
GA: Gaffer
G: Grip
Hair: Hairdresser
HMU: Head makeup artist
KG: Key grip
LT: lighting technician
M: Music
MA: Master of arms
Mix: Sound mixer
MU: Makeup
OE: Optical effects
PD: Production designer
PrM: Property manager
S: Story
2ndAD: 2nd Assistant director
SC: Screenplay
SD: Set decoration
SE: Special effects
SO: Sound

SOE: Special sound effects
SP: Still photographer
SS: Script supervisor / Script girl
ST: Sound technician
W: Wardrobe / Seamstress

Production
ADM: Administrator
AP: Associate producer
EP: Executive producer
GM: General manager / Production organizer
PA: Production assistant
PM: Production manager
PROD: Produced by
PS: Production supervisor
PSe: Production secretary
PseA: Production secretary assistant
UM: Unit manager
UPM: Unit production manager

As Assistant Director, Scriptwriter and Other

1961

I Love, You Love
(*Io amo, tu ami ... [Antologia universale dell'amore]*)
D: Alessandro Blasetti; S: Alessandro Blasetti; SC: Luigi Chiarini, Carlo Romano, Antonio Savignano, Alessandro Blasetti; DOP: Aldo Tonti (Ultrascope, Technicolor); M: Carlo Savina; E: Tatiana Casini Morigi; PD: Ottavio Garbuglia, Dario Cecchi; AD: Antonio Brandt. Cast: Chaz Chase, Coro Armata Rossa, Sophisticated Ballet, Trio Marny, Balletto Moisejev, Clowns Fattini, Cairoly & Co., Las Hermanas Benitez, Obrazkov, John and Masha, Giuliano Gemma (Young man on the beach), Giovanni Grasso (Sleeping coachman), Renato Speziali (Man on train), Alex Nicol (Man at the airport), Veronique (Herself). PROD: Mara Blasetti and Dino De Laurentiis for Dino De Laurentiis Cinematografica (Rome), Orsay Films (Paris); Distribution: De Laurentiis. Country: Italy/France. Running time: 132 min. (3626 m.); Visa n: 34319 (03/21/1961); Release date: 04/01/1961; Domestic gross: 655,644,000 lire. Also knows as: *L'Amour parte en vacances* (France).

Note: Valerii worked on the film uncredited, as Blasetti's volunteer assistant.

The Best of Enemies
(*I due nemici*)
D: Guy Hamilton [and Alessandro Blasetti]; S: Luciano Vincenzoni; *Adaptation*: Age [Agenore Incrocci], Furio Scarpelli, Suso Cecchi D'Amico; *SC*: Jack Pulman; *DOP*: Giuseppe Rotunno (Technirama, Technicolor); *M*: Nino Rota; *E*: Tatiana Morigi (English version: Bert Bates); *PD, ArtD*: Mario Garbuglia; *APD*: Mario Giovannoni; *SD*: Giorgio Herrmann; *CO*: Dario Cecchi, Ezio Frigerio; *AD*: Mario Maffei, Yoel Silbert, Tony [Antonio] Brandt; *SS*: Albino Cocco; *C*: Nino Cristiani; *SO*: Piero Cavazzuti, Bruno Brunacci; *MU*: Alberto De Rossi; *Hair*: Grazia De Rossi; *CC*: Aldo Puccini; *SE*: Cataldo Galiano, Vitantonio Ricci; *DialD*: Manuel Del Campo. *Cast*: Alberto Sordi (Captain Blasi), David Niven (Major Richardson), Amedeo Nazzari (Major Fornari), Michael Wilding (Burke), Harry Andrews (Lt. Rootes), David Opatoshu (Bernasconi), Aldo Giuffré (Sgt. Todini), Tiberio Mitri (Pvt. Mocca), Alessandro Ninchi (Lt. Del Prà), Pietro Marascalchi (Cpl. Bortolin), Bruno Cattaneo (Pvt. Mattone), Giuseppe Fazio (Sgt. Spadoni), Ignazio Dolce (Sentinel), Ronald Fraser ("Perfect"), Duncan Macrae (Trevethan), Bernard Cribbins (Col. Brownlow), Michael Trubshawe (Tanner), Robert Desmond (Pvt. Slinger), Noel Harrison (Lt. Hilary), Kenneth Fortescue (Lt. Tomlinson), Ahmed Alì Haggi, Don Powell, Abraham Mogos, Abrahama Elias, Abduraham Mohamed Elmi, Luigi Bracale. *PROD*: Dino De Laurentiis Cinematografica (Rome); *AP*: Luigi Luraschi; *PM*: Bruno Tolusso, Lazare Bianco, Giacomo Forzano; *PS*: Mara Blasetti; *PA*: Ralph B. Serpe; *Distribution*: De Laurentiis. *Country*: Italy. Exteriors filmed in Israel and Lavinio. *Running time*: 104 min. (3011 m.); Visa n. 34965 (10/11/1961); *Release dates*: Italy: 10/26/1961; U.S.A: 08/06/1962; *Domestic gross*: 1,088,041,000 lire. Also known as: *Liebenswerte Gegner* (West Germany, 03/30/1962); *Le Meilleur Ennemi* (Canada, France); *Dyo ahoristoi ehthroi* (Greece); *Hans bedste fjende* (Denmark); *Meidän vihollisten kesken* (Finland); *O Melhor dos Inimigos* (Portugal). *Home video*: DNC Home Entertainment (DVD, Italy).

Note: Valerii worked on the film uncredited, as Blasetti's assistant.

1962

I motorizzati
(The Motorized Ones)
D: Camillo Mastrocinque; *S, SC*: Castellano e Pipolo [Franco Castellano, Giuseppe Moccia]; *DOP*: Antonio Macasoli Hernandez (B&W); *M*: Ennio Morricone; *E*: Roberto Cinquini; *PD, SD*: Aurelio Crugnola; *AD*: Nino Zanchin; *2ndAD*: Tonino Valerii; *SS*: Ilde Muscio; *C*: Sandro Mancori; *AC*: Gino Santini; *AE*: Lisetta Lanni; *SO*: Roberto Matteoli; *B*: Roberto Cuomo. *Cast*: Nino Manfredi (Nino Borsetti), Ugo Tognazzi (rag. Achille Pestani), Franca Valeri (Velia), Walter Chiari (Valentino), José Luis López Vázquez (Mariano), Mercedes Alonzo [Alonso] (Claudia), Gianni Agus (Mario), Dolores Palumbo (Nino's mother-in-law), Luigi Pavese (head office), Gina Rovere (Elisa), Luigi Bonos (Franco), Paola Del Bosco (Clara), Mario Brega (Edoardo), Loredana Cappelletti (Paola), Peppino De Martino (Franco), Franco Giacobini (Alberto), Mario Pisu (Angelo), Marcella Rovena (Maria Grazia), Alberto Bonucci (Mario Bianchi), Mac Ronay [Germain René Sauvard] (Policeman), Aroldo Tieri (Dino), Franca Tamantini (Rita), Franco Franchi (Tires thief), Ciccio Ingrassia (Tires thief), Mimmo Poli (Vittorio), Consalvo Dell'Arti (Roberto), Tonino Valerii (Employee). *PROD*: Jolly Film (Trieste/Rome), Tecisa (Madrid); *PM*: Franco Serino; *PS*: Diego Alchimede; *PSe*: Nico Benetti; *Country*: Italy/Spain. Filmed at Titanus Farnesina studios (Rome). *Running time*: 90 min. (2746 m.); Visa n: 38912 (11/23/1962); *Release date*: 11/29/1962; *Distribution*: Unidis; *Domestic gross*: 735,681,000 lire. Also known as: *Los motorizados* (Spain; 02/10/1964). *Home video*: Ripley's (DVD, Italy).

Note: The song *Twist dei vigili* is sung by Edoardo Vianello, *Corri corri* is sung by Gianni Morandi. The film Ugo Tognazzi watches in the movie theater is *Black Sunday* (*La maschera del demonio*, 1960, Mario Bava).

1963

Tutto è musica
(Everything Is Music)
D: Domenico Modugno; *S and SC*: Domenico Modugno, Franco Migliacci, Tonino Valerii; *DOP*: Gábor Pogány (Technicolor); *M*: Domenico Modugno, conducted by Ennio Morricone, Luis Enriquez Bacalov, Nello Ciangherotti; *C*: Mario Capriotti; *E*: Roberto Cinquini; *AD*: Tonino Va-

lerii; *PD, CO*: Pasquale Romano; *AC*: Sabino Tonti; *AE*: Stefano Locchi; *MU*: Massimo Giustini; *SO*: Maria Ottavi, Mario Amari; *B*: Alvaro Orsini; *SS*: Bruna Malaguti. *Cast*: Domenico Modugno (Himself), Eddra Gale, Giustino Durano (Kurt), Franco Franchi (Anemia's friend), Ciccio Ingrassia (Anemia), Paolo Bergamaschi, Paola Del Bosco, Maria Teresa Orsini, Stefano Conti, Richard McNamara, Mario Laurentino, Mirella Machnich. *PROD*: Emme Film; *PM*: Lucio Bompani; *PS*: Romolo Germani; *PSe*: Ruggero Aprile. *Country*: Italy; *Running time*: 93 min. (2411 m.); Visa n. 40979 (08/10/1963); *Release date*: 08/18/1963; *Distribution*: Cineriz; *Domestic gross*: 150,427,000 lire.
Note: Valerii claims to have actually directed the film.

I terribili 7, a.k.a. *I cagasotto*
(The Terrible 7 / I cagasotto)
D: Raffaello Matarazzo; *S*: Guglielmo Santangelo; *SC*: Bruno Corbucci, Gianni Grimaldi, Guglielmo Santangelo, Raffaello Matarazzo; *DOP*: Marcello Masciocchi (B&W); *M*: Armando Trovajoli. Conducted by the author; *E*: Ornella Micheli; *PD*: Carlo Leva; *AD*: Ettore Maria Fizzarotti, Tonino Valerii; *2ndAD*: Aldo Grimaldi; *MU*: Telemaco Tilli; *AC*: Oddone Bernardini; *SO*: Giovanni Rosi; *SS*: Adolfo Aragone. *Cast*: Stefano Conti (Pecos Bill), Massimo Giuliani (Davy Crochett [sic]), Roberto Chevalier (Fantomas), Antonio Piretti (Pastaelenticchie), Stefano Tamborra (Cervellone), Claudio Maccari (Gambalesta), Loris Loddi (Biberò), Patrizia Canevari (Gianna), Angelo Secchi (Newborn Baby), Umberto D'Orsi (Marshall Toniolo, Pecos Bill's Father), Riccardo Garrone (Giorgio the Journalist, Pastaelenticchie's Father), Toni Ucci (Romolo the Streetcar Operator, Biberò's Father), Giacomo Furia (Ernesto, Fantomas' Father), Franco Volpi (The Lawyer, Cervellone's Father), Giuliana Lojodice (Newborn's Mother), Franca Tamantini (Romolo's Wife), Fulvia Mammi (Rosa, Toniolo's Wife), Dada Gallotti (Ernesto's Wife), Elsa Vazzoler (Vittoria, Davy Crockett's Mother), Armida De Pasquali (The Lawyer's Wife), Mario Chiocchio (Parish Priest), Antonella Della Porta (Gypsy Woman), Annie Gorassini (Giorgio's Fiancèe), Paola Piretti (Gianna's Sister), Nando Di Claudio (Public Security Guard), Mario Lavagetto (Gypsy), Bruno Scipioni (Reporter), Eugenio Galadini (Old Man), Mario De Simone (Nightwatchman), Rita Silenzi (Lauretta), Carol Smith (Ornella), Pino Ferrara (Sacristan). *PROD*: Gilberto Carbone for Film Columbus (Rome); *PM*: Lucio Bompani; *PSe*: Luciano Luna, Romano Di Casimiro. *Country*: Italy. Filmed at Titanus Studios (Rome). *Running time*: 93 min. (2541 m.); Visa n. 41900 (12/19/1963); *Release date*: 01/05/1964; *Distribution*: Titanus; *Domestic gross*: not available.

1964

Terror in the Crypt, a.k.a. *Crypt of the Vampire*
(*La cripta e l'incubo*)
D: Thomas Miller [Camillo Mastrocinque]. *S*: based on Joseph Sheridan Le Fanu's novel *Carmilla*; *SC*: Robert Bohr [Tonino Valerii], Julian Berry [Ernesto Gastaldi]; *DOP*: Julio Ortas (B&W, panoramic, Vistavision), Giuseppe Aquari (uncredited); *M*: Herbert Buckman [Carlo Savina], conducted by James Munshin [Carlo Savina]; *E*: Herbert Markle; *C*: Noel Lardner; *AC*: Charles Sundberg; *AE*: Judy Marlow; *AD*: Robert Bohr; *PD/SD*: Demos Filos [Demofilo Fidani]; *APD*: Remy Villar; *CO*: Milose [Mila Vitelli Valenza]; *MU*: Joe Carlin; *Hair*: Stephan Carlin; *SO*: Ferdinand Larkin [Fernando Pescetelli]; *SS*: Piper Samson [Paola Salvadori]; *DubD*: Mario Colli. *Cast*: Christopher Lee (Count Ludwig Karnstein), Audry Amber [Adriana Ambesi] (Laura Karnstein), Ursula Davis [Pier Anna Quaglia] (Ljuba/Sheena), José Campos (Friedrich Klauss), Véra Valmont (Annette), Cicely Clayton [Carla Calò] (Ljuba's mother), Vera Conjiù [Nela Conju] (Rowena), José Villasante (Cedric the butler), Angel Midlin [Angelo Midlino] (The hunchback), Bill Curtis [José Cortés], James Brightman; *uncredited*: John Karlsen (Franz Karnstein), Ignazio Balsamo, Lee Campos, Benito Carif, Angela Minervini (Tilde), Rafael Vaquero. *PROD*: William Mulligan [Marco Mariani] for MEC Cinematografica (Rome), Hispamer Films (Madrid); *PM*: Hector Corey; *PS*: Marcel Harrods; *PSe*: Heinz Bischop. *Country*: Italy / Spain. Filmed at Castle Piccolomini, Balsorano (Aquila). *Running time*: 82 min. (m. 2329); Visa n: 42808 (04/22/1964); *Rating*: V.M.14; *Release date*: 05/27/1964. *Distribution*: MEC (Italy, Regional); AIP-TV (U.S.A., TV). *Domestic gross*: 69,541,000 lire. *Also known as*: *La maldición de los Karnstein* (Spain: 08/01/1966); *La crypte du vampire* (France: 09/22/1965– 80 min.); *Ein Toter hing am Glockenseil* (West

Germany: 03/03/1967–85 min.); *Crypt of Horror* (U.K.: 1965–84 min.). *Home video*: Image (DVD, U.S.A.—as *Crypt of the Vampire*).

A Fistful of Dollars
(*Per un pugno di dollari*)
D: Bob Robertson [Sergio Leone]; *S*: Sergio Leone, Adriano Bolzoni; *SC*: Sergio Leone, Víctor Andrés Catena, Jaime Comas Gil [actually Fernando di Leo and Duccio Tessari]; *DOP*: Jack Dalmas [Massimo Dallamano] (Technicolor, Techniscope); *M*: Dan Savio [Ennio Morricone] (Ed. R.C.A.); *E*: Bob Quintle [Roberto Cinquini]; *C*: Steve Rock [Stelvio Massi]; *AC*: Ramón Sempere, Eduardo Noé; *ES*: Adriana Novelli; *PD, SD, CO*: Charles Simons [Carlo Simi]; *ACO*: Maria Pia Coen; *AD*: Frank Prestland [Franco Giraldi], Julio Sempere; *ASD*: Adolfo Cofiño, Rafael Pérez Murcia; *PrM*: Luis Ocaña; *HMU*: José María Sanchez; *MU*: Sam Watkins [Rino Carboni]; *Hair*: Dolores Clavel; *SO*: Edy Simson [Elio Pacella]; *SE*: John Speed [Giovanni Corridori]; *MA*: W. R. Thompkins; *Stunts*: Benito Stefanelli; *Title animation*: Iginio Lardani; *SS*: Tilde Watson [Ilde Muscio]; *DialD*: Tonino Valerii. *Cast*: Clint Eastwood (Joe), Marianne Koch (Marisol), John Wells [Gian Maria Volonté] (Ramón Rojo), Wolfgang Lukschy (John Baxter), Sieghardt Rupp (Esteban Rojo), Joe Edger [Joseph Egger] (Piripero), Antonio Prieto (Don Miguel Rojo), José Calvo (Silvanito), Margarita Lozano (Consuelo Baxter), Daniel Martín (Julián), Benny Reeves [Benito Stefanelli] (Rubio), Richard Stuyvesant [Mario Brega] (Chico), Carol Brown [Bruno Carotenuto] (Antonio Baxter), Aldo Sambreli [Sambrell] (Rojo gang member); *uncredited*: Luis Barboo (Baxter Gunman #2), José Canalejas (Rojo Gang Member), Juan Cortés (Mexican Army Captain), Álvaro De Luna (Rojo Gang Member), Nino Del Arco (Jesús), Jose Halufi (Rojo Gang Member unloading the corpses at Rio Bravo), Joe Kamel [Giuseppe Frisaldi] (Rojo Gang Member), Antonio Molino Rojo (Baxter Gang Member #3), Antonio Moreno (Juan de Dios), José Orjas, Manuel Peña, Antonio Pico (Rojo Gang Member), Julio Pérez Tabernero (Baxter Gunman #4), José Riesgo (Mexican Cavalry Captain), Lorenzo Robledo (Baxter Gunman #1), Fernando Sánchez Polack (Rojo Gang Member crushed by wine cask), Enrique Santiago (Fausto, Rojo Gang Member), Umberto Spadaro (Miguel, Rojo Gunman), William R. Thompkins (Baxter Gang Member), Edmondo Tieghi (Mexican Gold Coach Guard), Antonio Pico (Baxter Gang Member). *PROD*: Arrigo Colombo and Giorgio Papi for Jolly Film (Trieste/Rome), Ocean Film (Madrid), Constantin Film Produktion GmbH (Munich); *PM*: Frank Palance [Franco Palaggi], Günter Raguse; *PSe*: Peter Saint [Piero Santini]; *PS*: Fred Ross [Fernando Rossi]. *Country*: Italy/Spain/West Germany. *Running time*: 99' (2686 m.); Visa n. 43642 (08/31/1964); *Release dates*: Italy: 09/12/1964; U.S.A.: 01/18/1967; *Distribution*: P.E.A. (Italy), United Artists (U.S.A.); *Domestic gross*: 3,182,000,000 lire. *Also known as*: *Für eine Handvoll Dollar* (West Germany; 03/05/1965); *Por un puñado de dolares* (Spain; 09/27/1965); *Pour une poignée de dollars* (France; 03/16/1966). *Home video*: MGM (BD, U.S.A.)

Note: Technical cast based on the Italian credits. Sergio Leone and Gian Maria Volonté's real names were credited in Italian re-releases.

The Long Hair of Death
(*I lunghi capelli della morte*)
D: Anthony Dawson [Antonio Margheriti]. *S*: Julian Berry [Ernesto Gastaldi]; *SC*: Robert Bohr [Tonino Valerii], Anthony Dawson; *DOP*: Richard Thierry [Riccardo Pallottini] (B&W); *M*: Evirust [Carlo Rustichelli]; *E*: Mark Sirandrews [Mario Serandrei]; *ArtD*: George Greenwood [Giorgio Giovannini]; *SD*: Henry Fraser; *CO*: Humphrey Patterson; *AD*: Bob Parks [Roberto Pariante], Guy Farrell; *C*: Humbert Tennberg; *MU*: Edmund Stroll; *Hair*: Florence Clark; *SO*: John Tamblyn; *SS*: Eva Koltay. *Cast*: Barbara Steele (Helen Karnstein / Mary Karnstein), George [Giorgio] Ardisson (Kurt Humboldt), Halina Zalewska (Elizabeth Karnstein), Robert Rains [Umberto Raho] (Von Klage), Laureen Nuyen [Laura Nucci] (Grumalda), Jean Rafferty [Giuliano Raffaelli] (Count Humboldt), John Carey [Nello Pazzafini] (Monk), Jeffrey Darcey (Messenger). *PROD*: Felice Testa Gay for Cinegai (Rome); *PM*: Fred Dexter; *UM*: Paul Meredith, Dean Morris. *Country*: Italy. Filmed at Cinecittà (Rome) and at Castle Massimo, Arsoli (Rome). *Running time*: 100 min. (m. 2775); Visa n: 44461 (12/29/1964); *Rating*: V.M.14; *Release date*: 12/30/1964 (Italy). *Distribution*: Unidis (Italy); *Domestic gross*: 321,000,000 lire. *Also known as*: *La Sorcière sanglante* (France, 08.08.1970) *Hævnens flammer* (Denmark). *Home video*: East West Entertainment (DVD, U.S.A.—double feature w/ *Terror-Creatures from*

the Grave), Midnight Choir (DVD, U.S.A.—double feature w/*An Angel for Satan*), Raro (DVD, Italy), Artus (DVD, France).

1965

For a Few Dollars More
(*Per qualche dollaro in più*)
D: Sergio Leone; *S*: Sergio Leone, Fulvio Morsella [actually Fernando di Leo and Enzo Dell'Aquila]; *SC*: Luciano Vincenzoni, Sergio Donati, Sergio Leone [and Fernando di Leo]; *Dial*: Luciano Vincenzoni; *DOP*: Massimo Dallamano (35mm, Technicolor, Techniscope); *M*: Ennio Morricone, conducted by Bruno Nicolai; *E*: Eugenio Alabiso, Giorgio Serralonga; *C*: Eduardo Noé, Aldo Ricci; *AC*: Mario Lommi; *ES*: Adriana Novelli; *PD*: Carlo Simi; *APD, SD*: Carlo Leva, Rafael Ferri; *CO*: Carlo Simi; *AD*: Tonino Valerii; *2ndAD*: Fernando di Leo, Julio Sempere; *HMU*: Rino Carboni; *MU*: Amedeo Alessi [and Juan Farsac]; *MA*: Benito Stefanelli; *SO*: Oscar De Arcangelis, Guido Ortenzi; *SE*: Giovanni Corridori, Eros Bacciuchi, Manuel Baquero; *SS*: Maria Luisa Rosen; *Mix*: Renato Cadueri. *Cast*: Clint Eastwood (Monco), Lee Van Cleef (Col. Douglas Mortimer), Gian Maria Volonté (El Indio), Mara Krup [Krupp] (Mary), Luigi Pistilli (Groggy), Klaus Kinski (Wild), Josef [Joseph] Egger (Old prophet), Panos Papadopoulos (Sancho Perez), Benito Stefanelli (Luke), Robert [Roberto] Camardiel (Tucumcari station clerk), Aldo Sambrell (Cuchillo), Luis Rodríguez (Bandit), Tomás Blanco (Tucumcari Sheriff), Lorenzo Robledo (Tomaso), Sergio Mendizábal (Tucumcari bank manager), Dante Maggio (Carpenter in cell with Indio), Diana Rabito (Girl in bathtub), Giovanni Tarallo (Santa Cruz telegraphist), Mario Meniconi (Train conductor), Mario Brega (Niño), Werner Abrolat (Slim), Román Ariznavarreta (Half-shaved bounty hunter), Frank Braña (Blackie), José Canalejas (Chico), Rosemary Dexter (Mortimer's sister), Diana Faenza (Tomaso's wife), Jesús Guzmán (Carpetbagger on train), Karl Hirenbach (Mortimer's brother-in-law), Francesca Leone (Tomaso's baby), Rafael López Somoza, José Marco ("Baby" Red Cavanaugh), Guillermo Méndez (White Rocks Sheriff), Antonio Molino Rojo (Frisco), Nazzareno Natale (Paco), Enrique Navarro, Ricardo Palacios (Tucumcari Saloon Keeper), Antoñito Ruiz (Fernando), Enrique Santiago (Miguel), Carlo Simi (El Paso Bank Manager), José Terrón (Guy Calloway), Kurt Zips (Hotel manager), Eduardo García (Member of Indio's gang), José Félix Montoya, Aldo Ricci. *PROD*: Alberto Grimaldi for P.E.A. (Rome), Arturo González P.C (Madrid), Constantin Film (Munich); *PM*: Ottavio Oppo; *PA*: José Sánchez; *PS*: Norberto Soliño, Manuel Castedo, Fernando Rossi; *PSe*: Antonio Palombi. *Country*: Italy/Spain/West Germany; *Running time*: 130 min. (3200 m.); Visa n. 46186 (12/17/1965); *Release dates*: Italy: 12/18/1965; U.S.A.: 5/10/1967; *Distribution*: P.E.A. (Italy), United Artists (U.S.A.); *Domestic gross*: 3,492,268,000 lire. Also known as: *Für ein paar Dollar mehr* (West Germany; 03/25/1966); *La muerte tenía un precio* (Spain; 09/05/1966); *Et pour quelques dollars de plus* (France; 09/30/1966). *Home video*: MGM (BD, U.S.A.)

Note: Fernando di Leo, credited as second assistant director, did not take part in the shooting.

2007

All'amore assente (Andres and Me)
D: Andrea Adriatico; *S, SC*: Andrea Adriatico, Stefano Casi, Marco Mancassola; *DOP*: Andrea Locatelli; *M*: Roberto Passuti; *E*: Roberto Passuti; *PD*: Maurizio Bovi; *CO*: Andrea B. Cinelli; *SO*: Enrico Medri; *SP*: Raffaella Cavalieri. *Cast*: Massimo Poggio (Private detective), Francesca D'Aloja (Iris), Milena Vukotic (Magda), Maurizio Patella (Edoardo), Tonino Valerii (Andres' Father), Corso Salani (Carlo), Eva Robin's (Taxi Driver), Filippo Plancher, Ilaria Avanzi, Francesca Ballico, Patrizia Bernardi, Daniela Camboni, Daniela Cotti, Nahim Dali, Marco Mancassola, Francesca Mazza, Tomoko Matsubayashi, Luca Nunziata, Davide Sorlini, Carlo Strata, Franco Vazzoler. *PROD*: Cinemare (Bologna); *EP*: Monica Nicoli. *Country*: Italy. *Running time*: 95 min.

As Director

1956

Il diario di Anna Frank
(Anne Frank's Diary)
S: based on Anne Frank's diary; *SC*: Lili Veenman, Tonino Valerii, Luciano Arancio, Tersicore Kolosof; *DOP*: Alessandro Spina; *E*: Tonino Valerii, Maria Rosada; *C*: Pietro Morbidelli. *AC*: Hector Rios, Dupta Gupta; *ArtD*: Nato Frascà; *CO*: Vera Marzot; *AD*: Lili Veenman, Luciano

Arancio; *SO*: Adriano Taloni, Michelangelo Carosi; *B*: Giancarlo Penchini; *MU*: Franco Titi; *SS*: Gabriella Rossetto. *Cast*: Livia Contardi (Anna), Carlo D'Angelo (Anna's Father), Gian Carlo Tajo (Peter), Tersicore Kolosof (Margot). *PROD*: Centro Sperimentale di Cinematografia (Rome); *PM*: Armando Govoni; *PS*: Alfredo Tucci; *PSe*: Ugo Novello; *ADM*: Tonino Garzarelli; *Country*: Italy; *Running time*: 26 min.

Note: Valerii's directorial essay at Rome's Centro Sperimentale di Cinematografia. The opening titles specify that a whole treatment from the book was made, but only a part of it had been filmed.

1966

Taste of Killing
(*Per il gusto di uccidere*)

S and *SC*: Víctor Auz [actually Tonino Valerii] [English version: Frank Gregory]; *DOP*: Stelvio Massi (35mm, Eastmancolor, Cromoscope); *M*: Nico Fidenco, conducted by Willy Brezza; *E*: Yosi [Rosa G.] Salgado; *C*: Félix Mirón, Roberto Forges Davanzati; *ES*: Franco Fraticelli; *AD*: Julio Sempere; *2ndAD*: Ezio Palaggi; *ArtD, SD*: Pablo Gago; *PD*: Carlo Simi; *CO*: Rosalba Menichelli; *MU*: Adolfo Ponte Mancini; *SO*: Giuseppe Diliberto; *MA*: Remo De Angelis; *Stunts*: Miguel Pedregosa; *titles*: Ermanno Biamonte, Vladimiro Grisanti. *Cast*: Craig Hill (Hank "Lanky" Fellows), George Martin [Francisco Martínez Celeiro] (Gus Kennebeck), Peter Carter [Piero Lulli] (Collins), Diana Martín (Peggy Kennebeck / Molly Kennebeck), Frank [Franco] Ressel (Aarons), Rada Rassimov [Rada Djerasimovic] (Isabel), Fernando Sancho (Sanchez), Graham Sooty [Eugenio Galadini] (Jefferson), George Wang (Machete / Mingo), José Marco [José Joandó Roselló] (John Kennebeck), Lorenzo Robledo (Sheriff), Sancho Gracia (Bill Kilpatrick), José Canalejas (Peter), [José] Manuel Martín (Rodrigo), Dario De Grassi (Steve); *uncredited*: Enrique Santiago (Sanchez's henchman) Nazzareno Natale (Wylie), Manuel Bermudez (Juarez), Remo De Angelis (Vice Sheriff), Ulrich Müller (Poker Player). *PROD*: Francesco Genesi, Vincenzo Genesi, Daniele Senatore (and Stefano Melpignano) for Hercules Cinematografica (Rome), José López Moreno for Montana Films (Madrid); *EP*: Lucio Bompani; *PM*: Apolinar Robinal Huerta; *PS*: Luciano Luna, Ramón Baillo; *PSe*: Roberto Natrici. *Country*: Italy/Spain. Filmed in Spain and at Titanus Appia Studios (Rome); *Running time*: 88 min. (2440 m.); Visa n. 47125 (03/06/66); *Release date*: 06/08/66; *Distribution*: Titanus; *Domestic gross*: 495,749,000 lire. *Also known as*: *Cazador de recompensas* (Spain, 04/12/1967), *Lanky Fellow—Der einsame Rächer* (West Germany; 04/25/1967); *Lanky l'homme à la carabine* (France). *Home video*: Wild East (DVD, U.S.A.); SPO (Japan)

Note: The song *The Yankee Fellow* (Nico Fidenco/Giuseppe Cassia) is performed by The Wilder Brothers. Some sources wrongly credit Olga Karlatos as Molly.

1967

Day of Anger
(*I giorni dell'ira*)

S: based on the novel *Der Tod ritt dienstags* by Ron Barker [actually Ernesto Gastaldi and Renzo Genta]; *SC*: Ernesto Gastaldi, Tonino Valerii, Renzo Genta; *DOP*: Enzo Serafin (Technicolor, Techniscope); *M*: Riz Ortolani; *E*: Franco Fraticelli; *C*: Silvio Fraschetti; *AC*: Maurizio Lucchini; *AE*: Gabriele Reinecke; *ArtD, SD*: Piero Filippone; *ASD*: Carlo Gervasi; *PrM*: Carlo Simi; *CO*: Maria Baroni; *AD*: Mario Sacripanti; *2ndAD*: Fernando Popoli, Dietmar Belinke; *MA*: Benito Stefanelli; *SP*: Pietro Vesperini; *Title animation*: Iginio Lardani. *Cast*: Giuliano Gemma (Scott "Mary"), Lee Van Cleef (Frank Talby), Walter Rilla (Murph Allan Short), Christa Linder (Gwen), Yvonne Sanson (Vivien Skill), Ennio Balbo (Turner, the banker), Lukas Ammann (Judge Cutchell), Andrea Bosic [Ignacio Božič] (Abel Murray), Pepe [José] Calvo (Blind Bill), Anna Orso (Eileen Cutchell), Hans Otto [Karl-Otto] Alberty (Sam Corbitt), Nino Nini (Doctor), Virgilio Gazzolo (Mr. Barton, Owner of Arms Shop), Benito Stefanelli (Owen White, "The Saint"), Franco Balducci (Slim), Paolo Magalotti (Deputy Cross), Nazzareno Natale (Wild Jack's Man), Gianni Di Segni (Man washing his face), Eleonora Morana (Mrs. Barton), Giorgio Gargiullo (Marshall/Sheriff Nigel); *uncredited*: Román Ariznavarreta (Wild Jack's Man), Mirko Baiocchi [Canello Bajocchi] (Pianist), Giancarlo Bastianoni (Talby's Henchman), Dolores Calò (Courtroom observer), Omero Capanna (Head of Perkins' henchmen), Franz Colangeli (Gambler), Antonio Danesi (Rider), Álvaro De Luna (Wild Jack's Man), Fulvio Esposti (Gambler), Margherita [Margarethe] Horowitz (Card Player in Talby's Saloon), Enrico Marciani (Townsman),

Mauro Mannatrizio (Mackenzie Perkins), Vincenzo Matassi (Perkins' Henchman), Vladimir Medar (Old Man Perkins), Sergio Mendizábal [Hermenegildo Igarzabal Sánchez] (Wild Jack's Henchman), Mario Meniconi (Bank Guard), Fulvio Mingozzi (Turner's Assistant), Enzo Mondino (Gambler), Al Mulock (Wild Jack), Ricardo Palacios [Ricardo López-Nuño Diez] (Bowie Cantina Owner), Fulvio Pellegrino (Waiter in Talby's Saloon), Romano Puppo (Harve Perkins), Christian Consola, Ferruccio Viotti. *PROD*: Sansone e Chroscicky (sic) [Alfonso Sansone and Henryk Chrosicki] for Sancrosiap (Roma), Corona Filmproduktion (Berlino) and KG Divina Film, (Monaco); *PM*: Nino Milano; *GO*: Nicolò Pomilia, Alexander Gruter. *Country*: Italy/West Germany. Filmed in Spain, at Los Albaricoques and San José (Almería), and in Rome; *Running time*: 115 min. (3163 m); 111 min. (3050 m.); Visa n. 50380 (12/05/1967—V.M.14), 50875 (02/20/1968); *Release dates*: Italy: 12/19/1967; U.S.A.: November 1969; *Distribution*: Cidif. *Domestic gross*: 1,997,410 lire. *Also known as*: Der Tod ritt dienstags (West Germany; 01/12/1968–3170 m); Le Dernier Jour de la colère (France; 11/28/1968–90'); El día de la ira (Spagna). *Home video*: Arrow (BD, U.K.), Wild East (U.S.A.).

Note: In the Spanish version, Giuliano Gemma is dubbed by Simón Ramírez and Lee Van Cleef is dubbed by Francisco Sánchez. Pepe Calvo dubs himself.

1969

The Price of Power
(*Il prezzo del potere*)
S, SC: Massimo Patrizi [actually Ernesto Gastaldi and Tonino Valerii]; *DOP*: Stelvio Massi (Eastmancolor, Techniscope); *M*: Luís Enríquez Bacalov; *E*: Franco Fraticelli; *C*: Michele Pensato, Ricardo Andreu; *AD*: Giuseppe Bellecca, May [Mahnahén] Velasco; *PD*: Carlo Leva; *ArtD*: Ángel Arzuaga; *SD*: Francesco Antonacci; *CO*: Giorgio Desideri; *MU*: Walter Cossu; *Hair*: Anna Cristofani; *SO*: Attilio Nicolai; *B*: Tullio Petricca; *MA*: Benito Stefanelli; *SS*: Luigina Lovari. *Cast*: Giuliano Gemma (William "Bill" Willer), Warren Vanders [Warren John Vandeschuit] (Arthur McDonald), María Cuadra (Lucretia Garfield), Raï [Ray] Saunders (Jack Donovan), Fernando Rey [Fernando Casado Arambillet] (Mr. Pinkerton), Antonio Casas (Willer's father), Benito Stefanelli (Sheriff Jefferson), María Luisa Sala (Governor's wife), Ángel Del Pozo (Attorney), Julio Peña (Texas Governor), Franco Meroni (Sheriff's thug), Ángel Álvarez (Cotten), Francisco Sanz (Pat, Newspaper Editor), Norma Jordan (Annie Godard), Carlos Bravo (First Vice Sheriff), José Canalejas (Second Vice Sheriff), Joaquín Parra (Slim), Francisco Braña (Mortimer), Massimo Carocci (Anthony Ward, journalist), Lorenzo Robledo (Brett), Luis Rico Peláez (Dr. Hunter), Ralph Neville (Judge), Manuel Zarzo [Manuel López Zarza] (Nick), José Suárez (Vice President), Van Johnson [Charles Van Dell Johnson] (President James Garfield); *uncredited*: Michael Harvey (Wallace), José Calvo (Dr. Strips), Luigi Ciavarro (Third Vice Sheriff), Gene Collins (Audience member during the President's speech), Riccardo Pizzuti (Vice Sheriff in Saloon), Paolo Figlia (Wallace Henchman). *PROD*: Bianco Manini for Patry Film (Rome), Films Montana (Madrid); *PM*: Ferruccio De Martino, Jesús García Gárgoles; *PA*: Ofelia Minaldi; *PS*: Julio Parra Rubio; *PSe*: Fernando Piazza. *Country*: Italy/Spain. Filmed in Spain, at Tabernas (Almería) and La Calahorra (Granada), and at Elios Film Studios (Rome); *Carriages and horses*: Medina y García Morno S.A.. *Running time*: 111 min. (3041 m.); Visa n. 55121 (12/10/1969); *Release date*: 12/18/1969; *Distribution*: Cidif. *Domestic gross*: 1,273,858,000 lire. *Also known as*: La muerte de un presidente (Spain; 09/07/1970); Texas (France; 1974–89'); Blutiges Blei (West Germany; 09/04/1970–95'). *Home video*: Shendene & Moizzi (DVD, Italy).

Note: In the Spanish version, Giuliano Gemma is dubbed by Félix Acaso, and Van Johnson by José María Cordero; Rey, Suárez, Zarzo and Calvo dub themselves, but not so Ángel Álvarez, Antonio Casas (although they frequently did their own voices) or Paco Sanz (who was a professional dubber). Some sources also list Lisardo Iglesias and José Galera Balazote, but they don't seem to appear in the film.

1970

A Girl Called Jules
(*La ragazza di nome Giulio*)
S: Tonino Valerii and Francesco Mazzei, based on the novel *La ragazza di nome Giulio* by Milena Milani; *SC*: Marcello Coscia, Bruno Di Geronimo, Mauro Di Nardo, Francesco Mazzei,

Tonino Valerii [actually Pier Giuseppe Murgia, Giuseppe Bellecca and Tonino Valerii]; *DOP*: Stelvio Massi (Technicolor, Techniscope); *M*: Riz Ortolani; *E*: Franco Fraticelli; *C*: Sergio Rubini; *AC*: Michele Pensato; *AD*: Carlo Montanaro; *AE*: Agnese Putignani; *PD*: Carlo Leva; *CO*: Giorgio Desideri, Gloria Gardi; *W*: Velia Menchinelli; *MU*: Walter Cossu; *Hair*: Anna Cristofani; *SO*: Silvio Vallesi; *B*: Maurizio Ferrari; *GA*: Furio Rocchi; *KG*: Giuseppe Raimondi; *SS*: Marina Chierici. *Cast*: Silvia Dionisio (Jules), Gianni Macchia (Franco), Esmeralda Ruspoli (Laura, Jules' mother), Anna Moffo (Lia), Maurizio Degli Esposti (Lorenzo), John Steiner (Caretaker), Livio Barbo (Amerigo), Roberto Chevalier (Camillo), Raúl Martínez (Marco), Riccardo Garrone (Carvalli, the gynecologist), Malisa Longo (Serafina), Nino Nini (Priest at Santa Maria del Giglio), Umberto Raho (Father Dario, the confessor priest), Ivano Staccioli (Philosophy Professor), Claudio Trionfi. *PROD*: Francesco Mazzei for Julia Film (Rome); *PM*: Raniero Di Giovanbattista; *PS*: Franco Ballati, Claudio Vinale. *Country*: Italy. Filmed in Venezia, Perugia, Caorle and at Vides Studios (Rome); *Running time*: 110 min. (3024 m.); Visa n: 56202 (06/04/1970—V.M.18), 89097 (12/16/1995—V.M.14); *Release date*: 06/26/1970; *Distribution*: PAC; *Domestic gross*: 542,076,000 lire. Also known as: *Model Love* (UK—video); *Das Mädchen Julius* (West Germany; 05/07/1971), *Las perversiones sexuales de una chica llamada Julio* (Spain). *Home video*: KSM (DVD, Germany—as *Das Mädchen Julius*).

Note: This author has not been able to identify Claudio Trionfi in the film. Given that he is listed as a C.S.C. (the Italian National film school) member, it may well be that his participation was purely nominal, as it often happened, as a law in force until 1975 granted tax benefits to those Italian films that had two former C.S.C. students among cast and crew members, which often led to such scams.

1972

My Dear Killer
(*Mio caro assassino*)

S: Franco Bucceri, Roberto Leoni; *SC*: Franco Bucceri, Roberto Leoni, José Gutiérrez Maesso, Tonino Valerii; *DOP*: Manuel Rojas (Eastmancolor, Technochrome); *M*: Ennio Morricone, conducted by Bruno Nicolai; *E*: Franco Fraticelli; *PD*: Franco Cinini, Francisco Canet; *C*: Arcangelo Lannutti; *AE*: Alessandro Gabriele, Sergio Fraticelli; *CO*: Fiorenzo Senese; *AD*: Roberto Leoni; *2ndAD*: Remo De Angelis; *SO*: Pietro Ortolani; *MU*: Vittorio Biseo; *Hair*: Marisa Fraticelli; *G*: Mauro Pezzotti; *SS*: Renata Franceschi; *SP*: Angelo Novi. *Cast*: George Hilton (Commissioner Luca Peretti), Salvo Randone (Chief Inspector Marò), Marilù Tolo (Dr. Anna Borgese), William Berger (Giorgio Canavese), Manolo [Manuel] Zarzo (Brigadier Bozzi), Patty Shepard (Paola Rossi), Piero Lulli (Alessandro Moroni), Helga Liné (Mrs. Paradisi), Tullio Valli (Oliviero Moroni), Dante Maggio (Mattia Guardapelle), Dana Ghia (Eleonora Moroni), Alfredo Mayo (Beniamino), Mónica Randall (Carla Moroni), Corrado Gaipa (Head of Insurance Company), Daniela Rachele Barnes (Stefania Moroni), Francesco Di Federico (Vincenzo Paradisi), Lola Gaos (Adele), Elisa Mainardi (Maid at Moroni's house) Enzo Fiermonte (Jib crane owner), Andrea Scotti (Witness in Post Office), Guerrino Crivello (Barman), Sergio Mendizábal (Rag. Civitelli), Sofia Dionisio (Maid at Moroni's house), Luigi Antonio Guerra (Postman), Anna Maria Chio (Witness in Post Office), Antonio Spaccatini (Silvestri), Irio Fantini; *uncredited*: Pietro Ceccarelli (Canavese's Bodyguard), Jean-Pierre Clarain (Driver at Moroni's House), Remo De Angelis (Mario Ansuini), Giuseppe Marrocco (Policeman), Sergio Testori (Kidnapper). *PROD*: B.R.C. Produzione Films S.r.l. (Rome), Kramot Cinematografica S.r.l. (Rome), Tecisa Film (Madrid); *PM*: Roberto Cocco; *PS*: Carlo Giovagnorio, Anacleto Amadio. *Country*: Italy/Spain. Filmed in Rome, Madrid and at Incir—De Paolis Studios (Rome). *Running time*: 102 min. (2875 m.); Visa n: 59715 (01/29/1972—V.M.14); *Release date*: 02/03/1972; *Distribution*: Jumbo Cinematografica; *Domestic gross*: 250,524,000 lire. Also known as: *Sumario sangriento de la pequeña Estefanía* (Spain). *Home video*: Surf Film/Cecchi Gori ("Serie Z»); Shriek Show (Usa); X-Rated (Germany).

Note: José Gutiérrez Maesso did not actually contributed to the script, but was credited for co-production reasons. The film Patty Shepard watches on tv is *Django* (1966, Sergio Corbucci). Actor Irio Fantini (C.S.C.) is credited but does not appear in the film.

A Reason to Live, a Reason to Die!, a.k.a. *Massacre at Fort Holman*
(*Una ragione per vivere e una per morire*)

S: Ernesto Gastaldi, Tonino Valerii; *SC*: Ernesto

Gastaldi, Tonino Valerii, Rafael Azcona; *DOP*: Alejandro Ulloa (Technicolor, Techniscope); *M*: Riz Ortolani; *E*: Franco Fraticelli; *PD, CO*: Elio Micheli; *C*: Pasquale Rachini, Eduardo Noé; *AC*: Giorgio Aureli, Saturnino Pita; *AE*: Sergio Fraticelli, Anna Maria Roca, Maruja Soriano, Heidemarie Harschke; *AD*: Antonio Brandt, Giuseppe Pollini; *2ndAD*: Francisco Ardura; *SD*: Rafael Ferri; *ACO*: Osanna Guardini; *MU*: Luciano Giustini; *Hair*: Fausto De Lisio; *AMU*: Antonio Maltempo, Manuela Castro; *SO*: Kurt Doubrowsky; *SP*: Divo Cavicchioli; *SE*: Giovanni Corridori; *SS*: Fabio Pellarin; *Stunts*: Miguel Pedregosa; *Dial*: Albert Kantoff (France), F. A. Koeniger (Germany). *Cast*: James Coburn (Colonel Pembroke), Bud Spencer [Carlo Pedersoli] (Eli Sampson), Telly Savalas [Aristotelis Savalas] (Major Ward), Rene [Reinhard] Kolldehoff (Sgt. Brent), José Suárez (Major Charles Ballard), Ugo Fangareggi (Ted Wendel), Guy Mairesse (Donald MacIvers), Benito Stefanelli (Pvt. Samuel Piggott), Adolfo Lastretti (Will Culder), Turam Quibo [Joseph P. Persaud] (Jeremy), Fabrizio Moresco (Ward's Assistant), Paco [Francisco] Sanz (Farmer), Giuseppe Pollini (Unionist Sergeant), Georges Géret (Sgt. Spike), Rudolf G. Boeving, Carla Mancini; *uncredited*: Ángel Álvarez (Scully the Monger), Mario Pardo (Roger, the Farmer's son), Conchita Rabal (April), José Antonio López (Gatekeeper), Tomás Rudi. *PROD*: Alfonso Sansone, Henryk Chrosicki for Sancrosiap, Terza Film Produzione Indipendente (Rome), José Frade for Atlántida Films (Madrid), Europrodis (Marseille), Corona Filmproduktion (Munich); *PM*: Nino Milano, Luis Mendes; *PS*: Antonio Paoletti, Enrique Bellot; *GM*: Pietro Innocenzi. *Country*: Italy/Spain/France/West Germany. Filmed in Spain, in Gérgal (Almería) and at Elios Film Studios (Rome); *Running time*: 112 min. (3285 m.); Visa n. 61310 (10/26/1972—V.M.14); *Release dates*: Italy: 10/27/1972; U.S.A.: 08/28/1974; *Distribution*: Cidif; *Domestic gross*: 1,960,071,000 lire. *Also known as*: Sie verkaufen den Tod (West Germany; 12/27/1972), *Der Dicke und das Warzenschwein* (West Germany; 78') *La Horde des salopards*; *Une Raison pour vivre, une raison pour mourir* (France; 05/29/1974), *Una razón para vivir y una para morir* (Spain; 08/06/1973). *Home video*: Kino Lorber (BD, U.S.A.)

Note: French dialogue: Albert Kantoff; German dialogue: F.A. Koeniger.

1973

My Name Is Nobody
(*Il mio nome è Nessuno*)
S: Fulvio Morsella, Ernesto Gastaldi, from an idea by Sergio Leone; *SC*: Ernesto Gastaldi; *DOP*: Giuseppe Ruzzolini, Armando Nannuzzi [and Sergio Salvati, uncredited] (Technicolor, Panavision); *M*: Ennio Morricone; *E*: Nino Baragli; *PD*: Gianni Polidori; *C*: Giuseppe Bernardini, Elio Polacchi, Federico Del Zoppo; *AC*: Claudio Sabatini; *AD*: Stefano Rolla; *2nd unit director*: Sergio Leone; *AE*: Rossana Maiuri; *APD*: Dino Leonetti; *SD*: Massimo Tavazzi; *CO*: Vera Marzot; *MU*: Nilo Jacoponi; *Hair*: Grazia De Rossi; *SO*: Fernando Pescetelli; *AE*: Rossana Maiuri; *MA*: Benito Stefanelli; *SE*: Giovanni Corridori, Eros Bacciucchi; *Set constructor*: Gilberto Carbonaro; *Costruction coordinator*: Ben Zeller; *PrM*: Gianni Fiumi; *SOE*: Roberto Arcangeli; *Mix*: Fausto Ancillai; *SS*: Rita Agostini; *SP*: Angelo Novi. *Cast*: Terence Hill [Mario Girotti] (Nessuno/Nobody), Henry Fonda (Jack Beauregard), Jean Martin (Sullivan), R.G. Armstrong (Honest John), Leo Gordon (Red), Karl Braun (Jim), Piero Lulli (Sheriff), Mario Brega (Pedro), Mark Mazza [Marc Mazzacurati] (Don John), Benito Stefanelli (Porteley), Alexander Allerson (Rex), Remus [Rainer] Peets (Big Gun), Antoine Saint-John (Scape), Franco Angrisano (Train conductor), Tommy Polgar [Tamás Polgár] (Juan), Steve Kanaly (False barber), Geoffrey Lewis (Wild Bunch Leader), Neil [Nicholas] Summers (Squirrel), Emil Feist (Dwarf on stilts), Humbert [Hubert] Mittendorf (Carnival barker), Angelo Novi (Bartender), Carla Mancini (Mother), Antonio Luigi [Luigi Antonio] Guerra (Official), Ulrich Müller (Saloon Bouncer), Claus Schmidt (Saloon Bouncer), Antonio Palombi (Dirty); *uncredited*: West Buchanan (Saloon Patron), Charles Stocker Fontelieu (Longshoreman), Lance Gordon [Russell Stoughton] (Wild Bunch member), Jess Hill (Child with apple), Jackson D. Kane (Gunfighter outside barber shop), Maurice Kowalewski (New Orleans street photographer), Larry Melton (Gunslinger milking cow), Antonio Molino Rojo (U.S. Army Officer), Renato Pinciroli (Hotel Owner), José Terrón (Wild Bunch member), Frank Trolio (Indian). *PROD*: Fulvio Morsella for Rafran Cinematografica (Rome), Les Filmes Jacques Leitienne (Paris), La Société Imp. Ex. Ci. (Paris), La Société Alcinter (Paris), Rialto Film Preben Philipsen (Berlin); *EP*: Claudio Mancini; *GM*: Piero Lazzari

(U.S.A.); *UM*: Franco Coduti, Paolo Gargano. *Country*: Italy/France/West Germany. Filmed in the United States (New Mexico, Arizona, and Louisiana) and Spain (Granada and Almería); *Running time*: 118 min. (2960 m.); Visa n. 63655 del 01/12/73—*Release dates*: 12/21/1973; *Distribution*: Titanus; *Domestic gross*: 3,620,446,000 *lire*. *Also known as*: *Mon Nom est Personne* (France; 12/14/1973); *Mein Name ist Nobody* (West Germany; 12/13/1973); *Mi nombre es Ninguno* (Spain; 03/18/1974); *Mr. Nobody* (Japan; 11/08/1975). Home video: Image Entertainment (BD, U.S.A.)

Note: John Landis claimed in an interview that he had a role as an extra as one of the "Wild Bunch" riders together with James O'Rourke.

1975

Go Gorilla Go, a.k.a. *The Hired Gun*
(*Vai gorilla*)

S, SC: Massimo De Rita and Dino Maiuri; *DOP*: Mario Vulpiani (Technicolor, Technospes); *M*: Franco Bixio, Fabio Frizzi, Vince Tempera; *E*: Antonio Siciliano; *PD*: Luca Sabatelli; *C*: Pasquale Rachini; *AC*: Osvaldo Bagnato; *AE*: Giancarlo Morelli, Luigi Gorini; *APD*: Egidio Spugnini, Giancarlo Mentil; *AD*: Franco Cirino; *MU*: Massimo De Rossi; *AMU*: Feliziano Ciriaci; *Hair*: Agnese Pavarotto; *SO*: Luigi Salvi; *B*: Benito Alchimede; *Mix*: Gianni D'Amico; *SE*: Paolo Ricci; *SP*: Giuseppe Botteghi; *Stunt*: Angelo Ragusa; *MA*: Remo De Angelis; *SS*: Vivalda Vigorelli. *Cast*: Fabio Testi (Marco Sartori), Renzo Palmer (Engineer Gaetano Sampioni), Claudia Marsani (Vera Sampioni), Saverio Marconi (Piero Sartori), Al Lettieri (Ciro Musante), Adriano Amidei Migliano (Commissioner Vannuzzi), Tony [Antonio] Marsina (Berto, the Biker), Luciano Catenacci (Shooting Range Manager), Giuliana Calandra (Sampioni's Wife), Maria D'Incoronato (Elisa Sartori), Ernesto Colli (Watchman), Salvatore Billa (a "Gorilla"), Riccardo Petrazzi (Berto's Mustached Sidekick), Simone Santo (Old Man at racing track), Sergio Testori (Berto's Sidekick), Remo De Angelis (Berto's Sidekick), Furio Meniconi (the "Fence"), Franca Scagnetti (Fence's Wife), Angelo Ragusa (Thug). *PROD*: Mario Cecchi Gori for Capital Film (Rome); *GM*: Luciano Luna; *PM*: Marcello Crescenzi; *PS*: Mario Della Torre, Giandomenico Stellitano; *ADM*: Mario Lupi; *Cashier*: Marcello Tassi. *Country*: Italy. Filmed on location in Rome and at Incir—De Paolis Studios (Rome); *Running time*: 100 min. (2682 m.); Visa n. 67415 (11/08/1975—V.M.18), n. 88862 (05/03/1994); *Release date*: 11/14/1975; *Domestic gross*: 1,846,285,538 lire. *Also known as*: *De profesión: gorila* (Spain), *Der Gorilla* (West Germany). *Home video*: Domovideo (VHS, Italy).

1976

Bominaco, una scoperta

DOP: Eliseo Caponera; *M*: Mario Molino; *E*: Enzo Meniconi; *Text*: Augusto Frassineti, narrated by Riccardo Cucciolla. *PROD*: Istituto Luce. *GM*: Alberto Verdejo. *Country*: Italy. *Running time*: 18' (499 m.); Visa n. 68640 (09/10/1976).

1977

L'Abruzzo? Prendilo è tuo!...

Text: Augusto Frassineti; *narrated by*: Riccardo Cucciolla; *DOP*: Eliseo Caponera; *M*: Mario Molino (Ed. Luce-Usignolo); *E*: Enzo Meniconi. *PROD*: Istituto Luce. *GM*: Alberto Verdejo. *Country*: Italy. *Running time*: 51' (1458 m.); Visa n. 70515 (09/30/1977).

Sahara Cross

S: Adriano Belli; *SC*: Ernesto Gastaldi, Adriano Belli, Tonino Valerii; *DOP*: Franco Di Giacomo (Eastmancolor, Vistavision); *M*: Riz Ortolani; *E*: Mario Siciliano; *PD*: Aurelio Crugnola; *C*: Gianfranco Transunto; *AC*: Francesco Gagliardini, Luigi Conversi; *AE*: Giancarlo Morelli; *AD*: Franco Cirino; *APD*: Ivano Todeschi; *SD*: Gianfranco Fumagalli; *CO*: Lina [Nerli] Taviani; *MU*: Giancarlo Del Brocco; *AMU*: Alvaro Rossi; *Hair*: Gerardo Raffaelli; *SO*: Mario Bramonti; *B*: Giuseppe Muratori; *SP*: Mario Tursi; *KG*: Gastone Coppa; *GA*: Valerio Garzia; *Unit publicist*: Maria Rhule; *SS*: Elvira D'Amico; *W*: Maura Zuccherofino; *SE*: Giovanni Corridori, Pasquino Bennassati; *MA*: Nazzareno Zamperla; *Magic consultant*: Tony Binarelli. *Cast*: Franco Nero (Jean Bellard), Michel Constantin (Karl Mank), Pamela Villoresi (Nicole), Mauro Barabani (Kemal), Michael Coby [Antonio Cantafora] (George), Emilio Locurcio (Hamida), Luciano Bartoli (Eric), Luca Biagini (Grant), Geoffrey Copleston (Mr. Brown), Giorgio Del Bene (Captain Zaruck), Antonio Ferrante (Hospital patient), Pietro Valsecchi (Luis), Nazzareno Zamperla (Captain Zaaph). *PROD*: Donatella Senatore and Giorgio Cardelli for Cine Vera s.p.a. (Rome); *AP*: Carthago Films (Tunisia); *PM*: Stefano Pegoraro; *UM:* Tarak Ben Ammar; *PS*: Alfredo Petri, Anselmo Parrinello; *ADM*: Luigi Scardino. *Country*: Italy. Filmed on location in Tunisia and at Cinecittà Studios (Rome); *Running time*: 105 min. (2720 m.); Visa n. 70805 (09/09/1977); *Release date*: 10/09/77; *Distribution*: F.A.R.; *Domestic gross*: 706,960,000 lire. *Also known as*: *Les requins du désert* (France; 11/29/1978), *Peloton del desierto* (Spain). *Home video*: New Entertainment World (DVD, Germany).

Note: the screenplay kept at Rome's CSC is credited to the sole Gastaldi.

1984

Due assi per un turbo

(Two Aces for One Turbo)
PROD: Jacopo Capanna and Giuseppe Perugia for VI.RE.PRO s.r.l. (Rome), *in association with*: RaiUno, Vianco studio, Polivideo, Video realizzazione programmi, Zini Film; Miklós Salusinszky for Magyar TV (Hungary); *PM*: Mauro Ruspantini, Orazio Tassara, György Müller. *Country*: Italy/Hungary.

TV series in 12 episodes, 60' each, produced in 1984 and broadcast from March 11 to 28 June 1987. Valerii directed two episodes.

—Chi primo arriva

S, SC: Luigi Malerba, Luciano Perugia [and Tonino Valerii]; *DOP*: Gianfranco Transunto; *M*: Detto Mariano; *E*: Antonio Siciliano; *C*: Piero Clemente, Massimo Monico; *MU*: Franco Casagni; *AD*: Girolamo Marzano; *SO*: Filippo Pallottini; *SOE*: Edmondo Gintili; *Stunts*: Franco Salamon, Sándor Boros; *GA*: Francesco Rachini; *SS*: Gianna Bellavia, Endre Flórián; *Location manager*: Alessandro Scepi. *Cast*: Renato D'Amore (Franco), Christian Fremont (Vanni), Alba Mottura (Giò), Philippe Leroy (Orazio), Adolfo Celi (Oreste), Franco Angrisano, Scott Coffey, Antonio Diana, Vito Fornari, Franco Javarone, Elio Marconato.

—L'uomo dal turbante rosso.

S, SC: Luciano Perugia, Cristina Ambrosetti; *DOP*: Mohammed Soudani; *M*: Detto Mariano; *E*: Pedro del Rey; *AC*: Fabio Bernasconi, Giovanni Martello, Luca Olgiati; *CO*: Chiara Fabbri; *MU*: Ronald Hardimann; *AD*: Donato Rodoni; *SO*: Remo Belli, Claudio Crotta, Loris Minetti; *SOE*: Edmondo Gintili; *Stunts*: Franco Salamon, Sándor Boros; *GA*: Francesco Rachini; *SS*: Gianna Bellavia, Endre Flórián; *Location manager*: Andreas Buccheger, Marco Viecelli. *Cast*: Renato D'Amore (Franco), Christian Fremont (Vanni), Alba Mottura (Giò), Philippe Leroy (Orazio), Inge [Ingeborg] Prinz (Rosa), Mirella Banti (Elena), Ugo Bologna (Art dealer), Louis Ducreux (Rudi), Miro Bizzonero, Ezio Conforti, Ermes Dondé, Sergio Filippini, Fiorello Fiorini.

1985

Inail: 100 anni e non li dimostra

DOP: Franco Bergamini. *PROD*: Istituto Luce—Italnoleggio Cinematografico (Rome). *Country*: Italy. *Running time*: 15' (420 m.); Visa n. 80470 (06/26/1985).

Caccia al ladro d'autore

DOP: Giulio Albonico (Telecolor); *M*: Gianni Ferrio; *E*: Antonio Siciliano; *C*: Stefano Moser; *AC*: Roberto Orrù; *AE*: Andrea Caterini; *SD*: Massimo Tavazzi; *CO*: Barbara Pugliese; *Stunt*: Nazzareno Zamperla; *AD*: Rosanna Seregni; *MU*: Walter Cossu; *Hair*: Iolanda Conti; *SS*: Renata Franceschi; *SO*: Roberto Forrest; *W*: Lucia Baldacci; *Asst Dubbing*: Elvira De Majo. *PROD*: Fulvio Lucisano, Gianni Hecht Lucari for Multimedia Film (Rome), RaiUno; *PM*: Gino Usai; *PS*: Bruno Tribbioli; *RAI delegate*: Ippolita Tescari; *ADM*: Bruno Menegotti; *Mix*: Bruno Moreal; *SOE*: Roberto Sterbina, Sotir Gjika, Tullio Arcangeli; *Music coordinator*: Guido Cenciarelli. *Country*: Italy.

TV series in 7 episodes, 60' each, broadcast starting on Sunday November 20, 1985, at 8:30 p.m. on RaiUno. Valerii directed three episodes:

—Addio Raffaello

(Goodbye Raffaello)
S: Ugo Liberatore; *SC*: Ugo Liberatore, Tonino Valerii [and Ottavio Alessi, uncredited]. *Cast*: Giuliano Gemma (Captain Maffei), Vanni Corbellini (Brigadier Pernizio), Isabel Russinova (Dr Popescu), Néstor Garay (Francesco Moreno), Giovanni Bergesio (Miglio Diberti), Renzo Scarcella (Marco Comolli), Anna Melato (Laura Canetti), Leda Negroni (Mrs. Brini), Piero Nuti (Schwarzhauger), Carlo Cartier (Alain, French Commissioner), Enrico Arrighetti, Lorenzo Fineschi, Giorgio Naddi, Mario Viggiano.

—La foresta che vola

(The Flying Forest)
S: Ugo Liberatore; *SC*: Ugo Liberatore, Tonino

Valerii. *Cast*: Giuliano Gemma (Captain Maffei), Vanni Corbellini (Brigadier Pernizio), Ennio Fantastichini (Captain Marcolin), Pietro Biondi (Gero Memoli), Francesco De Rosa (Mario Scatozza "El Ratón"), Denise Du Chêne, Fiorenza Marchegiani (Countess Laura Venin).

—*Cartografia sacra*
(Sacred Cartography)
S: Ugo Liberatore; *SC*: Ugo Liberatore, Tonino Valerii. *Cast*: Giuliano Gemma (Captain Maffei), Vanni Corbellini (Brigadier Pernizio), Fabrizio Bentivoglio, Italo Dall'Orto, Memo Dini, Benedetto Fanna, Barbara Magnolfi, Michele Mirabella, Marco Morellini, Carola Stagnaro.

1986

Unscrupulous
(*Senza scrupoli*)
S: Mino Roli; *SC*: Riccardo Ghione, Tonino Valerii; *Dial*: Vinicio Marinucci; *DOP*: Giulio Albonico (35mm, Fujicolor, Telecolor); *M*: James Senese, Joe Amoruso; *E*: Antonio Siciliano; *PD*: Elio Micheli; *C*: Adolfo Bartoli, Enrico Lucidi; *AC*: Andrea Busirivici; *AE*: Andrea Caterini; *SD*: Anna Fasolo Franzetti; *CO*: Francesca Panicali; *MU*: Alvaro Rossi; *Hair*: Domenico Luzii; *AD*: Walter Italici; *SO*: Umberto Montesanti; *ST*: Tullio Arcangeli, Sotir Gjika; *SOE*: Roberto Sterbini; *Mix*: Bruno Moreal; *SP*: Pietro Cagnazzo; *GA*: Antonio Gasbarrini; *KG*: Francesco Mele; *W*: Valeria Sponsali; *Unit publicist*: Cristiana Caimmi; *SS*: Francesca Montani; *Dubbing supervisor*: Tonino Valerii; *Asst dubbing*: Elvira De Majo. *Cast*: Sandra Wey (Silvia Combi), Marzio Honorato (Diego Campus), Antonio Marsina (Massimo Combi), Cinzia de Ponti (Clara), Vincenzo Cavaliere (Diego's accomplice), Sandra Canale [Alessandra Pimpinella], Ferruccio Casacci, Antonio Cippo, Lorenzo Gobello, Nicola Il Grande, Giovanni Liboni, Tullio Lutrario, Marco Marchisio, Giuseppe Mendolicchio, Domiziano Arcangeli. *PROD*: Enzo Gallo, Lello [Domenico] Scarano for Grandangolo soc. cooperativa a r.l. (Turin/Rome); *PM*: Gino Usai; *PS*: Antonio Scarano; *PSe*: Franca Longo; *ADM*: Bruno Menegotti. *Country*: Italy. Filmed in Turin and at Incir—De Paolis Studios (Rome); *Running time*: 95 min. (2435 m.); Visa n. 81036 (11/21/1985—V.M.18); *Release date*: 01/09/1986; *Distribution*: 20th Century Fox; *Domestic gross*: 1,185,000,000 lire. *Home video*: Home Video Hellas (VHS, Greece—English language)

1987

Brothers in Blood
(*La sporca insegna del coraggio*)
S and SC: Roberto Leoni; *DOP*: Giancarlo Ferrando; *M*: Riz Ortolani, conducted by the composer; *E*: Antonio Siciliano; *PD*: Carlo Leva, Massimo Corevi; *C*: Bruno Cascio; *AC*: Alessandro Capuccio, Luigi Conversi; *AD*: Roberto Leoni; *SO*: Umberto Montesanti; *AE*: Minni Marani; *MU*: Alvaro Rossi, Rosario Prestopino; *KG*: Matteo Giordano, Amerigo Carlodani; *GA*: Armando Moreschini; *MA*: Franco Fantasia; *Weapons*: Giuseppe Carozza, Elio Terribili. *SS*: Luda Arlorio; *SP*: Vincenzo Savino, Franco Vitali. *Cast*: Bo Svenson (Steven Elliott Logan "Steel"), Carlo Mucari (Danny De Mayo), Peter Hooten (Richard), Werner Pochath (Travis), Nat Kelly Cole (Mark), Franklin Dominguez, Juan José Caballos, Martin Balsam (Major Briggs), Rocco Lerro, Sergio Testori, Pietro Torrisi. *PROD*: Eugenio Startari for Three International Sisters Film (Rome); *GM*: Maurizio Mattei; *PS*: Gaetano Di Leone. *Country*: Italy; Filmed on location in the United States (New York) and Dominican Republic (Santo Domingo, San Pedro de Maucoris); *Running time*: 90 min. (2500 m.); Visa n. 82569 (05/13/1987).

Note: The film was not released theatrically in Italy. According to Roberto Leoni, Franco Fantasia (credited as assistant director) was actually only the master of arms, while the actual assistant director was Leoni himself.

Shatterer
S: Tonino Valerii, Ernesto Gastaldi; *SC*: Yasuo Tanami, Ernesto Gastaldi, Tonino Valerii; *DOP*: Giulio Albonico; *M*: Tot Taylor; *E*: Antonio Siciliano; *ArtD*: Stefano Ortolani; *C*: Marco Onorato; *AC*: Andrea Busiri Vici, Pietro Clemente; *SD*: Livia Del Priore; *CO*: Francesca Panicali; *ACO*: Claudio Manzi; *Hair*: Teodora Bruno; *MU*: Rosario Prestopino; *1stAD*: Walter Italici; *2ndAD*: Mario Miyakawa; *AE*: Patrizia Malvestito, Fabrizio Di Blasi, Loretta Mattioli; *SO*: Roberto Alberghini; *B*: Marco Di Biase, Antonio Pantano; *Stunt*: Franco Salamon; *SP*: Gianfranco Salis; *Rally consultant*: Romano Fazio; *SS*: Francesca Ghiotto; *PrM*: Adriano Tiberi, Luciano Argento; *W*: Valeria Sponsali; *KG*: Italo Clemente; *GA*: Alberico Novelli. *Cast*: Kôji Kikkawa (Koichi Honda), Andy J. Forest (Victor Bridges), Marina Suma (Adriana, De Majo's Secretary), Orazio Orlando (Don Turi

Catalano), Marzio Honorato (Don Silvio), Mimmo Palmara (Dr. De Majo), Salvatore Billa (Tessio), Beatrice Ring (Lisa), Daniela Novak (Maria), Tano Cimarosa (Don Michele), Toshirô Mifune (Murai), Dalila Di Lazzaro (Secretary at SCD), Greta Vaillant [Vayan] (Sofia Catalano), Nando [Ferdinando] Murolo (Marco), Noburo Homma (Yanagida), Mario Miyakawa (Hiroshi), Lorenzo Flaherty (Salvatore Impellitteri), Francesco Torrisi (Mafia henchman), Giovanni [Nello] Pazzafini (1st Mafia Killer), Elio Bonadonna (2nd Mafia Killer), Riccardo [Parisio] Perrotti (New York Mafia boss), Tommaso Palladino (Mafia man in New York), John Learner (American Spy), Jack Gwillim (voice). *PROD*: Asao Kumada for Uanchi Corporation (Rome), Watanabe Production (Tokyo), Film Select (Geneve); *EP*: Shin Watanabe; *AP*: Francesco Martino de Carles; *PS*: Massimo Ferrero; *PSe*: Simona Mattei, Rossella Ferrero, Patrizia Pierucci; *Associate planners*: Komei Fujii, Toshirô Murayama; *GM (Japan)*: Yuichi Ino; *PM*: Mario Di Biase; *Accountants*: Silvana Olasio, Alessandra Sampaolo, Eleonora Profeta. *Country*: Japan/Italy/Switzerland. Filmed in Palermo and Ragusa (Sicily), Paestum (Campania), Rome and London; *Running time*: 110 min. Also known as: *Shataraa* (Japan), *Sicilian Connection* (Italy).

Note: The film was not submitted to the Italian board of censors. It was broadcast on Italian television in 1992, with the title *Sicilian Connection*. It was distributed in Japan by Toho. Original soundtrack album released by Sounds Marketing System, Inc. Japan.

1989

Il ricatto
(Blackmail)

D: Tonino Valerii, Ruggero Deodato; *S*: Ennio De Concini, Massimo Ranieri; *SC*: Ennio De Concini, Luca Rossi; *DOP*: Pasquale Rachini (Eastmancolor); *M*: Riz Ortolani, *played by* Orchestra Unione musicisti di Roma; *assistant and coordinator*: Danilo Salone; *engineer of the musical tracks*: Sergio Marcotulli; *E*: Antonio Siciliano; *PD*: Lorenzo Baraldi; *C*: Antonio Schiavo Lena; *AC*: Stefano Guidi, Rodolfo Angi; *SD*: Walter Caprara; *CO*: Bona Nasalli Rocca; *MU*: Fabrizio Sforza; *AMU*: Enrico Jacoponi; *W*: Angela Silighini, Bianca Erba; *AE*: Andrea Caterini, Valentina Curati, Pasquale Calone, Maria Luisa Lisci, Elena D'Antona; *AD*: Walter Italici, Bruno Nappi; *2ndAD*: Salvatore Chiosi; *SS*: Renata Franceschi; *Consultant Naples*: Franco Rapa; *MA*: Benito Stefanelli; *Stunts*: Gianlorenzo Bernini, Ottaviano Dell'Acqua, Bruno Di Luia, Marco Stefanelli, Marcello Verziera, Omero Capanna, Angelo Ragusa; *SP*: Benito Alchimede; *B*: Ettore Mancini; *GA*: Francesco Rachini; *KG*: Antonino Costantino; *PrM*: Remo Pizzaroni, Danilo Pagnotta; *Mix*: Alberto Doni; *Dubbing director*: Angelo Nicotra; *Asst dubbing*: Roberta Schiavon. *Cast*: Massimo Ranieri (Commissioner Fedeli), Fernando Rey (Judge Di Pola), Jacques Perrin (Grossi), Barbara Nascimbene (Leonetta Rasmo), Kim Rossi Stuart (Luca), Jean-Christophe Brétigniere (Francesco), Barbara Ricci (Giovanna Rasmo), Piero Pepe (Angelo Rasmo), Luca De Filippo (Don Vito), Leo Gullotta (Salvatore Musumeci "Carla"), Roberto Herlitzka (Baratti), Spiros Focas (Karsan), Orazio Orlando (Undersecretary Liscio), Vincenzo Romaniello ("Teresa"), Pasquale Russo ("Lucrezia"), Pastora Vega (Dora), Antonio Casagrande, Maurizio Berti, Kara Donati, Luigi De Filippo, Benito Artesi, Andrea Aureli, Pasquale Aveta, Aldo Barone, Rossella Baldari, Serena Bennato, Mario Colli, Giovanni Febbraro, Alessandro Fontana, Giovannella Gesmundo, Pippo Grasso, Giacomo Maisto, Carla Mancini, Camillo Milli, Tommaso Palladino, Fernando Pannullo, Salvatore Puccinelli, Patrizio Rispo, Gigi Savoia, Rosenda Scharschmidt, Massimiliano Ubaldi, Luigi Uzzo. *PROD*: Reteitalia (Milano), realized by Sergio Giussani for RA-MA 2000 (Rome), Telemax (Paris), TV3 (Barcelona); *PM*: Roberto Romoli, Gino Usai; *PS*: Enzo Canaldi; *PSe*: Franca Longo, Patrizia Nofroni; *ADM*: Giorgio Angelini; *Cashier*: Clara Mancini. *Country*: Italy/France/Spain. Filmed in Naples, Milan, Bergamo, Brianza, and at Incir—De Paolis Studios (Rome). *Running time*: 300 min.

Note: TV miniseries in 5 episodes, 60' each, broadcast from Sunday, April 23, 1989, to May 15, 1989, at 8:30 p.m., on Canale 5. Valerii directed the first three episodes and part of the fourth, completed by Ruggero Deodato, who directed the fifth and final one.

Due madri
(Two Mothers)

S, SC: Ugo Pirro, Massimo Russo, Marta Prandi [and Tonino Valerii, uncredited]; *DOP*: Giancarlo Ferrando (Eastmancolor); *M*: Franco Piersanti; *PD, ArtD*: Adriana Bellone, Renzo Gronchi;

C: Giuseppe Venditti; *AC*: Alessandro Capuccio; *CO*: Giovanna Cossia De Poli; *ACO*: Antonella Corno; *E*: Antonio Siciliano; *AE*: Giancarlo Morelli; *AD*: Walter Italici; *SO*: Bruno Pupparo; *B*: Renato Ciunfrini; *MU*: Pietro Tenoglio; *Hair*: Adriana Sforza; *SS*: Nicoletta Vegezzi; *SP*: Sebastiano Sfringola; *Asst dubbing*: Elvira De Majo. *Cast*: Barbara De Rossi (Dolores), Sonia Petrovna (Ester Stasi), Gianni Garko (Oscar Stasi), Pierluigi Misasi, Sabine Mazlo (Pinuccia/Pilar), Anna Maria Baratta, Barbara Berengo Gardin, Lidia Biondi, Carlo Cartier, Grace Dean, Angelica Del Solar Dorrego, Alicia Haydee Leoni, Gianni Olivieri, Dora Pamphili, Fernando Pannullo, Sonia Riva, Valeria Sabel, Luciano Tomadoni, Anita Zagaria, Gabriella Zito, and with the tango dancers of Maestro Carlos Valles. *PROD*: RAI, Plurivision (Rome); *PM*: Gino Usai; *PS*: Bruno Tribbioli; *PSe*: Mario Signoretti; *ADM*: Lavinia Gualino; *RAI delegate*: Fiorenza Fiorentino. *Country*: Italy. *Running time*: 95 min.

Note: TV movie broadcast on Sunday, April 30, 1989, at 8:30 p.m. on RaiUno, with over 5 million viewers. Some sources list it under the working title *Cronaca di un amore materno*.

1991

Una prova d'innocenza
(Evidence of Innocence)

S: Franco Verucci; *SC*: Franco Verucci, Tonino Valerii; *DOP*: Tonino Nardi; *M*: Claudio Piersanti; *E*: Mario Morra; *PD*: Luciano Spadoni; *C*: Claudio Morabito; *AC*: Emanuele Mazzilli; *2ndAC*: Maurizio Forconi; *SO*: Luciano Fiorentini; *CO*: Erica Biscossi; *AD*: Walter Italici; *SD*: Massimo Tavazzi; *APD*: Marta Maffucci; *ACO*: Angela Capuano; *HMU*: Gino Tamagnini; *MU*: Tiziana Sisi; *Hair*: Corrado Cristofori, Elisabetta De Leonardis; *SS*: Monica Raimondo; *AE*: Rita Triunveri; *2ndAE*: Mario Recupito, Severino Rossi; *B*: Maurizio Miani; *KG*: Italo Clemente; *GA*: Vittorio Pescetelli; *PrM*: Giulio Musto; *W*: Amedeo Monti; *MA*: Riccardo Mioni; *Stunts*: Omero Capanna, Giovanna Ciacchi, Benito Pacifico, Fabio Paiella, Ivano Silveri; *SE*: Paolo Ricci; *Color technician*: Giancarlo Barberi; *Post-production coordinator*: Antonella Galanti; *Dubbing sound*: Bartolomeo Messina; *Mix*: Roberto Moroni; *SOE*: Luciano Anzellotti; *Enrico Montesano's unit publicist*: Cristiana Caimmi. *Cast*: Enrico Montesano (Don Alessio), Corinne Dacla (Rita), Luigi Pistilli (Amleto), Angiola Baggi, Victor Cavallo, Renato Cestié, Paolo Baroni, Bruno Corazzari (Guido Marino), Antonella Della Porta, Vittorio Duse, Carmine Faraco, Ivano Marescotti (Filippelli), Claudio Gora (Gilberto Mantovani), Gianni Garko (Cremonese), Pino Ammendola (Police official), Laura Bacchiocchi (Wedding Guest), Gil Baroni (Magistrate), Clyde James Barret (Black man in round-up), Laura Campana (Wedding Guest), Elena Canali (Wedding Guest), Adelio Chitto (Don Alibrandi), Donatella Ciancarelli (Wedding Guest), Carlo Colombo Prison Chaplain), Franco Concilio (Dominican Friar), Francesco Dickmann (Groom), Stefano De Paolis (Marcello), Cristina Santini (Wedding Guest), Paola Fogagnolo (Wedding Guest), Lucia Frazzetto (Filippelli's secretary), Nino Fuscagni (Doctor at clinic), Anna Lelio (Don Alessio's mother), Teodosio Losito (Franco Cruciani), Nadia Mayer (Bride), Giuseppe Marini (2nd Bank clerk), Luigi Montini (Commissioner at the incident site), Tommaso Palladino (Cremonese's Bodyguard), Anacleto Papa (Marco Tessitore), Elisabetta Quaresima (Wedding Guest), Alessandra Sestan (Wedding Guest), Katia Silvetti (Wedding Guest), Silvano Spoletini (Poolhall boss), Sergio Stefanini (2nd Employee of the Land Registry), Pino Patti (1st Employee of the Land Registry), Nicoletta Via (Wedding Guest). *PROD*: Adriano Arié for Solaris Cinematografica; *PM*: Bruno Ricci; *GM*: Gianni Saragò; *PS*: Francesco Merolle; *ADM*: Carlo Gagliardi, Eleonora Fraternali; *PSe*: Francesco Lattuada. *Country*: Italy. Filmed at Incir—De Paolis Studios (Rome). *Running time*: 180 min.

Nota: TV movie in two parts, 90 minutes each, broadcast on February 12 and 14, 1991, on RaiDue.

1992

Il cielo non cade mai
(The Sky Never Falls)

D: Gianni Ricci [and Tonino Valerii]; *S*: Maria Venturi; *SC*: Veronica Salvi, Rodolfo Roberti; *M*: Guido and Maurizio De Angelis. *Cast*: Kim Rossi Stuart (Nicola Brentano), Anaïs Jeanneret (Francesca Fasser), Sandrine Caron (Camille Delaunay), Yves Collignon (Paul Delaunay), Stefano Davanzati (Roberto), Gianni Garko (Battista), Roberto Herlitzka (Vittorio Brentano), Lorenza Indovina (Angela Rossetti), Mita Medici (Clara Negroni), Anna Teresa Rossini (Silvia Brentano), Marcello Tusco (Giovanni

Fasser), Anita Zagaria (Diana Fasser). *Country*: Italy/France. *Running time*: 300 min.
Also known as: *Nur aus Liebe*.
Note: TV mini-series in 3 parts, broadcast on December 1, 2 and 3 1992, on RaiDue. Valerii was replaced after several days.

1997

Un bel dì vedremo
(One Fine Day We Will See)
S, SC: Enzo Azzolina, Arturo Orsini, from an idea by Kon Ichikawa; *DOP*: Mario Vulpiani; *M*: Stelvio Cipriani; *E*: Antonio Siciliano; *PD, CO*: Maria Luigia Battani; *C*: Filippo Neroni; *AC*: Franco Sterpa; *ACO*: Flavia Santorelli; *APD*: Carlo De Marino; *ArtD (Opera scenes)*: Setsu Asakura; *Stage lighting*: Sumio Yoshi; *AD*: Claudio Bernabei; *2ndAD*: Sabrina Ascani; *Sound Engineer*: Marco Treccioni; *Sound Designer*: Mick M. Sawaguchi; *HD Cinema Supervision*: Shin Naemura; *HD Head Technician*: Kôji Itakura; *HD Technicians*: Kazu Matsubayashi, Takayuki Ozasa, Norikazu Kuniwa, Naoto Ichioka; *SOE*: Yutaka Imai; *SO*: Marco Di Biase; *SOA*: Yutaka Otsuka, Yuji Aida; *B*: Alfredo Petti; *MU*: Franco Napoli; *Hair*: Maria Pia Petroni; *W*: Paola Perrilli; *SS*: Adele Parrillo; *PrM*: Giampiero Huber; *GA*: Marco Palermi; *El*: Carlo Alberto Pagura, Andrea Di Biase; *KG*: Sergio Fabriani; *G*: Marco Sallustri; *Groupman*: Gerlando Sergioli; *Unit publicist*: Elena Francot. *Cast*: Massimo Girotti (Emilio Venditti), Rajna Kabaivanska (Isabella Lucchese), Giuliano Gemma (Gianfranco), Massimo Wertmüller (Marco), Antonella Fattori (Claudia), Carlo Kumada (Bellomo), Eljana Popova (Fulvia), Jacopo Martino De Carles (Davide), Vera Gemma (Monica), Marilú Prati (Anna), Giovanna Trisolini (Rita), Teresa Ronchi (Teresa), Armando Cabassi (Alfonso), Augusto Palmas (Piero), William Bignami (Pino), Nadia Morani (Tiziana), Luigi Girati (Totò), Cataldo Di Leo (Antonio), Pierantonio Zoli (Giuseppe), Andrea Martino De Carles (Gigi), Federica Parisi (Chiara), Maria Pia Calzone (Young Isabella), Giorgia Cristiano (Micaela), Chisako Hara (Director), Gaetano Amato (Councilor), Antonio Buonopane, Clelia Santilli, Renato De Rienzo, Umberto Valentino, Mimmo Schiavone, Nunzia Schiavone, Renata Tafuri, Elena Parmense, Luigi Longobardi, Letizia Netti, Valerio Apice, Marco Esposito, Luigi Conte, Salvatore Ceccarini, Vanni Baiano, Roberto Nigro, Sergio Fornaiuolo, Nando Saino, Gino Tommasino. *PROD*: Asao Kumada for Uanchi Corporation (Rome) and Nhk Tokyo (Tokyo); in collaboration with Surf Film, TBS Vision, Comune di Salerno; *PM*: Nicolò Forte; *GM*: Francesco De Carles; *PS*: Vittoria Regano, Isabella Aldrovandi; *PSe*: Emanuele Ranesi; *ADM*: Angelo Frezza; *EP*: Nobuo Isobe, Yukio Tomizawa. *Country*: Italy/Japan. *Running time*: 90 min. *Also known as*: *Vom mai vedea* (Romania).
Note: The film was not submitted to the Italian board of censors.

Una vacanza all'inferno
(A Vacation in Hell)
S: loosely based on *Bangkwang* by Fabrizio Paladini; *SC*: Tonino Valerii; *Dialogue revision*: Lorenzo Cairoli; *Dialogue adaptation*: Ruggero Busetti; *DOP*: Sergio D'Offizi; *M*: Fabrizio Siciliano; *E*: Antonio Siciliano; *C*: Claudio Palmiere; *AC*: Andrea Fastella; *2ndAC*: Mario Palermi, Roberto Emidi; *AE*: Mario D'Ambrosio, *2ndAE*: Giulia D'Angeli; *PD*: Franco Vanorio; *APD*: Marco Conforti; *CO*: Stefano Giovani; *W*: Giovanna Russu; *MU*: Carla Catanzaro; *AMU*: Isabella Morelli; *Hair*: Luciano Paolo D'Apollonio; *AD*: Umberto Riccioni; *2ndAD*: Alessandro Trapani; *SO*: Riccardo Palmieri; *B*: Patrizia Palmieri; *Unit publicist*: Morabito-Nobile-Scarafone; *Dialogue coach*: Steven Luotto; *SS*: Fiammetta Nazzarri; *capo gruppo*: Giancarlo Bizzarri; *SP*: Pierfrancesco Bruni, Riccardo Caramanico; *GA*; Franco Caporale; *KG*: Marco Caporale; *El*: Efisio Usai, Pietro Emidi, Stefano Emidi; *G*: Eugenio Fortuna, Giampiero Manza; *Groupmen*: Antonino Rubino, Raffaele Battistelli; *Set construction*: Paolo Del Bravo, Corrado Ermacora; *PrM*: Roberto Masotti; *Camera Car Driver*: Giorgio Ricci; *Wardrobe Driver*: Nello Amato; *Roulotte Drivers*: Giuseppe Menegatti, Nicola Ciccarella; *Mix*: Romano Pampaloni; *Foley*: Mario Giacco. *Location shooting (Philippines)*. *Legal assistance*: Adv. Luciano Sovena; *Casting director*: Ine P. Radiasa; *Location supervisor*: Lope Juran, Jr.; *PM*: Lito Zebra Malabat; *PA*: Ray Serrano; *SO*: Juanito Clemente; *B*: Donald Santos; *AC*: Bernardo Gabilo; *PrM*: Ray Lachica; *G*: Angelo De Guzman, Gerardo Rey; *El*: Ernesto Baldonado, Francis Cumicad; *Groupman*: Anatalio Jurado; *Plature vehicles in charge*: Crispin Rebolledo; *Dubbing*: CDL doppiaggio edizioni; *Dubbing director*: Renzo Stacchi. *Cast*: Marco Leonardi (Angelo Ungarelli), F. Murray Abraham (Belis-

ario Salina), Mirca Viola (Michela Montini), Giancarlo Giannini (Raffaele Ortega), Rolando Ravello (Piero), Alessandro Zamattio (Luciano Risé), Federico Pacifici (Mario), Daryl Kwan (Lt. Prang), Giancarlo Cosentino (Daniel), Mark Wong (Kao), Marco Di Stefano (Gaston), Carlo Cumada (Morales), Eljana [Elzhana] Nikolova Popova (Gabriella, Belisario's Wife), Emanuele Carucci Viterbi (Sebastian), Luciano Roffi (Piero's Father), Gaetano Cafaro (Gonzales), Marcello di Martire (Angelo's Father), Francesco Gabriele (Inmate), Nouyen Khoa (Guard), Arnold Lee (Fok), Darry Lwin (Ministry of Interior's Inspector), Riccardo Montereali (Carlo), Beniamino Onorato (Paolo), Raffaella Panichi (Angelo's Mother), Vanna Rey (Luciano's Girlfriend), Bobby Rhodes (John), Richard Sammel (Bleer), Sua Julien (Agent), Hong Ping Tang (Guard), Abet Zealcida (Narcotics Agent), Willie Liami (Mickey Mouse), Eddie Llaneta (Narcotics Inspector), Tony Manalo (Custom Agent), Justice Ramon Mabutas (Judge), Archie Ventoza (Counselor Putri), Mike Casas (Public Prosecutor), Nitoy Clemente (Attorney General), Armando Cuneta (Minister's Secretary). *PROD*: Enzo Gallo for Metropolis Film; *PM*: Gino Usai; *PS*: Andrea Usai; *PSe*: Rosa Carta; *ADM*: Antonio Cesarini; *Drivers*: Domenico Ceci, Massimiliano Coramusi, Giuseppe Coletto. *Country*: Italy. Filmed in the Philippines and in Frosinone; *Running time*: 103 min. (2823 m.); Visa n. 92097 (11/06/1997—V.M.14); *Release date*: 28/11/97; *Distribution*: C.D.I.—Buena Vista International Italia; *Domestic gross*: 47,154,000 lire.

Note: Declared "Film of National Cultural Interest" by the Presidency of the Council of Ministers—Department of Spectacle.

Appearances as Himself

1983

Arrivano i vostri, ovvero storia avventurosa del western all'italiana

D: Isabella Bruno; *SC:* Duccio Tessari, with the collaboration of Isabella Bruno and Orio Caldiron; *M:* Guido and Maurizio De Angelis; *E:* Isabella Bruno. *PROD*: RaiDue, produced by L.P. Film s.r.l.; *EP*: Lucia Campione; *GM*: Fabiola Banzi. *Country*: Italy; *Running time*: 600 min.

Note: TV documentary in 10 installments, of 60 minutes each, broadcast from November 24 to December 25, 1983. Aside from Valerii, other interviewees were Age, Enzo Barboni, Maria Barony, Sergio Bergonzelli, Laura Betti, Mel Brooks, Enzo G. Castellari, David Carradine, Franco Castellano, Sergio Corbucci, Damiano Damiani, Mark Damon, Sergio Donati, Edoardo Fajardo, Paulo Roberto Falcao, Henry Fonda, Lucio Fulci, Gianni Garko, Giuliano Gemma, Franco Giraldi, Terence Hill, Klaus Kinski, Stelvio Massi, Tomas Milian, Franco Nero, Domenico Paolella, Leo Pescarolo, Pipolo, Fernando Sancho, Sergio Sollima, Lionel Stander, Rod Steiger, Lee Van Cleef, Luciano Vincenzoni, Nazzareno Zamperla, Manuel Zarzo.

1989

Viva Leone!

D: Nick Freand Jones; *C:* Angelo Uhana, Paul Morris; *Rostrum camera operator:* Ken Morse; *Graphic Designer*: Bob Cummins; *E:* Ian McKendrick, Jan Deas; *Dubbing Mixer*: Ron Edmonds; *Consultants*: Christopher Frayling (London), John Francis Lane (Rome). *PROD*: Nick Freand Jones for Acquisizione Programmativa; *PA*: Rosemary Braithwaite. *Country*: United Kingdom; *Running time*: 45 min.

Note: Documentary broadcast on BBC2 on December 24, 1989, at 11 p.m., to introduce a retrospective cycle of Leone's films. Aside from Valerii, other interviewees were Sir Christopher Frayling, Alex Cox, Ennio Morricone, Andrea Leone and (in archive footage dating back respectively to 1975, 1977 and 1984) Henry Fonda, Clint Eastwood and Sergio Leone.

2002

Érase una vez en Europa: Capítulo uno—Coproducción (50/50, 30/70, 70/30)

D: Manel Mayol; *Creator:* Carlos Prats; *SC and research*: Joan Ferré, Carlos Aguilar; *DOP*: Pere Ballesteros, Angel Puig, José Antonio de Álamo; *M:* Salvador Rey; *Graphic design*: Enric Jardí; *Graphic research*: Carlos Aguilar, Rafael Dalmau; *E:* Lola Muñoz; *Properties*: Frank Plant; *W:* María Domingo; *MU:* Silvia Parra; *SO:* Josep Perales; *El:* David Fernández, José María Tarradona; *Host*: Christopher Lee. *PROD*: Sara Gibbings for Media Park (Madrid); *AP*: Carles Ruiz, Patricia Lora, Ana Gutiérrez; *PA*: Frankie Colomer. *Country*: Spain; *Running time*: 30 min.

Note: TV documentary in 13 installments, 30 min. each, dedicated to European cinema, broadcast starting on March 3, 2002, on the satellite channel Via Digital. Aside from Valerii, other interviewees are Sir Christopher Frayling, Artur Brauner, Erika Blanc, Joaquín Romero Marchent, Eugenio Martín, Norbert Moutier, Giuliano Gemma, Carlo Rustichelli, José Giovanni, Carlos Aguilar, Jesús Franco, Lina Romay, Sergio Sollima, Horst Wendlandt, Alessandro Alessandroni, Ennio Morricone, Martine Beswick, Wolfgang Preiss, Antonio Margheriti, Jacques Deray, Dario Argento, Ingrid Pitt, Caroline Munro, Franco Nero, Jack Taylor, Bud Spencer, Marianne Koch, Riccardo Freda, Paul Naschy, Amando de Ossorio, Aldo Sambrell, Jorge Grau, Antonio Isasi.

Mi chiamo Tonino Valerii e faccio Western

D: Anna Fusaro, Antonio D'Orazio; *DOP*: Antonio D'Orazio, Claudio Di Giuliantonio (Betacam); *M*: Art of Noise, Ennio Morricone; *E*: Anna Fusaro, Antonio D'Orazio. *PROD*: Prodeo. *Country*: Italy; *Running time*: 42 min.

Note: Video interview with Tonino Valerii, interspersed with footage of the director returning to the "places of memory," footage from his films and still photographs.

2006

Sergio Leone—Il mio modo di vedere le cose

D: Giulio Reale; *DOP*: Marco Mangiarotti, Ferran Paredes, Alessandro Bosco, Stephanie Roth; *M*: Antonino Stella; *E*: Calin Hodis. *PROD*: Giulio Reale. *Country*: Italy; *Running time*: 62 min.

Note: Documentary on Sergio Leone with footage from his films and interviews with his collaborators, friends and the actors who worked with him. Aside from Valerii, other interviewees are Eugenio Alabisio, Nino Baragli, Claudia Cardinale, Damiano Damiani, Roberto Forges Davanzati, Alberto De Martino, Piero De Bernardi, Tonino Delli Colli, Franco Di Giacomo, Sir Christopher Frayling, Valerio Garzia, Vittorio Giacci, Franco Giraldi, Carla Leone, Gianni Maddaleni, Luigi Magni, Claudio Mancini, Giuliano Montaldo, Luca Morsella, Ennio Morricone, Gianfranco Pannone, José María Rodriguez, Giuseppe Ruzzolini, Giancarlo Santi, Antonio Scaramuzza, Carlo Tafani, Carlo Verdone, Luciano Vincenzoni, Eli Wallach.

2013

I Tarantiniani

D: Maurizio Tedesco, Steve [Stefano] Della Casa; *SC*: Maurizio Tedesco, Steve Della Casa; *DOP*: Alessandro Nardone; *E*: Alessandro Bianchi. *PROD*: Baires Produzioni, Rai Cinema, Surf Film. *Country*: Italy; *Running time*: 59 min.

Note: Documentary on Italian genre cinema, "rediscovered" by Quentin Tarantino (hence the title: The Tarantinians). Aside from Valerii, other interviewees are Tomas Milian, Enzo G. Castellari, Lamberto Bava, Ruggero Deodato, Barbara Bouchet, Sergio Martino, Luciano Martino, Umberto Lenzi, Fernando di Leo, Franco Nero.

Chapter Notes

Introduction

1. Tonino Valerii, "Le misteriose origini del western italiano," in Roberto Festi (edited by) *C'era una volta il ... western all'italiana. Mito e protagonisti* (Madonna di Campiglio: APT Madonna di Campiglio / Provincia di Trento / Stampalith, 2001), p. 21.
2. Aldo Viganò, "Giochi nel canyon del postmoderno," in *C'era una volta il ... western all'italiana*, p. 7.

Chapter One

1. Tommaso La Selva, *Tonino Valerii: mai temere il Leone* (Milan: Nocturno Libri, 2000), p. 67.
2. Il Solco, 14 September 1942, reported in Egidio Marinaro, *L'albo dei sindaci del comune montoriese. Suggestioni e risultati di una ricerca* (Montorio al Vomano: Comune di Montorio al Vomano, 2010).
3. *Podestà* (from the latin *potestas*, meaning "power") was the name given to the high officials in many Italian cities in the later Middle Ages. The term was exhumed during Fascism: in 1926 Mussolini's senate issued a decree which suspended elected local government and replaced it with an authoritarian figure appointed by the Fascist Party, called *podestà*.
4. Marinaro, *L'albo dei sindaci del comune montoriese.*
5. Adriano Baracco (1907–1976) was the editor-in-chief of many of post-World War II's most popular film magazines. He also acted as producer, founding Zenith Cinematografica with Mino Loy in 1961. Between 1962 and 1972 he worked as screenwriter on a number of films, including *The Treasure of San Gennaro* (*Operazione San Gennaro*, 1966, Dino Risi), *Bad Arabella* (*Arabella*, 1967, Mauro Bolognini), *Danger: Diabolik* (*Diabolik*, 1968, Mario Bava), *Gangsters '70* (1968, Mino Guerrini). He also wrote two science fiction novels under the pseudonym Audie Barr, *I figli della nuvola* (1957) and *Gli schiavi di Rox* (1958), both published in Mondadori's *Urania* series.
6. The Centro Sperimentale di Cinematografia (CSC), literally "Experimental film centre" is Italy's national film school, established in 1935. It is the oldest film school in Western Europe, and the country's most important institution for training, research and experimentation in the field of cinema.
7. Gastaldi is referring to the legal battle fought by Sacchi—the founder in 1971 of the local television channel Telebiella, Italy's first private TV channel—against RAI television (Italy's state television), which by the mid–1970s led to a new legislative framework that allowed a competitive system on the part of private broadcasters.
8. Email interview with the author, January 2008.
9. Ibid.
10. ANICA is an abbreviation for Associazione Nazionale Industrie Cinematografiche Audiovisive e multimediali (National Association of Cinema, Audiovisual and Multimedia Industries). Founded in 1944, it represents Italian film industries in their relationships with political institutions and in union negotiations. ANICA selects the Italian language films that will represent the country at the annual Academy Awards.
11. By then, the debuting Ferrari—who had been assistant to Rossellini, Antonioni and Bolognini—was considered the promise of Italian cinema. Unfortunately, *Laura nuda* was targeted by the censors, in no small measure because of the title: After being initially rejected, it was eventually granted a visa after a number of cuts were imposed, and given a V.M. 16 rating. Angelo Rizzoli's distribution company Cineriz made a backroom deal with the censorship commission (which promised to close one eye when revising the costly anthology *Boccaccio 70*, produced by Rizzoli and directed by De Sica, Fellini, Monicelli and Visconti) and released it in mid-August, in order for it to pass unnoticed among the public. And it did. Not only was *Laura nuda* a commercial flop, but it irreparably damaged Ferrari's career.
12. "Lu pisce spada" was one of Modugno's most popular songs, which originally appeared on the B-side of the singer's third single "La donna riccia."
13. Email interview with the author, January 2008.
14. As Julian Berry (a pen name adopted as an homage to a roommate by the name of Julian Birri) Gastaldi also found hospitality on the pages of the renowned science-fiction pocket book series *Urania*, published by Mondadori, with the novel *Iperbole infinita* (*Infinite Hyperbole*, 1960) and the serial novelette *Una storia da non credere* (*An Unbelievable Story*, 1961); previously, with other aliases (Freddy Foster, James Duffy), he published crime novels, such as *Brivido sulla schiena* (*Shiver on the Back*) and *Sangue in tasca* (*Blood in the Pocket*).
15. Riccardo Freda's *I vampiri* (1957) dealt with a peculiar kind of bloodsucker that had nothing to do with the traditional monster, whereas Steno's *Uncle Was a Vampire* (*Tempi duri per i vampiri*, 1959) was a spoof of Hammer Films, co-starring Christopher Lee, that played the genre stereotypes for laughs.

16. Email interview with the author, January 2014. Actress Mara Maryl (real name Maria Chianetta) is Gastaldi's wife.

17. La Selva, *Tonino Valerii: mai temere il Leone*, p. 104.

18. The so-called "Hand of Glory" is the dried and pickled hand of a hanged man (usually the left hand) which in Old European beliefs has a great magic power, if turned into a candlestick for which the candles are made from fat from the same corpse. The candle, so made, lighted and placed in the Hand of Glory (as if in a candlestick), would have rendered motionless all persons to whom it was presented.

19. In one of the episodes, Ugo Tognazzi plays an overtly impressionable horror movie fan who is terrified by Bava's film, and is then involved in a tragicomic adventure after he finds an apparently dead body in the back seat of his car. In the scene where Tognazzi leaves the vehicle out of town and goes looking for a place to call the police, the actor is preceded by a tracking shot backwards, from the bottom, similar to the scene in *Black Sunday* where the innkeeper's daughter ventures into the barn. A sign, perhaps, of a sincere tribute to Bava's technique that goes beyond the film's facetious context.

20. Tim Lucas, "What Are Those Strange Drops of Blood in the Scripts of Ernesto Gastaldi?," *Video Watchdog* n. 39, May/June 1997, p. 41.

21. *Ibid.* Valerii's name is also marginally related to another movie co-produced by Felice Testa Gay for Cinegai Films: the spy flick *Schüsse im 3/4 Takt* (1965, Alfred Weidelmann), starring Pierre Brice and Daliah Lavi, released in Italy as *Operazione terzo uomo* and broadcast on U.S. television as *Operation Solo*. The script kept at Rome's CSC, and titled *Quando la luce si spegne* (When the Light Goes Out) credits the scenario to Herbert Reinecker and the script to Rolf Thiele, Carl Merz and Antonio Valerii. The most likely explanation is that Valerii was only responsible for the dialogue adaptation for the Italian version.

Chapter Two

1. Franca Faldini and Goffredo Fofi, *L'avventurosa storia del cinema italiano raccontata dai suoi protagonisti 1960–1969* (Milan: Feltrinelli, 1981), p. 288.

2. Marco Giusti, *Dizionario del western all'italiana* (Milan: Mondadori, 2007), p. 358.

3. Adriano Bolzoni, "Il buono, il bravo e il bugiardo," *Il borghese*, November 11, 1978. By mentioning the Fox and the Cat and the Field of Miracles, Bolzoni is referring to Carlo Collodi's celebrated novel *The Adventures of Pinocchio*.

4. Paolo Albiero, Giacomo Cacciatore, *Il terrorista dei generi. Tutto il cinema di Lucio Fulci* (Rome: Un mondo a parte, 2004), p. 177.

5. Faldini and Fofi, *L'avventurosa storia del cinema italiano*, p. 288.

6. Walter Chiari was a well-known comedy actor, Leone's remark sharply underlining the excessively humorous content in Tessari's first draft.

7. Fernando di Leo, "Due o tre cose che so di me," *Nocturno Book #2*, January 2001, p. 4.

8. The title *Il magnifico straniero* was then used by Jolly Film for the Italian release (in August 1966) of a composite film assembled by splicing together with two episodes of the TV series *Rawhide* ("The Backshooter") and Incident of the "Running Man"), featuring a very young Clint Eastwood (who featured prominently on the poster). Colombo and Papi, after their breakup with Leone, were attempting to exploit the actor's outstanding popularity after Leone's films.

9. Noël Simsolo, *Conversations avec Sergio Leone* (Paris: Stock, 1987), pp. 89–90.

10. Stella explained in an interview: "In Rome there were two of us who rejected it: Giorgio Ardisson and I […] However, I did not do this film […] which no one wanted to do, because it was considered a low-budget flick." Stefano Ippoliti, Matteo Norcini, "Agente Tony Kendall operazione cinema," *Cine70 e dintorni #7*, 2006, p. 34. Actually, Ardisson had been approached for the role of Ramón, played in the film by Gian Maria Volonté; the part had initially been written for Mimmo Palmara.

11. Caiano confirmed the scarce initial feeling between the director and his lead: "I remember Sergio Leone's first encounter with Clint Eastwood, a meeting at which, I don't know why, I was present, perhaps because I spoke English. Sergio had chosen him after seeing him in some TV show, and I don't think he was enthusiastic about him." Mario Caiano, *Autobiografia di un regista di B-movies* (Piombino: Edizioni Il Foglio, 2014), p. 99.

12. Actually, Eastwood's character in *A Fistful of Dollars* does have a name—well, sort of. In an early scene a character (Piripero, played by Joseph Egger) calls him Joe—that is to say, anybody. Eastwood's character in *For a Few Dollars More*, on the other hand, is nicknamed "Monco" (Maimed) as he only uses one hand to shoot his gun. The whole "Man with No Name" mythology was actually a marketing creation on the part of the U.S. distributor, United Artists.

13. Tonino Valerii, *Una pistola per Arlecchino*, in Oreste De Fornari, *Tutti i film di Sergio Leone* (Milan: Ubulibri, 1984), p. 16.

14. Franco Grattarola, "Per qualche sceneggiatura in più … per un pugno di attori," *Cine70 e dintorni #7*, 2006, p. 64.

15. Giovanni Corridori was *A Fistful of Dollars*' special effect technician (credited as John Speed), and one of Italian cinema's most valuable experts in the field.

16. Valerii, *Una pistola per Arlecchino*, p. 167. Another inspiration, more immediate and evident, was Dashiell Hammett's *Red Harvest*: Kurosawa had drawn from Hammett's first novel (as well as from *The Glass Key* for the scene where Toshirô Mifune's character lies unconscious after being severely beaten, while a couple of thugs are playing and drinking near him), but neither Leone nor his associates noticed it—even though his film was actually closer to Hammett, as to escape his torturers Joe sets fire to the shack he is in, just like Ed Beaumont does in the novel. Interestingly, *Red Harvest* was later adapted, and rather faithfully, as a Western, by Juan Bosch as *La ciudad maldita* (1978), with Alberto Grimaldi acting as executive producer.

17. Tonino Valerii, *Fare l'aiuto regista nel cinema e nella TV* (Rome: Gremese, 1998), p. 50.

18. Di Leo, "Due o tre cose che so di me," p. 4.

19. Algerian revolutionary Ahmed Ben Bella became the first president of Algeria, from 1963 to 1965, after helping lead the struggle for the country's independence.

20. Davide Pulici, "Primo movimento: il tempo delle origini," in Davide Pulici, Manlio Gomarasca (eds.), "Calibro 9. Il cinema di Fernando di Leo," *Nocturno dossier* #14, September 2003, p. 8.

21. Marco Giusti, *Dizionario del western all'italiana* (Milan: Mondadori, 2007), p. 351.

22. Valerii's version here is confused, as Julio Sempere's brother, Ramón Sempere, is actually credited as first assistant cameraman on *A Fistful of Dollars*, where Noé is credited as second assistant cameraman. On *For a Few Dollars More*, Noé is credited as cameraman together with Aldo Ricci. The Spanish technician worked again with Valerii on *A Reason to Live, a Reason to Die!*

Chapter Three

1. The film is *A 001: Operazione Giamaica* (1965), credited to Richard Jackson [Ernst von Theumer], and starring Larry Pennell [Alessandro Pennelli] and Brad Harris. It was released in several European countries, and surfaced in the U.S. as well, directly on television, as *Our Man in Jamaica*.

2. The Cromoscope brand was not deposited, however, although there is no evidence that Technicolor took legal action against Francesco and Vincenzo Genesi. Calzini also created a highly automated printer which solved several issues related to the use of 2P: the lighting changes between scenes, the splice-jumps… Since the negative's interlines are too thin and close, it was necessary to avoid them being visible on the screen after the frame enlargement. The device was programmed in such a way that at the moment of the splice it jumped eight frames (four at the beginning and four at the end of each cut, left in excess by the editor when cutting the negative), so that the scene's original length remained unchanged. Calzini illustrated his invention in detail in the April 1966 issue (volume #75) of the *Journal of Society of Motion Picture and Television Engineers*, pp. 341–343.

3. In fact, besides the advantages listed above, the 2P involved some complications for the work at the moviola, caused primarily by the extremely thin interlines, and higher lab costs. Not being possible to use internegatives or matrices, since it would result in a further loss of quality and an increased graininess of the image, the printing of copies for distribution was done by printing directly from the negative in a standard projection format, reversing the frame from two to four perforations through a special printing machine, equipped with a prism that magnified the frame and turned it anamorphic.

4. In the following years, Hill worked in a number of Italian productions, mostly Westerns of varying success, such as *Seven Pistols for a Massacre* (*7 pistole per un massacro*, 1967, Mario Caiano), *No Graves on Boot Hill* (*Tre croci per non morire*, 1968, Sergio Garrone), *Trinity in Eldorado* (*Scansati … a Trinità arriva Eldorado*, 1972, Aristide Massaccesi), but he also co-starred in an impressive *giallo*, *The Bloodstained Shadow* (*Solamente nero*, 1978, Antonio Bido). Mostly active in Spain, to where he moved in the 1960s after his marriage to actress Teresa Gimpera, Hill also played in many Spanish horror and sci-fi pictures. Among his last film roles was *Second Name* (*El segundo nombre*, 2002, Paco Plaza), where he appeared alongside his wife.

5. In the English language version, several characters' names are changed: Peggy Kennebeck becomes Molly, and Machete becomes Mingo.

6. The board of censors asked the producers to "tone down the hot coffee scalding; cut from after the knife pierces a man in the saloon to the man's fall and the knife extraction."

7. "The timeless success that the Italian Western, all dripping blood and grimaces, meets with the public, is an alarming signal of the fascination increasingly exerted by the myth of violence. Pacifists chase doves in the clouds: for a conscientious objector there are ten, maybe a hundred or thousand men who dream of embracing a rifle, handling a gun or a knife to discharge their aggressive instincts on your skin. A generation that hates its neighbor as itself is growing in the darkness of movie theaters: war will come and it'll have its eyes. Those who want confirmation are kindly requested to watch *Taste of Killing* (produced by Italy and Spain, two hot-blooded countries), and overhear the satisfied murmurs from the audience, that follows with vibrant participation the carnage, and finally bursts into applause when Lanky Fellow, the cunning and ruthless hero whose motto is 'You can never have too much money,' aims at his rival's binoculars [sic], and with a masterful stroke shoots him through the eye and in the brain: the climax of a pic which since the opening credits cracks of gunfire, and where a bandit, to force his brother to reveal certain plans, spills hot coffee on his skull, and a grim mommy teaches her baby son how to manufacture bullets. These are among the most delicate and gentle passages […]. Tonino Valeri [sic], Sergio Leone's former assistant, is at his debut as a director, but already shows he knows what his public wants: characters with anger in the body and hate in their heart. *Taste of Killing* is not among the season's worst Westerns: although it washes up the remains of much more honorable banquets, it offers digestible crumbs, subsidized by the panoramic format, Nico Fidenco's music and a cute little old grouch. The lightning-fast drawing lead is called, or has himself called, Craig Hill." G. Gr. (Giovanni Grazzini), *Corriere della Sera*, August 10, 1966.

8. Christopher Frayling, *Sergio Leone: Something to Do with Death* (Minneapolis: University of Minnesota Press, 2000–2012), p. 188.

Chapter Four

1. "It has been repeatedly said that the novelty of the new trend of Italian Westerns is all in the exasperation of violence that's typical of the genre, and in its pigmentation with sadism, drugs, suggestively Mexican characters and setting. Tonino Valeri [sic] […] fit himself within the new current with not only the credentials, but with a few tricks up his sleeve for adding a new note

in the latest Western style, that's so rich already in features and in amazing, singular, entangling characters. Tonino Valeri [sic], in fact, has redeemed the character of the bounty killer from the monotony of an already worn cliché [...] by creating a brand new type of bounty hunter, full-bodied, elaborate, complex. [...] A unique operation, for the invention of the almost-clean system in its cold and calculated determination, for the James Bond-like rifle, for the evolution of the 'reward' motif transferred to valuable commodity, and, finally, for the strange but undeniable utility of the operation which, while it eliminates the robbers, saves the legitimate owners' gold. Loaded with bite and supported by a constantly tense pacing, the film stars Graig [sic] Hill [...]. The setting and the color cinematography are very accurate." (not signed), *Il Tempo*, August 10, 1966.

2. *Fists in the Pocket* (*I pugni in tasca*, 1965), Marco Bellocchio's extraordinary film debut, revealed the Colombian-born Castel as one of Italian cinema's most gifted actors: As the epileptic Alessandro, who murders his mother and his retarded brother, Castel embodied the then-growing dissatisfaction on the part of the younger generation towards the institution of family and authority in general, which would culminate in the 1968 protest movements.

3. Carlos Aguilar, *Giuliano Gemma. El factor romano* (Almería: Diputación de Almería, 2003), p. 23.

4. Paolo Micalizzi, "Tonino Valerii: i miei western da regista," *Quaderni di CinemaSud. Speciale western italiano*, August 2007, p. 117.

5. Email interview with the author, January 2008.

6. Aguilar, *Giuliano Gemma. El factor romano*, p. 56.

7. To film critic Kevin Grant, "Talby is like a ripened version of the short-lived henchmen Van Cleef had played in Hollywood. One particular role of note is that of Clanton, who executes the murderous will of 'respectable' banker Raymond Burr and other crooked burgers in *A Man Alone* (1955), a taut 'anti-populist' western directed by and starring Ray Milland." Kevin Grant, *Any Gun Can Play. The Essential Guide to Euro-Westerns* (Godalming, Surrey: FAB Press, 2011), p. 89.

8. "Wouldn't you be able to make 'em stop?" Talby asks in the Italian version, when Scott objects that his fellow villagers would tease him if he called himself Scott "Mary." The meaning is rather different compared with the English version, where Lee Van Cleef's line is "Who knows for sure whether they'd laugh at it."

9. La Selva, *Tonino Valerii: mai temere il Leone*, p. 100.

10. Italian Western scholar Howard Hughes noted the accuracy of the choice of weaponry in the film: "Each of the main characters is identified by his six shooter. Talby has a customized Colt .45 with two inches of the barrel missing and no sight. Scott and Murph have standard Colts (with seven-inch barrels). [...] Previously, Scott had honed his skill with a carved wooden pistol and a holster held up with rope. Hired gun Owen favours specialist hardware, while the sheriff prefers a shotgun—an authentic piece of period detail, as lawmen in the real West preferred 'scatter guns' for close shooting. At one point Talby boasts, 'The weapon that's gonna kill me hasn't been invented yet,' a variation on a quote from Dallas Stoudenmire (a Marshall of El Paso in the 1880s), who claimed, 'I don't believe the bullet was ever moulded that will kill me'; like Talby, he was wrong." Howard Hughes, *Once Upon a Time in the Italian West* (London/New York, I. B. Tauris, 2004), p. 188.

11. Armand Salacrou's stage play *Les Nuits de la colère* (1946). It must be noted, however, that another possible reference might be Carl Theodor Dreyer's *Day of Wrath* (*Vredens Dag*, 1943), released in Italy as *Dies Irae*, a further indication of the makers' ambitions, or at least an attempt to give the movie a powerful, Biblical-sounding title, compared to the more trivial ones sported by Leone's "Dollars Trilogy."

12. Tullio Kezich, *Il Millefilm* (Milan: Mondadori, 1983), p.286.

13. *Day of Anger* is Valerii's first film featuring music by Riz Ortolani. More will follow, namely *A Girl Called Jules*, *A Reason to Live, a Reason to Die!*, *Sahara Cross*, *Brothers In Blood* and *Il ricatto*. As Howard Hughes noted, "Ortolani's score also reinforces the best gag in a film noticeably lacking in humour. As Talby rides through the desert, he is accompanied by the brassy 'riding theme,' while Scott (in hot pursuit on a ragged mule) is accompanied by a knockabout, banjo-led version of the same piece." Hughes, *Once Upon a Time in the Italian West*, p. 189.

14. Email interview with the author, January 2008.

15. Aguilar, *Giuliano Gemma. El factor romano*, p. 55.

16. Valerii recounts the anecdote in Isabella Bruno's 1984 documentary *Arrivano i vostri, ovvero Storia avventurosa del western all'italiana*, hosted by Duccio Tessari.

Chapter Five

1. *Il Messaggero di Teramo*, March 12, 1967.
2. Email interview with the author, 2008.
3. Apparently, this was enough (paired with the presence of a number of Leone's tough-guy regulars and the wrong assumption that Valerii had been Leone's assistant on *Once Upon a Time in the West*) to make Alex Cox write that "Leone and his masterpiece cast long shadows over *The Price of Power*" ... if this was not enough, Cox goes as far as writing: "Why did Valerii, whose first solo Western [!!!—*author*], *Day of Anger*, was devoid of politics, make this intensely political film? I suspect the hand of Leone. The Master didn't direct a Western in 1969, but he was certainly in the vicinity [...]. Coincidence? Or was Leone, with his eye on the big picture, and the international dimension, pushing his collaborators somewhere he didn't dare to go?" Alex Cox, *10,000 Ways to Die. A Director's Take on the Spaghetti Western* (Harpenden, Hertfordshire: Kamera Books, 2009), p. 248.
4. During filming, Gemma's daughter Giuliana was born, and the actor flew home to stay by the side of his wife and daughter. The event was reported by a popular Italian tabloid, with quotes from Valerii, who explained that he allowed Gemma to return to Italy because "Giuliano did not reason anymore, he was incapable of concentrating, he looked as if in a trance." Anonymous, "La figlia di Ringo il pistolero," *Grazia* #1483, 20 July 1969.

5. Faldini and Fofi, *L'avventurosa storia del cinema italiano*, p. 311.
6. Grant, *Any Gun Can Play*, p. 429.
7. Giusti, *Dizionario del western all'italiana*, p. 392.
8. Anonymous, "Cavalcarono insieme. Sei domande ai registi italiani," *Almanacco Cinema 2*, Spring 1979 (Milan: Edizioni Il Formichiere, 1979), pp. 59–60. In the article, Valerii's surname is regularly misspelled as "Valeri."
9. Actually, the film does have its share of admirers. Sir Christopher Frayling, while dismissing *Day of Anger* as "a pedestrian 'young-man-meets-veteran-gunfighter'," calls *The Price of Power* "extraordinary" and makes an interesting, acute comparison with Anthony Mann's gripping period thriller, *The Tall Target* (1951). Christopher Frayling, *Spaghetti Westerns: Cowboys and Europeans from Karl May to Sergio Leone* (London: I.B. Tauris, 1998/2006), p. 96.

Chapter Six

1. *Capobastone*, or *capubastuni*, is the dialectic name given to the leaders of small local Mafia families. The term is mostly used for the Calabrian 'Ndrangheta, though.
2. *Campieri* were a typical figure of 19th century Sicily; they were private guards who were hired by the landowners, to overlook the cultivations in order to prevent thefts, fires and damages.
3. *La vigna di uve nere* was eventually adapted for television in 1984 by Sandro Bolchi, starring Mario Adorf and Lea Massari.
4. Milena Milani, afterword to *La ragazza di nome Giulio* (Milan: ES, 2001).
5. Gian Piero Brunetta, *Storia del cinema italiano. Dal miracolo economico agli anni Novanta* (Rome: Editori Riuniti, 2001), p. 499.
6. Callisto Cosulich, *La scalata al sesso* (Genoa: Immordino Editore, 1969), p. 187.
7. *Chi l'ha visto?* is a very popular TV program (broadcast since 1989) dedicated to missing people and unsolved mysteries.
8. Email interview with the author, 2008.
9. Anonymous, "Maria Schell sostituirà la Fontaine nel film di Valerii," *L'Unità*, January 25, 1970.
10. About 6 seconds.
11. About 8 seconds.
12. 8 seconds.
13. Bir [Guglielmo Biraghi], *Il Messaggero*, June 30, 1970.
14. Morando Morandini, "Due compromessi di segno opposto," *Il Tempo Illustrato*, September 19, 1970.
15. Morando Morandini, "Lascia la colt per l'attualità," *Il Giorno*, September 11, 1970.
16. *Una spia del regime* (1976) by Alberto Negrin, starring Vittorio Mezzogiorno.

Chapter Seven

1. Anonymous, "Un investigatore anti-eroe per Tonino Valeri [sic]," *L'Unità*, October 10, 1971.
2. The so-called "golden hours" are an additional amount of working hours to which producers may resort only in substantiated exceptional cases: the golden hour starts after the production's request and the positive evaluation on the part of the crew (which may reject the request if they do not consider as "exceptional" the motivations adduced). They were introduced in the collective agreement for cinema and television workers starting on December 7, 1999.
3. La Selva, *Tonino Valerii* cit., p. 108.
4. Once again, the English language version is sensibly different, and definitely worse: "Here was a child who at various times played with you ... she loved you ... and more to the point, she trusted you."

Chapter Eight

1. La Selva, *Tonino Valerii* cit., p. 106.
2. Anonymous, "Cavalcarono insieme. Sei domande ai registi italiani," p. 59.
3. "*A Reason to Live, a Reason to Die!* was my idea, and I wrote the script with Tonino. The idea came to me thinking of *The Dirty Dozen*." Ernesto Gastaldi, email interview with the author, October 2015.
4. Anonymous, "Cavalcarono insieme. Sei domande ai registi italiani," p. 59. The short story inspired a 1974 TV movie: *Parker Adderson, Philosopher*, directed by Arthur Barron and starring Harris Yulin and Colleen Dewhurst.
5. Ibid.
6. Giancarlo Albano, "Un miliardo di lire per riconquistare un fortino," *Bolero Teletutto* #1310, 11 June 1972, p. 39. The same article was published in Spain. Giancarlo Albano, "Almeria tierra quemada para el Western?," *Fotogramas* #1241, 28 July 1972.
7. Filming took place in other easily recognizable Spanish locations: the homestead seen when Pembroke's group leave the train is the same as the McBain homestead in *Once Upon a Time in the West*.
8. Albano, "Un miliardo di lire per riconquistare un fortino," p. 42. The anecdote was confirmed by Pedersoli to this writer.
9. In the Italian version, Fangareggi is dubbed by voice actor Oreste Lionello, Woody Allen's Italian voice, with perplexing results.
10. Some critics have pointed out the allegorical value of Pembroke's ascent to the fortress on the mountain. See Luca Beatrice, *Al cuore, Ramon, al cuore. La leggenda del western all'italiana* (Florence: Tarab, 1996), p. 49.
11. Giusti, *Dizionario del western all'italiana* cit., p. 418.
12. Incidentally, *The Dirty Dozen* had already been ripped off by the Italian Western: see *The Five Man Army* (*Un esercito di 5 uomini*, 1969, Don Taylor), written by Dario Argento and starring Bud Spencer himself, along with Peter Graves (while still going through his *Mission: Impossible* stint on TV), Tetsuro Tamba and Nino Castelnuovo.
13. The text goes as follows: "Joplin Gazette. Joplin, Missouri, April 10, 1872. Today, I walked through the ruins of what was once Fort Holman. 10 years ago, this civil war fortress, thought to be impregnable, was destroyed by a wild bunch of marauders. Eli Sampson, a survivor of the massacre, revealed in an interview that

the raid was the result of a blood feud between two bitter men: Colonel Pembroke, a union officer, thought to be a traitor and coward, led the mission to recapture the fort he had once surrendered. Major Ward, a ruthless 'Mad-Genius,' who joined the confederacy solely to gain command of Fort Holman, so that he could rule the vast surrounding Santa Fe territory after the war. But what motivated these two men and what caused this incredible blood bath, was explained by Eli Sampson in the story that follows…"

Chapter Nine

1. Gian Piero Brunetta, *Storia del cinema italiano. Dal miracolo economico agli anni Novanta* (Rome: Editori Riuniti, 2001), p. 405.
2. Francesco Mininni, *Sergio Leone* (Milan: Il Castoro Cinema, 1995), p. 11. It must be underlined that Leone's example is fictitious, as there is no film called *Se incontri Sartana digli che è un uomo morto*. The closest is … *Se incontri Sartana prega per la tua morte* (1968, Gianfranco Parolini), released in the U.S. as … *If You Meet Sartana Pray for Your Death*, a literal translation of the Italian title.
3. This and Donati's following declarations are part of a text which first appeared in the scriptwriter's own website and was then reprised by many other sources. It can currently be consulted on other websites, such as http://www.mymovies.it (the exact link is http://www.mymovies.it/dizionario/critica.asp?id=158815) and budterence.tk (on Bud Spencer and Terence Hill: the link is http://www.budterence.tk/interleone.php). When consulted by this author about said declarations, Donati confirmed "word by word" what he had previously written.
4. Interestingly, Donati went on to write the crime film *Mean Frank and Crazy Tony* (*Il suo nome faceva tremare… Interpol in allarme* a.k.a. *Dio, sei proprio un padreterno!*, 1973, Michele Lupo), starring Lee Van Cleef and Tony Lo Bianco, whose two main characters—veteran mobster Frankie Diomede, known as "Dio," and small-time crook Tony—share the same kind of relationship as Nobody and Beauregard. Given that the script liberally borrows from Donati's own novel *Mister Sharkey torna a casa*, published in 1956, it might well be that some of Donati's ideas eventually converged in Gastaldi's final script.
5. Email interviews with the author, January 2008, December 2015. As a bizarre footnote, an article on the prolific screenwriter and director Piero Regnoli dated 2002, which appeared on the Italian magazine *Cine70 e dintorni*, states: "Another script that passed through Regnoli's capable hands was *My Name Is Nobody* […]. Regnoli, who is not credited among the authors of the story and the screenplay, thought out the film's story with Leone and wrote most of the script; then, because of previous commitments, he had to leave the job. Silvia Innocenzi, Regnoli's wife and collaborator, still remembers the usual onset of Leone's phone calls: 'Lady, can you put Dante Alighieri on the phone?'" Franco Grattarola, Stefano Ippoliti and Matteo Norcini, "L'uomo delle stelle. Ricordo di Piero Regnoli," *Cine70 e dintorni* #2, Spring 2002, p. 37. Gastaldi's comment: "Regnoli might have taken part in the first phase, the Western version of the *Odyssey*, but I really don't know."
6. Fabio Melelli, *Eroi a Cinecittà. Stuntmen e maestri d'armi del cinema italiano* (Ellera, Perugia: Mercurio Editrice, 1998), p. 142. See also Frayling, *Sergio Leone: Something to Do with Death*, p. 349.
7. Giusti, *Dizionario dei film western* cit., p. 307.
8. *Cavalcarono insieme. Sei domande ai registi italiani*, "Almanacco Cinema 2," spring 1979 (Milan: Edizioni Il Formichiere, 1979), p. 56.
9. Tonino Valerii, *Il vero e il falso*, in appendice of La Selva, *Tonino Valerii: mai temere il Leone* (Milan: Nocturno Libri, 2000), p. 122.
10. Tonino Valerii, *Bud e Terence: due grandi attori, due grandi amici*, in AA.VV., *Bud Spencer & Terence Hill. West botte da orbi e buoni sentimenti. XXV rassegna del cinema italiano "Primo piano sull'autore"* (Assisi: ANCCI, 2005), p. 179.
11. Frayling, *Sergio Leone: Something to Do with Death*, p. 358.
12. Email interview with the author, January 2008.
13. "Situated four miles north of Glenwood on Highway 180, then nine miles on the paved narrow road NM 159, Mogollón lies tucked in a narrow valley with several old buildings still standing. In the 1880s the town, named for the Mogollón Mountains, roared into existence with a rich production of gold and silver, which went down the long trail to Silver City in clanking ore wagons pulled by 18-mule teams. The town contained over 2,000 people and had a theater, the usual saloons and general merchandise. A decreased demand for gold and silver during World War I spelled the end of Mogollón. Picturesque original buildings were used in *My Name Is Nobody*, but some movie sets were also created, such as a saloon on the south side of main street and a general store for scenes with Henry Fonda and Terence Hill. Some scenes were shot in the huge Little Fannie Mine structures above the town (at 7,000 feet)." Carlo Gaberscek, Kenny Stier, *In Search of Western Movie Sites* (Lulu.com, 2014), p. 96.
14. La Selva, *Tonino Valerii: mai temere il Leone*, p. 89.
15. Frayling, *Sergio Leone: Something to Do with Death*, p. 361.
16. Donati, http://www.budterence.tk/interleone.php.
17. La Selva, *Tonino Valerii: mai temere il Leone*, p. 93.
18. *Ivi*.
19. Frayling, *Sergio Leone: Something to Do with Death*, p. 362.
20. Giulia D'Agnolo Vallan, *John Landis* (Turin: Torino Film Festival, 2004), p. 46. Actually, only about 60 extras at best can be spotted in the scene.
21. Frayling, *Sergio Leone: Something to Do with Death*, pp. 361–362. Summers adds: "I was also to do the house of mirrors scenes in Spain but they could not find enough mirrors to satisfy Sergio, so I was told I would have to go to Rome for the reminder of my scenes."
22. Marco Giusti, *Dizionario del western all'italiana* (Milan: Mondadori, 2007), p. 308.
23. *Ibid.*, p. 309.
24. In his blind love for all things Leone, Alex Cox

picks up a line from Giusti's book and builds a castle in the air: "According to Giusti, Leone directed 'second unit' for Valerii: no small assignment, since it included all the American shooting—the first 40 minutes of the film, plus the gunfight in New Orleans, and the epilogue—*and* the scenes with the Wild Bunch. [...] If Leone shot these scenes, all that remained for Valerii to shoot were the dreadful 'hall of mirrors' and circus freak scenes featuring Hill, Mazza and Stefanelli; the long, boring scene involving Fonda, Hill and a 'cute/funny' old man; and a 'funny' drinking and shooting scene in a bar, also involving Hill, Stefanelli and Mazza. These are the worst scenes in the film, but, according to some sources, Leone directed them, too." Cox, *10,000 Ways to Die*, p. 301.

25. In capital letters in the original email.

26. Email interview with the author, January 2008.

27. Frayling, *Sergio Leone: Something to Do with Death*, p. 378.

28. Italo Moscati, *Sergio Leone. Quando il cinema era grande* (Turin: Lindau, 2007), p. 187.

29. The following Western produced by Leone *Un genio, due compari, un pollo* (1975), directed by Damiano Damiani and starring Hill, Miou Miou, Patrick McGoohan and Klaus Kinski, was distributed in West Germany as *Nobody ist der Groesste* (Nobody is the Best) to exploit the success of *My Name Is Nobody* (and Hill actually wore the same costume). Damiani's film was not released theatrically in the U.S.

30. *Variety*, 16 January 1974. On the other hand, *The Chicago Reader*'s Myron Meisel included the film in his runners-up list of the year's best, with such company as Terrence Malick's *Badlands*, Francis Ford Coppola's *The Conversation* and *The Godfather: Part II* and Altman's *California Split* and *Images*.

31. Peter Bogdanovich, "Two Beeg Green Eyes." *New York*, vol. 6, no. 48, November 26, 1973, p. 78.

32. Laurence Staig, Tony Williams, *Italian Western: The Opera of Violence* (London: Lorrimer, 1975), p. 87. Even most recent film studies on Leone featured blatant errors and oversimplifications: although conceding that "Valerii was a credited director several times over," Robert Cumbow writes that *My Name Is Nobody* (which he wrongly states as being the director's fifth film, instead of his seventh) "made his reputation," as if, say, *Day of Anger* had never existed. What is more, he concludes that "Valerii has his own style and voice, but is so closely indebted to Leone that he seems on surest ground when dealing with avowed parody." Robert Cumbow, *The Films of Sergio Leone* (Lanham, ML: Scarecrow Press, 2008), pp. 95–124.

33. Tim Lucas, "What Are Those Strange Drops of Blood in the Scripts of Ernesto Gastaldi?," *Video Watchdog* #39, May/June 1997, pp. 48–51.

34. Email interview with the author, January 2008.

35. Noël Simsolo, *Conversations avec Sergio Leone* (Paris: Petite Bibliothéque des Cahiers du Cinéma, 1999), pp. 156–158.

36. Sergio Leone, *Sergio Leone: fuori il regista!*, in Edoardo Tiboni and Paolo Smoglica (eds.), *L'Abruzzo e il cinema. Atti del Convegno Internazionale premi Flaiano, 16–17 giugno 1995* (Pescara: EDIARS, 1995–2008), pp. 261–262.

37. Francesco Mininni, *Sergio Leone* (Milan: Il Castoro Cinema, 1995), p. 11.

38. Namely, Fernando di Leo, A "Due o tre cose che so di me," *Nocturno Book* #2, gennaio 2001, pp. 5–6; Tonino Valerii, "Killer vs. Killer," *Nocturno Book* #4, March 2001, pp.4–5; Fernando di Leo, "L'ultimo duello," *Nocturno Book* #6, May 2001, pp. 7–8.

39. Al Mangini, "Breve Intervista a Ernesto Gastaldi," www.spaghettiwestern.altervista.org.

40. Frayling, *Sergio Leone: Something to Do with Death*, p. 350.

41. The "Wild Bunch" whistled theme draws its origins from the song "Quello che conta," sung by Luigi Tenco in *La cuccagna* (1962, Luciano Salce). Robert Cumbow notes how the musical piece is "deliberately evoking the self-conscious mythic obtrusiveness of the Italian Western." Cumbow, *The Films of Sergio Leone*, p. 97.

42. Regarding the references to Ford's masterpiece, Valerii recalled: "I wanted to dress Henry Fonda in exactly the same clothes he wore in *My Darling Clementine*. Bravo, perfect. In my opinion, that *is* Henry Fonda. But Sergio had taken it into his head that he should wear a shirt with an enormous ruffle on the front, a lace ruffle. 'Yes,' I'd say. 'Shirts like that are sometimes seen in Westerns, but this is a type of wardrobe more suited to an adventurer, or a professional gambler or a minor character in the story.'" Yet Valerii obliged. Then, one night during shooting, he was awoken by a phone call from Rome. "I went to the phone and it was Sergio, who said, 'What's that shirt you've put on Henry Fonda, with that horrible ruffle?' So much hot air! These are the contradictions of the man. Another director had been watching the rushes with him and asked him to make a note about his shirt, so wrong and so out of place… And just to keep *him* happy, we finally dressed him as I wanted." Frayling, *Sergio Leone: Something to Do with Death*, p. 360.

43. Federico Patrizi, *Intervista ad Ernesto Gastaldi*, in www.antoniomargheriti.com.

44. Frayling, *Sergio Leone: Something to Do with Death*, p. 357.

45. Cumbow, *The Films of Sergio Leone*, p. 99. Cumbow then opines: "Nobody is to Beauregard as Valerii is to Leone? [...] The carnival sequence that begins with Nobody's shooting away the dwarf's stilts and appropriating his cigar is a series of trials–*tours de force* of cinematic technique–planned as much for Valerii to show his stuff as for Nobody to impress both us and Sullivan." Too bad most of the scene was actually shot by Leone's second unit, as Valerii himself stated!

46. Frayling, *Sergio Leone: Something to Do with Death*, p. 352.

47. "To make the horses fall, right where we'd put the powder for the explosions, in my first film I resorted to a technique which I then re-used later: you decide where the horse must fall, then you dig a hole which you fill with magnesium and other stuff (these are materials that are used for the explosions, but it is the sound which makes the 'boom' [...]). The horses start galloping two hundred yards before, and to their front legs steel cables are attached, which are stretched at the right time, and when it happens the horses fall … it is that simple. Of course there is the danger that the horse is left crippled, and so for such scenes we used horses that were not of great value, old horses [...] And when

Leone asked: 'But how are we gonna do these things?' I simply replied, 'Let me explain it to you, it's not difficult, we're gonna do it this way....'" La Selva, *Tonino Valerii* cit., p. 94.

48. Hughes, *Once Upon a Time in the Italian West* cit., p. 246.

49. Gastaldi did not like the joust scene, not the least bit. "Too bad they added a stupid scene, inventing a joust in a Wild West village." Ernesto Gastaldi, *Voglio entrare nel cinema—Storia di uno che ce l'ha fatta* (Milan: Mondadori, 1991), p. 229. According to Hughes, the mirror sequence in the Horror House owes to Parolini's *Sabata* films. Hughes, *Once Upon a Time in the Italian West* cit., p. 247.

50. Alberto Crespi, *Segnocinema* #68, July/August 1994, pp. 23 ss.

51. Cumbow, *The Films of Sergio Leone*, p. 97.

52. Roberto Donati, "Il mio nome è Nessuno: il canto del cigno del western italiano," in *Quaderni di Cinema-Sud. Speciale western italiano*, August 2007, pp. 25–26.

53. Dario Zanelli, "Il mio nome è Nessuno," *Il resto del Carlino*, December 20, 1973.

54. Terence Hill claimed Beauregard's letter was his idea, "because at the time a beautiful film by Kon Ichikawa came out, *The Burmese Harp*, where there was a letter which the protagonist wrote to his companions on a boat: hence Fonda's letter to Nobody was born. I also remember that Leone and I went to see *The Sting* and noticed that it featured the same idea of the fake death (Redford killing Newman)." Beatrice, *Al cuore, Ramon, al cuore*, p. 154. Hill's claims are hard to believe, given that *The Burmese Harp* (1956) came out in Italy in 1958, not 1973. As for *The Sting*, it came out in Italy in June 1974 but was released in the U.S. on December 25, 1973, five days after the release of *My Name Is Nobody* in Italy. It is then pretty unlikely (to use a mild understatement) that George Roy Hill and his scriptwriter David S. Ward ripped off Valerii's film, as the actor seems to imply...

55. Cumbow, *The Films of Sergio Leone*, p. 99–100.

Chapter Ten

1. The script was written by De Rita and Valerii. According to the director, Dino Maiuri (credited with the former as co-scripter) did not actually take part in the film.

2. La Selva, *Tonino Valerii: mai temere il Leone*, p. 101.

3. Email interview with the author, October 2015. The unfilmed project is listed as *Scalpman* in Giusti, *Dizionario del western all'italiana*, p. 666.

4. La Selva, *Tonino Valerii: mai temere il Leone*, p. 100.

5. Born in February 1959 in Nairobi, Kenya, Marsani had been Miss Teenage Italy in 1973. Her film career was very brief: after debuting in Luchino Visconti's *Conversation Piece* (*Gruppo di famiglia in un interno*, 1974) she appeared in a handful of films before retiring. Besides *Vai gorilla*, she was also in the TV mini-series *La signora Ava* (1975), *The Probability Factor* (*L'ordinateur des pompes funèbres*, 1976, Gérard Pirès), starring Jean-Louis Trintignant, Lea Massari and Mireille Darc, and the erotic drama *Submission* (*Scandalo*, 1976, Salvatore Samperi), alongside Franco Nero, Lisa Gastoni, Raymond Pellegrin and Andréa Ferréol. She also graced the cover of a 1975 issue of *Playboy*.

Chapter Eleven

1. David Ballerini, *Steadicam. Una rivoluzione nel modo di fare cinema* (Alessandria: Falsopiano, 1999), p. 76.

2. *Ibid.*, p. 77.

3. *Ibid.*, pp. 70–72.

4. "And right on *chott* [...] a scene of particular interest takes place, for the weaving it shows between technical device and stylistic result. [...] It starts with the camera moving forward (obviously done with the Steadicam) in order to frame the flat and arid land that runs in front of the cameraman [...]; when, after a few steps, the Steadicam raises its eye to frame the formless and limitless expanse of the salt lake, one can see in the distance, entering the frame and crossing it roughly from right to left, the technicians' jeep [...] advancing to a crawl, and one of the technicians themselves preceding it on foot, acting as a guide to avoid the quicksand. Slowly, the camera approaches them more and more, subtly correcting its trajectory (initially perpendicular to that of the technicians) until it is in full shadowing mode, directly behind the guide: placing itself in the latter's semi-POV, the gaze of the camera on the expanse of salt (perfectly homogeneous to the eye), becomes one with the guide's and demonstrates the impotence of those who are lost and can not find any reference point with which to orientate themselves. The guide stops disheartened and turns back; the Steadicam stops too, interrupting the stalking. A Steadicam POV shot of the guide retracing his steps (with a 360-degree reversal) to consult with his companions in the car, shows the jeep (which then had to be directly behind him) at the center of the frame; but if the jeep was still behind him, then the Steadicam, in the previous shadowing, not only had imperceptibly placed itself in a semi-POV regime with the guidance that preceded it, but even more imperceptibly would necessarily have taken in the subjective point of view of those who followed the guide on the jeep. Here, then, its POV must be not only the helpless one of a guide who does not see any reference point, but also (and simultaneously) the one—full of expectation and tension, and therefore of suspense—of those who must rely on that guidance while seeing all around themselves the impossibility of the enterprise. Hence, precisely that use of the Steadicam that had been necessary on a technical level (the one on the *chott*, on which any other more traditional camera would have sunk) and that, therefore, could have more easily remained a mere technical gimmick [...] simply instrumental, turns into [...] a sequence of particular effectiveness and stylistic weight." *Ibid.*, p. 71.

5. *Ibid.*, p. 75. Some sequences were used for a demonstration at Cinecittà on the Steadicam's technical potential. Soon, the camera would be purchased by the Rome studio. However, the first Italian Steadicam remained unused for a long period, since there were no cameramen who could use it, except for Transunto. The

latter was eventually asked to train another operator, Otello Spila.

6. In the Italian version, while seducing Nicole, Jean says, "People should not make war ... they should only make love." In the English version, the line is replaced as follows: "Poor George ... he didn't live to see if his idea would work..." (!)

Chapter Twelve

1. Email interview with the author, October 2015.
2. Valerii is referring to *Tex and the Lord of the Deep* (*Tex e il signore degli abissi*, 1985), starring Giuliano Gemma, which was a commercial and critical flop.
3. Anonymous, "Cavalcarono insieme. Sei domande ai registi italiani," p. 56.
4. *Ibid.*
5. Amidei (1904–1981) was one of Italian cinema's most renowned screenwriters: he was active since the 1930s and collaborated with many of Italy's greatest filmmakers: he was Rossellini's frequent collaborator, starting with *Rome Open City* (*Roma città aperta*, 1945), and worked among others with De Sica—on *Shoeshine* (*Sciuscià*, 1946)—Luigi Zampa, Carlo Lizzani, Ettore Scola, Marco Ferreri…
6. The British Film Institute site credits Valerii as the director of the mysterious *Dodici papà per Marcellino* (A Dozen Fathers for Marcellino), dated 1982 and produced by Mondial Baia Cinematografica, mentioned in *Foreign Sales, Italian Movie Trade* vol. 8, no. 4/5, April-May 1982, which is not mentioned in any Valerii filmography. The synopsis goes as follows: during World War II, a small boy is brought up by a dozen strange characters who survive by taking refuge in a monastery and disguising themselves as monks. There is no trace of the film, which probably never reached shooting stage. When asked about *Dodici papà per Marcellino* by this author, Valerii exclaimed: "But for heaven's sake … never heard of it in my whole life!" Mondial Baia's only other produced film was the little-seen comedy *Venni, vidi e m'arrapaoh* (1984, Vincenzo Salviani).
7. Luigi Malerba (real name Luigi Bonardi, 1927–2008) was a renowned novelist and screenwriter. Among his works for the cinema were Alberto Lattuada's *The Overcoat* (*Il cappotto*, 1952) and *Matchless* (1967), and Pasquale Festa Campanile's *The Gamecock* (*La sculacciata*, 1974).
8. The coffee's brand was Sanka, advertised in the U.S. by actor Robert Young.
9. Anonymous, "Giuliano Gemma carabiniere per una serie di tredici telefilm," *L'Unità*, August 3, 1982.
10. However, the series' original project, as it appears from the pilot "Il ratto di Proserpina," directed by Duccio Tessari, was quite different from the following episodes: Maffei (a former Decathlon champion at the Mediterranean Games) is set in Rome; has an office with a view on Piazza Sant'Ignazio; a superior, Colonel Raimondi (Luciano Stella), a family (a sister who is an art restorer, and whose daughter—Fiorenza Tessari—haunts her uncle with jokes about Carabinieri, and a girlfriend, journalist Laura (Assumpta Serna), who is only mentioned in the pilot. She will eventually appear in the episode *Il calice di Murano*.

11. Silvia Garambois, "E Tex imparò l'arte," *L'Unità*, November 20, 1985.

Chapter Thirteen

1. A. Duanelli, Video, 1986.
2. Ettore Nuara, "Ciak Proibito: *Senza scrupoli*," *Ciak* #7, November 1985, p. 106.
3. Actually, erotic…
4. Marco Giusti, "La stagione 1985/86," in *Il Patalogo 8/9. Annuario 1986 dello spettacolo* (Milan: Ubulibri, 1986), p. 130.
5. In his harsh review of *Senza scrupoli*, critic Michele Anselmi pointed out the similarities between Valerii's film and Eriprando Visconti's *La orca* (1976), about the unhealthy affair between a proletarian criminal (Michele Placido) and the rich girl (Rena Niehaus). Michele Anselmi, "Senza scrupoli è il regista," *L'Unità*, January 15, 1986.

Chapter Fourteen

1. Langdon Hammer, *James Merrill: Life and Art* (New York: Knopf, 2015), pp. 686–688.

Chapter Fifteen

1. Anonymous, "Toshiro Mifune gira in Italia," *Repubblica*, February 4, 1987.
2. Kikkawa, still very popular in Japan, continued his acting career in his home country. Among his films, the best-known in the West is probably *City of Lost Souls* (2000) by Takashi Miike.
3. Stuart Galbraith IV, *The Toho Studios Story: A History and Complete Filmography* (Lanham, MD: Scarecrow, 2008), p. 356.
4. Carlo Alberto Dalla Chiesa (1920–1982) was a General of the Italian Carabinieri, who campaigned against terrorism in the 1970s and was assassinated by the Mafia in Palermo, along with his wife, on September 3, 1982. Dalla Chiesa's figure had inspired the lead character of Leonardo Sciascia's novel *The Day of the Owl*, and was portrayed by Lino Ventura, in his last film role, in Giuseppe Ferrara's *Cento giorni a Palermo* (1984).

Chapter Sixteen

1. Aldo Grasso, *Enciclopedia della televisione* (Milan: Garzanti, 2002), p. 612.
2. In the 1980s and 1990s, RaiDue was under the political influence of the Italian Socialist Party (whereas RaiUno was under Democrazia Cristiana and RaiTre was a fief of the Communist Party).

Chapter Seventeen

1. Katia Ippaso, "L'aristocratico Abraham nella Bangkok dei dannati," *L'Unità*, June 6, 1997.
2. Curiously, a couple of years later Jonathan Kaplan would helm a similarly themed flick, *Brokedown Palace* (1999), starring Claire Danes and Kate Beckinsale.
3. The film also failed to find an International dis-

tribution—no wonder since *Variety* panned it without appeal: "This abysmal concoction of prison-movie cliches set in a nightmarish Thai lockup has neither dramatic tension, character development nor narrative flow. Name cast appears to have been assembled with an eye on international markets, but their efforts likely will languish in video bargain bins." David Rooney, "Vacation in Hell," *Variety*, December 7, 1997.

4. Ippaso, "L'aristocratico Abraham nella Bangkok dei dannati."

5. The quote can be found in Verrecchia's introduction to Schopenhauer's *Aforismi per una vita saggia* (Milan: BUR, 1993), and in Verrecchia's own book, *Giordano Bruno: la falena dello spirito* (Rome: Donzelli, 2002), p. VIII.

Epilogue

1. "Intervista a Tonino Valerii," December 10, 2003, www.terencehill.it.

2. The book Valerii is referring to is *Eroi a Cinecittà* by Fabio Melelli (see Bibliography).

Afterword

1. *Sora* is Roman dialect for *Signora*, "lady."

Appendix: Interviews

George Hilton

1. The protagonist of *Return of Halleluja* (*Il West ti va stretto amico ... è arrivato Alleluja*, 1972, Giuliano Carnimeo).

2. The protagonist of *Man Called Invincible* (*Lo chiamavano Tresette ... giocava sempre col morto* (1973, Giuliano Carnimeo) and *The Crazy Bunch* (*Di Tresette ce n'è uno, tutti gli altri son nessuno*, 1974, Giuliano Carnimeo). The character was renamed Tricky Dicky in the English version.

3. *Coartada en disco rojo*, a.k.a. *I due volti della paura* (1972, Tulio Demicheli).

Roberto Leoni

1. The 13-year-old girl Milena Sutter, the daughter of Swiss industrialist Arturo Sutter, was kidnapped on May 6, 1971, at 5 p.m., at the exit of the private school she attended in Genoa. The day after, the family received an anonymous phone call with a ransom request of 50 million *lire*. Then, there were no more communications on the part of the kidnapper(s). Two weeks later, on May 20, Milena's body was found in the Ligurian Sea, a few hundred yards from the shore. The autopsy revealed that she had been killed on the very day of the kidnapping, then buried in a grave for several days and eventually thrown into the sea, weighed down with six lead weights of one kilo each. That very evening, a 25-year-old man, Lorenzo Bozano, was arrested and put on trial. First acquitted for lack of evidence in 1973, he was condemned to a life sentence in appeal, in 1975. Soon after, he fled to France. He was arrested by sheer chance in 1979 and extradited to Italy. He eventually came out on probation in 1989.

2. Actually, the space of time between the kidnapping and the film's release amounted to nine months.

Franco Nero

1. Giorgio Strehler (1921—1997) was one of Italy's most important and innovative opera and theater directors. His work (including plays by Brecht and Alban Berg, and operas by Verdi, Mozart and Mascagni) influenced and inspired stage actors and directors around the world. In 1982 he was President of the jury at the Cannes Film Festival, and in 1985 he was given the prestigious Légion d'honneur.

2. Checco Zalone (real name Luca Medici) is Italy's most popular comic actor. He became popular on TV as a stand-up comedian, before starring in four films that were all box-office hits and record breakers: his latest movie, *Quo vado?* (2016, Gennaro Nunziante), was released on January 1, 2016, in 1,500 theaters (a record in Italy), topping *Star Wars: The Force Awakens* (2015, J. J. Abrams), and within a mere ten days it became Italy's highest grossing film of all time. Zalone's films are broad but sometimes biting satires of the average Italian guy.

Bibliography

On Italian Cinema

Brunetta, Gian Piero. *Storia del cinema italiano: Dal miracolo economico agli anni Novanta*. Rome: Editori Riuniti, 2001.

Faldini. Franca, and Goffredo Fofi, eds. *L'avventurosa storia del cinema italiano raccontata dai suoi protagonisti 1960–1969*. Milan: Feltrinelli, 1981.

Gastaldi, Ernesto. *Voglio entrare nel cinema—Storia di uno che ce l'ha fatta*. Milan: Mondadori, 1991.

Melelli, Fabio. *Eroi a Cinecittà: Stuntmen e maestri d'armi del cinema italiano*. Perugia: Mercurio editrice, 1998.

On Italian and Euro Westerns

Books, Monographs

Bud Spencer & Terence Hill: West botte da orbi e buoni sentimenti. Assisi: ANCCI, 2005.

Aguilar, Carlos. *Giuliano Gemma: El factor romano*. Almería: Diputación de Almería, 2003.

Beatrice, Luca. *Al cuore, Ramon, al cuore: La leggenda del western all'italiana*. Florence: Tarab, 1996.

Bertolino, Marco and Ridola Ettore. *Bud Spencer & Terence Hill* (Rome: Gremese, 2002).

Bruschini, Antonio, and Antonio Tentori. *Western all'italiana. Book One—The Specialists* (Florence: Glittering Press, 1998).

BruschinI, Antonio, and Federico De Zigno. *Western all'italiana. Book Two—The Wild, the Sadist and the Outsiders* (Florence: Glittering Press, 1998).

Bruschini, Antonio, Federico De Zigno and Stefano Piselli. *Western all'italiana. Book Three—100 More Must-See Movies* (Florence: Glittering Press, 1998).

Castagna, Alberto, and Maurizio Cesare Graziosi. *Il western all'italiana*. Milan: Federico Motta Editore, 2005.

Cox, Alex. *10,000 Ways to Die: A Director's Take on the Spaghetti Western*. Harpenden, Hertfordshire: Kamera Books, 2009.

Cumbow, Robert C. *The Films of Sergio Leone*. Lanham, MD: Scarecrow Press, 2008.

Curti, Roberto. *James Coburn: El samurai del Oeste*. Almería: Diputación de Almería, 2005.

De Fornari, Oreste, *Tutti i film di Sergio Leone* (Milan: Ubulibri, 1984).

Donati, Sergio, *C'era una volta il West (ma c'ero anch'io)* (Rome: Omero, 2007).

Festi, Roberto (a cura di). *C'era una volta il ... western all'italiana: Mito e protagonisti* (Madonna di Campiglio: APT Madonna di Campiglio / Provincia di Trento / Stampalith, 2001).

Frayling, Christopher. *Spaghetti Westerns: Cowboys and Europeans from Karl May to Sergio Leone*. London: I. B. Tauris, 2006).

_____. *Sergio Leone: Something to Do with Death* (Minneapolis: University of Minnesota Press, 2012.

Gagliani Caputo, Marcello. *...Altrimenti ci arrabbiamo: Il cinema di Bud Spencer e Terence Hill* (Rome: Un Mondo A Parte, 2004).

Garofalo, Marcello. *Tutto il cinema di Sergio Leone* (Milan: Baldini & Castoldi, 1999).

Giusti, Marco. *Dizionario del western all'italiana* (Milan: Mondadori, 2007).

Grant, Kevin. *Any Gun Can Play: The Essential Guide to Euro-Westerns* (Godalming, Surrey: FAB Press, 2012).

Hughes, Howard. *Once Upon a Time in the Italian West* (London/New York: I. B. Tauris, 2004).

Malloy, Mike. *Lee Van Cleef: A Biographical, Film and Television Reference*. Jefferson NC: McFarland, 2005.

Mininni, Francesco. *Sergio Leone* (Milan: Il Castoro Cinema, 1995).

Moscati, Massimo. *Western all'italiana* (Milan: Il Timone, 1978).

Pezzotta, Alberto. *Il western italiano* (Milan: Il Castoro, 2012).

Prickette, James. *Actors of the Spaghetti Western* (Xlibris, 2012).

Rège, Philippe. *Lee Van Cleef. Soledad y muerte* (Almería: Diputación de Almería, 2004).

Simsolo, Nöel. *Conversations avec Sergio Leone* (Paris: Petite Bibliothèque des Cahiers du Cinéma, 1999).

Staig, Laurence, and Tony Williams. *Italian Western: The Opera of Violence* (London: Lorrimer, 1975).

Articles, Interviews, Special Magazine Issues

Bruschini, Antonio, and Igor Molino Padovan. "Non solo Ringo—Intervista a Giuliano Gemma," *Amarcord* #4, 1996.

"Eurowestern," *Nosferatu* # 41–42, October 2002. Various authors.

Fratter, Roger A., and Manlio Gomarasca. "Wanted: Dieci ricercati dello spaghetti western," *Nocturno Dossier* # 62, September 2007.

Fratter, Roger A., and Pulici Davide. "Ai confini del western: Zone d'ombra del genere all'italiana," *Nocturno Dossier* #31, February 2005.

Grattarola, Franco. "Per qualche sceneggiatura in più ... per un pugno di attori," *Cine70 e dintorni* #7, 2006.

Ippoliti, Stefano, and Matteo Norcini. "Agente Tony Kendall operazione cinema," *Cine70 e dintorni* #7, 2006.

Lucas, Tim. "Ernesto Gastaldi interviewed," *Video Watchdog* #39, 1997.

Navarro, Antonio José. "El western all'italiana," *Dirigido Por* #316, 2002.

"Speciale western italiano," *Quaderni di CinemaSud* # 2/2007, August 2007. Various authors.

On Tonino Valerii: Articles, Interviews, Monographs

Albano, Giancarlo. "Un miliardo di lire per riconquistare un fortino," *Bolero Teletutto* #1310, 11 June 1972.

Ballerini, David. *Steadicam: Una rivoluzione nel modo di fare cinema* (Alessandria: Falsopiano, 1999).

"Cavalcarono insieme: Sei domande ai registi italiani," *Almanacco Cinema—Il Formichiere* #1, Spring 1979.

Curti, Roberto. "Tonino Valerii: El más clásico de los posmodernos," in "Eurowestern," *Nosferatu* # 41–42 (San Sebastián: Donostia Kultura, October 2002).

Curti, Roberto. "Vai gorilla," in "Anni di piombo," *Nocturno Book* #18, April 2001.

La Selva, Tommaso. *Tonino Valerii: mai temere il Leone* (Milan: Nocturno Libri, 2000).

Micalizzi, Paolo. "Tonino Valerii: i miei western da regista," *Quaderni di CinemaSud*, # 2/2007.

Tiboni, Edoardo, and Paolo Smoglica, eds. *L'Abruzzo e il cinema: Atti del Convegno Internazionale premi Flaiano*, 16–17 giugno 1995 (Pescara: EDIARS, 1995–2008).

Vitti, Antonio Carlo. "Tonino Valerii," in *Lezioni di cinema e di regia* (Florence: Società Editrice Fiorentina, 2013).

Zanello, Fabio. "Mi chiamo Tonino Valerii ... e faccio il western," *Amarcord* #14–15, July-October 1998.

Index

Page numbers in bold italics indicate pages with illustrations.

A 001: operazione Giamaica see *Our Man in Jamaica*
Abraham, F. Murray 144, 164
Abrams, J. J. 216
L'Abruzzo? Prendilo è tuo!... (documentary) 107
Adorf, Mario 27, 211
Adriatico, Andrea 148
The Adventures of Pinocchio (novel) 208
Aguilar, Carlos 6, 210
The Alcove (film) 121
Aldrich, Robert 25, 43, 73
Alessi, Ottavio 119
Alive or Preferably Dead (film) 56
All the Colors of the Dark (film) 71
All'amore assente (film) 146
Allen, Woody 211
Almanacco del cinema (magazine) 116, 117, 211, 212
Altman, Robert 213
Altri tempi (Zibaldone n. 1) (film) 20
Ambesi, Adriana 22, 191
Amendola, Mario 24
An American in Rome (film) 100
Amidei, Sergio 117, 118, 215
Anderson, Michael 59
Andreotti, Giulio 19
An Angel for Satan (film) 23
ANICA 17, 207
Anime nere (film) 165
Anselmi, Michele 215
Antonelli, Laura 87, 122
Antonioni, Michelangelo 15, 19, 61, 207
Arau, Alfonso 163
Ardisson, Giorgio 208
Argento, Dario 10, 38, 66, 67, 68, 69, 79, 128, 144, 160, 163, 211
Arizona Colt (film) 8
Arlecchino servitore di due padroni (comedy play) 28, 29
Armstrong, R.G. [Robert Golden Armstrong, Jr.] 94
Arrivano i vostri, ovvero Storia avventurosa del western all'italiana (TV series) 210
Ash Wednesday (film) 85
L'assedio dell'Alcazar (film) 2, 77
August, Bille 164
Ausino, Carlo 122
Autant-Lara, Claude 19, 57

Auz Castro, Víctor 33
L'avventura (film) 61
L'avventurosa storia del cinema italiano raccontata dai suoi protagonisti (book) 26, 208, 211
Azcona, Rafael 73, 75
Azzolina, Enzo 141

Baba Yaga (film) 71
Bad Arabella (film) 207
Badlands (film) 213
Badroots—Cattive radici (novel) 160
Bain, Donald 65
Balbo, Ennio 40
Baldi, Ferdinando 168
Ballad of Death Valley see *A Pistol for Ringo*
Ballerini, David 112, 214
Balsam, Martin 8, 126, 127, 134, 172, 173, 186
Banderas, Antonio 160, 164
Bandidos (film) 43
Banfi, Lino 125, 167
Bangkwang. Tre anni per droga nelle carceri thailandesi (book) 142
Baracco, Adriano 15, 207
Barboni, Enzo 8, 25, 30, 77, 79, 80, 96, 147
Barker, Ron 40
Baron Blood (film) 71
Barron, Arthur 211
Basehart, Jackie 162
Basinger, Kim 124
Battaglia, Rik 86
Battistrada, Lucio 117, 146
Battleship Potemkin (film) 17
Bauer, Alfred 64
Bava, Lamberto 147, 180, 182
Bava, Mario 21, 23, 71, 150, 207, 208
Becker, Jacques 110
Beckinsale, Kate 215
Un bel dì vedremo (film) 11, 141–142, 154, 157
Bellecca, Giuseppe "Beppe" 59
Belli, Adriano 107, 108
Bellocchio, Marco 39, 186, 210
Ben Ammar, Tarak 107
Ben Bella, Ahmed 29, 209
Ben-Hur (1959 film) 41
Beneck, Bruno 17

Bentivoglio, Fabrizio 119
Benvenuti, Nino 56
Berg, Alban 216
Berger, Debra 161
Berger, Helmut 162
Berger, William 160
Berlusconi, Silvio 125, 133, 140
Berry, Julian see Gastaldi, Ernesto
Bertolucci, Bernardo 63, 80
The Best of Enemies (film) 20, 130
Beyond the Law (film) 77
Bianchi, Pietro 86
Bido, Antonio 209
Bierce, Ambrose 9, 53, 73
The Big Gundown (film) 8
The Big Heat (1953 film) 36
The Big Racket (film) 102
Billa, Salvatore 132
Billian, Hans 26
Binarelli, Tony 109
The Bird with the Crystal Plumage (film) 66
Black Grapes (novel) 7, 57
Black Patch (film) 43
Black Sunday (film) 21, 22, 23, 208
Black Turin (film) 184
Blasco, Ricardo 32
Blasetti, Alessandro 1, 3, 7, 15, 16, 20, 29, 32, 116, 147, 148, 149
Blood and Roses (film) 22
Blood at Sundown see *The Return of Ringo*
Blood for a Silver Dollar (film) 40, 158
The Bloodstained Shadow (film) 209
Boccaccio 70 (film) 207
Boetticher, Budd 40
Bogdanovich, Peter 88, 213
Bohr, Robert see Valerii, Tonino
Bolchi, Sandro 211
Bolkan, Florinda 71
Bolognini, Manolo 66, 160, 166, 167, 170
Bolognini, Mauro 66, 134, 207
Bolzoni, Adriano 25, 26, 208
Bominaco: una scoperta (documentary) 107
Bompani, Lucio 33, 41
Bonadonna, Elio 132
Bonanza (TV series) 24, 51
Bonelli, Gian Luigi 116, 117
Boot Hill (film) 56

219

Bora Bora (film) 58, 59
Boratto, Caterina 119
Bordella (film) 105
Il borghese (magazine) 26, 208
Bosch, Juan 208
Bosic, Andrea [Ignacio Božič] 40
Bouchet, Barbara 134
Bozano, Lorenzo 216
Brancaleone's Army (film) 99
Brass, Tinto 9, 63, 121, 123, 131, 151, 152
The Bravados (film) 40
Brazzi, Oscar 125
Brazzi, Rossano 125
Brecht, Bertolt 216
Brega, Mario 94
Brokedown Palace (film) 215
Bronson, Charles 27
Bronston, Samuel 24
Brothers in Blood, a.k.a. *Savage Attack* (film) 8, 13, 125–129, 132, 137, 161, 162–163, 165, 171–174, 185–186
Brown, Garrett 111
Brunetta, Gian Piero 58, 79, 211, 212
Bruno, Isabella 204, 210
Brynner, Yul 134
Bubù (film) 66
Bucceri, Franco 66, 71, 167, 170
Buchs, Julio 75
A Bullet for Sandoval (film) 75
A Bullet for the General (film) 8
Bullets Don't Argue (film) 27
Buñuel, Luis 75
The Burmese Harp (film) 214
Burn! (film) 56, 132
Burn, Boy, Burn see *A Woman on Fire*
Busey, Gary 184

Cabiria (magazine) 146
Cabot, Sebastian 43
Caccia al ladro d'autore (TV series) 118, 119, 121, 154, 157
Cagney, James 17
Caiano, Mario 27, 71, 147, 208, 209
Calhoun, Rory 25, 27
California (film) 125, 166
California Split (film) 213
Caligari, Claudio 187
Calvo, José "Pepe" 40, 45, **55**
Calzini, Mario 32, 209
Cameron, Rod 27
Candelori, Francesca 13
Canevari, Cesare 9
Cantafora, Antonio 109, 177
Canutt, Yakima 41
Capitani, Giorgio 159, 160
Capriccio (film) 131, 151
Carati, Lilli [Ileana Caravati] 121
Cardinale, Claudia 160
Carmilla (novella) 22
Carnera, Primo 147
Carnimeo, Giuliano 80, 159, 216
Carraro, Nicola 117
La casa del sorriso (film) 142
Casablanca Express (film) 171
Cascio, Bruno 174, 200

The Case of the Scorpion's Tail (film) 159, 160
Castel, Lou 39, 47, 210
Castellano, Franco 120
Castellari, Enzo G. [Enzo Girolami] 44, 98, 99, 102, 126, 128, 147, 160, 161, 171
Castelnuovo, Nino 19
Castle of Blood (film) 21
The Cat O'Nine Tails (film) 128
Catena, Víctor Andrés 26
Catenacci, Luciano 105
Cavani, Liliana 17
Cecchi Gori, Mario 99, 100, 102, 105, 106, 171, 176
Celi, Adolfo 120
Cento giorni a Palermo (film) 215
Centro Sperimentale di Cinematografia (CSC) 1, 7, 15, 16, 33, 108, 146, 149, 207, 208
Chaney, Lon, Jr. 77
Che tempo che fa (TV show) 92
Chevalier, Roberto 63
Chi l'ha visto? (TV show) 59, 211
Chiari, Walter 20, 26, 208
Chicago Reader (newspaper) 213
La chienne (1972 film) 179
China Gate (film) 40
Christie, Agatha 70
Chrosicki, Henryk 39, 49
Ciak (magazine) 121, 215
Ciampi, Yves 19
Cicero, Nando 43
El Cid (film) 24
Il cielo non cade mai (1992) 139
Cimarosa, Tano 132
Cin... cin... cianuro (film) 109
Cinema (magazine) 15
Cinema Paradiso (film) 14, 144, 163, 165
Cinesex (magazine) 58
I cinque del Condor see *Squadra selvaggia*
Cinquini, Roberto 28
Citizen Kane (film) 55
La città e la memoria (documentary) 107
City of Lost Souls (film) 215
La ciudad maldita (film) 208
Close, Glenn 164
Clouzot, Henri-Georges 23
Coburn, James 7, 27, 75, 77, 178, 184
El Cochecito (film) 73
Coffee, Tea or Me? (TV movie) 65
Coffee, Tea or Me? The Unhibited Memoirs of Two Airline Stewardesses (novel) 65
Cole, Nat Kelly 126, 128, 137, 162, 173, 186
Colizzi, Giuseppe 49, 56
Colli, Ernesto 176
Collodi, Carlo 208
Colombo, Arrigo 3, 17, 23, 27, 29, 208
The Colossus of Rhodes (film) 25
Comas Gil, Jaime 26
Combat Shock (film) 127
Comencini, Luigi 50, 77, 176

Comradeship (film) 19, 28
El Condor (film) 74
Confessions of a Police Captain (film) 134
The Conformist (film) 63
The Conjugal Bed (film) 39, 73
Connery, Sean 33
Constantin, Michel 109, 110, 112, 114
Contraband (film) 176
Conversation Piece (film) 214
The Conversation (film) 213
Conversations avec Sergio Leone (book) 89, 208, 213
Conversi, Cleofe 17
Cooper, Gary 75, 116
Coppola, Francis Ford 102, 213
Corbucci, Sergio 8, 25, 36, 53, 66, 96, 100, 115, 147
Cormack of the Mounties (film) 102
Corman, Roger 23
La corona di ferro (film) 15
Corridori, Giovanni 28, 147, 208
Corriere della Sera (newspaper) 117, 209
Cortini, Pippo 34
Coscia, Marcello 59
Cosulich, Callisto 58, 211
Cotten, Joseph 78
Could It Happen Here? (film) 115
Cox, Alex 210, 212, 213
El Coyote (film) 24
The Crazy Bunch (film) 216
Crescenzi, Marcello 86
Crespi, Alberto 96, 214
Crime Busters (film) 115
Cristaldi, Franco 117, 165
Cruise, Tom 180
Crypt of the Vampire see *Terror in the Crypt*
CSC see Centro Sperimentale di Cinematografia
Cuadra, María **55**, 56
La cuccagna (film) 213
Cumbow, Robert 95, 213, 214

Dacla, Corinne 139
D'Agata, Giuseppe 117
Dalla, Lucio 122
Dalla Chiesa, Carlo Alberto 132, 134, 215
Dalla parte giusta (film) 174
Dallamano, Massimo 43
Damiani, Damiano 8, 57, 99, 115, 132, 133, 134, 213
The Damned (film) 58, 162
D'Amore, Renato 120
Danes, Claire 215
Danger: Diabolik (film) 207
Daniel Boone (TV series) 51
Darc, Mireille 214
Davis, Bette 78, 122
Davis, Brad 144
A Day in Court (film) 100
Day of Anger (film) 1, 5, 6, 7, 8, 9, 36, 39–49, 50, 53, 55, 57, 62, 70, 71, 77, 95, 96, 97, 103, 130, 146, 147, 154, 155, 156, 210, 211, 213

The Day of the Owl (film) 57
The Day of the Owl (novel) 215
Day of Wrath (film) 210
De Angelis, Remo 41, 67, 69
Death Rage (film) 134
Death Rides a Horse (film) 43
Death Wish (film) 100
De Concini, Ennio 134
De Curtis, Cinzia 151
De Filippo, Luca 135
De Fornari, Oreste 124, 208
Degli Esposti, Maurizio 59
De Larderel, François 31
De Laurentiis, Alfredo 161
De Laurentiis, Dino 99, 151, 161
Del Buono, Oreste 95
Dell'Aquila, Enzo 29
Delli Colli, Tonino 87, 147
Delon, Alain 153
Del Re, Carlo 65
De Luca, Lorella 162
Delvaux, Paul 63
Demicheli, Tulio 216
De Niro, Robert 80
Deodato, Ruggero 136, 147, 152, 173, 179
De Palma, Brian 112
De Rita, Massimo 80, 100, 104, 214
De Rossi, Barbara 137
De Santis, Attilio 185
De Santis, Giuseppe 15
Desert Attack see *Ice Cold in Alex*
De Seta, Vittorio 21
De Sica, Vittorio 61, 99, 181
De Sisti, Vittorio 136
De Stefani, Livia 7, 57
Devil Hunter 128
Devil in the Flesh (1947 film) 19
Dewhurst, Colleen 211
Di che segno sei? (film) 100
Diabolique (film) 23
Il diario di Anna Frank (featurette) 16
Diary of a Chambermaid (1964 film) 75
The Diary of Anne Frank (book) 16
Di Biase, Mario 151
1900 (film) 80
1860 (film) 15
Di Clemente, Giovanni 144
Der Dicke und das Warzenschwein see *A Reason to Live, a Reason to Die!*
Di Geronimo, Bruno 59
Di Giacomo, Franco 111
Di Giulio, Ed 111
Di Lazzaro, Dalila 131, 151, 183
Di Leo, Fernando 26, 29, 59, 91, 109, 116, 208
Dillinger Is Dead (film) 105
Di Nardo, Mauro 59
Dionisio, Silvia 59, 61, 63
The Dirty Dozen (film) 25, 73, 77, 211
Distretto di polizia (TV series) 187
Divine Comedies (book of poetry) 126
Divorce—Italian Style (film) 23

Django (1966 film) 36, 39, 66, 132
Django Unchained (film) 146
Dmytryk, Edward 47
Dodici papà per Marcellino (film) 215
La Dolce Vita (film) 80
Donati, Sergio 6, 29, 79, 80, 82, 84, 87, 90, 212, 214
Una donna allo specchio (film) 122
Dor, Karin 27
Douglas, Gordon 77
Douglas, Kirk 71, 170
Dreyer, Carl Theodor 210
Duck, You Sucker (film) 54, 56, 77, 84, 87
Due assi per un turbo (TV series) 119–120
Due madri (film) 136–138, 145, 153, 154
Duel (film) 89
The Duel at Silver Creek (film) 38

Eastwood, Clint 1, 2, 26, 27, 28, 29, 35, 40, 87, 208
The Easy Life (film) 20
Eccezziunale ... veramente (film) 120
Edera (soap opera) 154
8½ (film) 21
1860 (film) 15
Eisenhower, Dwight E. 24
Eisenstein, Sergei M. 15, 17
El Cid (film) 24
Empire (TV series) 51
Erotic Games (film) 121
Estrada, Carlos 34
European Nights (film) 20
Even Angels Eat Beans (film) 87
Execution Squad (film) 77, 99
Executive Action (film) 53

Fabiola (film) 16
Facing Windows (film) 142
The Facts of Murder (film) 67, 169
Fago, Giovanni 120
Fajrajzen, Stefano 46
Faldini, Franca 26, 208, 211
Fangareggi, Ugo 75, 211
Fantasia, Franco 172, 173
Fantastichini, Ennio 119
Fare l'aiuto regista (book) 146
Farina, Corrado 71
The Fastest Gun Alive (film) 94
Fattori, Antonella 142
Fazio, Fabio 92
Fellini, Federico 21, 58, 132, 176
Fellini—Satyricon (film) 207
Fenech, Edwige 71, 134
Ferrando, Giancarlo 172, 173
Ferrara, Giuseppe 215
Ferrari, Nicolò 19, 207
Ferreol, Andréa 214
Ferreri, Marco 39, 73, 105, 122, 123, 142, 215
Ferroni, Giorgio 39, 40, 47
Fersen, Alessandro 46
Ferzetti, Fausto 139
Ferzetti, Gabriele 139
Festa Campanile, Pasquale 215

Fidenco, Nico 35
15 from Rome see *Opiate '67*
The Fifth Commandment (film) 126, 162
55 Days at Peking (film) 24
The Fighting Fists of Shanghai Joe (film) 71
Film Form and the Film Sense (book) 15
The Final Executioner (film) 166
First Blood (film) 125
A Fistful of Dollars (film) 1, 2, 7, 25–29, 32, 33, 38, 41, 103, 208, 209
Fists in the Pocket (film) 39, 47, 210
Fitzgerald, Francis Scott 95
The Five Man Army (film) 211
Flaherty, Lorenzo 131
Fofi, Goffredo 26, 208, 211
Fonda, Henry 3, 7, 56, 81, 82, 84, 85, 86, 87, **88**, 89, 90, 94, 97, 181, 212, 213, 214
Fonda, Peter 82
Fontaine, Joan 61, 211
For a Few Dollars More (film) 1, 2, 7, 26, 28, 29–30, 33, 34, 35, 36, 79, 90, 93, 139, 150, 208, 209
For a Few Extra Dollars (film) 39, 40, 157
Forest, Andy J. 6, 131, 132, 151–153, 183, 200
Forty Guns (film) 94
Four of the Apocalypse (film) 102
Fraga, Manuel 24
Franchi, Franco 20, 21
Franco, Francisco 24, 77
Franco, Jesús "Jess" 40, 128
Frank, Anne 16
Frank, Margot 16
Frank, Otto 16
Frayling, Christopher 1–3, 6, 38, 86, 87, 95, 209, 211, 212, 213
Freda, Riccardo 21, 40, 75, 128, 150, 207
Frederick II of Swabia 182
Fremont, Christian 120
The French Sex Murders (film) 71
Freud, Sigmund 15, 45
Frizzi, Fulvio 102, 115
Fulci, Lucio 102, 150, 159, 176, 182, 208
Full Metal Jacket (film) 143
Fuller, Samuel 40, 94
Fury of Johnny Kid (film) 43

Gaburro, Bruno 121
Gadda, Carlo Emilio 169
Galadini, Eugenio 35
Gale, Eddra 21
Galeppini, Aurelio 116
Gallo, Enzo 121, 122, 123, 142
The Gamecock (film) 215
Gangsters '70 (film) 207
Gaos, Lola 68, 169
Garbo, Greta 17, 52
Garbuglia, Mario 161
Garfield, James A. 50, 52, 53, 54, 55
Garko, Gianni [Gianni Garkovich] 6, 27, 137, 139, 153–154

Garrone, Matteo 176
Garrone, Sergio 209
Gassman, Vittorio 125, 160
Gastaldi, Ernesto 3, 6, 16, 17, 21, 22, 23, 28, 32, 39, 40, 43, 44, 47, 51, 53, 54, 72, 73, 77, 80, 81, 86, 88, 92, 93, 95, 96, 101, 107, 108, 109, 116, 132, 149–150, 207, 208, 211, 212, 213, 214
Gastoni, Lisa 214
Gemma, Giuliana 210
Gemma, Giuliano 6, 7, 8, 20, 39, 40, 41, *42*, 47, 48, 49, 51, 52, *53*, *55*, 56, 71, 87, 96, 118, 119, 125, 130, 141, 147, 154–158, 210, 215
Genesi, Francesco 32, 39
Genesi, Vincenzo 32, 39
Genina, Augusto 2, 77
Un genio, due compari, un pollo (film) 213
Genta, Renzo 39
Géret, Georges 75
Germi, Pietro 23, 67, 158, 169
The Getaway (1972 film) 102
Ghione, Franco 122
Ghione, Riccardo 121, 122
The Ghost (film) 21
Giannini, Giancarlo 145, 164, 165, 168, 169
Gibson, Mel 184
Gimpera, Teresa 209
Giornale dello spettacolo (magazine) 111, 118
Un giorno in Europa (documentary) 150
Giovinazzo, Buddy 127
A Girl Called Jules (film) 10, 33, 57–64, 80, 124, 168, 210
Giro girotondo... con il sesso è bello il mondo (film) 125
Girolami, Marino 104, 161
Girotti, Massimo 2, 141, 142
Giusti, Marco 80, 86, 123, 213
The Glass Key (novel) 208
Go Gorilla Go, a.k.a. *The Hired Gun* (film) 3, 5, 10, 11, 38, 99–106, 107, 112, 115, 132, 141, 144, 171, 175, 176, 178, 179, 214
God Forgives... I Don't! (film) 49
The Godfather (film) 102, 183
The Godfather—Part II (film) 80, 213
Goldoni, Carlo 2, 28, 29, 119
The Good, the Bad and the Ugly (film) 1, 32, 38, 39, 40, 46, 49, 75, 77, 90, 93
Gordon, Leo 43, 82, 94
Gould, Elliot 169
The Grand Duel (film) 43, 179
La Grande Bouffe (film) 105, 179
Grandi, Serena 121
Grant, Kevin 210
Grasso, Aldo 134, 215
Graves, Peter 211
Graveyard Disturbance (film) 180
The Great Silence (film) 8
Greenflowers, John J. [Antonio Scutari] 160
Grimaldi, Alberto 29, 31, 208

Grunt! (film) 120
Guerrieri, Romolo 99, 166
Guerrini, Mino 207
Guillermin, John 74
Guiteau, Charles J. 53
The Gunfighter (film) 94

Hackman, Gene 171
Hadley Chase, James [René Lodge Brabazon Raymond] 134
Hamilton, Guy 20
Hammer, Langdon 6, 126, 215
Hammett, Dashiell 208
Hands of a Gunfighter (film) 34
Hanlin, Tom 31, 32
Harakiri (1962 film) 101
Hardy, Robin 23
Harris, Brad 209
Harrison, Richard 27
Harvey, Michael 56
Hawks, Howard 88
Heartbreak Ridge (film) 126, 185
Hecht Lucari, Gianni 118
Heflin, Van 102, 160
The Hellbenders (film) 53
Hellman, Monte 36
Hercules (1958 film) 25
Heston, Charlton 116
High and Low (film) 70
High Noon (film) 40
Hill, Craig 34, 35, 102, 209, 210
Hill, George Roy 109, 214
Hill, Terence [Mario Girotti] 3, 7, 8, 25, 49, 56, 77, 78, 80, 81, 82, 84, 85, 86, 87, 88, *91*, 92, *94*, 96, 97, 115, 120, 181, 185, 212, 213, 214
Hilton, George [Jorge Hill Acosta y Lara] 6, 43, 68, 159–161, 168, 169
The Hired Gun see *Go Gorilla Go*
The Hired Hand (film) 82
Hitchcock, Alfred 61, 107, 119, 139
Hollywood (magazine) 15
Homer 79
Honorato, Marzio 122, 123
Hooten, John Peter 6, 126, 161–163, 173, 186
The Horrible Dr. Hichcock (film) 21
A Horseman in the Sky (short story) 53
The House of the Spirits (film) 164
How to Kill a Judge (film) 179
The Howl (film) 63
Hudson, William Henry 118
Hughes, Howard (film historian) 96, 210, 214
Huston, John 153

I Am Afraid (film) 115
I Confess (film) 139
I Love, You Love (film) 20
Ice Cold in Alex (film) 112
Ichikawa, Kon 132, 141, 214
If You Meet Sartana Pray for Your Death (film) 212
The Iguana with the Tongue of Fire (film) 128
Images (film) 213
INAIL: 100 anni e non sentirli (documentary) 118

Indian Summer (film) 153
The Inglorious Bastards (film) 126, 161, 162
Ingrassia, Ciccio 20, 21
An Innocent Man (film) 144
Innocenzi, Pietro 77
Innocenzi, Silvia 212
Intervista (film) 132
Interzone (film) 180
Investigation of a Citizen Above Suspicion (film) 115, 168
Ionesco, Eva 59
Irons, Jeremy 139
It Can Be Done Amigo (film) 77
Italian Western: The Opera of Violence (book) 88, 213

Jancsó, Miklos 110, 186
The Jester's Supper (film) 15–16
Jet-Set Swingers (film) 64
The Jeweller's Shop (film) 59
Jodorowsky, Alejandro 166
Johnson, Van 51, 52, *55*, 56, 157
Jolly Film/Unidis 1, 3, 17, 20, 23, 26, 27, 28, 29, 104, 208
Judgement of Coyote (film) 24

Kabaivanska, Raina 141, 142, 157, 158
Kaplan, Jonathan 215
Karis, Vassili [Vassili Karamenisis] 27
Keach, Stacy 125
Kendall, Tony [Luciano Stella] 27, 208, 215
Kennedy, John Fitzgerald 50, 52, 53, 156
The Key (film) 121
Kezich, Tullio 45, 46, 49
Khasoggi, Adnan 120
Kikkawa, Kôji 131, 151, 180, 181, 183, 215
Kill Bill vol. 1 (film) 146, 158
Kill Bill vol. 2 (film) 146, 158
Kill the Fatted Calf and Roast It (film) 59
King, Henry 40, 94
King, Martin Luther 54
Kinski, Klaus 160, 213
Kleinhoff Hotel (film) 115
Kobayashi, Masaki 101
Koch, Marianne 27, 215
Kolldehoff, René 75
Kotcheff, Ted 125
Kubert, Joe 116
Kumada, Asao 93, 130, 141
Kurosawa, Akira 1, 2, 24, 25, 26, 28, 29, 70, 77, 101, 131, 132, 153, 208
Kuveiller, Luigi 167

Lady of the Night (film) 121
Landis, John 86, 212
Lang, Fritz 36, 94
Lardani, Iginio 46
La Selva, Tommaso 1, 6, 91
Last of the Badmen (film) 43
The Last Round (film) 103
Lattuada, Alberto 40, 64, 182, 215
Laura nuda (film) 19, 207

Index

Laura nuda (novelization) 19
Law, John Phillip 43
Lawrence, Peter Lee [Karl Hyrenbach] 43
Lazzari, Piero 80, 84
Le Fanu, Joseph Sheridan 22
Lelouch, Claude 181
Lenzi, Umberto 152, 173
Leonardi, Marco 6, 144, 163–165
Leone, Carla 27
Leone, Sergio 1, 2, 3, 5, 6, 7, 8, 9, 10, 23, 24–30, 32, 33, 35, 36, 38, 40, 41, 45, 46, 47, 57, 77, 79–98, 101, 116, 146, 147, 150, 154, 156, 163, 170, 208
Leoni, Roberto 6, 66, 71, 125, 127, 165–175
Leopold II, Grand Duke of Tuscany 31
Lerro, Rocco 126, 161, 172
Lethal Weapon (film) 184
Lettieri, Al 102, 104, 176
Levi Bianchini, Marco 15
Lewis, Geoffrey 94, 197
Liberatore, Ugo 50, 119
Like Water for Chocolate (film) 163
Linder, Christa 40
Liné, Helga 66, 69, 160
Lionello, Oreste 211
Lizzani, Carlo 6, 116, 184, 215
Lo Bianco, Tony 212
Lombardo, Goffredo 39, 50, 65, 138, 139, 154
Long Days of Vengeance (film) 47
The Long Goodbye (film) 169
The Long Hair of Death (film) 23
Longo, Malisa 63
Love & Passion see *Capriccio*
Loy, Mino 207
Lucas, Tim 23, 208, 213
Lucidi, Maurizio 77, 125
Lucisano, Fulvio 106
Lulli, Piero 33, 38, 86
Luotto, Andy 120
Lupo, Michele 8, 64, 71, 80, 125, 166, 170, 212
A Lustful Mind (film) 121

Macchia, Gianni 6, 59, 61, 64
Madan, Geoffrey 162
Madison, Guy 27
Maesso, José 169
Maggio, Dante 68, 169
The Magnificent Cuckold (film) 39
Il magnifico straniero (film) 208
Mairesse, Guy 75
Maiuri, Dino 214
Makavejev, Dušan 64
Maladolescenza (film) 59
Maladonna (film) 121
Malatesta, Guido 41
Malcolm X [Malcolm Little] 144
Malerba, Luigi [Luigi Bonardi] 119, 215
Malicious (film) 87
Malick, Terrence 213
A Man and a Woman (film) 181
Man Called Invincible (film) 216
Man of the East (film) 77, 96

The Man Who Shot Liberty Valance (film) 94
Mancini, Claudio 84, 85, 171
Mancini, Henri 183
Manfredi, Nino 20, 182
Mangano, Silvana 78
Mankiewicz, Joseph L. 97
Mann, Anthony 9, 211
Marathon Man (film) 111
Marconi, Saverio 6, 102, 175
Margheriti, Antonio 21, 22, 23, 71, 134, 150
Mariano, Detto 119
Marinucci, Vinicio 17, 28
Márquez, Evaristo 132
Marsani, Claudia 104, 214
Marsili, Emilio 150
Marsina, Antonio 38, 102, 122, 124, 176
Martin, George [Francisco Martínez Celeiro] 33, 102
Martin, Jean 84
Martino, Luciano 160
Martino, Sergio 71, 119, 150, 159, 171, 172
Maryl, Mara (Maria Chianetta) 22, 208
Mascagni, Pietro 216
Massaccesi, Aristide 102, 121, 126, 209
Massacre at Fort Holman see *A Reason to Live, a Reason to Die!*
Massacre Time (film) 159
Massari, Lea 211, 214
Massi, Stelvio 25, 33, 39, 55, 103, 120
The Master Touch (film) 71, 75, 170
Mastocinque, Camillo 20, 22, 23, 150
Mastroianni, Marcello 32
Matalo! (film) 9
Matarazzo, Raffaello 20, 40
Matchless (film) 215
Mattei, Maurizio 172
Mayo, Alfredo 66, 68, 169
Mazzei, Francesco 57, 59, 61
McGoohan, Patrick 213
McQueen, Steve 102
Mean Frank and Crazy Tony (film) 212
Meisel, Myron 213
Mendizábal, Sergio 66
Meniconi, Nello 80
Merighi, Ferdinando 71
Merli, Maurizio 25, 104, 134
Merrill, James 126, 162, 215
Merz, Carl 208
Metello (film) 134
Mezzogiorno, Vittorio 211
Mia madre (film) 176
Miami Vice (TV series) 125, 152
Midnight Express (film) 144, 164
Midnight Gigolo (film) 121
Mifune, Toshirô 8, 70, 131, 132, 151, 152, 153, 180, 183, 208, 215
Migliacci, Franco 21
Mihályfy, Sándor 120
Miike, Takashi 215
Milan Calibre 9 (film) 29

Milani, Milena 57, 58, 59, 63, 211
Milian, Tomas 19, 96
Miller, David 53
Miner, Allen H. 43
Mininni, Francesco 90, 212, 213
Miou Miou [Sylvette Herry] 213
Miranda (film) 131
Mission: Impossible (TV series) 211
Mister Sharkey torna a casa (novel) 212
Miyakawa, Mario 181
Mizoguchi, Kenji 131
Modugno, Domenico 21, 33, 207
Moffo, Anna 59, 63, 64
Mohr, Gerald 38
Molino Rojo, Antonio 94
Moll, Giorgia 19
Monicelli, Mario 32, 99, 207
Montagnana, Luisa 80
Montaldo, Giuliano 116
Montanari, Sergio 174
Monteleoni, Giulio 32
Montesano, Enrico 138, 139
Montgomery, George 43
Monti, Mario 57
Moore, Roger 125
Morandini, Morando 64, 102, 211
Moreno, José López 32, 33
Moresco, Fabrizio 75
Moretti, Marino 118
Moretti, Nanni 176
Morricone, Ennio 3, 70, 87, 94
Morsella, Fulvio 79, 80, 84, **85**, 89
Morti noi, morto il mondo... see *A Reason to Live, a Reason to Die!*
Moscati, Italo 87, 213
I motorizzati (film) 20, 23
Mozart, Wolfgang Amadeus 216
Mucari, Carlo 126, 163
Mulock, Al 41
Munzi, Francesco 165
Murder on the Orient Express (novel) 70
Murgia, Pier Giuseppe 59
Mussolini, Benito 207
Muti, Ornella 125
My Darling Clementine (film) 3, 94
My Dear Killer (film) 10, 11, 66–70, 71, 80, 159, 160, 165–170
My Name Is Nobody (film) 1, 2, 3, 5, 7, 8, 9, 42, 79–98, 116, 117, 121, 146, 147, 150, 170, 171, 178, 181, 212, 213, 214
My Son, the Hero (film) 40

Nannuzzi, Armando 82, 84
Negrin, Alberto 211
Nero, Franco 6, 99, 109, 110, 112, **113**, 115, 134, 159, 167, 177–178, 187, 214
Nick the Sting (film) 109
Nicolodi, Daria 38
Niehaus, Rena 215
9½ Weeks (film) 124
1900 (film) 80
Niven, David 20
No Graves on Boot Hill (film) 209

Nocturno Cinema (magazine) 5, 26, 91
Noé, Eduardo 30, 178
Non essere cattivo (film) 187
North Dallas Forty (film) 126
Nosferatu (magazine) 5
Novelle Film (magazine) 15
Nudo di donna (film) 182
Les Nuits de la colère (play) 210
Nunziante, Gennaro 216
Nyby, Christian 88

Obsession (1943 film) 2, 141
Oceano (TV series) 173
The Octopus (TV series) 132, 133, 134
Odyssey (poem) 79, 80, 212
Ogro (film) 176
o.k. (film) 64
Once in Every Lifetime (novel) 31
Once Upon a Time in America (film) 62, 88, 183
Once Upon a Time in the West (film) 3, 8, 51, 56, 87, 93, 94, 95, 210, 211
Ongaro, Alberto 117
Only the Valiant (film) 77
Opera (film) 38
Operation Solo (film) 208
Opiate '67 (film) 99
Orca (film) 161
La orca (film) 215
The Organizer (film) 32
Orgasmo (film) 58
Orlando, Orazio 131
Orsini, Arturo 141
Ortolani, Riz 46, 57, 77, 112, 128, 146, 210
Oswald, Lee Harvey 53
8½ (film) 21
Our Man in Jamaica (film) 31, 209
The Overcoat (film) 215
Ozpetek, Ferzan 142

Pabst, Georg Wilhelm 19, 57
Palacios, Ricardo 40
Paladini, Fabrizio 142
Palaggi, Franco "Checco" 26, 27
Palance, Jack 102, 116
The Palermo Connection (film) 163, 182
Palladino, Tommaso 132
Palmara, Domenico "Mimmo" 25, 26
Palmer, Renzo 101, 102, 144
Panama, Norman 65
Papi, Giorgio 3, 17, 19, 23, 27, 28, 29, 208
Papillon (film) 144
Parker, Alan 144
Parker Adderson, Philosopher (short story) 73
Parker Adderson, Philosopher (TV movie) 211
Parolini, Gianfranco 56, 212, 214
La patata bollente (1979) 134
Patrizi, Massimo 50, 51
Pazzafini, Nello 132
Peck, Gregory 77, 94

Peckinpah, Sam 77, 94, 95
Peepshow see *Midnight Gigolo*
Peerce, Larry 85
Pellegrin, Raymond 214
Pennell, Larry [Alessandro Pennelli] 209
Penombra (film) 121
Perugia, Luciano 119
Petri, Elio 99, 158, 167
Petroni, Giulio 8, 43, 54
Petrovna, Sonia 137, 153
Philippe, Gérard 19
Pietrangeli, Antonio 39
Pipolo [Giuseppe Moccia] 120
Pires, Gérard 214
Pirri, Massimo 115
Pirro, Ugo 137, 138, 153
El Pisito (film) 73
Pistilli, Luigi 139
A Pistol for Ringo (film) 40
The Pit and the Pendulum (film) 23
Pittman, Tom 43
A Place for Lovers (film) 61
Placido, Michele 215
Playboy (magazine) 214
Plaza, Paco 209
The Pleasure (film) 121
Pochath, Werner 128, 163, 171, 173, 186
Poe, Edgar Allan 38
Pogány, Gábor 21
Polidoro, Gian Luigi 39
Politoff, Haydée 59
La polizia è al servizio del cittadino? (film) 99
Pontecorvo, Gillo 56, 132, 176
Ponti, Carlo 50
Power, Romina 59
Power, Taryn 59
Pozzetto, Renato 134
Die Prairie am Jacinto (novel) 117
Prandi, Marta 137
Il prato (film) 176
Il prato macchiato di rosso (film) 122
Presle, Micheline 19
The Price of Power (film) 2, 8, 9, **10**, 33, 42, 50–56, **51**, **53**, **55**, 57, 59, 68, 70, 80, 95, 96, 97, 103, 154, **155**, 156, 157, 210, 211
Private Vices, Public Pleasures (film) 110, 177
The Probability Factor (film) 214
Una prova d'innocenza (film) 138, 139, 153, 154
Puccini, Giacomo 142
Puccini, Gianni 43, 44
Puccini, Massimo 5
Pudovkin, Vsevolod 15
Puppo, Romano 44
Pure as a Lily (film) 125
The Purloined Letter (short story) 38
The Purple Land (novel) 118

Quaglia, Pier Anna 22
Quel nostro cinema (weekly TV broadcast) 17

Quer pasticciaccio brutto de Via Merulana (novel) 169
Quo vado? (film) 216

Rachini, Pasquale 6, **103**, **105**, **135**, **136**, **177**, 178–180
La ragazza di nome Giulio (novel) 8, 10, 57–58
Il ragazzo di campagna (film) 120
Il ragazzo di fuoco (novel) 59
Raho, Umberto 62
Rancho Notorious (film) 94
Randone, Salvo 67, 160, 168
Ranieri, Massimo 134, 135, 136, 174
Rashomon (film) 25
Rassimov, Rada 38
Rawhide (TV series) 24, 27, 208
Razza selvaggia (film) 176
A Reason to Live, a Reason to Die! (film) 2, 7, 8, 9, 42, 71–78, 96, 146, **177**, 178, 184–185, 209, 210
Red Harvest (novel) 208
Reder, Gigi 17
Reeves, Steve 27
Regnoli, Piero 212
Reich, Wilhelm 122
Reservoir Dogs (film) 158
Ressel, Franco 33, 34
Return of Halleluja (film) 216
The Return of Ringo (film) 40
Rey, Fernando 51, 54, 134, 157, 160
Rhodes, Bobby 145
Il ricatto (TV series) 42, 133–136, 139, 174, 178, 179, 210
Il ricatto 2—Bambini nell'ombra (film) 136
Ricci, Aldo 209
Ricci, Gianni 140
Richard III (play) 46
Ride Lonesome (film) 40
Rilla, Walter 40
Rilla, Wolf 40
Ring, Beatrice 6, 131, **179**, 180–184
R.I.S.—Delitti imperfetti (TV series) 187
Risi, Dino 20, 23, 87, 99, 207
Ritual of Love (film) 182
La rivoluzione sessuale (film) 122
Rizzoli, Angelo 71, 207
Road of the Giants (film) 41
Robin's, Eva [Roberto Coatti] 146
Robinson, Edward G. 17
Rochat, Éric 122
Roger la Honte (film) 75
Roland, Gilbert 160
Roli, Mino 121
Romanzo criminale—La serie (TV series) 154
Rome Open City (film) 215
Romero Marchent, Joaquín Luis 24
Romero Marchent, Rafael 34
Rosi, Francesco 158, 163, 182
Rossellini, Roberto 207, 215
Rossi, Ernesto 65
Rossi, Franco 125
Rossi Stuart, Giacomo 135
Rossi Stuart, Kim 135, 139
Rouse, Russell 94

Run for Your Wife (film) 39
Ruspoli, Dado 161
Ruspoli, Esmeralda 61
Russinova, Isabel 119
The Ruthless Four (film) 159, 160
Ruzzolini, Giuseppe 84

Sabata (film) 56, 214
Sabatello, Dario 17
Sacchi, Giuseppe "Peppo" 18, 207
The Saga of Gosta Berling (film) 17
Sahara Cross (film) 3, 10, 11, 107–114, 115, 116, 119, 121, 161, 171, 177–178, 186–187, 210
Salacrou, Armand 45, 210
Le salamandre (film) 58
Salani, Corso 146
Salce, Luciano 116, 125, 213
Salerno, Enrico Maria 160
Salino, Sesto 147
Salvati, Sergio 84
Salviani, Vincenzo 215
Samperi, Salvatore 87, 214
Sancho, Fernando 33, 36
Sandrelli, Stefania 121, 122
Sanson, Yvonne 40
Sansone, Alfonso 39, 49, 73, 74, 75
Santa Sangre (film) 166, 167
Santi, Giancarlo 43
Sarafian, Deran 179, 180, 182, 183, 184
Sartori, Claudia 27
Savage Attack see *Brothers in Blood*
Savalas, Telly 7, 75, **76**, 77, 184
Saxon, John 69
Sbarigia, Roberto 162
Schaffner, Franklin J. 144
Schell, Maria 61, 211
Schivazappa, Piero 121
Schlesinger, John 111
Schmiederer, Walther 64
Sciascia, Leonardo 215
Scola, Ettore 215
The Scopone Game (film) 77
Sealsfield, Charles [Karl Anton Postl] 117
Second Name (film) 209
Selznick, David O. 95
Sempere, Julio 30, 209
Sempere, Ramón 209
Senatore, Daniele 115
Senatore, Donatella 115
Senatore, Paola 121
Senese, James 124
Senilità (novel) 121
Senza scrupoli 2 (film) 122
Serandrei, Mario 19
Serna, Assumpta 215
Sessomatto (film) 87
Seven Beauties (film) 169
Seven Deaths in the Cat's Eye (film) 71
Seven Keys to Baldpate (play) 22
Seven Pistols for a Massacre (film) 209
The Seven Samurai (film) 77
La sfida del samurai see *Yojimbo*
Shane (film) 101, 102

The Shark Hunter (film) 128
Shatterer (film) 8, **18**, 122, 130–132, 141, 151–153, **179**, 180–184
Shepard, Patty 66, 69, 160, 169
Shepherd, Peter 130, 152
The Shining (film) 132
Shoeshine (film) 215
Shoot First... Ask Questions Later (film) 96
Sicilian Connection see *Shatterer*
Siegel, Don 38
La signora Ava (film) 214
Simi, Carlo 27, 33
Simsolo, Nöel 89
Soavi, Michele 139
Sodom and Gomorrah (film) 25
Solinas, Franco 8, 53
Sollima, Sergio 8
Sollima, Stefano 154
Sordi, Alberto 20, 78, 100
Sorrentino, Paolo 176
Soviet Spy (film) 19, 28
Spencer, Bud [Carlo Pedersoli] 6, 7, 8, 25, 49, 56, 74, 77, 78, 87, 96, 115, 120, 178, 184–185
Una spia del regime (TV mini-series) 65, 211
Spielberg, Steven 3, 89, 153
Spila, Aristide 147
Spila, Otello 215
Springsteen, Bruce 134
Squadra selvaggia (film) 173
Stagecoach (film) 14, 102
Staig, Laurence 88
Star Wars: The Force Awakens (film) 216
Steele, Barbara 21, 23
Stefanelli, Benito 41, 42, 54, 75, 80, 94, 147, 156, 185, 213
Steffen, Anthony [Antonio De Teffé] 27
Stegani, Giorgio 77
Steiner, John 62
The Stendhal Syndrome (film) 144, 163
Steno [Stefano Vanzina] 77, 99, 134, 207
Stevens, George 64, 101, 102
The Sting (film) 109, 214
The Story of O 2 (film) 122
Stoudenmire, Dallas 210
La strada che porta lontano (film) 16
The Strange Vice of Mrs. Wardh (film) 160
Street Law (film) 99
Street People (film) 125
Strehler, Giorgio 177, 216
Strindberg, Anita 160
Submission (film) 214
Suma, Marina 131, 151, 152
Summers, Neil 86, 212
The Sunday Woman (film) 119
Sunset Blvd. (film) 97
Suspicion (film) 61
Sutter, Arturo 216
Sutter, Milena 165, 166, 216
Svenson, Bo 6, 125, 126, 127, 162, 172, 173, 185–186

Svevo, Italo 121
The Sweet Body of Deborah (film) 58

The Tale of Tales (film) 176
Tales of Soldiers and Civilians (short story anthology) 73
The Tall Target (film) 211
Tamba, Tetsuro 211
Tanabe, Yasushi 141
I Tarantiniani (documentary) 147
Tarantino, Quentin 6, 132, 146, 158
Taste of Killing (film) 7, 31–38, 39, 41, 46, 47, 50, 99, 102, 113, 114, 209
Taviani, Paolo 176
Taviani, Vittorio 176
Taylor, Don 211
Tempi nostri (Zibaldone n. 2) (film) 20
Tenco, Luigi 213
Tenebrae (film) 69
Teorema (film) 58, 66
Tepepa (film) 8, 54
I terribili 7 (I cagasotto) (film) 20
Terribili, Elio 174
Terror in the Crypt, a.k.a. *Crypt of the Vampire* (film) 21, 22, 23, 32
Terror of Oklahoma (film) 24
Tessari, Duccio 8, 26, 29, 40, 47, 56, 117, 119, 126, 147, 161, 162, 208, 210, 215
Tessari, Fiorenza 215
Testa Gay, Felice 23, 208
Testi, Fabio 38, 101, 102, 104, 105, 115, 175, 176
Testori, Sergio 126
Tex and the Lord of the Deep (film) 119, 126
There Was a Crooked Man... (film) 97
They Call Me Trinity (film) 8, 9, 25, 79, 80, 81, 87, 90
Thiele, Rolf 208
The Thing from Another World (film) 88
Thompson, J. Lee 112
Tieri, Aroldo 20
Der Tod ritt dienstags (novel) 40
Tognazzi, Ugo 20, 208
Toland, Gregg 55
Tolo, Marilù 67, 160, 168
Torrisi, Pietro 126, 172
Totò [Antonio De Curtis] 23
Touch of Evil (film) 109
Transunto, Gianfranco 111, 214
La traversata (TV documentary) 59
Treasure Island (novel) 14
The Treasure of San Gennaro (film) 207
The Treasure of the Silver Lake (film) 24
Trinity in Eldorado (film) 209
Trinity Is Still My Name (film) 25, 87, 96
Trintignant, Jean-Louis 214
Le trou (film) 110
Tutto è musica (film) 21, 33

2020 Freedom Fighters (film) 126
The Two Faces of Fear (film) 160

Ulloa, Alejandro 178
Ultimo (TV series) 187
Uncle Was a Vampire (film) 99, 207
Uncommon Valor (film) 171
Ungaretti, Giuseppe 58
L'Unità (newspaper) 90
Unscrupulous (film) 8, 63, 121–124, 142
Urzì, Saro 67
Una vacanza all'inferno (film) 143–145, 146, 163–165

Vadim, Roger 22
Valerii, Andrea 50
Valerii, Francesca 39
Valerii, Luca 50
Valerii, Riccardo 13, 14
Valerii, Rita 6, **18**, 33, 50
Valerii, Tonino: as actor 20, 146; apprenticeship at Jolly/Unidis 17–19, 23, 28–29; as assistant director 20–21; birth and childhood 13–15; books written by 19, 146; censorship issues 36, 49, 63–64, 105–106, 123; cinephilia 14–15, 77, 131; controversy regarding *My Name Is Nobody* 86–92, 116, 146, 170; family 13, 14, 18, 46; film studies at CSC 16–17; film style 9, 36, 46–47, 55–56, 62–63, 68–69, 77, 95, 105, 109, 111–113, 123–124, 126–127, 132, 139, 141, 144, 164, 178, 181, 187, 214; key themes 9, 44–46, 53–54, 62, 81, 103, 144–145; marriage with Rita 32, 33; meeting with Ernesto Gastaldi, 16–17; meeting with Sergio Leone, 23; as scriptwriter 21–23; television works 118–120, 133–140; unfilmed projects 7, 31–32, 50, 57, 65, 80, 93, 101, 116–118, 146

Valmarana, Paolo 119
Valsecchi, Pietro 177, 187
I vampiri (film) 207
Vancini, Florestano 47
Van Cleef, Lee 2, 7, 40, 41, 42, 43, 44, 48, 49, 50, 56, 62, 75, 155, 156, 210, 212
Van Daan, Peter 16
Vanders, Warren [Warren John Vanderschuit] 51, 56
Van Eyck, Jan 120
Vanzina, Carlo 120
Variety (magazine) 88, 216
Vattimo, Gianni 147
Venni, vidi e m'arrapaoh (film) 215
Ventimiglia, Giovanni 32
Ventura, Lino 215
Venturi, Maria 139
Veo, Carlo 150
Vera Cruz (film) 43
Verdi, Giuseppe 216
Verhoeven, Michael 64
Verrecchia, Anacleto 145
Verucci, Franco 138
Videla, Jorge Rafael 138
Video Watchdog (magazine) 88
Vieni avanti cretino (1982) 125
La vigna di uve nere (TV movie) 211
Village of the Damned (1960 film) 40
Villoresi, Pamela 6, 109, 110, 111, 115, 177, 186–187
Vincenzoni, Luciano 26, 29
Viola, Mirca 144
Violent Rome (film) 104
Visconti, Eriprando 215
Visconti, Luchino 2, 58, 119, 141, 162, 207
Volonté, Gian Maria 27
Voltati Eugenio (film) 176
Von Theumer, Ernst 209
Vukotic, Milena 146
Vulpiani, Mario 105, 141, 158, 179

Wagner, Richard 94
Wallach, Eli 74
Waltz of the Toreadors (play) 74
Ward, David S. 214
Warlock (1959 film) 47, 94
Watanabe, Shin 131, 151
Wayne, John 102
The Wedding March (film) 39, 73
Weidelmann, Alfred 208
Wendel, Lara [Daniela Barnes] 59, 68
Wertmüller, Lina 169
Wertmüller, Massimo 142
Western Union (film) 94
Wey, Sandra 122, 123
Whirlybirds (TV series) 34
The Wicker Man (1973 film) 23
The Widower (film) 23
The Wild Bunch (film) 77
Wilder, Billy 97
Williams, John 183
Williams, Tony 88
Wolff, Frank 27, 43
A Woman on Fire (film) 59
A Wrong Way to Love (film) 61

Yankee (film) 9
Yates, Peter 144
Yojimbo (film) 1, 2, 25, 26, 28, 101, 132
Young, Robert 215
Youth (film) 176
Yulin, Harris 211

Zalone, Checco [Luca Medici] 177, 178, 216
Zampa, Luigi 215
Zamperla, Nazzareno 41, 156, 157
Zanchin, Nino 20
Zanelli, Dario 97
Zarzo, Manuel "Manolo" 67, 68, **156**, 157, 160
Zingarelli, Italo 160
Zinnemann, Fred 40
Zurlini, Valerio 138, 153

www.ingramcontent.com/pod-product-compliance
Ingram Content Group UK Ltd.
Pitfield, Milton Keynes, MK11 3LW, UK
UKHW050530150426
5217IPUK00026B/1879